ABOUT THE AUTHORS

For five decades, award-winning writer **Brad Steiger** has been devoted to exploring and examining unusual, hidden, secret, and otherwise strange occurrences. A former high school teacher and college instructor, Brad published his first articles on the unexplained in 1956. Since then he has written more than two thousand articles with paranormal themes. He is author or coauthor of more than 170 titles, including *Real Ghosts, Restless Spirits, and Haunted Places; The Werewolf Book; Mysteries of Time and Space;* and *Real Monsters, Gruesome Creatures, and Beasts from the Darkside*.

Brad is a veteran of broadcast news magazines, ranging from *Nightline* to the *NBC Nightly News*, and a wide variety of cable programs. He is also a regular radio guest on Jeff Rense's *Sightings, The Allan Handelman Show,* and *Coast to Coast* with George Noory. Brad has been interviewed and featured in numerous newspapers and magazines, including the *New York Times, Los Angeles Times, San Francisco Chronicle,* and *Chicago Tribune*.

For over forty-five years, **Sherry Hansen Steiger** has actively studied the mysteries of the paranormal, as well as the dynamic interaction between the body, mind, and spirit and the effects of environment and technology on health and wellness. Sherry has been the keynote speaker and addressed audiences and corporate groups from coast to coast.

Sherry has served as counselor to troubled youth, the homeless, migrant workers, and families in need of crisis intervention. In the 1970s she formed a nonprofit holistic research and education school, and in the 1980s she served as public relations director for astronomer Dr. J. Allen Hynek in the Phoenix branch of the Center for UFO Research. She has authored or coauthored more than forty-four books, including the best-selling "Miracles" series.

Together, the Steigers have researched mysteries and miracles throughout the globe and lectured and conducted workshops for over twenty years. They have been interviewed on many national radio programs and have guested on such television programs as *The Joan Rivers Show, Hard Copy, Inside Edition,* and *Entertainment Tonight,* as well as appearing in specials on HBO, The Learning Channel, Discovery, History, and A&E channels, among others. They were also featured in twenty-two episodes of the syndicated series *Could It Be a Miracle?*

Between them, Sherry and Brad have two sons, three daughters, and ten grandchildren. Information on their continuing research can be found at www.bradandsherry.com.

OTHER VISIBLE INK PRESS BOOKS BY BRAD STEIGER

Conspiracies and Secret Societies:
  The Complete Dossier, 2nd edition
With Sherry Hansen Steiger
ISBN: 978-1-57859-368-2

Real Aliens, Space Beings, and Creatures
  from Other Worlds,
With Sherry Hansen Steiger
ISBN: 978-1-57859-333-0

Real Ghosts, Restless Spirits, and
  Haunted Places, 2nd edition
ISBN: 978-1-57859-401-6

Real Miracles, Divine Intervention,
  and Feats of Incredible Survival
With Sherry Hansen Steiger
ISBN: 978-1-57859-214-2

Real Monsters, Gruesome Critters,
  and Beasts from the Darkside
With Sherry Hansen Steiger
ISBN: 978-1-57859-220-3

Real Vampires, Night Stalkers,
  and Creatures from the Darkside
ISBN: 978-1-57859-255-5

Real Zombies, the Living Dead,
  and Creatures of the Apocalypse,
ISBN: 978-1-57859-296-8

The Werewolf Book: The Encyclopedia of
  Shape-Shifting Beings, 2nd edition
ISBN: 978-1-57859-367-5

"Real Nightmares" E-Books
by Brad Steiger
Book 1: *True and Truly Scary*
  Unexplained Phenomenon
Book 2: *The Unexplained Phenomena*
  and Tales of the Unknown
Book 3: *Things That Go Bump in the*
  Night
Book 4: *Things That Prowl and Growl i*
  the Night
Book 5: *Fiends That Want Your Blood*
Book 6: *Unexpected Visitors and*
  Unwanted Guests
Book 7: *Dark and Deadly Demons*
Book 8: *Phantoms, Apparitions, and*
  Ghosts

ALSO FROM VISIBLE INK PRESS

Alien Mysteries, Conspiracies,
  and Cover-Ups
by Kevin D. Randle
ISBN: 978-1-57859-418-4

Angels A to Z, 2nd edition
by Evelyn Dorothy Oliver and
  James R Lewis
ISBN: 978-1-57859-212-8

Armageddon Now: The End of the World
  A to Z
by Jim Willis and Barbara Willis
ISBN: 978-1-57859-168-8

The Astrology Book: The Encyclopedia of
  Heavenly Influences, 2nd edition
by James R Lewis
ISBN: 978-1-57859-144-2

The Dream Encyclopedia, 2nd edition
by James R Lewis and Evelyn
  Dorothy Oliver
ISBN: 978-1-57859-216-6

The Encyclopedia of Religious
  Phenomena
by J. Gordon Melton
ISBN: 978-1-57859-209-8

The Fortune-Telling Book:
  The Encyclopedia of Divination
  and Soothsaying
by Raymond Buckland
ISBN: 978-1-57859-147-3

Hidden Realms, Lost Civilizations, and
  Beings from Other Worlds
by Jerome Clark
ISBN: 978-1-57859-175-6

The Religion Book: Places, Prophets,
  Saints, and Seers
by Jim Willis
ISBN: 978-1-57859-151-0

The Spirit Book: The Encyclopedia of
  Clairvoyance, Channeling, and Spirit
  Communication
by Raymond Buckland
ISBN: 978-1-57859-172-5

Unexplained! Strange Sightings,
  Incredible Occurrences, and Puzzling
  Physical Phenomena, 3rd edition
by Jerome Clark
ISBN: 978-1-57859-344-6

The Vampire Book: The Encyclopedia of
  the Undead, 3rd edition
by J. Gordon Melton
ISBN: 978-1-57859-281-4

The Witch Book: The Encyclopedia
  of Witchcraft, Wicca, and Neo-
  paganism
by Raymond Buckland
ISBN: 978-1-57859-114-5

PLEASE VISIT US AT VISIBLEINKPRESS.COM

Real Encounters,
Different Dimensions,
and
Otherworldly Beings

REAL ENCOUNTERS, DIFFERENT DIMENSIONS, AND OTHERWORLDLY BEINGS

Visible Ink Press®
43311 Joy Rd., #414
Canton, MI 48187-2075

Visible Ink Press is a registered trademark of Visible Ink Press LLC.

Most Visible Ink Press books are available at special quantity discounts when purchased in bulk by corporations, organizations, or groups. Customized printings, special imprints, messages, and excerpts can be produced to meet your needs. For more information, contact Special Markets Director, Visible Ink Press, www.visibleinkpress.com, or 734-667-3211.

Managing Editor: Kevin S. Hile
Art Director: Mary Claire Krzewinski
Typesetting: Marco Di Vita
Proofreaders: Barbara Lyon and Chrystal Rozsa
Indexing: Shoshana Hurwitz

Cover images: Shutterstock.com.

Library of Congress Cataloging-in-Publication Data

Steiger, Brad.
    Real encounters, different dimensions, and otherworldy beings / by Brad Steiger and Sherry Hansen Steiger.
        pages cm
    Includes bibliographical references and index.
    ISBN 978-1-57859-455-9 (pbk. : alk. paper)
    1. Parapsychology—Anecdotes. 2. Occultism—Anecdotes. 3. Human-alien encounters. 4. Unidentified flying objects—Sightings and encounters. I. Title.
    BF1029.S74 2013   001.94—dc23

Printed in the United States of America

10 9 8 7 6 5 4 3 2

Real Encounters, Different Dimensions, and Otherworldly Beings

Brad Steiger with
Sherry Hansen Steiger

VISIBLE
INK
PRESS

Detroit

CONTENTS

Acknowledgments   [ix] • Photo Credits   [xi] • Introduction   [xiii]

Visitors from Extraterrestrial Worlds 1
Contact with Space Brothers and Sisters 23
Taken Away to Other Worlds 43
Sky Critters and Orbs 69
Old Gods from the Sea or Visitors from the Stars? 83
The Master Race from the Inner Earth 103
The Wee People: Guardians of the Earth Mother 121
Meeting Strange Creatures in Dark Forests 139
Unknown Beings of Terror and the Darkside 155
Encounters with a Menagerie of Monsters 183
Angelic Helpers and Messengers 201
Encountering Spirit Guides and Teachers 219
Communicating with Animal Totems and Nature Spirits 235
Ghosts, Poltergeists, and Recording Spirit Voices 251
People and Places from Other Dimensions 273
Visiting the Astral World 289
The Flexible Dimensions of the Dream World 305
Mind Traveling through Time and Space 319
Voyages during Near-Death Experiences 333
On Stage in the Magic Theater 351

Bibliography   [363] • Index   [371]

ACKNOWLEDGMENTS

We wish to give special thanks to the remarkable Ricardo Pustanio, who took time from designing award-winning floats for the New Orleans' Mardi Gras to contribute so many unique and compelling illustrations for the book. We also thank Bill Oliver for his enchanting creations that captured so well the hidden kingdom of the wee folk, as well as visitors from other worlds.

We are indebted to the following contributors, who enabled us to explore the farthest reaches of inner and outer space and to include a vast array of Real Encounters: Paul Dale Roberts, Brent Raynes, Sandy Nichols, Sean Casteel, Brandie, Patricia Ress, Don and Peggy Avery, Nick Redfern, Tom T. Moore, Z. Peterson, Pastor Robin Swope, Dan Wolfman Allen, Noe Torres, Angela Thomas, Tuesday Miles, and William Kern. In addition, there are many contributors to this book who chose to remain anonymous or to use pseudonyms, and we are grateful for their sincerity in sharing their fascinating accounts.

Once again, we had the great pleasure of collaborating with the talented staff of Visible Ink, helmed by Roger Jänecke, our always helpful publisher; Kevin Hile, editor extraordinaire; Mary Claire Krzewinski, creative art director; Marco Di Vita, tireless typesetter; and Barbara Lyon and Chrystal Rozsa, meticulous proofreaders. As always, we thank our steadfast agent, Agnes Birnbaum, who has stood by us while we explored UFOs, ghosts, restless spirits, and all manner of phenomena for over twenty-five years.

CREDITS

When not credited in the caption underneath the photo or illustration, all photos in this book are courtesy of Shutterstock, with the following exceptions: page 8 (Finlay McWalter), page 41 (Larry D. Moore), page 217 (KOMU News)

"Conversations with My Brother on Another Planet" copyright © Tom T. Moore.

INTRODUCTION: REAL ENCOUNTERS WITH THE OTHER

Those individuals who have encountered what they perceived as an extraterrestrial visitor, a ghost, an angel, an elfin creature, or a nightmarish monster have never forgotten the experience. Their lives have never been the same. Their concept of reality has been forever expanded. Upon reflection, some may consider the encounter a life-altering experience, an illumination, an epiphany; but whether the encounter occurred to them a few months ago, a few years ago, or when they were very young children, they remember it as clearly as if no time at all has elapsed. The experience remains with them in an Eternal Now.

We have been engaged in UFO and paranormal research since the early 1950s, and we have come to the conclusion that throughout history some external intelligence has interacted with *Homo sapiens* in an effort to learn more about us and/or to communicate certain basic truths. In this book we present the thesis that the aliens, angels, spirit guides, demons, and gods or goddesses encountered by unaware, yet somehow receptive percipients may actually be the product of a multidimensional intelligence that masks itself in physical forms that are more acceptable to humans than its true image—if it does, indeed, have a perceivable form at all. We choose to define and to name this multidimensional intelligence and its multitude of manifestations as the Other.

The many guises of the Other exist only a frequency away in the background of the unconscious, waiting for some triggering mechanism to bring it into focus. The so-called "collective unconscious" of modern psychology is nothing less than a subliminal doorway to that immaterial domain that the physicists are so busily mapping on a different level. Once that "doorway" has been opened, an as-yet-unknown psychic mechanism activates the unconscious mind, the "higher self," and summons the Other. Once activated, the

Other is able to absorb, reflect, and imitate human intelligence, thereby creating a host of entities that are fashioned by the dramatic by-products of our collective unconscious. Once the Other draws upon a human's belief construct, it may produce an independent image that can sustain itself on the vagaries of centuries of legend and myth. If there is truly but one Life Force and a common, collective unconscious for *Homo sapiens*, then, in the larger sense, any contact with the Other becomes part of the common experience of all humankind, whether the incident is reported in the popular press or pondered quietly in the mind of the individual observer.

The messages relayed by the images that have been created by the Other are always relevant to the time context of human observers, but the symbolism that it employs is always timeless, archetypal, and instantly recognizable by one level of the percipient's consciousness. Angels, genies, wee people, devils, and gods, it would seem, have been popular in all cultures throughout history.

Many of the messages conveyed by the Other seem, upon first examination, to contain creative symbolic myths rather than literal truths. We maintain that, in addition to mystical and spiritual insights, numerous literal truths have been prompted by the Other. We believe that, through the ages, the gods, angels, and alien messengers have been provoking humankind into ever higher spirals of intellectual and technological maturity, guiding men and women toward ever-expanding mental and spiritual awareness, pulling our species into the future.

Throughout history it has seemed that the Other has been content merely to show us that the impossible can be accomplished. The Other has already demonstrated the possibility of air flight, radio communication, television, computers, and a host of technological extensions of our five senses. Today, the maneuvers of this manifold intelligence might be demonstrating the possibility of dematerialization, invisibility, and rematerialization. Perhaps these cosmic tutors are showing us that the best way of dealing with space travel over great distances is not to travel through space but to avoid it altogether.

Although the paraphysical, multidimensional "gods" and "messengers" have always co-existed with us, in the last forty years they have been accelerating their interaction with us in preparation for what has been defined as a fast-approaching time of transition and transformation. This period, we have been told, will be a difficult one; and for generations many of our prophets and revelators have been referring to it as The Great Cleansing, Judgment Day, or Armageddon.

What answers does the Other offer for this turbulent time ahead? Has this multidimensional intelligence that has interacted with us throughout our physical, mental, and spiritual evolution manifested to prepare us for the acceptance of the grim reality that our reign as the dominant species on the planet has come to an end? Or has it accelerated its program of real encounters to help us gain a deeper understanding of the dimensions that exist without and within us, our true role in the cosmic scheme of things, and the destiny that awaits us?

VISITORS FROM EXTRATERRESTRIAL WORLDS

If you believe that the "modern era" of UFOs began in 1947 with Kenneth Arnold's famous sighting near Mt. Rainier, Washington, you are sorely mistaken. If you further believe that this was the first time that anyone saw flying discs moving "like saucers skipping off the surface of water" in the skies over North America, you would again be very mistaken. People have been recording the sightings of strange lights and objects moving in the skies above them since the earliest days in the nation's history.

In 1804, a report concerning an Unidentified Flying Object was written and submitted by a naturalist named William Dunbar and communicated, or presented, to the American Philosophical Society by Thomas Jefferson, who was president of the Society and also Vice President of the United States. A one-page notice appeared in the *Transactions of the American Philosophical Society* (Volume 6, Part 1 [Philadelphia, 1804], p. 25).

Description of a singular Phenomenon seen at Baton Rouge, by William Dunbar, Esq. communicated by Thomas Jefferson, President A. P. S. Natchez, June 30, 1800. Read 16 January 1801.

> A phenomenon was seen to pass Baton Rouge on the night of the 5th April 1800, of which the following is the best description I have been able to obtain. It was first seen in the South West, and moved so rapidly, passing over the heads of the spectators, as to disappear in the North East in about a quarter of a minute. It appeared to be of the size of a large house, 70 or 80 feet long....
>
> It appeared to be about 200 yards above the surface of the earth, wholly luminous, but not emitting sparks; of a color resembling the

sun near the horizon in a cold frosty evening, which may be called crimson red. When passing right over the heads of the spectators, the light on the surface of the earth, was little short of the effect of sunbeams, though at the same time, looking another way, the stars were visible, which appears to be a confirmation of the opinion formed of its moderate elevation. In passing, a considerable degree of heat was felt but no electric sensation. Immediately after it disappeared in the North East, a violent rushing noise was heard, as if the phenomenon was bearing down the forest before it, and in a few seconds a tremendous crash was heard similar to that of the largest piece of ordnance, causing a very sensible earthquake.

I have been informed, that search has been made in the place where the burning body fell, and that a considerable portion of the surface of the earth was found broken up, and every vegetable body burned or greatly scorched. I have not yet received answers to a number of queries I have sent on, which may perhaps bring to light more particulars.

[Thanks to Dr. Robert G. Bedrosian and *UFO Digest* (http://www.ufo digest.com). The entire volume, which is in the public domain, may be downloaded from http://rbedrosian.com/Downloads/TAPS_1804_Jefferson_Ufo.pdf]

SIGHTING OF A TRIANGLE-SHAPED UFO: MT. RAINIER, 1996

By Dan Wolfman Allen

Although Mt. Rainier should have by no means received the credit for being the "birthplace" of the flying saucers in the modern era, all UFO researchers will have to admit that there is "something" about that region that remains a hot spot for mysterious phenomena. Our friend, artist, writer, and researcher Dan Allen, had his first major sighting in that area. Here is his account of that dramatic initiation into a confrontation with the Other.

When I lived in Northwestern Washington in the mid-1990s, one of my favorite activities during the late summer/early fall was camping and fishing trips on the Eastern side of Mt. Rainier. On the mountain there are several small cut-offs located by rivers and canyons that are just big enough for one or two vehicles to camp overnight. These cut-offs are quiet and peaceful because only the locals know about them. On this particular evening, we had pulled into one of those areas to camp. These spots did not have fire pits or tent areas, and when you stayed there, you slept in the bed of your pickup truck.

I was along with my uncle and fourteen-year-old cousin on this particular trip. When they got settled down for the night, I decided to hike on my own about a quarter of a mile along a steep hillside, which led into a rocky canyon.

As I took a seat on one of the huge stones next to the creek, I began to feel a very slight tremor coming up through the rocks. What was bizarre was that I could not tell from which direction the noise was emanating. And it was really more of a vibration than a noise. I could see no extra light coming from anywhere. Somehow, I had the urge to draw my attention upward, and what I saw was something I will not forget.

I cannot give you exact dimensions of the object, only what I could perceive. The cliff face was at least fifty to seventy feet, and I would estimate the trees in that place to be about one hundred feet tall. Floating not two hundred feet above the trees was a giant, black, triangular-shaped craft. The best I could estimate the speed was around fifteen miles per hour. As best as I could describe the movement, it was a slow, lazy float.

The sound the craft made, if it could be called a sound, was omnidirectional. If you were to wear a blindfold, you would not be able to locate from where the sound was emanating. The best example I could possibly use as a description is if you would tune a high-performance stereo system to cancel out the treble, turn the bass up all the way, and play a tape of a slow, constant vibration. Not the "Boom Boom bass" you might hear from a car playing modern hip-hop, but an ultra-low tone where you can barely hear the audio, but enough to vibrate the earth below you.

As for the shape of the craft, from my point of perception it was that of an equilateral triangle, or very close to it on the bottom. There were no peripheral lights, common to the crafts seen over Phoenix or Hudson Valley, only four points of illumination from below. Mounted inward from each point of the triangle were half orbs.

The only point of reference I can give you is at the altitude which the craft was levitated, were you to hold your arm upward, bend your forearm at a 90-degree angle, and ball your hand into a fist; it was about the length from your elbow to the knuckle of your forefinger. As for the three orbs themselves, they were a very dark purple with a light violet crackle. If you have ever seen underwater volcanic activity where tube pressure continually forces fresh plugs of lava into the ocean, where the lava glows for a few seconds, then cools into black stone, it would be the closest thing to the lights within the orbs, making a purple or violet tint. Though the craft gave out an illumination, it did not seem enough to light the bottom of the craft.

The sound the craft made, if it could be called a sound, was omnidirectional. If you were to wear a blindfold, you would not be able to locate from where the sound was emanating.

Real Encounters, Different Dimensions, and Otherworldly Beings

The center of the craft contained a white light. Again, the best real world example I could give would be similar to a parking lot bulb light, though the light was close to pure white and never changed tint. The center light was intense enough to illuminate a small part of the bottom of the craft, though even at its low altitude, it did not backlight/highlight the top of the trees. From what I could see in the illuminated part of the underside of the craft was a series of I-beams and tubing. I was probably at least three hundred feet below the craft, but from what I recall, I could not see either rivets or bolts; all the joints were either completely welded or fused. The white light produced a dull, medium battleship-grey color on all the beams and tubes.

I wasn't wearing a wristwatch, but in my perception, it probably took about fifteen minutes for the craft to pass overhead. It made a lazy turn and continued over the valley above a small town and disappeared into the distance. I estimate the length of the total sighting to be around two hours.

As the craft turned and continued into the distance, all I noticed was a complete symmetrical, dome-shaped top; a continuous curve from each point to a curve on the top. There were no noticeable "floors," windows, or lit portals. With the ambient light of the night, the rest of the craft seemed to be black. No wavering or animated patterns or markings, just a satin-finish black.

I walked back to my truck, lay in the bed, and stared up at the stars for the rest of the night in awe. I didn't want to mention what had happened to my uncle that night, for he was extremely conservative. This was before I knew about serious research into UFOs or the local Center for UFO Studies. I only mentioned this to friends with open enough minds to take this somewhat seriously. When I finally contacted Brad and Sherry Steiger three years later, I listed this sighting on their paranormal survey.

In the years following, I got deeply into UFO studies and learned that Mt. Rainier is a UFO hot spot. I have also heard about deep black operations, stealth dirigibles, counter-rotating mercury anti-gravity experiments by the Nazis, and I am up to date about the latest experimental craft. The one thing that continues to bug me is that most of the other sightings of huge, triangular craft report steady red lights on the three corners. I have yet to come across another report that describes the crackling, mutating, purple and violet orbs that I witnessed.

SHAPE-SHIFTING UFOs

By Tim R. Swartz

Tim R. Swartz is an Indiana native and Emmy-Award winning television producer/videographer. He is the author of a number of popular books, including The Lost Journals of Nikola Tesla; Time Travel:

UFOs can behave in peculiar ways that sometimes make them seem as if they are not solid objects at all, changing in shape and size. (*Art by Ricardo Pustanio*)

A How-To Insiders Guide; *and is a contributing writer for such books as* The Paranormal World of Sherlock Holmes: Sir Arthur Conan Doyle First Ghostbuster and Psychic Sleuth *and Brad Steiger's* Real Monsters, Gruesome Critters, and Beasts from the Darkside.

As a photojournalist, Swartz has traveled extensively and investigated paranormal phenomena and other unusual mysteries from such diverse locations as the Great Pyramid of Giza in Egypt to the Great Wall in China. He has worked with television networks such as PBS, ABC, NBC, CBS, CNN, ESPN, and the BBC. Tim R. Swartz is the writer and editor of Conspiracy Journal, *a free, weekly email newsletter, considered essential reading by paranormal researchers worldwide.*

There is no doubt that UFOs are strange. The fact that they are usually seen silently zipping around in our skies is weird enough, but throw in the fact that many UFOs that appear solid are seen to be constantly changing shape and size, it's enough to drive any serious UFO researcher to take up butterfly collecting instead.

It is one of the great mysteries of UFOs: How can something that looks so real not behave like a solid object and change shape as rapidly as smoke in the wind? This has led to wild speculations on the true nature of UFOs and allowed skeptics to dismiss the entire phenomenon as simply misinterpreted natural events.

What hard-core skeptics fail to take into consideration is the thousands of diverse UFO sightings that have come in over the years that exhibit the same shape-shifting characteristics. A reported sighting of a weird object that changes shape can be a good way to distinguish a real UFO from one that is fraudulent.

UFOs are reported to come in all kinds of different shapes and sizes, ranging from saucers, ovals, cigars, spheres, rocket, and triangular shaped. They can suddenly appear and disappear, only to reappear in a completely different location. They can split in two and rejoin again instantly. This has led to all sorts of heated arguments between UFO researchers who have a preferred shape, choosing to throw out cases that don't meet their criteria. However, if you take into account all of the reports of UFOs seen to morph from one shape into another, then possibly the vast diversity of UFOs is not so difficult to explain after all.

Classic Report of a Morphing UFO

On June 29, 1954, the British Overseas Airways Corporation (BOAC) Stratocruiser Centaurus left New York's Idlewild airport bound for London. Just after 9:00 P.M. the aircraft passed 170 miles southwest of Goose Bay, Labrador, flying northeast at nineteen thousand feet. The crew suddenly noticed an object to the west of the plane that was roughly five degrees aft of the port wing at a distance of about five miles. As they drew closer, the crew could see a large, pear-shaped UFO flying in formation with six other smaller objects.

Against the sunset these objects appeared dark, with the six smaller UFOs changing their positions around the larger craft which seemed to change from its original pear shape to a telephone handset shape and, in the words of Captain Howard: "[W]hat looked like a flying arrow—an enormous delta-winged plane turning in to close with us." The anomalous, shape-shifting object seemed to be solid with definite, clearly-defined edges.

As the jetliner drew closer, the smaller UFOs formed into a regular line and seemed to merge into the larger object. Then the remaining large UFO appeared to suddenly shrink and vanish right before the eyes of the startled crew.

Captain Howard remarked later: "… they were obviously not aircraft as we know them. All appeared black and I will swear they were solid. There was a big central object that appeared to keep changing shape. The six smaller objects dodged about either in front or behind …"

In another case a Baptist pastor, while traveling with his family in the western part of the United States on June 8, 2002, observed a silver, aluminum object flying above the mountains.

The pastor said, "When I first noticed the object it was in the shape of a box and about the size of a small private plane. I tried to show it to my family and I was pointing where to look. Taking my eyes off of it for a moment, it changed to a round bottom cup shape without the handle (the round section being at the top). The sighting lasted about 30 seconds. The craft was not in a hurry really but seemed to be just cruising around. I don't know how it disappeared. I lost sight of it trying to point it out to my family after looking away for just a second."

UFO Changes Shape Right before Witnesses' Eyes

On June 5, 2005, a man was stopped at a traffic light on Route 422 in Niles, Ohio, when he noticed a bright silver, metallic UFO in the clear blue sky in front of his car.

According to his description: "It was thin, cigar shaped with rounded ends and there was a large spot of sun glare shining from the left (back end). With my arm completely extended, its length would have been about the width across of a quarter."

About six to seven seconds after he first spotted the unusual object, it seemed to change shape, with the front end moving slightly inward so that the object took on more of a boomerang shape with one side shorter than the other. The glare from the sun that had been so bright at the left end moved in a quick flash and settled more in the center of the object and there seemed to be a darker spot right in the middle.

At that point the UFO was seen to ripple and get fuzzy at the edges. After the hazy ripple, it completely vanished, leaving the eyewitness wondering what he had just seen.

One odd, shape-shifting UFO was actually captured on camera in 1994, at an undisclosed location within the Nellis Air Force Base Bombing and Gunnery Range Complex in Nevada. The videotape is said to have been smuggled out by contractor personnel who had operated tracking stations on the Nellis range. Even though the UFO was photographed by a very good remote-controlled, fixed mounted camera, it still has that fuzzy, cotton-ball look about it, which seems to be common among UFOs.

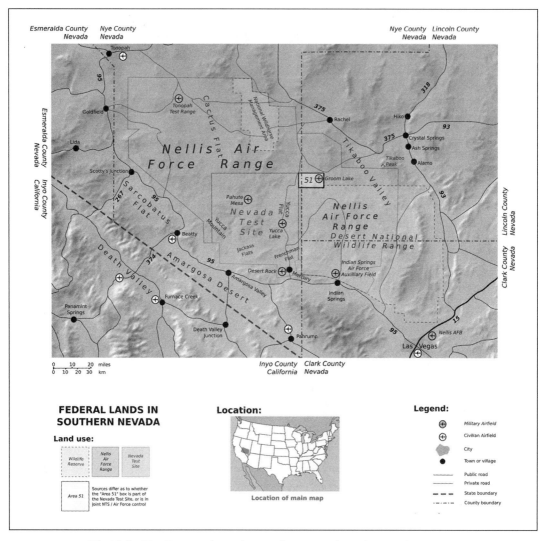

The Nellis Test Range is located in southern Nevada. Military radar and cameras have captured evidence of UFOs flying in the area.

The Nellis Test Range UFO footage is an excellent example of what seems to be a real UFO caught on tape. This object, tracked by military radar and cameras, flies boldly around in a bright, clear sky seemingly unconcerned that it is being watched and photographed.

The object recorded on videotape flying over the desert terrain that day appears to be constantly changing shape. At first it appears to be disc-shaped, then it looks somewhat like a small jet with round, stubby wings. Then it changes into three balls; at no point in the video is the object ever clearly defined. It is as if it is surrounded by fog or mist, keeping it just out of focus.

What kind of object are we dealing with that is never still, is always changing shape, and seems to be not quite solid?

As the object slowly spins, a projection of some kind can also be seen. There is also a shifting "coal black" region. More often than not, the craft has a morphing, indefinite profile that appears to be self-luminous.

Physicists have speculated that what we see around shape-shifting UFOs may not be the UFO itself, but rather the energy change occurring around the UFO as it moves between dimensions. Apparent "vehicles" that seem to change shape while in the air may not be spacecraft at all, but cross-sections of four-dimensional objects that bisect familiar three-dimensional reality. For example, a three-dimensional cross section of a four-dimensional tube would appear spherical. If the tube was irregular in shape, we would expect it to "change shape" in our three dimensions as it moved, much as a sphere passing through a two-dimensional plane would appear like a rapidly growing disc to any watching flatlanders.

Alan Holt and David Froening, at the end of the 1970s, worked on an extension of Einstein's Unified Field Theory involving what they referred to as a "field propulsion" craft. This spacecraft would change color and shape as it entered different stages of flight—this phenomenon is similar to that described about many UFOs that have been reported

Have UFOs Inspired Morphing Aircraft Designs?

Rumors have circulated among the UFO community that modern aircraft designs have been influenced by back-engineered extraterrestrial spacecraft. According to the website LiveScience.com, NASA and U.S. Department of Defense engineers are trying to create a plane that can morph into new shapes during flight by flexing or twisting, due to being made of new metals that form a kind of "flexible skin."

Amazing advances are being made in the development of new metal alloys. These alloys have remarkable characteristics, in that they will change shape upon the application of an electric current or magnetic field. They change shape, or morph rapidly and with some considerable force. They are termed "compact hybrid actuators," alloys that incorporate advanced nanotechnology that is designed to enable them to mimic living systems in their versatility and dynamism.

The list of potential applications seems endless, and the U.S. military is funding a variety of related research programs exploring the full range of options. Self-healing wings that flex and react like living organisms, versatile bombers that double as agile jet fighters, and swarms of tiny, unmanned aircraft are just a few of the science-fiction-like possibilities that these next-generation technologies could make feasible in the decades ahead.

Might alien aircraft be inspiring NASA and the U.S. Department of Defense in their own designs? (*Art by Ricardo Pustanio*)

In his 1997 book, *The Day after Roswell*, the late Col. Philip J. Corso described his own experience of examining unusual material alleged to have come from the 1947 UFO crash site in New Mexico:

> There was a dull, grayish-silvery foil-like swatch of cloth among these artifacts that you could not fold, bend, tear, or wad up but that bounded right back into its original shape without any creases. It was a metallic fiber with physical characteristics that would later be called "supertenacity," but when I tried to cut it

with scissors, the arms just slid right off without even making a nick in the fibers. If you tried to stretch it, it bounced back, but I noticed that all the threads seemed to be going in one direction. When I tried to stretch it width-wise instead of length-wise, it looked like the fibers had re-orientated themselves to the direction I was pulling in. This couldn't be cloth, but it obviously wasn't metal. It was a combination, to my unscientific eye, of a cloth woven with metal strands that had the drape and malleability of a fabric and the strength and resistance of a metal.

Corso claimed in his book that he "seeded" the alien material to the research departments of Monsanto and Dow. Furthermore, Corso claims that the material had previously been delivered to the Air Material Command at Wright Field. Wright-Patterson Air Force Base is famous in UFO circles for its Foreign Technology Division, purported to hold extra-terrestrial craft and artifacts. It could be that the new morphing technologies being used in new, top secret aircraft are the results of years of study on the UFO debris captured by the United States in the 1940s.

The entire UFO phenomenon is always changing and never clearly defined. When you think that you finally have something definite, the phenomenon changes again and you are back at square one. For more than fifty years, this is what has constantly confounded UFO researchers—when it comes to shape-changing UFOs, there appear to be no real truths or answers.

———◦◦◦—————

THE UFO AS A "LIVING MYTHOLOGICAL SYMBOL"

Throughout the millennia of humankind's spiritual and intellectual evolution the UFO has become a living mythological symbol designed to awaken, and to give guidance to, the energies of life.

The distinguished scholar Joseph Campbell has observed that the most important function of such a mythological symbol not only "turns a person on," but it turns him in a specific direction that enables him to participate effectively in a functioning social group.

Jungian psychotherapist Dr. John W. Perry has identified a living mythological symbol as an "affect image"—an image that speaks directly to the feeling system and instantly elicits a response. Only after the image has affected the percipient where it really counts does the brain provide interpretive and appreciative comments. If a symbol must first be "read" by the brain, it is already a dead symbol and will not produce a responding resonance within the percipient, "… like the answer of a musical string to another equally tuned." When the vital symbols of any given social group are able to evoke such resonances within all its members, "… a sort of magical accord unites them as one spiritual organism, functioning through members, who, though separate in space, are yet one in being and belief."

It is our contention that the UFO continues to provide contemporary humans with a vital, living mythological symbol, an "affect image" that communicates directly to our essential selves, bypassing our brains, evading acculturation, and manipulating historical conditioning. We believe that the image of the UFO somehow serves humankind as a transformative symbol that will unite our entire species as one spiritual organism, functioning through members who (as noted above) "though separate in space, are yet one in being and belief."

For many individuals, the act of staring up at a UFO that remains hovering above them for any length of time may become comparable to the experience of fixing one's attention on a mandala while meditating in order to achieve an altered state of consciousness. After a period of time, the percipient may feel that a mental connection has been made, and the percipient may feel that he or she is receiving "messages" from the object.

Aliens might be starship travelers, but they could also be visitors from other dimensions. (Art by Ricardo Pustanio)

At other times, the flight of the UFO is so erratic that observers may compare its pattern of movement to that of a water bug skimming across the surface of a pond, and wonder whether or not the object might actually be a living thing.

And then there are those UFOs that appear to alter their appearance, becoming, as Tim R. Swartz suggests, as if they were craft with bizarre cloaking mechanisms, or as if they were phantom entities with powers that make them capable of shape-shifting.

Do Extraterrestrial Visitors Walk among Us?

We do not dogmatically exclude the extraterrestrial hypothesis, but we think it more probable that the UFO Intelligences may be manifestations of the Other, and could even be our neighbors right around the corner in another Space-Time continuum.

Because we do believe that there is intelligent life elsewhere in the universe, we can envision the day when an alien astronaut from an extraterrestrial world may indeed request a startled Earthling to take him to his leader. However, what we have thus far been labeling "spaceships," we propose might be multidimensional mechanisms or psychic constructs of our paraphysical companions. We have even come to suspect that, in some instances, what we have been calling "spaceships" may actually be forms of higher intelligences rather than vehicles transporting occupants.

We have also come to respect those who maintain that the Other may fashion bodies that allow entities to walk among us appearing as regular (or almost regular) human beings.

⊸⊸⊸

THE DAY AN EXTRATERRESTRIAL VISITED THE ROSWELL UFO MUSEUM

By E. J. Wilson

E. J. Wilson is the co-author of a book with UFO researcher Noe Torres called Ultimate Guide to the Roswell UFO Crash. *Wilson made contact with us after our appearance on the Jeff Rense radio program with Dennis Balthaser and Noe Torres on July 13, 2012, in which we invited anyone with an ET experience to contact us about it. Wilson, who was the tour guide at the Roswell UFO Museum from March 2000 to May 2008, wrote to inform us about his encounter "with an actual alien being." He assured us that he was not "being funny" or "messing" with us; his account was "simply what happened," and he had a witness to back up his story.*

About 165,000 visitors come to the UFO museum every year. "We got all kinds," Wilson said, beginning his account, "We had every kind of human you can imagine. Some of them were different or strange, but they were all humans, as far as any of us could tell. That changed in September of 2009."

Here is Wilson's account of that strange day when an extraterrestrial visitor stopped by the Roswell UFO Museum.

My co-worker, Gail, and myself were checking in guests at the front counter. I had a strange pair of gentlemen check in with a Dallas zip code. One looked like a normal Texas cowboy, complete with cowboy hat, jeans, plaid shirt, and cowboy boots. He spoke with a Texas accent. The only thing unusual about him was that he was no taller than five feet two inches.

His companion was every bit of seven feet tall and three hundred pounds. In appearance he was humanoid, but not strictly human. His eyes were twice the size of yours and mine, and set on the side of his head.

Now, I want to be very clear about that—his eyes were *huge*—at least twice the size of a human's and set on the *side of his head*, like a horse's. His eyes were perhaps a little back behind where our own temples would be, or the front edges of our ears.

If you're familiar with the 1960s TV show *Bonanza*, I think of these two as Hoss and Little Joe.

Of course, everyone should be aware that some people are born different. That's not what I'm referring to. When this being looked at me, I got a funny feeling in my stomach, and the thought "off-worlder" came into my head. I never had that sensation before or since, presumably because I have not encountered any other off-worlders, or, if I have, none has transmitted that sensation to me.

I speak a few languages, and I'm always interested in accents and regionalisms, so I was dying to hear this being talk.

"So, y'all are from Dallas?" But every time I asked Hoss a question, Little Joe answered! It was infuriating! I wanted to say to Little Joe, "Would you *please* let Hoss answer?" The large being did not say a single word the entire time he was there!

By this time, my co-worker, Gail, was through with whatever she was doing, and the strange pair from "Dallas" had completed check-in and gone into the exhibit area. Without planting a suggestion of any kind, I told her, "Get a look at the big fellow when he comes back around." I didn't say anything about his being alien, an ET hybrid, *nothing*. I wanted her to form her own opinion.

I kept an eye on them. They never spoke to each other, either. But I noticed they would look at something together on the exhibit, and then look back at each other, and then look at something, and look back at each other again. It was as though they were in telepathic communication.

They came out of the exhibit hall and Gail was out in the lobby, so she got a good look at the big one. Face to face, it was clear she made eye contact, the same way I had. She ran over to me and said, "Oh my God, E.J., he's not from this Earth!"

We watched as he went through the door to the gift shop; he filled the entire door frame.

The tallest human I've ever met is a computer salesman in the Atlanta, Georgia, area. He was six feet 8 inches tall and pretty stout, also, but he was a

About 165,000 tourists visit the Roswell UFO Museum in New Mexico. Apparently, the museum is even a draw for out-of-this-world visitors.

good bit shorter than the alien. I want to point out that every tall human I've ever known has been self-conscious about his height. Not necessarily shy, but they do have to be careful about overhead light fixtures, even going through doors and stuff, in case something is hanging down they could bump into. Very often, with the tall people I've known, they develop a slumped posture in an effort to minimize their height. This is because a tall person has to adapt to a shorter environment here on Earth.

That was not the case with this alien. He walked through the museum without a care, as though, wherever he grew up, he did not have to adapt to a shorter world. As though everything was the appropriate size and height for him, and he never had to concern himself with it. If you've been in the UFO museum, there actually is a lot of overhead room, so after they got in the door, there were no hanging obstructions.

[E. J. Wilson told us that the above account has been published in a book called *Roswell USA: Towns That Celebrate UFOs, Lake Monsters, Bigfoot, and Other Weirdness* by UFO researcher and Roswell historian John LeMay.

Real Encounters, Different Dimensions, and Otherworldly Beings

Wilson said that he has read the book, and he felt that LeMay "did an out-standing job of accurately publishing what happened." There was some information that Wilson did not tell LeMay that he considered a follow-up to his encounter with the odd couple because it occurred after the book had come out. This information follows.]

I was in the Roswell Planet UFO shop in the summer of 2011, chatting with the owners, Rick and Dagmar Schupe, when I heard a female voice say, "You're E.J. Wilson."

I was surprised to be recognized, because I didn't think I was at all famous, so I responded, "Wow! If I knew I was famous, I would have shaved and put on a nicer shirt."

The lady, who had just entered the store was with some other people, stated that she recognized me from my website and wanted me to meet "Commander Sanni Ceto."

Sanni Ceto claims to be a Human/Grey hybrid. She's got Asperger syndrome, so she needs help with regular day-to-day activities, like keeping a schedule, attending meetings, etc. Her helper was the lady who introduced us. Now, I am not convinced Sanni is what she claims to be, but she sure looks the part. Sanni is short with very light skin.

We sat down with Sanni at a table. She asked for some paper and pens, and she started drawing all types of art work. Beautiful stuff—mostly alien figures. The weird part is that she didn't orient the paper to herself. She had it angled all over the place, so that sometimes she was drawing sideways or upside-down, etc. It also seemed she was hardly paying attention to what she was doing, but the artwork was fantastic.

I was intrigued by the aliens she was drawing. Sanni's helper told us that Sanni was in telepathic communication with the Greys, and she would try to answer questions.

I asked Sanni about the tall, unusual being that Gail and I had encountered at the UFO museum. Sanni asked me to describe the entity, which I did. She seemed to meditate for a moment, as though in telepathic communication with a mothership or whatever, and then said, "That was a reptilian or reptoid shape-shifter."

Now, if you remember from my original account of meeting the alien, I was trying very hard to get him to speak so I would know what an alien sounds like, but the alien (whom I still think of as "Hoss") never said a word. I asked Sanni if he *could* speak, and what would he sound like? She replied that they can speak, and if he had, his voice would have been very, very deep.

This follow-up part with Sanni, I rarely share with anyone, just because there's no substantiation. I am not sure I believe her myself, only that everything she said fits with the observations I had.

I have had people ask me if the being was a shape-shifter, why didn't he at least move his eyes around to the front?

I have given that a good amount of thought. Have you ever got new glasses or contact lenses? Even though the prescription is correct, it's not what you had before, so there's an adjustment period where things don't look right.

If you're used to your vision being from eyes on the side of your head, then moved them around to the front, that would, I'm sure, necessitate an adjustment period, which might not have been worthwhile for a forty-five-minute visit to the UFO museum.

WHO IS THE ALIEN?

Our dear friend Barbara May is a well-known astrologer who started her career as an accountant until she began studying the stars in 1967. In 1976 she became a professional astrologer and she has never looked back. She is a native Californian, who celebrated fifty years of marriage with her husband, Hoyt, in July 2012. They have two daughters, four granddaughters, and two great-grandchildren. She is as normal as blueberry pie. But in the early 1950s, Barbara had a very eventful day when, she believes, she encountered two aliens—and she, herself, was mistaken as an alien.

Here is her memory of that remarkable occasion:

In January of 1954, my first husband, his best friend, my mother-in-law, and I drove from the Pasadena area in southern California to a restaurant about halfway up Mount Palomar where we heard a man named George Adamski [1891–1965; the first of the famous UFO contactees], who described his encounters with beings from outer space and sold a book that he'd written on the subject. I remember vividly starting the drive to climb that mountain road. I got very nauseous, and soon I was throwing up with my head hanging out the window.

This went on for about half an hour and was awful. Later I learned, with the only

Barbara May could identify aliens in an audience by perceiving how their auras were different. Underneath their human forms were aliens! (*Art by Ricardo Pustanio*)

other pregnancy I ever had, that this was what I did when newly pregnant. I thought at the time I was tossing my cookies in fear of what we might see and hear, but four years later I discovered that I throw up once with each pregnancy, and that's it!

When we reached the restaurant, I saw that the restrooms were outside, so I went into the Ladies to clean up, wash my face, drink some water, and repair my hair and makeup. When I had refreshed myself, I joined the others in a large room where an older man with graying hair was talking about being in a spaceship, interacting with extraterrestrials, and other outer space information.

I had started seeing auras when I was around five years old. As I looked over the audience, I saw two auras that were totally different from any that I'd ever seen before—and they were right next to Mr. Adamski. The auras were very large, and at first I could not make out the faces or shapes of their bodies. Then I saw two young men that I judged to be in their early twenties, slender, and quite tall when they stood up. They were staring at me intently, and I realized that they had sensed that I could see their auras. We had direct communication at that point, but although I was listening to Mr. Adamski, I was openly staring at these two strangers—who were "strangers" in a new way to me.

Within a few minutes, those two strangers and I were sharing thoughts without speaking. Not a conversation, just the sharing.

I settled down, directing my attention to Mr. Adamski, and the day passed with talking to others in the room during breaks. I noticed that the two young men with the strange auras never left Mr. Adamski's side. At one point there was a definite break in the "Q and A" with Mr. Adamski, and I again went to the Ladies room outside. When I returned to the main room, I met a young man who asked me if I was from this planet! He seemed half serious and half teasing, so the imp in me replied, "No, I'm from Venus."

The young man got very pale and ran away from me. I laughed, looked up, and saw the two young men with the strange auras looking at me and laughing with delight. I joined the laughter and went on my way back inside the restaurant.

Were those two young men really from another planet? I've always thought so, because in the fifty-eight years since, I've traveled the world and never seen auras like the ones I saw that day coming from them. I recall in sharp relief everything that happened that day: the colors, the smells and my feelings. I was never afraid of those two young men with the strange auras. They felt like old friends.

Why do I recall that day so clearly after all this time? As a curious aside, the baby I was carrying nearly cost me my life as well as her own, and she's always been fascinated by science fiction. In fact, *both* of our girls are like that. I haven't told many people about this, just my husband, Hoyt.

⤛⫷∿⫸⤜

MY PERSONAL ENCOUNTER STORY

By Sean Casteel

Sean Casteel has written about UFOs, alien abduction, and related phenomena since 1989. Casteell contributed regularly to Tim Beckley's magazine UFO Universe, *eventually being given the title associate editor. He continued to write special reports and books for both of Beckley's publishing companies, Inner Light Publications and Global Communications. To date, Casteel's book titles include* UFOs, Prophecy and the End of Time, Nikola Tesla's Death Ray and the Columbia Space Shuttle Disaster, *and, coauthored with Beckley,* Our Alien Planet: This Eerie Earth. *Casteel's personal take on UFOs is biblical, meaning, as he says, "I believe the aliens are basically angelic creatures, not demons or mad scientists from outer space. I realize I am probably in a very small minority, but there it is."*

Like many who come into the UFO field, or rather get dragged kicking and screaming into it, Sean Casteel had no particular interest in UFOs or aliens, and would have sneered at anyone who did. But of course that all changed once he had an encounter of his own, which he shares below.

I was nineteen years old and living in Austin, Texas, working as a dishwasher while I tried to form a band to back me while I sang my own original songs. I was obsessed with following in the path of Bob Dylan and writing lyrics that were genuinely poetic and meaningful.

I was sharing an apartment with two other musicians but not having much luck in assembling the needed players. One of my roommates suggested that a local fiddle player he knew might be interested in joining us. I was sitting in our living room one spring day in 1977 when the person I thought was the fiddle player knocked on our door and warmly greeted my roommate. The fiddle player was wearing very black sunglasses and cowboy boots with shorts. Not the height of fashion at the time.

At that point, I was plunged into blackness. I had no idea what was going on. I began to hear a voice speaking to me telepathically, but I don't recall anything the voice actually said. I knew whatever it was, it was reading my mind, and I became ecstatic at the thought that I could communicate so easily, that I could be understood completely without the effort to put things into words. I have a very clear memory of looking into jet black eyes, which I assumed at the time were the dark sunglasses of the fiddle player. I now realize the black eyes were more likely that of the standard gray alien. I also heard the repeated sound of a vault door slamming, which I read in later years was reported by other people as well.

I remember conversing about my music for a little while and I also recall moments of heart-pounding terror, though I don't remember any specific cause for that feeling. I somehow came out of the trance or whatever it was and was back in the living room. The fiddle player was leaving and I could hear the grinding of the gears on his pickup truck, like something was wrong with his engine. The idea of that seemed to please me for some reason.

When I spoke to one of my roommates from the Austin period ten years later, in 1987, he told me that the other roommate had found me wandering around in the front yard babbling incoherently the night following the living-room-telepathy encounter. I apparently hadn't been returned safely to the living room as I thought I was, but was missing for several hours and couldn't even speak intelligibly on my return. Needless to say, I was asked to find another place to live.

In 1982, I was living in Norman, Oklahoma, in a basement apartment near the campus of The University of Oklahoma. It was in the springtime, and I left my apartment to walk a short distance down the street to a pizza delivery place. I placed my order and then started walking back to my apartment to await the pizza. A voice spoke to me, saying something like, "Look up if you want to see something interesting."

So I looked up, and in the darkening sky above my apartment building, I saw two ships pass by in close formation less than fifty yards from where I stood. They were shiny and metallic, one a bright green and the other a polished gold color. Their shape is hard to describe, but they weren't the standard disc shape or cigar shape. They were completely silent except for the slightest sound of the wind passing around them as they flew.

My next recollection is of waking up in my bed the next day. I never got the pizza and I'm sure the delivery person was miffed that I wasn't there to pay him anything, or give him a tip.

I realize now, after more than twenty years of studying the UFO and alien abduction phenomena, that these are the exact kinds of experiences—including the amnesia associated with certain aspects of them—that are often studied under regressive hypnosis in order to retrieve those minutes or hours of "missing time."

During one of my many conversations with the late abduction research pioneer, Budd Hopkins, he advised me not to submit to regressive hypnosis, even though he used it all the time, because after so many years of researching abduction myself, I probably wouldn't be able to "trust" what I remembered. I would quite naturally think that I was at least partially generating the mental images, etc., from unconscious memories of my own research and would be

It is common for people to experience amnesia after being abducted by aliens. (*Art by Bill Oliver*)

plunged into even worse doubt and uncertainty about what had happened. Budd said that unless not knowing what happened to me was disrupting my life, I should just leave it all alone.

It was reading Whitley Strieber's *Communion* in 1989 that led to the first real breakthrough for me, and I'll always be grateful for having the presence of mind to check it out of the local library in Norman, Oklahoma. I suddenly realized that so much of the "high strangeness" of my life since the experience in Austin was also happening to millions of other people and we were all just beginning to explore a completely different reality that was both terrifying and beautiful.

Somewhere along the line I read that the initial experience with this kind of paranormal thing is almost always viewed in negative terms because of the extreme shock involved in realizing that this other reality even exists at all, something the late Harvard psychiatrist Dr. John Mack called "ontological shock" and the subsequent uncomfortable realignment of everything you formerly held to be true.

After I got my journalism degree at The University of Oklahoma, I did freelance work for some local newspapers, but after reading Whitley's *Communion* and Budd's *Intruders*, most of my writing concerned itself with UFOs and alien abduction. That has been the case for many years now.

I still don't know what memories are there, hiding just beneath the surface. To this day, I have no memory of seeing a gray alien even once, beyond the grip of those large black eyes I saw in Austin. I can only hope that the overall experience is happening for a good reason and that people are being "chosen" to take part in some kind of blessed transformation of this planet and ourselves, leading to something like the paradise that is promised at the end of the Book of Revelation, where God will actually come to dwell alongside mankind. Perhaps the New Jerusalem will be a large, bejeweled ship from "out there" somewhere. Once you allow for aliens in the mix, anything becomes possible.

REAL ENCOUNTERS ARE LEARNING EXPERIENCES

We believe that if there are paraphysical beings who walk among us, they may have the ability to influence the human mind telepathically in order to project what may appear to be three-dimensional images. The image seen may depend in large part upon the preconceptions the human observer has about alien life forms. Thus, reported accounts of spaceship occupants run the gamut from Bug-Eyed Monsters to Little Green Men to Metaphysical Space Brothers to Slender Young Men with Large Auras.

Although we may not perceive these intelligences in their true form—if, indeed, they even possess physical forms—it seems clear that most people would be more likely to communicate with a "Visitor" that is fairly conventional in appearance, and that once human attention has been attracted, the intelligence-mechanism of the Other could quite easily alter human consciousness. We believe that many of the "chance" encounters that occur between human witnesses and the Other are in reality learning experiences for the human percipients; that is, they were designed to assist the percipients to become aware that humankind is not alone in the universe or on this planet. After extensive research, we have come to the conclusion that it may not really matter *who* perceives the many divergent beings fashioned by the multidimensional intelligences; the important thing is that *someone* acknowledges and interacts with them on either a conscious or an unconscious level.

CONTACT WITH SPACE BROTHERS AND SISTERS

In the previous chapter, Barbara May told of having attended a seminar by George Adamski when she was a young woman in 1954. Adamski (1891–1965) was the first of the New Age UFO prophets to gain national and international attention. According to his account, just as the prophets of old went out into the desert to receive their revelations directly from God or the angels, Adamski went out into the night near Desert Center, California, on November 20, 1952, and received his first encounter with Orthon, a Venusian Space Brother. Their communication occurred through telepathic transfer, and Adamski learned that the space traveler had come in peace and that he was greatly concerned with the spiritual growth of humankind.

After Adamski published *Flying Saucers Have Landed*, co-authored with Desmond Leslie, he became popular as a lecturer, as our friend Barbara May witnessed firsthand. Flying saucer mania was rampant in the early 1950s, with steady sightings of unidentified flying objects keeping the rampant rumors about the alleged saucer crash in Roswell, New Mexico, in 1947, ever in public awareness. There was an eager segment of the population who wanted to know who was piloting the mysterious craft in the sky, where they were from, what they looked like, and whether they were friendly or hostile. Adamski had the answers. Orthon had come in peace, eager to warn earthlings about radiation from the nuclear tests that were being conducted. There were universal laws and principles established by the Creator of All, and the people of Earth would do well to begin to practice those laws at once.

Adamski described his Space Brother as smooth-skinned, beardless, with shoulder-length, blond hair, who stood about five feet six inches tall, and wore what appeared to be some kind of jumpsuit-like uniform. Adamski

George Adamski first encountered the Venusian people in 1952, encountering a being named Orthon. (*Art by Bill Oliver.*)

received the first of the messages telepathically, but later, after he had been taken for a trip into outer space, he was able to communicate verbally with such entities as Firkon, the Martian, and Ramu, from Saturn, as well as his friend Orthon.

The death of George Adamski on April 23, 1965, by no means termi-nated the heated controversy that had never stopped swirling around the pro-lific and articulate contactee. Throughout his career as a contactee, Adamski's believers steadfastly declared him to be one of the most saintly of men, com-pletely devoted to the teachings of universal laws. After his death, a number of his followers provided their disciple of intergalactic peace with a kind of instant resurrection. In the book *The Scoriton Mystery* by Eileen Buckle, a con-tactee named Ernest Bryant claims to have met three spacemen on April 24,

1965, one of whom was a youth named Yamski, whose body already housed the reincarnated spirit of George Adamski.

Adamski's desert encounter with a Venusian and Robert Wise's motion picture *The Day the Earth Stood Still*, with its warning from the alien messenger Klaatu that the people of Earth had better clean up their act, were probably the two most contributive factors in birthing the UFO contactee movement in the United States.

⸺⬥⸺

PROFILE OF A UFO CONTACTEE AND THE COSMIC GOSPEL

UFO contactees are men and women who are convinced that they have encountered alien "space intelligences" and that they remain in direct communication with them through telepathic thought transference. The contact experience with the Space Brothers and Sisters follows very much the same pattern all over the world.

1. The contactees first saw a UFO on the ground, hovering low overhead. Sometimes they report having heard a slight humming sound above them which drew their attention to a mysterious craft.

2. A warm ray of "light" emanated from the craft and touched the contactees on the neck, the crown of the head, or the middle of the forehead where the "third eye" of higher awareness is located. Many state that they lost consciousness at this point and, upon awakening, may have discovered that they could not account for anywhere from a minute or two to an hour or two of their time.

3. None of the flying saucer contactees report feeling any fear of their solar brothers and sisters, and most of them eagerly look forward to a return visit from them. The contactees agree that the Space Beings' most prominent characteristic is wisdom, and they seem to take their space siblings' scientific knowledge for granted. If they have traveled through space from other worlds to Earth, then they have to be extremely and sublimely intelligent.

4. After the initial contact experience, nearly all contactees seem to suffer through several days of restlessness, irritability, sleeplessness, and unusual dreams or nightmares. Many contactees are told that they were selected for contact because they really are aliens or hybrids, who were planted on Earth as

very small children. They are advised that their cosmic abilities will soon begin to manifest. In some cases, UFO researchers have observed that there does seem to be a heightening of what one would normally consider manifestations of extrasensory perception after the contact experience with an alleged benevolent Space Being. Along with psychic abilities, the contactee is often left with a timetable of certain predictions of future events.

5. Family and friends of the contactees report that they appear to be changed persons after their alleged experience with the Space Beings.

6. After a period of a week to several months, the contactee who has received a message from the Space Beings feels compelled to go forth and share it with others.

The essence of the Cosmic Gospel of the Space Brothers contains such concepts as the following:

1. Humankind is not alone in the solar system, and what humans do somehow affects the entire universe. After the explosions of atomic bombs in 1945 signaled that Earth had entered the nuclear age, brothers and sisters from outer space have come to Earth to help those humans who will listen to their promise of a larger universe and heed their warnings to become better caretakers of the planet.

2. The Space Beings want humankind to become eligible to join an intergalactic spiritual federation.

3. The Space Beings have come to assist the people of Earth to lift their spiritual vibratory rate so they may enter new dimensions. (According to the Space Beings, Jesus, Krishna, Confucius, and many of the other leaders of the great religions came to Earth to teach humanity these very same abilities.)

4. The citizens of Earth stand now in a transitional period before the dawn of a New Age of peace, love, and understanding.

5. If the Earthlings should not raise their vibratory rate within a set period of time, severe earth changes and major cataclysms will take place and a larger portion of the human population will be destroyed.

In spite of such setbacks as public humiliations when unfulfilled prophecies have received wide publicity and do not come to pass, a good many of the contactees continue to be imbued with an almost religious fervor to spread the message that has been given to them by the Space Beings.

Some researchers have observed that the Space Beings appear to function as do the angels of more conventional theologies. Both beings are concerned about Earth, and they seem to be actively trying to protect it and the people on it. Both the Space Beings and the angels are entities who appear to have control over the physical limitations of time and space—yet they are benevolent in their actions toward humankind. It seems that Space Beings have deliberately placed themselves in the role of messengers of God, which is the biblical definition of the word "angel."

George Van Tassel (1910–1978) published his first booklet in 1952 and introduced the world to "Ashtar," commandant of station Schare, said to be one of several saucer stations in Blaau, the fourth sector of Bela, into which our solar system is moving. Van Tassel, operator of the Giant Rock Airport in California's Mojave Desert, received most of this information directly from the Council of Seven Lights, a group of discarnate earthlings inhabiting a space ship orbiting our planet. He received these messages when he went into a trance while sitting at the base of the huge rock that gave the region its name. "Shan" was the name that Van Tassel's contact gave for planet Earth. Van Tassel's Ashtar also decreed the universe to be ruled by the Council of Seven Lights, which had divided the Cosmos into sector systems and sectors.

Some researchers have observed that the Space Beings appear to function as do the angels of more conventional theologies.

Van Tassel founded the Ministry of Universal Wisdom based on his revelations of the Space Brothers. This ministry teaches the universal law, which operates on humankind in seven states: gender (male and female); the creator as cause; polarity of negative and positive; vibration; rhythm; ruled by the Council of Seven Lights, which had divided the Cosmos into sector systems and sectors.

On August 24, 1952, an alien named Solgonda invited Van Tassel to travel aboard a spaceship. When Van Tassel returned to Earth, he knew that it would be his special mission to host space conventions at Giant Rock. And this the genial, colorful contactee did until his death in 1978. During his lifetime, he also found time to travel the United States, presenting nearly three hundred lectures and appearing on over four hundred radio and television programs.

SIMILARITIES BETWEEN SPACE CONTACTEES AND SPIRIT MEDIUMS

Although most of the contactees claim an initial physical contact with a Space Being, the operable mechanics of the experience seem very reminiscent of what can be seen in Spiritualism when the medium works with a spirit guide or a control from the "Other Side." In Spiritualistic or mediumistic channeling, the medium enters the trance state and relays information from the guide, an entity who contacts various spirits from the other side. The mechanism in the Flying Saucer Movement is very often that of the contactee going into some state of trance and channeling information from Space Beings. Because the trigger mechanism that the facets of the Other employ in making contact has something to do with the psychological state of the individual contactee, subjective elements invariably infuse mystic and paranormal experiences into the experience.

Perhaps the most revealing "mythic" giveaway in UFO contactee cases, pointed out by such researchers as Michael Talbot (1953–1992), is the delivering of the Cosmic Gospel. Many UFO-entity encounters feature figures suggestive of various spiritual avatars who appear to exhibit the characteristics of divine revelation. The entities' avowed purpose for appearing to the witness is to convey a sort of heavenly message, or "orgalogue."

In his thought-provoking paper, "A Mile to Midsummer," Talbot refers to such phenomena as appearances of the Virgin Mary, fairies, and so forth, as "protean-psychoid." Talbot states that they are "protean" because they are all part of the same chameleon-like phenomenon that changes to reflect the belief structures of the time. He goes on to say that they are "psychoid" in that they are a paraphysical phenomenon and are related to the psychological state of the observer.

Talbot states that it is the subjective and paraphysical aspect of UFOs that sheds the most light on their nature. If UFOs appeared to be totally a physical phenomenon, Talbot points out, it would be easier to deal with them as extraterrestrial or even ultra-terrestrial. An astronomer does not experience "headaches," "strange voices," "visions," or "poltergeist phenomena" every time he discovers a redshifted galaxy. The phenomena with which astronomers, and the majority of scientists, deal are objective and physical.

"The paraphysical nature of UFOs has always suggested that they are somehow 'less real' than redshifted galaxies," Talbot comments.

"In any case, three facts remain: (1) People *are* experiencing UFO phenomena and contacts. (2) The phenomenon strongly suggests an 'objective' nature. (3) The phenomenon also strongly suggests a 'subjective' nature.

"The fact that we have not been able to resolve the conflict between their subjective and objective nature indicates that perhaps the only conflict is in our assumptions concerning experience. Not only must UFOs be considered in both their subjective and objective light; that is, as an 'omnijective' phenomenon, but the categories of 'real' and 'unreal' become meaningless."

THE "SILENT" CONTACTEES

It is impossible to estimate how many men and women claim to receive messages from Space Beings. Groups continue to rise from dynamic contactees, each with their variations of previous revelations and their own occasional individual input.

There is also the category of revelators that UFO researchers term the "silent contactees"—men and women who have not gathered groups about them, but who have established contact with what they feel to be entities from other worlds and who have directed their lives according to the dictates of those Space Beings. Many of these men and women continue to work in conventional jobs, confiding their experiences only to close associates and family members.

We would term Don Avery a silent contactee. He has been active in civic life in his community. He is a former Democratic candidate for County Commissioner and Flatland County, Montana, administrator. He quietly researches the phenomenon of contact by using his own experience as the case study. He told us that he does not travel the country advertising himself as a channel for the Space Brothers. He has prepared the below *UFO Diary* especially for this book.

UFO DIARY: KINGMAN & PARKER, ARIZONA: WINTERS OF 2010 THROUGH 2012 UFO SIGHTINGS

By Don Avery

The time frame was mid-April 2010. My wife, Peggy, and I had recently arrived in Kingman, Arizona, to pick up a fifth-wheel trailer. This was just a few days before the BP oil well blowout. I was standing behind the trailer in a KOA campground, taking a photo for use in a book being published by Brad Steiger dealing with various real monsters. I was one of the contributors.

While waiting for my wife to retrieve the camera for the photo, I noticed a sharp glint or reflection in my eyes coming from above and slightly to the left. I observed that an object was slowly ascending. It did not have wings or emit any noticeable emissions. It was also silent. Having been down this road many times before, I attempted to grasp an idea of time loss. [Contactees often report "missing time" during their visits from the communicating entity.] It couldn't have been much, maybe a few minutes. But, they don't need much. I knew that they had something for me.

"The attitude of the Star People toward the oil spill was one of complete outrage. I was quite surprised to see the level of emotion that was displayed by these entities." (*Art by Bill Oliver*)

The attitude of the Star People toward the oil spill was one of complete outrage. I was quite surprised to see the level of emotion that was displayed by these entities.

These beings are very dark, red-brown and fairly large in stature. I'm guessing five feet nine inches to five feet eleven inches. I was ten at my first encounter experience and the smallest of the entities was about an inch taller than me.

They claim that the well disaster in the Gulf of Mexico was already under way and that BP had lied and was down some forty thousand feet under the sea floor creating a long-term disaster that even they [Star People] could not repair. There is now long-term geological damage to the sea floor and the consequences could be devastating.

Humankind has been a poor steward of this planet and the Star People are so angry about this current disaster that they don't know what to do next.

They will consult with the other groups of Star People who are utilizing this planet.

I wanted to know what they expected me to do about all of this. Why are you venting at me?

I was told, "We will be back." I was instructed to continue paying attention to these things and to prepare.

I then realized that after the last visit that I remember (July 2008) I earnestly began to store and prepare for almost any eventuality. In fact, I have stored up food and necessary survival items for almost twenty years. I got the impression that they were deceived by BP and our government and that there was some serious retribution coming our way.

On January 12, 2011, I was driving from the RV park that we were staying at in Parker Dam, Arizona, to Parker, a distance of fifteen miles. I left at 11:30 A.M. and arrived in Parker at approximately 12:15 P.M. The speed limit was fifty mph. The drive normally takes seventeen to eighteen minutes. I remember leaving and arriving, but that's about it. I'm missing twenty to twenty-five minutes.

My wife, Peggy, watched a disc hovering above the Colorado River below Parker Dam for several minutes in mid-February 2011, after dark, around 9:30 P.M. She came running into our fifth-wheeler all excited. When she ran back outside, it was still there hovering across the river from us.

I experienced a stationary object hovering silently over the desert near Parker, Arizona, on October 27, 2011. It was stationary for several minutes and had a number of flashing lights. It exited in a blur of speed. I'm not aware of time lost.

My wife spotted a stationary red light over our area on the night of January 13, 2012. She seems to spot peculiar night light displays about once a week in the Arizona skies during the winter.

On January 14, 2012, at approximately 6:20 P.M. I went for a walk around the south half of the RV park where we are spending the winter on the Colorado River near Parker, Arizona, I had covered about two-thirds of the route when I noticed a bright, reddish light off to the west over the river. At first I thought that it might be a planet that I had failed to notice earlier because there was some light cloud cover. But, the clouds slid behind it and a commercial jet was high overhead above it. Its height is hard to estimate, maybe 1,200 to 1,500 feet. It was slowly sliding south and

Avery drew this sketch of the UFO he and his wife, Peggy, saw hovering over the Colorado River.

Real Encounters, Different Dimensions, and Otherworldly Beings

gave off no emissions. It did not have any appendages or emit any sound. It began to ascend as I rounded the corner en route to our fifth-wheeler. It was now dark. At that point, I saw another one (or maybe the same one) off to the north about one-half mile from where I saw the first one. This one was very bright, lower in altitude, and sliding west above the park to our northwest.

I yelled at my wife to come outside. We both watched it for several minutes. I grabbed the camera, but at this point, it was starting to ascend. It was identical to the first one that I saw. That's four sightings in two days. What gives? I'm not aware of any time lost.

On January 18, 2012, at 7:06 P.M., I stepped out of our fifth-wheeler when I observed a glowing red light hovering to the north at about one thousand feet. It made no sound or emissions. I beckoned to my wife to come and watch. We both observed it for about a minute before it ascended and disappeared. I have bought a new camera and came close to getting a photo. If it keeps showing up, I will get a picture of this craft. This also occurred on the 29th of January, but it was not close enough to get a decent picture.

February 8, 2012, at 7:15 P.M., my wife called me outside to observe a light moving across the eastern sky (north to south). It was silent and exhibited no emissions or appendages. It proceeded parallel to us, ascended, and then made a 90 degree turn and headed east. You can't see much, just a light. I will use a telephoto the next time. The moving light is at the center of the photo and is the largest light

On Friday, February 10, 2012, at approximately 7:45 P.M., my wife and I watched a reddish light approaching us from the northwest at a slow rate of speed. It stopped and hovered for several minutes and then headed north at a rapid rate of speed. It seems that we see this type of light every couple of weeks. What it is, I do not know [but I made] a sketch of what it appeared to resemble through binoculars.

A sketch by Don Avery of the UFO he and his wife saw in 2012.

On Saturday, February 25, 2012, at 7:14 P.M., we were driving back from having dinner out and spotted a reddish light off to the north. By the time I parked the truck and retrieved the camera it had accelerated to the north and disappeared. This event replicates many of the other sightings reported in this blog.

On Sunday, April 1, 2012, at about 12:05 P.M., I was out for a walk, heading north to a marina and restaurant located on the Colorado River about one-quarter mile north of the RV park where we are spending the winter. As I rounded the end of the marina, I noticed a silver object above the California side of the river. Based upon the height of the adjoining hills I would place its elevation at five to six thousand feet and horizontal distance at about one-half mile. The time was 12:23 P.M.

I watched it for about forty-five seconds as it slid to the southwest and began to ascend. It had a top or upper deck. It did not have any wings. No emissions were evident and it made no noise that I could hear. I returned home, arriving at 12:32 P.M. I'm missing about eight to nine minutes.

From almost sixty years of contact experience, I can assure others of several things:

1. There is something coming our way. What and when, I do not know. But I think that our government has a feel for this and has constructed a number of underground facilities that they think are safe havens from whatever awaits us. I have some bad news for them. Your best chance is topside. Don't be a mole in a hole with nowhere to go.

2. They (this group of Star People) do not communicate with our government because of the extreme level of corruption.

3. They cannot stand being lied to. They absolutely abhor it. They prefer putting up with my bad attitude and previous efforts to engage in extreme violence than being jerked around by a species of beings that barely registers on the intelligence scale. Whatever you do, stand up straight and get counted. They may not like it, but they will respect it.

4. They do have their tolerance level. I feel a very ancient connection to them. I believe that many of our life experiences are predicated upon prenatal accords in an effort to advance ourselves in a very positive sense. Those that revert to prior conduct have a very serious problem. There is no place to hide.

Stand up strong and be true to honesty and yourself, no matter what the consequences. In the long run, you will advance.

[Don and his wife, Peggy, have a blog preppingmadeeasy.blogspot.com in which they demonstrate a ten-step process to help individuals think their way through any emergency. Don has another blog, destroyedby-oil.blogspot.com, that deals with all kinds of interesting experiences ranging from Bigfoot and the paranormal to conspiracy theories and articles related to health issues and history. It has had many thousands of visitors.]

HE COMMUNICATES WITH HIS BROTHER ON ANOTHER PLANET

Our good friend Tom T. Moore of Plano, Texas, surprised us when he told us that he was in touch with "his brother on another planet." Over the past forty years, we have interviewed dozens of men and women who claim to be in regular communication with Space Intelligences, but in this case the contactee was a man that Brad had known for more than thirty years and who we considered a very down-to-earth businessman. Now we did know that Tom had always been interested in mystical and spiritual explorations and had quite recently published a book and established a website titled "The Gentle Way: A Self Help Guide for Those Who Believe in Angels." But now we had a serious Texas gentleman telling us that he had established contact with an amphibian gentleman on another planet.

We had to learn more, and Tom was generous to his usual standard of benevolently expecting great things, and he allowed us to include in this book a portion of his forthcoming book on his conversations with Antura in the Sirius B Star System.

CONVERSATIONS WITH MY BROTHER ON ANOTHER PLANET
By Tom T. Moore

In July of 2005 I discovered that I could communicate with other beings while in a light Alpha-altered state. This took place during a seminar put on by the master hypnotist Richard Sutphen, who is well known for his books on past lives.

I had decided to try and communicate with an American Indian shaman living in the western United States during the 1600s by the name of "Reveals the Mysteries." He had been "channeled" for me by my friend Robert Shapiro. When Richard put us under, ostensibly to try our hand at automatic writing, I thought in my mind, "Reveals the Mysteries, are you there?" He responded, "Yes I am, Tom," and I thought to myself, "Wow!"

He went on to tell me I was an Indian shaman by the name of "Still Water," living at that same time, and I had decided to "… reintroduce people to The Gentle Way," in the twentieth and twenty-first centuries. That became the title of my first book, from that very first conversation with Reveals the Mysteries. Later I would begin to communicate with Gaia, the Soul of the Earth and my own Guardian Angel, whom I named Theo, as he said our vocal chords were not made to say angelic names. Theo told me we can communicate with anyone anywhere in the universe because we receive "thought packets" which we filter according to our education, knowledge, and spiritual beliefs. But it's even easier if the person is part of your soul group or "cluster," as Theo calls them, which on average is six to twelve fragments of your soul. Reveals the Mysteries turned out to be part of my soul "cluster."

A couple of years later, I was communicating with Theo in meditation one morning on the subject of ancient ET ruins on earth, and Theo told me, "They will be able to point these artifacts out to you at some future point." I asked if he meant "you" generally or "you" personally. He responded, "It will be you personally, Tom. You will have the privilege of meeting a Sirian one day."

He then asked if I would like to speak to him, as he was tuning in to us. After I got over the surprise that we were on a "party line" and not having a confidential conversation, I declined and said I would put together some questions for my next meditation. And thus began many, many questions for my soul "cluster" brother living a life in the Sirius B Star System.

Texas native Tom T. Moore asserted that he was in touch with an alien who lived on another planet. (*Art by Ricardo Pustanio*)

I would have difficulty receiving his name correctly for several weeks. First it was "Antu," then "Anturara," and finally one day he almost shouted out the word (thought packet-wise) "AntuRAH!" He explained that we had several lives together, the last one being in Atlantis. He said he had more lives on earth after that, just not with me.

I would have another big surprise after we began communicating. I had always heard first public contact would be with people that looked just like us—probably the Pleiadians. So naturally I assumed since he would be coming to see us he would appear just like any earth human—more or less.

In one of our early conversations I was asking him about his planet and he explained that it had a small landmass, with most of the planet covered by water. I then asked if he lived on land or in the ocean, and he replied he was a water being—an amphibian! He likes the term coined by the host of a radio show I appeared on—"Aqua Man."

If you saw any of the *Hellboy* movies, there is an amphibian character by the name of Abe Sapien. If you do a search for images from that movie, you'll get as close as we possibly can to a photographic description of him. He has gills behind rounded ears. He has "strikingly beautiful" (he says) blue skin, tinged with white and yellow to blend with the ocean for protection in their early lives on the planet. His eyes are round, but smaller than the Zeta eyes, with eyelids, and a smaller nose. He has four digits—no thumbs, as they say they don't need them—and four toes. Naturally they are webbed. They're vegetarians and not oxygen breathers.

Antura says they live to be 1,200 to 1,500 years old, as their lives are not as difficult as ours. He is already between 450 and 500 years of age. They do excrete waste, just not as often as we do. Their females typically do not have children until after their 125th year and no periods until they are ready to conceive. Gestation is six months to birth their "little tadpoles" as he humorously says. They sleep a little less than earth humans and dream, as do most beings in the universe. Their universal greeting is to wish a long life or good life. They were amused at the Star Trek greeting (but I still like it!).

Antura's water planet is one of more than twenty planets in the Sirius B Star System. Only 10 to 12 percent of the planet is landmass and there are beings that live on the land, which they are friends with. Their city is approximately one mile below the surface, with a large percentage of it dry, but also many places with access to water. He and his family live in what we would consider an apartment building. As is typical, it seems, of other societies in the universe they do not play competitive games, as that involves negativity. He says that's what earth people will bring to the rest of the universe—small amounts of negativity—typically 0.2 percent to 2 percent maximum. Even though it will be several hundred years this seems to make them nervous. We're supposed to be the catalysts to get these societies moving again to raise their vibrational levels. I thought they would be at 5.85 on the fifth-focus frequency scale but was told it was more like 5.35, and his planet has been inhabited for around eighteen million years!

He said I originated on that planet, and in fact was one of the first souls to have a life there; he also said I was one of the first to have a life on earth. It seems each life I have is as some sort of spiritual master, as that is my soul's main interest. He further stated that my next life will be back on the water planet before my next earth life as a female space pilot of one of seventeen earth starships in the 3400 era. Antura said we will not begin traveling to the stars until around 3250. One earth ship will actually leave for one of the nearer star systems without the advantage of "portal hopping" as Antura calls it, but will be rescued by one of the very first starships using portals to travel a few years later.

He explains that you cannot go from one side of the universe to the other with one portal hop; it takes several. He compared it to Southwest Airlines going from one part of the United States to the other, making three or four stops. When I expressed surprise at the comparison, he explained that they know "everything" about us, having studied us for years and years. The best explanation I could get out of him is that there are folds in space. I asked for a better explanation and he said he could not, as our scientists must figure that out themselves. He said to imagine waves in the ocean.

So why did he contact me? He's part of a "first contact team" that contacts other planets as they find them all over the universe. I asked him what was the last planet he performed this duty on, and he said it was a planet inhabited by what we might call sloths. They're a few thousand years away from more development, but they like to introduce themselves at an early stage. They somehow used the form of a wise sloth so as not to frighten the local population.

> **S**o why did he contact me? He's part of a "first contact team" that contacts other planets as they find them all over the universe.

When asked what was his background that made him ideal for the first contact team, he said he had lived eight hundred lives on earth and that had given him the "gift of gab." It seems he does grassroots-type contacts, as compared to the team members who work with governments and scientists. Which is where I come in. Since I'm one of his soul cluster "brothers," he said he planned to meet with me and two other people when they come in 2017, two years after the Pleiadians (who do look just like us) make first public contact in Europe in 2015. One of the other people is a lady living in Provence in southern France. She's also a member of our soul cluster. He says I have even visited the town during my many trips to Cannes as part of my international film and TV program distribution business. The other person lives in Asia and is not a soul cluster member, but Antura has had a number of lives with him on earth.

So I thought, this will be interesting, getting to meet a real-life alien. He explained that I would be given instructions to go to a remote location where he would meet me. Naturally I asked if I could have a ride in the "scout craft," which he described as typically saucer shaped, about forty feet in diameter, and capable of carrying five to eight passengers. He said of course I could. Now after hundreds of more questions I've discovered that I'll actually go to his "mothership" and stay for a month or two, if I wish, getting to know all the crew members.

He says that the mothership, which is thousands of years old, holds seven hundred to one thousand crew members. He told me my senses would be on overload, as there will be so many different types of ETs I'll meet, mostly from the Sirius B System—but others too, including two reptilians who "like to stay to themselves." He explained that several million years ago there was a real star wars started by the reptilians. It was really nasty, as instead of blowing up a planet as we've seen in the sci-fi movies, they would blow up the sun, destroying all the planets in that solar system. And this went on for several thousand universal years (which are different from earth years). Finally peace came again. Supposedly I had a hand in the peace process during one of my spiritual master lives. I suggested that the reptilians be allowed to take part in the "earth experiment" by providing souls, too. I've been told that one of my current friends has a reptilian soul and was put in my path so that I could see how they're faring.

Recently I found that we would also visit our moon in Antura's scout craft. We'll probably go the "conventional" way of a speedy trip there and then he'll demonstrate a "portal hop" back to the mothership.

Of course I had many questions about the mothership, especially when I learned how many different beings would be on board. He explained that when the crew is known, they are able to insert "modules" to accommodate each being according to its needs. There will be birds, insects, amphibians, and all sorts of humanoids on board, as best I understand. I did make sure my module would have a toilet! He said no problem.

It seems the mothership, at least in the common areas, has a mild temperature setting, but I'll be wearing sort of a mini force field, which will supply me with slightly higher oxygen content than is normal on earth, with my own temperature setting. There are translation devices far beyond what we have today, which will enable me to speak to anyone on board and vice versa. The crew does not wear uniforms, just the normal attire they wear on their home planets (assuming they wear anything). Antura says that some beings meet in common areas for meals and some beings eat elsewhere and join for discussion later. He said I wouldn't want to see some of the eating habits—even he doesn't wish to. Not sure if I wish to find out too much more about that, but we'll see.

There doesn't seem to be a real work schedule. Beings work when they feel like it or are motivated to do some specific work—taking readings or whatever they do when they're studying earth. Antura says, "Parking is at a premium," as there can be upwards of fifty ships, from multiple galaxies and universes, as we seem to be the big story—switching from the third to the fifth focus. That's never been done before by any other society.

It's my understanding that it will be my job to introduce the beings of the Sirius B Star System to the people on earth, as they look so different from the Pleiadians. It's one thing to meet people from another star system whose appearance is very close to yours, but I think there's a fear-factor of meeting intelligent beings—and even much more intelligent perhaps than you—who look quite strange indeed. Although they probably will not be on his ship, Antura says there are humanoids with horns, some with snouts, some who are fifteen feet tall, and others who are very short or even tiny.

As I mentioned earlier, they're millions of years ahead of us in technology, but they are not progressing vibrationally, and that's what our contribution to the universe will be—as catalysts.

We will be invited to join this Federation of Planets. There are approximately two hundred planets in this particular group. Antura says there are several other groups or federations of planets just in the Milky Way galaxy, all but one of them friendly. That one just wishes to be left alone. But of course, earthlings like a challenge!

So in conclusion, it will be interesting to see if the timeline holds up. The last time I asked Antura, he said it was more solidified than ever. If 2015 rolls around and the Pleiadians show up, I might start to be excited, but for now I'm just passing along some of the many things I've learned from my "brother on another planet."

POWER OF MIND IS THE ULTIMATE POWER

On one occasion in the Ossining, New York, home of our friend Andrija Puharich (1918–1995), the well-known inventor, scientist, physician, and parapsychologist, we were discussing the UFO phenomenon and, especially, the subject of contactees and their messages to the world. Because the famous television screenwriter and producer Gene Roddenberry (1921–1991) was taking part in the discussion, we posed the question regarding whether or not the Space Brothers, with their preachments and their alleged physical activities on Earth, were performing outside interference with the historical progression of our planet. On Roddenberry's classic television series *Star Trek*, the space explorers on the Starship Enterprise are careful to follow "The Prime Directive," a Federation law which forbids them from performing any act that might unduly influence the evolutionary progression of any primitive planet that they may visit.

Dr. Puharich chuckled and suggested that we take a quick skip through the history of Earth.

I think there's evidence textually in Egyptian, Hebrew, early Greek literature, Hindu literature, and many other ancient texts, that there have been 'people' from some other place

It is the power of the mind that allows us to cross barriers into new worlds and encounter other beings. (*Art by Ricardo Pustanio*)

Real Encounters, Different Dimensions, and Otherworldly Beings

arriving here on Earth in things that we now call spacecraft. Whoever these visitors were, they set down instructions for humanity, but not with a very heavy hand, because teaching should be a gentle thing. The heaviest hand that we seem to have seen laid on man from some other place is in the Old Testament when Jehovah lays down the law and says, "Do it my way or else!'"

But if you look over five thousand years of history that we've got on the books, it seems to me that the presence of the UFO intelligence has been seen, but scarcely felt. It's not obvious. It's not accepted by religion, not accepted by scientists. So I'd say the influence from a historical point of view has been very gentle, like a father who's seldom around, but his presence is still there.

Roddenberry agreed, noting that if all these "gods" from the sky had indeed been all-powerful, they could have gone "Zap!" and all men would have been good.

We asked Puharich if, when he spoke of space and spacecraft, he had ever considered whether the entities may have come from other dimensions, rather than from outer space.

"I'm glad you brought that up," he responded enthusiastically. "People immediately get the idea when you talk about spacecraft that they are from our three- or four-dimensional frame of reference. Forget it! Absolutely not! The one conclusion I have about the nature of spacecraft, having watched them all over the world, photographed them, having actually seen them on the ground, is that the one thing they can do is to transform from this dimension to somewhere else. My basic assumption is that what is called the spacecraft is indeed a time machine that can transform from one dimension to another.

"We have very good analogies in modern physics for this," he continued. "For example, consider a so-called three-dimensional particle, such as an electron, in a so-called tunnel effect. You see the electron here, and then it appears over there, instantly."

In Puharich's opinion, the visitors who make contact with people cannot be dealt with on a three- or four-dimensional scale.

"You have to get into higher-dimensional phenomena," he said. "This is what bugs all of us. We'd like to be able to package it in cellophane in three-dimensional and say we've got it all wrapped up, but the phenomenon is not like that.

"The 'big picture,' as you phrase it, extends outside of our dimension, beyond our scope of vision, of hearing, of communication. We're very much like a prisoner who's in a cell who doesn't know what's going on outside. He has no doors, no windows. Every once in a while somebody shoves food under the door, and he tries to imagine who's on the other side, but he doesn't really know who or what. He can only decode the message in terms of his own little black box, and this is the kind of black box all of us live in. I think it's very much a bigger picture than any of our speculations from theological to science fiction to philosophical to physical science have considered."

Roddenberry predicted that "... when we start dividing up the neuron and proton and understand the tachyon, and when we cut these things up still further, maybe then we will find that the ultimate particle, the ultimate reality, is thought. I think this possibility has a bearing on everything we've been talking about."

He went on to admit that he didn't know whether the contactees who saw themselves in a spaceship or on other worlds actually went to another planet or a spaceship as we presently know such things. "But," he said, "I think it is possible that the power of thought allows them to create a place, not an imaginary place, but a place that is as real to them as reality.

Gene Roddenberry (1921–1991) created the popular science fiction television series *Star Trek*. It was not just space ships and aliens; he created an entire futuristic society, including principles such as the Prime Directive that said Federation officers should not interfere with other cultures. It is a concept perhaps similar to what extraterrestrials followed in the past and in the present.

"I know that when I am writing very well, and I create (I don't know where that comes from either) a different planet, a different society, during the time I'm writing, it's as real to me and as solid as this table top," Roddenberry continued. "I have smelled the smell of a campfire with an odor from no wood you'd ever have on Earth. There has been quite a reality there. I sometimes wonder how much farther one would have to go until indeed it became real. I don't know how many worlds are going on all at once. All of us here may be living in a different one in which we just sort of correspond. We may be reaching each other through those dimensions. I think an exciting explanation, an exciting way to look at things, is that the ultimate power, the ultimate particle, the ultimate meaning, is thought itself."

Excited by Roddenberry's declaration of thought being the ultimate power, Puharich wanted to pick up on that idea: "My experience leads me to believe that the power of the mind to travel across these barriers is the only

Real Encounters, Different Dimensions, and Otherworldly Beings

means we have of transporting across the dimensions. That same power may be able to create four-dimensional worlds or five-dimensional worlds. The only problem is, it's still a private world. We've not got to the point where it is public, where a large number of people can share this world."

In the next chapter we shall meet some individuals who have encountered beings who may wish to create human hybrids capable of creating and inhabiting four- or five-dimensional worlds.

TAKEN AWAY TO OTHER WORLDS

While the number of UFO contactees remains nebulous at best, estimates presented at a conference on the alien-abduction phenomenon at the Massachusetts Institute of Technology in June 1992 suggested that as many as several hundred thousand to more than three million adults in the United States alone have had abduction experiences with UFO beings. More recent estimates by some researchers place the number of abductees at 5 to 6 percent of the population, which would total more about two million. While such figures seem mind-boggling to say the least—and terrifying if true—some UFO researchers say that the actual numbers of humans examined by alien intelligences could be much higher.

⚓⚓⚓

EERIE ABDUCTION BY A HUGE, GLOWING JELLY FISH

In November 2010, we received an intriguing, detailed account of the UFO abduction encounters of Z. Peterson, a mental health technician at an in-patient psychiatric hospital in Oklahoma.

I wanted to share some of my own ET and UFO experiences with you. I have included my most personal account of what I believe to be an abduction experience without memory of events involved, as well as another abduction experience with what appears to be complete conscious recall. I have not included those events which I cannot recall to a degree of certainty or those which seem far too dreamlike to call real. I should note that I frequently dream about UFO craft as well as ETs and have had hundreds of what I can only describe as "abduction dreams." I have also encountered the phenomena known as "missing time," and on several occasions, a sort of time-warping

Peterson's sketch of the entity he calls the "Heart of the Deep."

effect in which I will suddenly notice that what seemed like half a day's time has transpired in about two minutes.

I am currently working as a health care professional here in Lawton, Oklahoma. I have not published a formal account of these incidents and have not reported them yet. I have documented them completely, though, and look forward to publishing them in some form or fashion as time permits.

Attached you will find a sketch that I made in April of 2010, of the entity I call "Heart of the Deep." This reference is from what I believe to be a telepathic-tactile transmission that took place later, in the summer of 2010. I have tried to remain objective, if not skeptical, when possible, concerning my own experiences, but I realize this is not always possible. I do, however, welcome the skepticism of others. As I told a longtime friend of mine, "It seems that the 'true believers' and the 'hard-core skeptics' in the field of ufology have one really big thing in common: The skeptics are secretly worried that they are actually wrong, and the believers are secretly worried that they are actually right."

In February of 2004, 2:30 A.M., I witnessed my first UFO. I had been awakened by bright red light shining through my windows and a deep resonant humming sound that vibrated the ground as well as my entire duplex.

Residing not more than five miles from the Fort Sill Army post, I assumed that the light could be caused by some low-flying helicopter or else some kind of flare. I have seen both in my time here in Lawton/Fort Sill. I was leery to venture outside, but absolutely compelled to find out what had made that strange hum as well as the bright red glow. I threw on my robe and slippers and headed to the front door to look outside from the porch. The view from the porch was totally unproductive. There were no lights to be seen. I listened intently. The hum had stopped. In fact, there was no noise to be heard at all. It was as if all sound had been stopped.

As I stepped out onto the porch and began my way down the stone walk toward my driveway, I felt the newly fallen snow blowing about my feet, and the strong, northern Oklahoma wind began to pick up again. I was beginning to feel ridiculous, so I resigned myself to take one quick check back into the alleyway behind my truck and then to return inside to warm myself by the heater before returning to bed.

As I turned back around I saw something I will never forget. Hanging up in the sky was a huge, glowing jellyfish. Its body appeared to be made of radiant light, and below it flickered strange tendrils of pure white light scattering patchwork patterns on the darkened alleyway ground. Its color was that of lavender to hot pink and parts were bluish as well. (I have set to work drawing it in colored pencil many times but can't seem to render it exactly as I remember it.)

I can recall actually saying out loud at that point, "What in the hell is that big glowing jellyfish doing up there in the sky?"

Even as the last few words left my mouth I can recall feeling as if maybe I was thinking the words rather than being able to finish them audibly. The last thing I knew was the sensation of extreme dizziness and the faint sensation of cold and damp as I passed out into the snow beneath my feet.

When I awoke I was in my bed, dressed in my scrubs, ready for work. I felt dizzy and light-headed. A mild case of nausea seemed to pass after I ate a plate of fried eggs and some bacon. An occasional faint, buzzing sensation was present in my left ear and occasionally in my limbs and in my head also (but rarely).

I passed the entire incident off as an episode brought on by too much stress and too much sleep deprivation. At the time I was working long hours as a mental health technician at an in-patient psychiatric hospital, working my way through a degree in experimental psychology and biology. I did not tell anyone, even though I wanted to at times. Later I would confide in a friend who was a psychiatrist, asking him about the incident. His response was that I was probably under too much stress and that I should take a week off and relax. The week off helped, but I never could seem to shake the feeling that what I saw and experienced was just not normal at all!

As the years went by I noticed profound changes in my consciousness as well as my physiology. I needed far less sleep than I had grown accustomed to. I had taken up Transcendental Meditation as well as more traditional forms of yoga and Buddhist meditation. My stress level was manageable, and I had all but forgotten the strange incident of 2004.

My sense of normalcy was shattered once again on March 11, 2010, from 6:35 to 7:30 A.M. I was lying half-awake, half-asleep in my bed; my wife, Becca, was lying next to me about four feet to the left (king-size bed). I had glanced at the alarm clock just a few moments before. Abby would soon be standing at the bars of her crib, petitioning to watch Elmo with us and with her big, neon green stuffed bunny she named "Boppy." A strangely familiar feeling overtook me, I felt a vibration that turned into a sense of profound numbness, and I knew that I was going to blackout.

This time I didn't wake up in my bed. In fact, I didn't seem to wake up at all. Instead I felt myself walking down a darkened stone corridor towards a brilliant light. At first I thought that I might be dead or dying, having some kind of out-of-body-experience or near-death-experience episode. As I made my way out of the passageway into unbelievably bright sunlight, I was relieved to find myself feeling perfectly alive.

I checked myself all over: I was breathing properly; my heart was still beating (albeit at a much quickened pace); and the warm sun felt good on my naked skin. Cautiously, I made my way out towards what looked like a series of huge, open, glass or plexiglass aquarium tanks where dolphins and humans were swimming together and playing. I stood for a moment and watched them, marveling at the strange and beautiful sights I was seeing.

Then I noticed a strange person (at the time I thought it was a black man with funny looking skin). He was climbing out of a large stone pool next to the tanks. Once again, I began to get very dizzy and nauseated. I wanted to leave, I wanted to wake up and be safe in my bed, watching Elmo with Abby. I began to look more closely at the "man," knowing that (just like that "jellyfish" object I had seen in the night sky) there was something so strange and so out of place about him, that something was horribly wrong with this whole experience.

With much trepidation and an ever-growing feeling of sickness in my stomach, I approached this strange person and the other people who had been swimming with the dolphins. They were reclining now against the base of a large white stone column that supported a tiled Romanesque roof that slightly overhung the huge stone pools. The whole area reminded me of some strange, futuristic, outdoor Roman bath house. The sunlight blinded me as I approached the people, and then it receded behind an alabaster pillar and I could see them clearly.

They were about nine feet tall, maybe a bit over. They had a vaguely familiar humanoid structure to their physique. Curling around their jaws on both sides of their face were hot pink- to magenta-colored gill-like structures in sets of three. The color and hue of these structures deepened to a dark crimson to purple to black as they entered their bodies. They had indigo to deep blue-colored, iridescent skin (from a distance it looked almost black). Upon closer inspection their skin appeared to be partially translucent in nature, as I could peer through the first few layers of tissue to see blood vessels underneath and the dense, almost grainy structures of their muscles underneath their skin.

Their eyes were huge and looked at once both human and alien. The color of their irises appeared to change even as I looked at them, but then became a bright apple green color that blended into a bright yellow and finally orange, approaching their big black pupils. Their eyes had a mirror quality to them. I could actually see myself reflected (nearly perfectly) in them. They

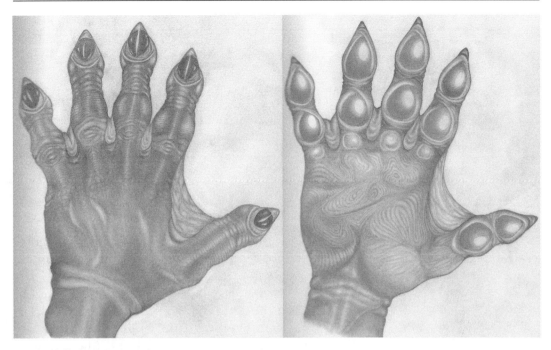

Peterson drew these alien hands as he remembers them "because I feel that there is so much information that can be taken in simply ... seeing someone's hands."

had milky, clear eyelids that reminded me of a frog's or fish's. They had another set of jet black opaque eyelids that remained open the entire time.

They had no hair, anywhere. And they, too, were completely naked. My dizziness increased, and I was absolutely frozen like a deer stuck in the headlights of an oncoming car. I had to sit down. I could not look away. I was transfixed. I knew that they were not human. I just kept praying that it was all a bad dream and that I would soon awaken, shake it all off, and go on with my life.

My ability to move was still restricted to some extent, and I felt as if every move I made was being allowed for. This sense of loss of control really angered me.

Then I heard a voice, calm and smooth in my head. The being was using my own words and concepts to generate perfect human speech telepathically.

[Using their collective consciousness, they said in one voice,] "Hello," plain as day. I began to reply, and they told me, "Relax, it's OK." They said it just like I would have said those exact words. I was beginning to ask "Why?" and they answered telepathically again, "This has been arranged."

I remarked that they looked very human in some ways, the shape of their body's frame, their facial features, their smile and movements. By this time all I had to do was think the thoughts, and I knew they would "hear" me.

They gave a little chuckle, and I saw their mouths open slightly to reveal razor-sharp, milky-clear, small, cone-shaped, pointed teeth and a huge shiny, smooth, magenta-colored tongue.

I felt an odd resonant feeling, as if their bodies had emanated a deep low-pitch tone (like when a sub woofer thumps). I felt it in my diaphragm.

The frame of their bodies seemed almost top heavy, with a very deep and large muscular chest and a strongly defined ribcage. Their hips seemed oddly shaped, but properly proportioned for their anatomy. The deep sound of their laughter was eerily silent except for its low frequency echo.

They Said They Were from the Star System Sirius

They explained that they were from a planet in the star system Sirius. (They actually showed it to me within my own mind, like guiding me

through a big map of the night sky. I saw the huge, looming constellation of Orion, his belt stars glinting, pointing like an arrow toward the bright star, Sirius A.) They also explained that their race of beings was spawned by the being (known to ancient Egypt) as the god Osiris. It was made clear that they do not worship Osiris, and that he is not a god at all, rather a transcendent being (an extraterrestrial formerly from the constellation Orion) who now resides within another plane of existence. They also said that their own species had been responsible for the birth of both earth-bound cetaceans as well as primates, including humans. They made it very clear that concerning deities—and any beings of an advanced sort—I should never bow before any being that wanted me to do so, that any submission of a worshipful nature that I might make unto them would be an insult to both of us and that I was never to consider them as gods or God, or godlike.

An image of the Egyptian god Osiris as depicted on the tomb of Queen Nefertari. According to one story, the being known as Osiris is a transcendent being who long ago spawned a race from Sirius, as well as humans and cetaceans here on Earth.

Looking around the being I sensed to be speaking, I saw small, "hidden," almost invisible beings that were congregating around him. They were making a commotion, like a crowded hall or room full of voices, and my head was now filled with telepathic noise.

The Being Appeared Humanoid, Fishlike, and Reptilian

Some of the beings, more visible than others, appeared like fish, some like reptiles, and others like humans. Some of them were too hideous for me to look at. I became very uneasy, and the being sensed that. He waved his left hand to the side, and they all disappeared in a flash, like they had never existed at all. He explained that they were simply observing and that they meant no ill will or offense to me.

At this point my nausea was beginning to get the best of me, and I really felt like vomiting onto the ground next to me. I began to cough and double over, and I felt a wave of calm hit me like warm water.

I looked up to see the being looking directly into my eyes. The nausea passed instantly. I broke out in a cold sweat, and all at once I felt very calm and content. It was as if they were hypnotizing me.

I held their gaze for what seemed like a few minutes, and then they began to send me visual images, slowly at first and then more quickly. Some of the visions were from my childhood, some seemed totally out of place, some made no sense to me at all.

I do not recall all of the images. Some of them were totally abstract, like geometrical shapes and symbols. It did not seem to matter to this being that I had absolutely no understanding of the symbols, just that I was comfortable and fully aware, taking it all in.

Suddenly they stopped "feeding" images into my head, and I was just sitting there wondering what I was supposed to do. With my nausea gone and my head cleared of dizziness, I slowly rose to my feet and approached the being.

The Encounter Became Up Close and Personal

I had been approximately ten to fifteen feet away from them. When I came closer to them, I had a thought in my mind, one of pure childish curiosity. I wondered what it would feel like to touch them. I was too nervous to say anything, but of course this did not matter. They knew my thoughts entirely. One of them extended his hand to me (palm up), and I reluctantly placed my hand onto his.

Their hands seemed so huge compared to mine, as if mine was a toddler's hand—almost like the size of Abby's hand compared to mine (Abby was two at the time.) Though very beautiful, their hands were absolutely alien looking. They had thick, shiny, circular pads on their fingers and swirls and ridges of shimmering iridescent patterns all over their palms. Their fingernails appeared much thicker than mine and were completely translucent, slightly milky, and opalescent in quality. They had thick, milky-clear webbing (nearly invisible at a distance) between each of their ten fingers and ten toes. When I touched them, they felt warm and smooth, slightly moist, almost like a child's skin after it gets out of a bath.

The very moment that my hand made contact with one of theirs, I got a message transmitted through my skin (cell to cell). The concept was completely foreign to me, just like the telepathy had been, and startled, I jerked back my hand. The message was something like a thought and yet again something like a memory of a concept from childhood. It was like a memory of seeing something, or touching something, that was so impossibly ancient that somehow it shouldn't exist. It's hard to explain. That's my best attempt.

The being seemed to understand and smiled warmly at me, sending me that same calm feeling all over my body. My childish curiosity returned, and I began to touch and visually explore his body, trying to understand it all, as if I somehow could.

A time came when the being explained that they needed to refresh themselves and get into the pool. They were amphibious and needed to keep their skin moist or it would become quite painful to them. When they approached the edge of the pool they suddenly changed shape and became like big black dolphins.

This really bothered me for some reason (yet another concept that was completely foreign to me) and I was beginning to find that maybe I wasn't as open-minded as I thought I was. This was really challenging me!

The Beings Could Shape-Shift at Will

I shuddered when I saw the beings swimming about in the pool with those same big eyes winking back at me from the water. They sensed that it bothered me and changed quickly back into their humanoid forms.

In response they explained that the dolphin-like shape was one of the forms that their species could take. It was a default setting, so to speak, within their own DNA. They could also change into a pale-white, human-like form with a strange looking tale with flukes, which fascinated me. (I have yet to capture this form into a satisfactory sketch, but will continue to try.) They also explained that their species had evolved into what is known as a "transitional form." They have many qualities with which humanity is familiar: telepathy, shape-shifting, precognition, telekinesis—and one that I found particularly fascinating: they can manipulate water by changing its salinity and electrical charge.

Their own world is largely covered with pure, clean salt water and has many small islands. It is this water that is their life force. It provides them with nutrition that they absorb directly through their skin. Their food is made up of primarily fish and sea life as well as some aquatic vegetation.

They have no individual names, and they communicate through a collective mind that transmits through their water much like dolphins use sound in the water to communicate here on Earth. Most of this information was "poured" into me in a fraction of a second through the tactile mode of communication.

[Z. Peterson warned us that some of his abduction experience was sexually explicit and graphic. He said that he had debated if he could find the words to abbreviate the additional formation or else leave it out altogether. In the end, he decided not to sacrifice the more functional elements of his disclosure for some small measure of personal modesty.]

Their own world is largely covered with pure, clean salt water and has many small islands. It is this water that is their life force.

A Sexual Experience Transmits an Alien Teaching

As I studied their bodies, I stood in front of them and knelt occasionally to see them more clearly. They had a rather large organ that looked very much like a huge, prehensile, salmon-orange tongue curling and extending out from beneath folds of skin (not unlike the human female's vulva); this tongue was approximately ten inches long and four inches wide at its thickest point and appeared to consist of a very dense muscular tissue (the being explained that it was much like a clitoris or prostate on humans). It actually curled around my forearm when I touched it. It was covered in small, smooth, shiny round nodules all over its dorsal surface.

All this time I felt both nervous and curious. At a moment I felt almost ashamed, because it aroused me; actually, it aroused me mentally and physically, because it was so fascinating to me. The being again sent me a wave of calm and told me, "Nothing we are doing here is wrong. You need not feel ashamed or bad inside. This is about learning and growing."

I was still feeling very odd about this, but my curiosity was far too strong to back away again. As I looked back down I could see what appeared to be a rather large male organ protruding from those genital folds. It looked very similar to a human penis except that it had a slightly different shape. It was jet black and shiny, smooth, and about the size of my entire forearm. Below the tongue-like organ was a slit that appeared analogous to a human female's vagina. Almost identical to humans, it had a rectum just after a small bump on what appeared to be a perineum-like region of their anatomy.

They explained that their species had always been this way. Their sex was (as they put it) undifferentiated, thus their bodies had both male and female qualities. They could become pregnant and impregnate one another.

They formed mated pairs like humans do, and the idea of sex was seen as something both sacred and spiritual. They made love (face to face, belly to belly) in the water, and they interpenetrated one another simultaneously. (All of this was transmitted instantly through their skin into mine.)

We were very close now, and our legs touched. The beings made their intention clear to me: They wanted to touch me, too, but they wanted to make sure that I was absolutely clear that this was not a sexual act but a mental, spiritual, and emotional one that just happened to have physical components. I felt one of them reach their hand down and come to rest with the smooth warm pads of their fingers now directly on my perineum (known as the root chakra, or root gate of the chakra).

At this point I felt information being read from my body, from my chakra and essentially from all the cells in my body. They told me that they knew my entire life, every cell in my body, and my entire family. They also explained that this process required a great deal of openness, and I felt another huge wave of induced calm pulse through my entire body, pushing me nearly to the point of sleep.

Their bodies had both female and male qualities, and their urge to touch was not so much sexual as a need to connect in mental, emotional, and spiritual ways. (*Art by Ricardo Pustanio*)

They explained that this act would allow for direct communication from their chakra system into and through my own. They had me place my hand in the same place on their body and hold it there. I began to feel a sensation very much like an orgasm building in my genitals and continuing to move through my spine until my entire body felt like I was going to have a massive orgasm. Every cell in my body filled with indescribable ecstasy. I did not have an orgasm, but the sensation continued to build to a very uncomfortable level, and I could feel my body beginning to shake and shudder in waves of tremendous energy. The being continued to send waves of calm into me, through my chakra, (by this time my eyes had rolled backward into my head and I was convulsing). As the feeling built and built many times over, I felt suddenly like I was going to leave my body altogether, like I might simply fall out of my own body into the blue sky above me.

Then I lost all comprehension of my body altogether. It was as if I was no longer myself, but a combination of the being and myself, just thoughts and feelings pulsing back and forth—a dynamic communication with consciousness. I had no contact with my bodily senses, and the very concept of time seemed to not apply to this experience.

As we hung there feeling suspended in a great void of light and energy, I felt great volumes of information being fed into my spirit chakra from the being. In fact, the information was being sent back and forth freely like waves of energy and light. Gradually I began to perceive a feeling of instability within my portion of the "link" (as I call it), and I then felt my body again, being overcome with tidal waves of energy. It felt as if my body was being dragged behind the wake of a huge fast moving ship, like the energy might literally tear me apart, even unto an atomic level!

My body could no longer withstand all that energy, and I was beginning to overload. I felt as if physical death was imminent. What a horrible feeling that is! The being knew it, and in an instant I was let go.

I can recall a violent flash of blinding light and an indescribable sound/feeling—something like a horrible SNAP—as I was slammed back into my bed. I awoke, shaking and crying, dizzy, and completely overwhelmed with emotion, naked and covered in sweat.

Abby soon awoke and I got up, dressed, and just sat in our big leather recliner and rocked her in my arms, tears silently rolling down my cheeks.

In the days and months that followed, I found myself in a new chapter of my life. I could no longer go back. I felt compelled to hurl myself headlong into full-time research of this phenomena. I have learned much since my own experiences, but I honestly cannot say that I am any closer to truly feeling some kind of ease with my own memory. I think that someday I may be willing to undergo hypnosis and see if I am able to put more of the puzzle pieces together, but for now I am content to learn and grow as naturally as is possible.

> *Has Z. Peterson shared with us a vivid account of a profound illumination or visionary experience, or could it have been an actual abduction experience in which his very essence became one with an alien intelligence? Although his abduction experience involved a powerful sexual element, this facet of his encounter was much more like that of a mystical, tantric energy exchange than the rough, invasive sexual examination reported by, perhaps, the majority of abductees. Indeed, Peterson's gentle amphibious humanoids seemed far more gentle than the great majority of inquisitive aliens that are alleged to be snatching humans for what seems to be some kind of process of selection, as well as examination.*

---◁◖◗▷---

DR. SPRINKLE'S LIST OF CHARACTERISTICS COMMON TO PEOPLE WHO CLAIM ABDUCTION BY ALIENS

Dr. R. Leo Sprinkle, formerly on staff at the University of Wyoming in Laramie and currently in private practice, has speculated that there may well be hundreds of thousands of people who experience the phenomenon of a UFO abduction, but who were not even aware of it at the time. Dr. Sprinkle lists several characteristics common among people who have had such experiences:

1. An episode of missing time. Under hypnosis many people remember driving down the road and then being back in their car. They know that "something" happened between the two points of consciousness, but they can't fill in the missing time.

2. Disturbing dreams. The abductee will dream about flying saucers, about being pursued and captured, and being examined by doctors in white coats.

3. Daytime flashbacks of UFO experiences. While they are doing tasks in their normal daytime activities, abductees will flash back to some kind of UFO image or UFO entity.

4. Strange compulsions. Dr. Sprinkle told of one man who for seven years felt compelled to dig a well at a particular spot. Under hypnosis he revealed that a UFO being had told him they would contact him if he dug a well.

5. A sudden interest in UFOs. The abductee may suddenly give evidence of a compulsion to read about UFOs, ancient history, or pyramids and crystals, without knowing why.

---◁◖◗▷---

TOP SOLAR PHYSICIST BELIEVES ONE OUT OF EIGHT PEOPLE MAY HAVE BEEN ABDUCTED BY ALIENS

David Webb, an Arlington, Massachusetts, solar physicist, cochairman of the Mutual UFO Network (MUFON), a top UFO research organization, believes that space aliens have abducted one out of every eight people who have reported seeing UFOs. According to Webb's research, in many cases the victims undergo some kind of examination, but they usually remember nothing of the on-board experience.

In the course of numerous hypnotic regressions that he conducted with UFO abductees, Dr. James Harder (1926–2006) said that he had found a great deal of evidence to support the theory that alien abductors return to find and to reexamine abductees at various intervals, sometimes throughout a person's lifetime and sometimes without his or her being aware of it. Dr. Harder observed that it is as if some sort of extraterrestrial group of psychologists is making a study of humans.

Dr. Harder and other researchers have discovered that a high percentage of people who have been abducted appear to have undergone multiple experiences with UFO entities. Most abductees who have had more than one experience with UFO aliens usually undergo the first encounter between the ages of five and nine. These abductees remember the alien as friendly and quite human in appearance. Upon further hypnotic regression and careful probing, however, the investigators have learned that the entity did not look human at all.

> **Most abductees who have had more than one experience with UFO aliens usually undergo the first encounter between the ages of five and nine.**

In most cases, the entity usually tells the children that he will be back to see them throughout the course of their life. He also admonishes the children not to tell their parents about the encounter.

Dr. Harder has also discovered that during the adult-abductee experience, those men and women undergoing the encounter will often report having a vague memory of their abductor, and they will later say that they feel as though they have seen the entity before. In Dr. Harder's opinion, the multiple UFO abduction is not a random occurrence.

THE WELL-DOCUMENTED HILL CASE: PROTOTYPE FOR THE INTERRUPTED JOURNEY ALIEN ABDUCTION ENCOUNTER

The other-worldly abduction of Betty and Barney Hill by occupants from a UFO has become the prototype for the "interrupted journey," in which humans are taken on board a spacecraft and examined by aliens. Their encounter, familiar to many since the details have been made available in numerous books, magazine articles, and a made-for-television movie with James Earl Jones and Estelle Parsons playing Barney and Betty, occurred on September 19, 1961.

Betty, a social worker, and Barney, a mail carrier, both in their forties, were returning to their home in New Hampshire from a short Canadian vacation when they noticed a bright object in the night sky. Barney stopped the car and used a pair of binoculars to get a better look at it. As he studied the object, its own illumination showed a well-defined, disc-like shape moving in an irregular pattern across the moonlit sky.

RICARDO PUSTANIO 2012

Many alien abductees later recall strong feelings ranging from unease to outright fear. (*Art by Ricardo Pustanio*)

Intrigued by the strange aerial phenomenon, Barney walked into a nearby field to get a better look. He could now see what appeared to be windows—and, from the windows, beings looking back at him. Realizing that he was being watched frightened Barney, and he ran back to the car, got in, and began to race down the road. Then, as if obeying some mysterious internal directive, he drove down a side road—where the Hills found five humanoid aliens standing in their path. Suddenly unable to control their own bodies and under another's control, Betty and Barney were taken from their car and, in a trancelike condition, led to the UFO by the humanoids. Later, under hypnosis, the Hills would recall that for nearly two hours they were the guests of the UFOnauts before they returned them unharmed to their car with the mental command that they would forget all about their abduction experience.

After experiencing strange and disconcerting dreams that they could not understand, Betty decided to seek the help of a psychiatrist friend, who suggested that the memory of the two missing hours on their journey home from Canada would return in time. But the details of that unexplained "interruption" remained in a troubled limbo of fragmented memories until the Hills began weekly hypnosis sessions with Dr. Benjamin Simon, a Boston psychiatrist.

Under Dr. Simon's guidance, the couple revealed an astonishing story of being treated by aliens from space in much the same manner as human scientists treat laboratory animals. Although much has been made of the Hills' alien medical examinations, in the larger view, the key to the whole event and the single aspect that may be most essential in giving their story credibility is the star map that Betty said she was shown while on board the UFO.

Under hypnosis in 1964, Betty, with little or no understanding of astronomy, drew her impressions of the map with a remarkable expertise that concurred with other, professionally drawn, star maps. As an important bonus, Betty's map showed the location of two stars called Zeta 1 and Zeta 2 Reticuli, allegedly the home base of the space travelers who abducted them. Interestingly, the existence of the two stars was not confirmed by astronomers until 1969— eight years after Betty remembered seeing the star map aboard an alien spaceship. As an added element of intrigue, the two fifth-magnitude stars, Zeta 1 and Zeta 2 Reticuli, are invisible to observers north of the latitude of Mexico City.

STRIEBER'S COMMUNION WITH ALIEN ABDUCTORS

Whitley Strieber, author of the best-selling book *Communion*, has said that he attempted to deal with his tension and anxiety over having undergone an abduction experience by writing about his encounter. Strieber has told audiences at various conferences, and repeated the account during numerous radio and television interviews, that when he first realized what had happened to him, he was suicidal. Then he began to investigate some UFO literature and discovered that others had experienced similar abductions by alien intelligences. He sought out the services of a hypnotist, thinking that perhaps that would be the last of the ordeal. It wasn't, and he wrote the book hoping that the memories and the feelings would go away. Regrettably, the memories returned.

Strieber has received thousands of letters from other abductees—people who do not welcome publicity, including entertainers, political leaders, and members of the armed forces in high positions. According to Strieber, all of these abductees had reported a basic progression of emotions, moving from uneasy, fragmented recollections to a clear memory accompanied by fear. If the abductees consented to undergo hypnotic regression, they usually became even more terrified. Instead of attempting to glean more and more information about the abductee through hypnotic regression, Strieber suggested that concerned researchers should be trying to help these individuals with their fright, and focus on helping them gain more understanding about what had happened to them.

Perhaps a majority of abductees remember the frightening and disorienting aspects of their abduction experiences only in fragments and flashes until they undergo hypnotic regression. Even after counseling, it seems that most abductees regard their interaction with the UFO entities to be negative. The frustration of being partially paralyzed and taken on board a craft without their consent in order to undergo a medical examination against their will has left them with resentment as well as disturbing memories.

ABDUCTED IN CHINA BY BLUISH ALIEN BEINGS

Our colleague Paul Dale Roberts, a paranormal investigator and author, reported receiving a telephone call from "Ming," who was very fascinated with his UFO articles.

"She explained to me over the phone," Paul said, "that she had a very interesting story about a UFO abduction in the fields of China in which she was not taken, but her girlfriend Li Zhao (not her real name) was. Ming caught my interest, and I agreed to meet her."

Ming told Paul that in May of 1999 she was outside of Wulumuqi, with her girlfriend Li Zhao, walking through some open fields. As they looked upward, they saw the cumulus clouds seem to open. Then, after a few moments, from the clouds a very bright disc descended upon them. Both Li and Ming collapsed as the disc came closer. In a few minutes Ming awakened and she found herself alone in the field. Li was nowhere to be found.

Under the condition of complete anonymity, Li agreed to be interviewed by Paul by telephone concerning her abduction.

Paul: Hi, Li, I am sitting here with Ming, and she tells me that you were possibly abducted, is this true?

Li: I was taken as I walked with Ming in a field. At first, I did not remember much of the experience, but now, in a series of dreams, I remember being taken aboard a strange craft. Around me were light bluish colored creatures with dark, black oval eyes. The dreams have stopped, and I know exactly what happened to me. I was shown a series of light images that would appear in the air, inside the ship. I saw chaos and destruction. The light images seemed to display an impact from some kind of meteorite or maybe a comet. There were high waters covering cities, there were buildings collapsing, fires everywhere. The largest alien pointed to the light images and wanted me to focus on the images.

Paul: Do you believe that your abductors were trying to show you the end of the world?

Li: I don't know if it was the end of the world, but I could see people running in the street. Everyone looked scared. After they showed me the light images, I was taken back into a room filled with lights. As my eyes became focused, I could see the tall alien with oval eyes talking with two men dressed in black with black caps on. There was some sort of insignia on their uniforms, but I could not make out the writing or drawing.

> "I don't know if it was the end of the world, but I could see people running in the street. Everyone looked scared."

Paul: Did the Men in Black look human?

Li: Yes, they looked American. One had olive complexion, the other was white. [Authors' note: In the United States, many abductees have reported their temporary captors to be Asian in appearance.]

Paul: Could you hear what they were talking about?

Li: No, but one of the Men in Black looked at me with piercing eyes. He was not smiling. When he looked at me, I felt nauseated. I think I fainted. When I opened my eyes, I was back in the field again with Ming. Ming looked like she was passed out in the field. She was lying there asleep.

Paul: Ming … how is it that you were out again?

Ming: I actually passed out once when Li was taken, and just before she returned, I passed out again. When I awoke, Li was back.

Journalist Recalls Missing Time Experience of Five Hours

We have been friends with Patricia Ress for many years. An accomplished journalist, author-coauthor-contributor of eleven books, such as Beyond Earthly Knowledge: The Time and Interdimensional Time Revelations of Rick Lipani, *and an occasional co-host of the*

Eddie Middleton radio program Night Search, *Patty told us that she had experienced "missing time" when she was a young girl in Iowa.*

I was raised in a small town of three thousand souls in western Iowa, growing up in the late 1940s and 1950s and graduating from high school in 1963. My dad, a pharmacist, owned a small, multigenerational drug store, and we lived on the floor above it. From about 1954 to about 1961, I owned a nice little horse, mostly white with brown spots, a Morgan-Arabian cross named Joker. Most of my classmates and friends were farmers' daughters or sons, and many—if not most of them—also rode horses and belonged to the local county saddle club.

One summer afternoon in 1955 when I was ten years old, I promised to go riding with a friend of mine named Suzi, who lived eight or nine miles out in the country. Usually, I would ride out to her place, then we'd go riding together around her folks' farm or maybe to visit other friends nearby. There had been some tornados the night before, and Suzi and I looked upward at the sky and saw several funnels that we believed had been generated by the storm that had passed through earlier. We rode around, decided to fish for a while in the pond across the road from her parents' house, and then returned to her mother's kitchen to see when we'd be having supper.

By then it was nearly 6:30 P.M., and since it was about an hour and fifteen minutes' ride to get home, her mother always felt I should eat some supper with them. This was fine with me as her mother made a most heavenly cream of tomato soup with a huge biscuit in the middle and dream bars with cherries and whipped cream for dessert. Nothing anywhere tastes as good as fresh Iowa farm food.

Anyhow, we finished supper, and I called my dad and told him I would be leaving soon—about 7:15 P.M., so not to get worried if I didn't get home until around nine. No problem there. So, at 7:15 P.M. I set out on my horse heading for home, but I apparently was waylaid into a somewhere or someplace I do not remember. Not far from Suzi's farm was the home of another friend, and I waved to her as I trotted along that sunny summer night so long ago.

I was just blissfully enjoying the scenery, so imagine my surprise when I reached the exit of the long gravel road onto the highway (the old 141) and found it pitch dark! What seemed like only a few minutes ago, the countryside had been bright and sunny! Now it was even blacker outside than at midnight. As I rode into town, the place seemed deserted. It had to be later than my usual 10:30 or 11 P.M. bedtime. Just then I noticed the large clock on the corner bank. It said 3:30 A.M.!

I was aghast! I would have believed 10 P.M.—possibly. But even that was a stretch. Anytime I had stayed for supper at Suzi's, I had always been home by 9 or 9:15 P.M. tops! One time I had stopped for a short time to visit a friend.

Her mother had just made a fresh pie and invited me in for a piece. That was my 9:15 P.M. arrival. Nothing like that had happened this time.

When I approached the barn where I kept my horse, my brother drove up in his car and scolded me with great anger. Didn't I realize that my parents had the town police alert to my missing? That even the county sheriff had been called? Where had I been? What had I been doing?

Imagine his surprise when I said, "Nothing! I just rode back from Suzi's. I called Dad around seven and left about ten minutes later."

My parents later verified my story with Suzi's parents, and everyone wondered the same thing: Where had this ten-year-old been for about five and a half hours?

Well, my life went on the same as usual and within a couple of weeks nearly everyone had forgotten the whole thing—except for Joker. Joker had been seven years old when I bought him. He was well trained and had been used as a cutting horse at the Sioux City Stockyards for the two years before I bought him. It was the cutting horse's job to separate cattle from the herd for vaccinating, castrating, and sorting. When I took him riding, we passed pig farm after pig farm, but now Joker seemed terribly frightened of the porkers. If pigs so much as looked at him and so much as snorted, Joker was off on a run! Thankfully the run only lasted until we were out of sight of the pigs, but while it lasted it was frightening! Seeing my horse so suddenly and strangely frightened by swine was the worst part of all the confusion about my mysterious tardiness in getting home so late that night.

Twenty-two years later, in 1977, I was working on a newspaper in central Nebraska when *Star Wars* had its first release. "Long, long ago in a galaxy far, far away" was a bar scene in which a pirate character named Han Solo shot and killed a small, blackmailing alien that looked like a pig! But wait a minute! Wasn't my old horse, Joker, afraid of pigs?

Something was definitely going on in my mind, and I didn't like what I was thinking. As it happened, shortly after this, I had occasion to write my first book about UFOs in the American heartland. I had to contact a well-known hypnotist-college professor who taught psychology at a western university. I happened to tell him my horse story, which involved my missing five and a half hours in 1955. He knew about horses and rode them, so when he said, "Perhaps your horse hadn't become afraid of pigs, perhaps he was frightened by aliens that looked and behaved like pigs!" It rang a bell!

In 1997 I became a part-time host on a paranormal radio talk show. A frequent visitor to the show was a very intelligent lady who claimed to be in contact with aliens. Before one of our shows, I asked her via email if I had ever been abducted. Her answer was, yes. In fact, in 1955! The aliens with whom she claimed to be in contact did not look like pigs, but they may have been "in cahoots" with that other race. More than one abduction story involved contact with more than one race in one abduction! Whitley Strieber noticed this in his own well-known experiences.

I may never know what happened to me that night in 1955, but once in a while when I stop someplace where people are riding horses, I wonder what they might have encountered on some of their night rides.

ARE ALIENS IMPREGNATING EARTH WOMEN TO PRODUCE HYBRID BABIES?

In the 1960s, we began receiving correspondence from women who claimed that they had been impregnated by alien visitors and that they had delivered healthy "hybrid" babies who had exhibited various extraordinary abilities as they matured into adolescence. While there were only occasional such

claims in the era of Flower Children and the dawning of the Age of Aquarius, today in 2013, it has become commonplace to hear about Star Children, Indigo Children, Cosmic Kids, Crystal Children, and other progeny suggestive of a special or extraterrestrial heritage. We believe that the Other, the multidimensional visitors, are paraphysical in that they can manifest physical bodies when it suits their purpose and their mission. Have they developed a Grand Plan to elevate the bloodline of *Homo sapiens* as well as their consciousness by cosmic insemination?

More women are claiming that aliens have impregnated them, resulting in the births of children with extraordinary abilities. (*Art by Ricardo Pustanio*)

IMPREGNATED BY ALIENS AT THIRTEEN YEARS OLD

An abductee we will call Jane stated in her report to us that she began having dreams about UFO people when she was only five years old. In these apparent dream scenarios, she would see a large ship hovering over her parents' home, and then on a beam of light, entities would come into her room and look at her. They seemed always to be examining her, she recalled, as if they were doctors. They never spoke to her, and their mouths seemed to be fixed in a permanent kind of half-quizzical smile. She was never alarmed. She was fascinated.

As she grew older, the examinations continued. Shortly after she turned ten, she recalls the entities coming to her, taking her by the hand, and apparently lifting her out of her body in a kind of astral dream.

She remembers being taken to a lovely, pink room where everything was soft, gentle, and loving. She has a clear memory of very pleasant music playing. She cannot identify the music as any melody familiar to her, but it relaxed her, made her feel very comfortable.

Her most dramatic occurrence took place when she was thirteen. She was visited in her room by the same entities, who on this occasion stood back in the corner while a more humanlike-appearing entity approached her. She knew, in spite of her youth and her inexperience, that she was engaging in normal sexual intercourse. Within two or three months, she stated, she knew she was pregnant.

She was very frightened. She could not work up the nerve to tell her parents about the strange visitation. She considered telling her school counselor, but she could not bear the shame or the humiliation in attempting to explain how she had become pregnant. She knew that she had not had any type of physical experience with any human male—not a boy her own age or any older man or boy.

Just when she was beginning to experience morning sickness, she reports, she had another dream in which the entities came to her room and examined her. This time she felt a bit of pain, and she remembers lying as if she were paralyzed while the visitors performed some kind of operation on her. When she awakened, she knew that she was no longer pregnant. A short time later, her monthly periods resumed.

> Once again she was in that beautiful, pink room, and this time she was looking at a beautiful baby boy.

Several months later, she had the last of her UFO dreams. She dreamed that she was taken aboard a spacecraft. Once again she was in that beautiful, pink room, and this time she was looking at a beautiful baby boy. The entities smiled and indicated that she could pick up the baby. She did so, and had the strongest feeling that she was holding her own child.

Everything then became hazy. The pink room seemed to get smaller and smaller, and Jane seemed to be enveloped in a pink mist. She awakened back in her room. She never again had another UFO dream of that type.

—◁◁◁∫∫∫▷▷▷—

AN ALIEN TOLD LILA HE IS HER TRUE FATHER

Lila said that she no longer has any doubts regarding the identity of her real father. Lila, twenty-two years old when she filed a report with us, stated that she has been communicating telepathically with an alien being that she calls "Father," an entity who says he is her true male parent.

As it appears to be with so many individuals who have such memories, Lila was an unexpected child, and now her "Father" has awakened her to the knowledge of who her real parents are and where her home planet is. Lila says that she cannot wait to go home. The alien being who identifies itself as her father also states that Joyce, Lila's two-year-old daughter, is his granddaughter.

—◁◁◁∫∫∫▷▷▷—

DECLARED STERILE,
SHE MIGHT HAVE BEEN IMPREGNATED BY AN ALIEN

Theresa was a twenty-seven-year-old accountant when she wrote to us that it was not until she had been out on her own, away from her family home for three or four years, that her mother told her the following story:

Theresa's mother had been declared sterile, and in spite of repeated attempts to become pregnant, it was to no avail. The doctors had begun to suggest adoption, and Theresa's parents were strongly considering this option.

Then, Theresa's mother, according to her story, was awakened one night by a strange buzzing sound that she described as sounding something like a metallic bumblebee. She looked up from the bed to see a bright light about the size of a soccer ball moving across the bedroom. Before she could say anything to her sleeping husband—before she could shout or scream or express alarm or fear—she felt herself entering an altered state of consciousness.

Dimly she remembered the light hovering above her husband.

At that point, her husband, although he was asleep, became animated as if he were a marionette being pulled into sudden life. And although her husband never opened his eyes, he performed the act of love with her.

And it was roughly nine months after that strange act of cosmic sex that Theresa was born.

Her mother told Theresa that on the way home from the hospital she became aware of a bright light in the sky above the automobile.

As she walked into the house with baby Theresa in her arms, the light seemed to hover at treetop level. The light, according to her mother, was witnessed by several neighbors and by Theresa's father. After hovering at treetop level for ten or fifteen minutes, it moved into the night sky at an enormous rate of speed.

After hearing her mother's peculiar story, Theresa said that she felt a little uneasy about exactly who her true father might be. She admitted that ever since she had been a small child she had a fascination for outer space and UFOs. It was during such a discussion of various science fiction and scientific concepts, including the possibility that extraterrestrial visitations could be occurring, that Theresa's mother had told her the strange account of her conception and birth.

ARE "STARSEED" AND "SPACE KIDS" ACCELERATING HUMAN EVOLUTION?

In a discussion with Dr. Andrija Puharich and his associates about the reality of those who claim to be Starseed, the "Space Kids," awakening among us to accelerate human evolution, he commented:

> I think it's a phenomenon that will eventually become clear, but it's not going to become clear with the ordinary three-dimensional vision that we exercise in contemporary science. I think we're going to have to develop what I call a whole race of "psychonauts"—talented people who are able to cross dimensional barriers. And there are such people. I've worked with them. They can see into the future. They can see into the next dimension. They can bring back reliable, hard information that can be verified in the three-dimensional world.

> I think it's going to take an enormous amount of data collection with these psychonauts, who can escape from the fourth dimension and the fifth dimension and the sixth dimension and tap other civilizations, get aboard spacecraft physically, be tele-transported from here to some other civilization. I think we're just at the beginning of a whole new age of exploration; and, to me, it's probably much more exciting than the time when the first little old Neanderthal man dug out a canoe and sailed forth. That little Neanderthal and his canoe led to the great age of exploration, but the exploration on which we are now embarking will be much greater than landing on the moon or going to Jupiter.

> I think that everybody should be aware that we are dealing with exciting new phenomenon which will make the present way of

life seem archaic and primitive, as we look at man in the Paleolithic Age. I think we are on the threshold, and we have all the tools, all the opportunities. All we have to do is remain cool about it and not try to preserve old ideas, old systems, old philosophies of science, old religions, old political forms.

I think we should imagine that the world never existed before and we're starting out from scratch. We've got the opportunity to create a whole new world.

THE COMING TRANSFORMATION OF HUMANKIND

One of Dr. Puharich's associates, John Whitmore, said that the big picture is the transformation of humankind: "This comes in so many different forms. Even sociologists are writing about some sort of a transformation. I think each group perceives it in the context in which they're working. I think that too few people are drawing connections between all these things. We have been conditioned to the specialized, focused ways of perception. I think the New Age, so to speak, is a holistic age."

Are we heading toward a new era for humankind when we are all transformed in a very deep and spiritual way? (*Art by Ricardo Pustanio*)

Melanie Toyofuku, also in attendance at our group discussion, agreed that both a biological and a spiritual evolution is occurring right now:

In Queen Victoria's time, for example, some women began menstruating at the age of 21. Today girls are menstruating at the young age of ten. I think that a kind of biological evolution makes it a lot easier for people to accept a psychological and a spiritual evolution, and the children are in that kind of evolution.

The children have evolved to the point where they're transcending. All that's happening is transcendence. I think that transcendence is the important thing. Some people transcend on a religious level. They commune with God, and that's enough for them. You mention space civilizations to them, and they get very upset. With the space children, religion upsets them. They're in another kind of space with another civilization. All of that to me is comfortable.

I think the arguments we create, whether it's a UFO, whether it's a Jungian thought-form, whether it's collective unconscious, all that is less important to me in terms of an argument. All of it is totally acceptable to me, and I think it depends upon your personal belief system as to whichever cosmology you wish to believe. The important thing is that if we are indeed here as part of the evolutionary process, which I believe we are, then our commitment is to be effective in creating a transcended planet, so that we survive in light and be the best that man can be.

SKY CRITTERS AND ORBS

In the mid-1960s, when Brad Steiger left teaching to explore full time the strange, the unusual, and the unknown, and when his writings had received national attention because of a number of bestselling books, he still found it rather difficult to come out of the cosmic closet in his native Iowa, the buckle in America's Bible Belt. At that time Fay Clark, the author of *Beyond the Light* and publisher of Hiawatha Books (Hiawatha, Iowa), became an early supporter and mentor of Brad's. It seemed that Fay, who had close ties with the Association for Research and Enlightenment (ARE), also knew many key members in the psychic, paranormal, and UFO fields from coast to coast. Clark opened many doors for Brad—and he also opened corners of Brad's mind that might have remained shut far longer if not for his guidance and inspiration. It seemed as though wherever Brad lectured in those early days, there was Fay; his wife; Mary, and two Methodist pastors, Rev. Milton Nothdurft and Rev. Mark Weston, members of the Spiritual Frontiers Fellowship, an organization also very supportive of Brad's early work.

An extra bonus for movie buff Brad was that Fay was an absolute dead-ringer for the great motion-picture actor Claude Rains, even to his manner of speaking. Sometimes Brad truly felt as though he was receiving instruction from the Invisible Man, Sir John Talbot, or Mr. Jordan.

Here is a remarkable account from Fay, who died on October 23, 1991, telling in his own words about his sighting of what he believed to be a "living UFO," circa 1973.

SIGHTING A "LIVING UFO"

By Fay Clark

I had been investigating UFOs for twenty-two years, but the sighting that completely changed my view of the phenomenon occurred at Lone Pine,

Light from UFOs is usually reported to be extremely bright and many times varies in intensity. (**Art by Bill Oliver**)

California. My wife and I observed a UFO resting on a small grove of aspen trees. We had been attracted to the area by a terrifically bright light that was so intense we were unable to look directly at it.

Then the light subsided somewhat and we could see the clear outline of the object. All the way around it were openings in its side. The light began to grow until it covered nearly the entire area of the object. As it grew in size, it lost its brilliance and became a lavender color. When the light reached nearly the entire size of the object, the illumination began to shrink down until it got to the very brilliant white portion again, which, if my judgment was correct, would probably have been about twenty feet in diameter. Then the light would again increase its size to maybe three-quarters or four-fifths of the size of the entire object, and it would be that lavender color.

This process of expansion and contraction of light continued, and my wife and I realized that *it was matching the rhythm of our respiration rates*.

We became aware that the object was increasing its tempo. We saw one edge of the UFO raise so that it was no longer level with the tops of the trees. In the length of time that it took me to turn my head, the object had moved ten miles out over Death Valley. I know it was ten miles, because we drove out underneath it.

The thing that really amazed my wife and me was that it took off at that tremendous speed *instantly*—with no sound, no fire, no smoke. And all of the trees leaned with it, rather than being blasted backward. We looked the area over carefully and found no more small limbs and leaves on the ground than one would find under any grove of trees.

The word that kept coming to me was that the object was *impelled*, rather than *propelled*. It was *drawn*, rather than *pushed*. If there would have been any force pushing it, it certainly would have blasted limbs and leaves off the trees.

We drove out in the desert and stayed with the object for probably an hour and a half, directly underneath it. When we first stopped the car, some substance that looked like whipped cream or heavy fog rolled out of the openings in its sides. It was probably not more than three hundred feet above the ground, but it was completely hidden from view after it produced its own "cloud" of this substance.

We knew it was there, though, so we drove back a distance so that we could clearly see it sitting on top of its artificial cloud.

What we were observing, I believe, was a phenomenon going on *inside* the object. I believe that the thing was breathing, and I see no reason to change my thought on that matter.

My wife and I both had the feeling that we were witnessing the ultimate in creation. The closer we came to the object, the more we were suffused with a feeling of reverence and beauty and humbleness.

I'll tell about another object we witnessed, and I will illustrate why I know there were no occupants inside it. This sighting occurred outside of Seligman, Arizona. We watched the object coming, then observed it change its course to come and hover not more than fifteen feet above our Volkswagen. It seemed to me that it was just looking at us, as if it were studying our little car.

I jumped out with my Hasselblad camera and swung it up to take a picture. But before I could even touch the shutter, the UFO zipped right toward a little butte.

I had a terrible, sick feeling that anything so beautiful was going to crash and be destroyed. Instead of crashing, though, just before it touched the butte it shot *straight up*. It didn't stop; it just changed direction—a right angle, straight up—and disappeared.

No crew could have been in this craft and survived such a maneuver. They would have been mashed against the sides of the vehicle, then pulled apart by the acceleration straight up.

I do not believe that we observed a craft made by beings from some other planet. I believe that we were watching a living creature, a form of life that moved into our dimension.

Different people throughout the years have said to me, "Fay, you know a lot more than you are telling. Come on now, tell us the truth. Admit that you made contact with the aliens *inside* the object. At least tell us they contacted you."

But Brad, we were not contacted, and there were *no occupants* inside the object. We only had the most wonderful feeling of peace and harmony, and the knowledge that we were witnessing the beauty of the ultimate of creation.

I firmly believe that UFOs are a form of life that come not from another planet but from another dimension. I believe that they are probably all around us all the time—just outside of our own dimension.

<hr>

⊸⊸≪∩≫⊷⊷

TREVOR J. CONSTABLE AND THE SKY CRITTERS

In 1975, when Brad discussed the matter of living UFOs with another old friend, highly respected military and aviation historian Trevor James Constable, "T. J." said that biological life in the upper octave of terrestrial existence has been overlooked by too many UFO investigators who early on were in favor of the foregone conclusion that UFOs were vehicles from outer space.

T.J. handed Brad a stack of photos of UFOs that he had taken with a Leica G IR 135 infrared film at f-3.5, 1/30.

"These are plainly biological forms," he said. "These are plasmic living organisms native to our atmosphere. As they appear in these photographs, they give one the impression of looking through the side of an aquarium."

Constable continued:

The daily etheric breathings of the Earth produce a barometric pressure wave twice daily, which formal science has never been able to explain. There is enough energy in these barometric waves to run the world's machines—if we can but find the transducer. The torque drive of the Earth itself is an inexhaustible, life-positive energy source of staggering magnitude. That's what civilization depends on—making material substance spin. We see the discs in our skies manifesting these spinning motions over and over again, pressed down upon us in such profusion that one wonders how there can be any vestige of skepticism remaining. Wilhelm Reich has already shown that motors can be run directly from the cosmic life energy, or orgone, as he discovered and refined that energy.

The characteristic of this coming epoch—heralded by UFOs—is that free primary energy will run the world. No one can put etheric force into a wire and sell it. No sheik can say that tomorrow etheric force is going to cost four times what it does today. No one can confine it within storage tanks and demand money for it. Everyone is going to have energy to do the world's work without pollution and without financial price.

Before long, someone will uncover that all-important step (discovered by Wilhelm Reich but not disclosed by him) by which etheric force can be transduced into existing electric motors or simple adaptations of them. Orgone and magnetism are cheek by jowl. The UFO evidence screams this at the world. The era of free primary energy is imminent, and its imminence is reinforced

RICARDO PUSTANIO 2012

Sky critters are ethereal beings whose breathing generates barometric waves in the atmosphere that could potentially be harnessed as an energy source. (*Art by Ricardo Pustanio*)

by the absolute necessity for its appearance. The UFO shows the feasibility and potential of etheric force in technological use. With etheric force comes not just a new technical epoch, but a cultural and educational change forced by the need to understand etheric energies as we now understand other energy forms.

The price for this new technical epoch is a forced overhaul of our whole mode of existence. We will see the beginning of a reunion between science and religion as the cosmic energies—pervaded with life and themselves the milieu of living beings—come into technical utility. Man will find the central parts of his own physical existence inseparably bound up with etheric energies, and he will be opened to a widened understanding of himself and the cosmos that produced him. The ultimate consequence will be a new humanity.

Constable handed Brad a photograph of a partially materialized UFO that Dr. James O. Woods had taken in the Mojave Desert in April 1958. According to T.J., whose own shadowed image appears in the lower right of the picture, this photo provided basic keys to the propulsion system of this type of living UFO. The black dot on top of the two-tiered object, he said, was a lens for focusing primary energy from the Sun. Plasmic fields that appeared as white lobes whirled around the rim of the disc and created a plasma in the atmosphere that Dr. Woods had recorded with infrared film.

A photograph taken by Constable captured a rather large "space critter" near Giant Rock, California, on May 17, 1958. "It is such critters as this that account for so many UFO sightings," he said. "I maintain that such atmospheric animal forms exist in an adjacent, but invisible, physical continuum. Normally, these creatures are invisible to human sight, but they occasionally drop into the visible spectrum as a result of far-reaching changes in the biosphere brought about by human activity."

After many years of research, Constable came to the conclusion that it is the Ahrimanic powers that are trying to seize control of our planet. He believes that Inner Space, not Outer Space, is the invasion route chosen by the Ahrimanic powers. The choices we make, Constable says, and the extent to which we utilize balancing forces to neutralize the Ahrimanic attacks, will bring us victory or defeat.

Ahrimanic entities are fallen angels, according to Persian and Chaldean traditions, who travel in high-tech vehicles and inhabit the space between Earth and the heavens. Today they are mistaken for alien, interstellar space travellers. (*Art by Ricardo Pustanio*)

According to Persian and Chaldean tradition, the *Ahrimanes* are fallen angels, who out of revenge for being expelled from heaven continually torment the apex of God's creation—the human inhabitants of Earth. The old legends have it that the Ahrimanes decided to inhabit the *Ahrimane-Abad*, the space between the Earth and the fixed stars.

Because from time to time the Ahrimanic entities have revealed themselves riding in etherically propelled vehicles that appear to represent a material technology far in advance of that possessed by humans, people have assumed that such UFOs are spacecraft from a scientifically superior extraterrestrial world. In addition, the Ahrimanic beings have devised contact encounters with ingenuous human beings who can be used to serve certain ends in promulgating the thought that the Space Brothers come from outer space, rather than being deceivers from a nonmaterial dimension near at hand.

Constable decrees that the overall consequence of such deceptive contact encounters, wherein humans are set upon by the Ahrimanic humanoids, is that the world is led to believe that material craft and physical alien beings are involved. And if people are not convinced by the contactee, then he or she is labeled just another "flying saucer nut." Either way, the world gets a lie overlaid with confusion and ridicule, while the Ahrimanic humanoids depart from view.

The Ahrimanic deceivers are everywhere, Constable warns, unrecognized and often aided by humans who don't know that the Devil is indeed and well—and coming to Earth within the lifetime of millions now living. One is always wise to "test the spirits" and attempt to determine if the counseling entity serves the dark side or the light side of the force. And caution should be doubled in reports of UFO encounters, for in Constable's opinion, the Ahrimanic messengers inject themselves into such events in order to sow confusion, disorientation, and distrust among UFO investigators. Humans are constantly being seduced into doing the work of the nether forces because they simply do not acknowledge that such forces exist, let alone recognize how they work *into* and *upon* Earth life. "Incomprehension of spiritual forces and the institutionalized denigration of the spirit in formal education make humanity pitifully vulnerable in dehumanizing, life-negative, and destructive trends," Constable says. "The Ahrimanic intelligences confront humankind with a bewildering armory of advanced technical devices, transcendental abilities, and mind-bending powers. Armed only with mechanistic thought and an unbalanced technology, the human posture for meeting this stupendous and unavoidable event is both unstable and inadequate."

Constable maintains that the hope of humankind lies in the expansion of human awareness. "If man can be shown where the battlefield is, the nature of the terrain, and the ways in which he is already being assaulted in this inner war, then the right tactics and strategy can be brought to bear against inimical forces."

For centuries, the Ahrimanic entities have held as their goal the enslavement of humankind. If they are unopposed, they will overwhelm humanity and take evolution wholly under their control. We must realize that in the struggle for mastery of Earth, we human beings, and our souls, are at once the goal of the battle and the battleground itself.

⊸⪼⟐⪻⊷

REAL ENCOUNTERS WITH ORBS

One summer's night in 1953, as seventeen-year-old Brad Steiger was driving home in his 1948 maroon Ford coupe, he was startled to see a greenish, glowing orb of light bobbing right ahead of him, square in the middle of the

RICARDO PUSTANIO 2012

Ball lightning? Swamp gas? Will-o'-the-wisps? Even camera flares or other optical illusions? People have tried explaining strange lights for years without much success. (*Art by Ricardo Pustanio*)

country road at the end of a neighbor's lane. It appeared to be about the size of a volleyball or basketball.

Brad really didn't have time to hit the brakes in order to avoid striking the mysterious illuminated ball because it came right at him and passed right through the windshield. It remained for a couple of disconcerting moments at Brad's chest level, in front of the steering wheel, then it veered around him to pass out an open back window.

Although the object had appeared to be a solid ball of some luminous substance, it had passed through the windshield of the Ford without causing the automobile or the driver any discernible damage. Brad was shaken by the encounter and had no idea what the thing was. The next day, describing the experience to some of his friends, he learned that three teenage girls claim to have been chased home after encountering a glowing ball of light at the same place on the same country road.

Incredibly, the glowing globe was waiting for Brad near the same clump of trees on the next two consecutive evenings. On each occasion, it seemed eager to demonstrate its ability to pass through solid matter without leaving any trace of its entrance or exit.

After three nights of close encounters with the enigmatic, glowing green light, Brad did not witness another until several years later while driving late at night. On that occasion, the light swerved away from his car and shot at great speed across an open, freshly planted cornfield.

A study of perplexing phenomenon yielded information about manifestations of will-o'-the-wisps, swamp gas, and ball lightning. None of these theories seemed to explain the remarkable faculties of the glowing, green globe that could pass through an automobile's windshield without leaving any evidence of penetration.

THE ORB THAT FOLLOWED HER HOME

Some years ago, we received a letter from an elderly woman who had a rather frightening encounter with such a glowing object in 1916. Mrs. B.K. was teaching at a rural school near Wellsburg, Iowa, and boarding with a farm family. One night in May, near the end of the school year, she was restless and unable to sleep. So even though the hour was very late, around eleven, she got up, dressed, crept silently down the stairs, walked out the door, and went for a walk.

Then, as she tells it in her own words:

It was a beautiful night, and a full moon was riding high in the sky. I felt quite exhilarated and not at all afraid. All the farm families in the neighborhood were fast asleep, so there was little chance of meeting anyone on the little-traveled dirt road. I was enjoying my walk so much that 1 didn't notice how far I had gone, but it must have been two or three miles.

As I realized that I must start back, the sky became overcast, covering the full moon and making the night darker and darker. My mood changed to an eerie sort of fear, and I kept walking faster and faster.

At last I reached the crossroads near where I was staying. Then I suddenly turned my head and looked over my shoulder. There, just a few yards behind me, floating about three feet above the ground, was an orange-red ball or disc, following me at the same pace as I was walking. It glowed dully, but shed no light around it or on the ground. As soon as I saw it, it veered off to the side of the road, rose a bit, then sailed over the barbed-wire fence and disappeared in some shrubbery on the other side. It was with great relief that I reached the house and went back to bed.

I did not want my landlady to know about my midnight walk, but finally my curiosity got the better of me and I did tell her about what I had seen. She merely nodded and said, "We call them jack-o'- lanterns," From her response it was obvious that lots of other folks had seen them, but I sensed that she didn't care to talk more about the subject so I dropped it.

I'd heard of such things as the will-o'-the-wisp, but I always pictured that as a rather formless white light, and this had been an orange-colored globe. There were no swamps or marshes around, so it couldn't have been "swamp gas." My father once said something vague about "ball lightning," but if it had been that, it should have exploded. This strange ball of reddish light behaved as if it were intelligent, for it had been following me in a straight line—but as soon as it was discovered, it swerved aside and went into the bushes as if in hiding. And hadn't there been something unnatural about the sudden darkness? This experience remains among my unsolved mysteries.

—◦◦◦◦◦—

Are Orbs Ball Lightning?

Ball lightning, the most often cited suspect for such encounters as the ones above, remains a mystery. On June 7, 2006, *National Geographic News* stated that in spite of around ten thousand written reports of observations of ball lightning, the phenomenon had thus far defied precise scientific explanation. Ball lightning is most often described as a floating, glowing, round object similar in size to a tennis ball or even a beach ball. The mysterious ball floats near the ground, sometimes rebounding off other objects, and always defying the known laws of gravity. Although contact with the glowing orbs are usually not fatal, people have been killed by touching ball lightning, and there are reports of the objects melting through glass windows and burning through window screens. Notice that the reports state *melting* through glass, not passing through without leaving a sign of its sizzling passage.

Graham K. Hubler, a physicist at the U.S. Naval Research Laboratory in Washington, D.C., told Brian Handwerk of *National Geographic News* (May 31, 2006) that ball lightning is "a real, physical phenomenon that's out there in nature, and we don't have the foggiest idea what it is … It's possible that there's some new physics in it that could be very profound."

⟶⟶⟶

THE SHINING ONES

What if such manifestations as these glowing balls of light should be intelligent entities—or what if they should be the vehicle of transport for multidimensional beings?

We have a folklore and a religion at least two thousand years old that links these mysterious globes of light with the Devas, "the Shining Ones." Although Hinduism does not specifically refer to the Devas as angelic beings, they do act in ways similar to angels and they can play a protective role toward humans. And just as there are Devas who dwell in the higher astral planes, there are fallen Devas who live in the lower astral plane. Devas may also assist in humans' spiritual development and concern themselves with the fruitful growth of the earthly environment.

The manipulation of glowing balls of light as a means of transportation may also be employed by angels and spirit guides. Indeed, the globes of light may be the form these benevolent beings assume before fully materializing in our dimension. As a word of caution, however, we must remind the reader that not-so-benevolent beings may also utilize orbs for more nefarious purposes. Throughout the centuries, men and women have encountered elves, fairies, huddlefolk—or whatever one chooses to label our earthly companion species—arriving in illuminated globes. Remember Glinda, the Good Witch in the Wizard of Oz, who soared and descended in a large ball of light? Other observers of the metaphysical scene theorize that the balls of light are themselves an intelligence that can shape-shift into the physical form most compatible with the level of understanding of each individual witness, appearing to some as an angel, to others as a Deva, and to those of more conventional beliefs, as a saint or a holy figure.

⟶⟶⟶

ENCOUNTERS WITH ORBS ARE ON THE INCREASE

Paranormal researchers have taken notice that encounters with spheres of light have been on the increase in recent years. Balls of light have been reported moving above fields of wheat and corn, apparently responsible for the crop circles found there the next morning. Paranormal investigators have photographed orbs while recording phenomena in houses said to be haunted—and they aren't talking about dust motes or droplets of water captured by their digital cameras, but about glowing spheres that moved toward them. Skeptics attribute such manifestations to balls of plasma energy or natural phenomena,

Real Encounters, Different Dimensions, and Otherworldly Beings

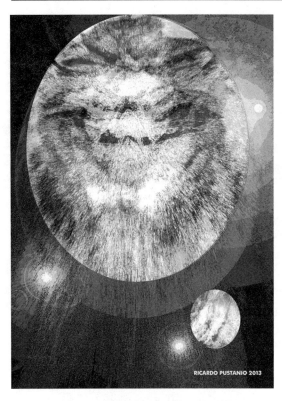

RICARDO PUSTANIO 2013

Glowing globes of light might not be vehicles for transportation but, rather, simply the form otherworldly beings take before they fully materialize within our dimension. (Art by Ricardo Pustanio)

but others are convinced that these objects are under the control of angels, spirit guides, nature spirits, or other multidimensional beings.

Consider, for example, the essential message which may lie in the basic shape of the orbs moving about in "haunted" places, the mysterious discs darting across the skies—all are most often reported as circular in form. In numerous instances the UFO seems almost to have been mandala-like, and like the mandala, which is often used for purposes of meditation, has precipitated in the observers a state similar to that of trance.

In his *Ego and Archetype*, Jungian analyst Edward E. Edinger discusses Rhoda D. Kellogg's studies of pre-school art. Ms. Kellogg observed that the mandala, or circle image, appears to be the predominant one expressed by young children learning how to draw. Initially, a two-year-old merely scribbles, but "soon he seems to be attracted by the intersection of lines and begins to make crosses." The cross soon becomes enclosed by a circle, thus presenting us with the basic pattern of the mandala. As the child endeavors to replicate human figures, Ms. Kellog noted, "they first emerge as circles, contrary to all visual experience, with the arms and legs being represented only as ray-like extensions of the circle."

Edinger assesses Ms. Kellog's studies as providing "clear empirical data indicating that the young child experiences the human being as a round, mandala-like structure and verifying in an impressive way the psychological truth of Plato's myth of the round man." Child therapists, Edinger notes, often find the mandala an effective healing image in young children. "All of this indicates that, symbolically speaking, the human psyche was originally round, whole, complete—in a state of oneness and self-sufficiency that is equivalent to deity itself.

It may be that the message of these orbs moving about our fields and forests, or these discs moving across our skies, is a call to humankind to return to that original state of wholeness, that sense of oneness with the Cosmos. Surely, the holistic view, that which maintains that all life is one, and that each single cell maintains a signal link-up with every other cell, is becoming increasingly popular. Humankind is reawakening to the necessity of becoming truly and totally integrated with its environment. Contemporary men and women by the hundreds of thousands are becoming vitally interested in meditative practices which will permit them to regain, even fleetingly, that state of union for which humankind apparently feels so much nostalgia.

⊰─◄║◊║►─⊱

A RENOWNED RESEARCHER TELLS OF HER LIFE-LONG ENCOUNTER WITH ORBS

Dr. P.M.H. Atwater grew up in the reclaimed deserts of southern Idaho and is today an accomplished and successful writer of many books and an internationally known researcher and lecturer on the near-death experience. She is also the author of *Children of the Fifth World: A Guide to the Coming Changes in Human Consciousness*. As a child, she may have seen the orbs of the nature spirits as they really are.

As P.M.H. tells it:

As a child, I could readily see, hear, and talk to other human souls; and I honestly believed that everyone else could, too. But it was when I went outdoors that the fun really began. I never really saw little *people*, not ever! But I did see colored vortexes of swirling, pulsating energy that I played with and watched. It is strange now, looking back, but I never had any desire to give them names or to place them in any kind of human role, It simply was not necessary to me for them even to have human forms. It was always all right for them simply to be what they were, and for me to be what I was. We didn't have to be models of each other to communicate or to share life.

Perhaps I really shouldn't call them "vortexes," either. Perhaps the best description would be to call them "energy masses," for that's exactly what they were—pure energy. They made little movements and sometimes big ones without the benefit of wind. They behaved in playful fashion, sometimes kicking up a little dust here and there, sometimes ducking under a leaf or parting the grass. The energy masses I saw spun when they moved, like miniature whirlygigs. Whenever they would spin onto the palm of my outstretched hand, they really tickled and I found that to be a lot of fun.

They had colors, sounds, and odor. Their colors, though, were not as the ones I see in the regular world around me. No, their colors were more like shimmering, translucent colors that you could taste! Each little energy mass created its own sounds that I am at a total loss to describe. Everything was so natural, so complete.

> Perhaps the best description would be to call them "energy masses," for that's exactly what they were—pure energy.

I enjoyed my little friends whenever I could. They were not "bigger than life" things to me—they were simply another part of life. They were not separate ever, but they were a part of my total existence.

As I grew older, they did not disappear, but they did become less important to me. It was seeing other human souls, observing living numbers, and perceiving sounds that bounced like tiny cubes in the air that caused me trouble growing up. These things and others like them are what I quickly learned to be quiet about—for to talk about them became a "sin."

When I reached puberty and throughout my teen years, the Spirit Keepers became a very important part of my life. Without their total acceptance of me and the training I received from them, I would not have survived my teen years with an intact personality.

In the February 28, 2013, issue of her newsletter, Dr. Atwater dealt with the question of orbs and made some very interesting observations:

"Orbs, or any form of plasma, are attracted to and follow consciousness. Plasma is a perfect 'container' for the deceased, or whatever seems 'alien,' guides and guardians, or 'visitors,' and are frequently seen at funerals or doorways in-between the many worlds of spirit. Notice that I said plasma will respond to consciousness—yours, mine, anyone else's. So of course those who grieve a loved one's death often see the face of that loved one in an orb or sense that he or she is the orb itself; perhaps contact has been made (even after many years) and communication in some form begins."

Known internationally for her extensive research on the near-death experience, Dr. Atwater observed, "Near-death experiencers see lots of orbs. Young people going through puberty do, too. Anyone involved in energetic, emotional displays (positive or negative) often produce orbs. When I crossed the United States, leaving Idaho to move to Virginia, alone, totally dedicated to my 'mission,' with no sense of fear, I saw orbs following along on either side of my car, small ones, but always there, every day, just out there, in the air, just there. I had no sense of beings or guides or anything other than the comfort of having orbs around. Were they protecting me? I don't know. I had no reason or desire to imagine a purpose for them, nor did they assume any special shape. Orbs can simply exist as an outplay of our own consciousness. Sometimes that's enough."

OLD GODS FROM THE SEA OR VISITORS FROM THE STARS?

STARS OR UFOS DIVE INTO THE MEDITERRANEAN SEA

On January 28, 2012, a young couple was walking on the promenade near the beach of the ancient seaport of Ashkelon, Israel, when they spotted "two stars that were flickering in light above the Mediterranean Sea." According to the report that they submitted to the National UFO Reporting Center, "The lights moved slowly west like they were floating." As they watched, they saw the color of the lights "suddenly change to red, with a three-second gap between each flicker of each object." The two objects continued to move to the west until one of them began to fall "very slowly" to the sea. There was no noise as the object struck the water, and its companion hovered motionless, still flickering, for several seconds until it began to move to the west. Two other objects appeared above the one on the sea. "After several minutes," the witnesses said in their report, "the three objects flew away at super-high speed." [Thanks to Peter Davenport, National UFO Reporting Center.]

FIVE BRIGHT ORANGE DISCS OVER LITTLE GASPARILLA ISLAND

Another 2012 report from the files of Peter Davenport recounts the sighting of five bright orange discs by a group watching evening fireworks on the beach of Little Gasparilla Island, a barrier island midway between Sarasota and Fort Myers on Florida's tropical southwest coast. The discs, or orbs—four in

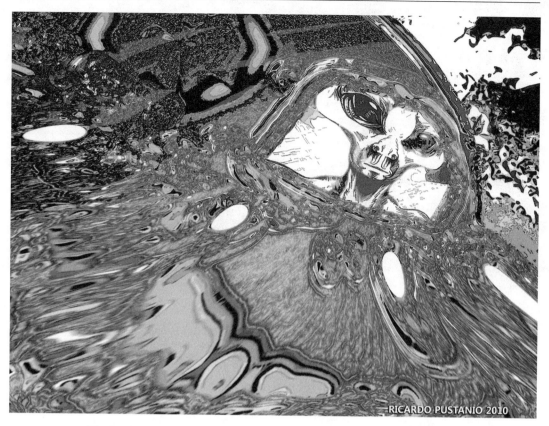

The UFOs seen by a young couple in Israel fell into the sea in slow motion. (*Art by Ricardo Pustanio*)

back and one in the front—moved north along the coastline into the clouds. Hundreds were in the crowd on the beach watching fireworks about 9 P.M., and they saw the objects coming up the island's shoreline. According to witnesses, the glowing orange discs moved up the shoreline at a steady pace.

The witness who made the report to the National UFO Reporting Center said that they did have one of the objects on a cell phone camera: "When you zoom into the thing, it is a bright orange with red along the edges that were very strange."

A Light "Brighter Than Venus" Appears to Follow a Cruise Ship

A Mutual UFO Network (MUFON) Case Management System (CMS) report carries the account of a couple on cruise on September 6, 2010, through the Alaskan Inside Passage aboard the MS *Norwegian Pearl.* "It was about 9:30 P.M.," begins the witness, "and our ship was traveling at 22 knots with a compass bearing of about 338 degrees. Ahead of the ship and about 10 to 20 degrees off her port bow and above us, I noticed a bright light heading in a straight line along the side of the ship. It was coming directly toward the ship but on a parallel, not an intercept course."

The witness describes the light as being "brighter than Venus … a dingy yellowish white with no flicker to it." He called his wife's attention to the object, and they observed that the slow-moving object progressed "… above and along the length of the ship and passed by our position over a period lasting about 5 minutes." The couple saw no signs of a strobe light or any navigation lights. It passed them "by probably no less than 1000 feet." After about five minutes, the slow-moving, silent object faded from view, "then it reappeared in its full brightness at about the same position relative to the ship. This time it kept exact pace with the ship, but was now moving on an intercept course perpendicular to the ship."

According to the witness, the mysterious object took two minutes to traverse a distance equal to the length of his thumb held at arm's length. "At that point," he said, the yellowish-white object "… made a course deviation away from the ship before correcting once again in the opposite way so that it was again approaching."

<hr />

Chinese-U.S. Armada Investigates Underwater Base near San Francisco

In mid-September 2012, Gordon Duff, senior editor of *Veterans Today,* reported on a classified memo which had first been confirmed, then denied, that detailed an account of a combined fleet operation of Chinese and U.S. Navy vessels gathering off the U.S. coast near San Francisco to confront extraterrestrial craft operating from underwater bases. Duff credited Kerry Cassidy of Project Camelot, WhistleBlower Radio, as an early source for the rumored assemblage of the multinational military force.

The rumors flying around the event included the following: 1) Extraterrestrial craft were operating from underwater bases; 2) In order to deal with the extraterrestrial threat, advanced U.S. sub-orbital weapons platforms had been deployed from Vandenberg Air Force Base; 3) The process of UFO tracking was now employing nanotechnology microscopic sensors to detect such eventualities as distortions in time.

The reasons for the formation of the Chinese-U.S. armada were the conclusions of high-ranking military officers that the extraterrestrial opposition was extremely aggressive and unfriendly, and that the threat represented a clear and present danger to the topside residents of Earth. China, so said the rumors, was forced to cover for a more extensive U.S. presence in confronting the extraterrestrial threat because the U.S. Navy had deployed a large number of its vessels to the Persian Gulf. Echoing a warning that attempts to seek confirmations or to directly verify these multinational operations could lead to "fatal consequences," Gordon Duff gave the rumors a "70 percent" reliability grade.

⸺⫘⫘⫘⸺

RESEARCHERS STATE UNDERSEA ALIEN BASES ARE FOUND IN OCEANS WORLDWIDE

Our contemporary mysteries of the sea contain innumerable accounts of mysterious "lights in the skies" (UFOs), as well as unidentified submersible objects cruising our oceans, seacoasts, and large bodies of inland waters. The USOs' apparent affinity for water has long been noted by ufologists and flying saucer buffs. Perhaps the UFO enigma might be traced to the inner space of our seas rather than the outer space of our solar system.

There is no question that claims of mysterious underwater bases have been circulating since before and after pilot Kenneth Arnold, who while flying near Mt. Rainier on June 24, 1947, sighted the "flying saucers" that signaled the beginning of the modern era of the UFO mystery. On July 7, just two days after the alleged crash of an alien space vehicle near Roswell, New Mexico, two teenagers walking on the beach at San Rafael, California, were astonished to see an unusual craft emerge from the ocean. According to writer-researcher Preston Dennett, the teenagers watched as a "flat, glistening object" flew for a short distance, then dove back into the water four hundred yards from shore.

Dennett, who has been researching underwater UFO bases since the late 1980s, reports in *Fate* (February 2006) that in August 1947, steamers and other sea traffic going into and out of San Francisco Bay encountered a mysterious object that was large enough to earn descriptions of being "an undersea mountain," "a reef," or a "submarine mountain" before it decided to leave the Golden Gate behind and move out to sea.

Dennett documents an early morning sighting near Playa del Rey on November 6, 1957, in which three motorists driving along the Pacific Coast Highway were startled to see a large "egg-shaped object" enveloped in a blue haze descend on the beach only a few yards away. The witnesses Richard Kehoe, Ronald Burke, and Joe Thomas got out of their cars and warily approached the strange craft. As they drew nearer, they saw two strange looking occupants disembarking from the UFO.

According to the three witnesses' reports, the UFOnauts had "yellow-ish-green skin," and wore "black leather pants, white belts, and light-colored jerseys." The strange beings walked up to the three men and began to attempt to converse with them. The men later said that the occupants seemed to be trying to ask them questions, but the language in which they spoke was completely unintelligible to them and they could not recognize it as any language with which they had any familiarity. After a few minutes, the occupants of the craft walked back to their craft in obvious disappointment with their failure to communicate. After entering the egg-shaped vehicle, they quickly took off and seemingly within seconds had accelerated out of sight.

"That same day at 3:50 P.M.," writes Dennett, author of *UFOs Over California: A True History of Extraterrestrial Encounters in the Golden State*, "an officer and 12 airmen from an Air Force detachment in nearby Long Beach observed six saucer-shaped objects zooming across the sky. Two hours later, officers at Los Alamitos Naval Air Station reported seeing 'numerous' objects criss-crossing the sky. At the same time, police stations in Long Beach received more than 100 calls from residents reporting UFOs."

USOs Evade Argentine Navy

The reports of USOs in the early years of UFO research are by no means confined to the shores of California.

Early in February 1960, the Argentine Navy, with the assistance of United States experts, alternately depth-bombed and demanded the surrender of submarines thought to be lying at the bottom of Golfo Nuevo, a forty-by-twenty-mile bay separated from the South Atlantic by a narrow entrance. On a number of occasions the Argentines declared that they had the mystery submarines trapped. Once, they announced that they had crippled one of the unidentified subs.

The mysterious submarines (there were at least two) had peculiar characteristics. They were able to function and maneuver in the narrow gulfs for many days without surfacing. They easily outran and hid from surface ships. They were at last able to escape completely, in spite of the combined forces of the Argentine fleet and the most modern U.S. sub-hunting equipment.

Skeptics of the bizarre undersea chase accused the Argentine Navy of timing their dramatic confrontation with mystery submarines with the evaluation of the new navy budget by the Argentine Congress. On the other hand, UFO buffs enumerated the many reports of strange vehicles seen entering and leaving the sea off the coast of Argentina and pronounced that

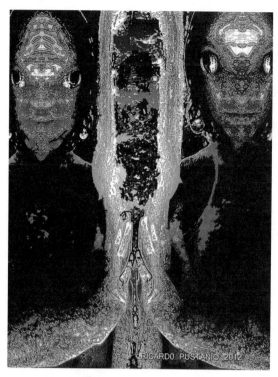

the unknown objects were underwater spacecraft, rather than terrestrial submarines. As a third alternative, might we envision a Council of the Cosmic Tutors severely reprimanding two captains of their reconnaissance fleet for allowing themselves to get boxed in and nearly caught by an earthling navy?

Who might be piloting these strange USOs that have been spotted not only by private citizens but also chased after by the U.S. Navy? (*Art by Ricardo Pustanio*)

FAMOUS MARINE SCIENTIST DETECTS USO OFF FLORIDA KEYS

Dr. Dmitri Rebikoff, a marine scientist making preparations to explore the Gulf Stream's depths, found himself faced with a puzzle when, on July 5, 1965, he detected and attempted to photograph a fast-moving undersea USO on the bottom of the warm-water stream that flows from the Florida Keys to Newfoundland and onward to northern Europe. Dr. Rebikoff told Captain Jacques Nicholas, a project coordinator, that a pear-shaped object, moving at approximately three and one-half knots, appeared beneath the various schools of fish.

"At first, from its size, we thought it to be a shark," Dr. Rebikoff reported. "However, its direction and speed were too constant. It may have been running on robot pilot. We received no signal from it and therefore we do not know what it was."

AIRLINE PILOT SPOTS USOs IN NEW ZEALAND

On January 12, 1965, according to Issue No. 43 of New Zealand's *Spaceview*, Captain K, an airline pilot on a flight between Whenuapai and Kaitaia, New Zealand, spotted another of the mysterious underwater unidentifiables. He was about one-third of the way across Kaipara Harbor when he saw what he at first believed to be a stranded, gray-white whale in an estuary. As he veered his DC-3 for a closer look at the object, it became evident to him that he was observing a metallic structure of some sort.

According to *Spaceview*, Captain K noted that the thing was perfectly streamlined and symmetrical in shape "… had no external control surfaces or protrusions … appeared metallic with the suggestion of a hatch on top … was resting on the bottom of the estuary and headed toward the south as suggested by the streamlined shape … was harbored in no more than 30 feet of water … was not shaped like a normal submarine, but approximately 100 feet in length with a diameter of fifteen feet at its widest part."

The journal made inquiries of the Navy upon receipt of Captain K's report and learned that it would have been impossible for any known model of submarine to have been in that particular area, due to the configuration of harbor and coastline. The surrounding mud flats and mangrove swamps would make the spot in which Captain K saw his underwater USO inaccessible to conventional undersea craft.

POWERFUL ELECTROMAGNETIC USO
DETECTED UNDERWATER OFF LONG ISLAND SOUND

On October 24, 1965, the auxiliary sloop *Vision 4* was cruising off Milford, Connecticut, skippered by Alfred Stanford, a retired U.S. Navy captain. Aboard as Stanford's guest was the noted explorer Dr. Paul Sheldon, holder of the Cruising Club's Blue Water Medal.

The sloop was about four miles off Charles Island, steering for the harbor entrance from out in Long Island Sound, when the compass suddenly began a strange, clockwise circling. The engine was running slowly, about 1,000 R.P.M., and there was no excessive amount of vibration; yet the compass continued its clockwise circling for about ten minutes, or three-quarters of a mile, before it steadied.

Captain Stanford later noted that he had the compass on the *Vision 4* adjusted for zero error by an experienced navigator, and he commented that the compass had been free of error during a full, intensive season of cruising.

Such erratic behavior on the part of the sloop's compass suggests a very powerful electromagnetic field beneath the surface of the coastal waters over which the *Vision 4* was cruising. Captain Stanford told newsmen that the peculiar rotation of his compass could not have come from the sloop's engine, because he had a disconnect switch on the generator field coil, which he had pulled without effect. There had to have been a submerged *something* beneath his sloop, Captain Stanford said, that had been playing havoc with his compass.

———∈⟪⟫∋———

SHAG HARBOR RESIDENTS WITNESS
SIXTY-FOOT USO DIVE INTO OCEAN

On October 3, 1967, several residents of Shag Harbor, Nova Scotia, were not able to think of any other term than "flying saucer" to describe the sixty-foot-long object with a series of bright portholes that they saw glide into the harbor and submerge in the ocean. Within twenty minutes several constables of the Royal Canadian Mounted Police were on the scene, attempting to reach by boat the spot where about a half mile off shore the sizzling UFO was seen to float and to submerge beneath the surface of Shag Harbor.

A Coast Guard boat and eight fishing vessels joined the constables in time to observe a large patch of yellowish foam and bubbling water. Divers from the Royal Canadian Navy searched the area for two days, but found no physical evidence of any kind. The Halifax *Chronicle-Herald* quoted Squadron Leader Bain of the Royal Canadian Air Force as saying: "We get hundreds of reports every week, but the Shag Harbor incident is one of the few where we may get something concrete on it."

The incident at Shag Harbor has become one of the most highly investigated cases in the annals of ufology, and even many skeptical researchers consider it one of the most convincing of alleged reports of UFOs submerging or crashing into the sea.

———∈⟪⟫∋———

RUSSIAN NAVY OFFICIALS ADMIT
NUMEROUS ENCOUNTERS WITH USOS

In September 2009, the website *Russia Today* released information that allegedly came from Russian Navy officials, who admitted that the Russian Navy had not only experienced numerous encounters with USOs in the seas, but that responsible members of Russian crews had sighted alien beings below the surface. Trustworthy naval personnel stated that it is very possible that underwater alien bases exist.

Vladimir Azhazha, spokesman for *Russia Today*, observed that, since even submarines rarely visited the great depths of the oceans, it was very possible for such alien bases to exist. Documents recording such encounters with USOs have existed since the time of the Soviet Union, Azhazha said, and the information that Soviet seamen discovered is of great value. Fifty percent of UFO encounters are connected with oceans, Azhazha commented. Fifteen percent more with lakes. So, it would appear, USOs tend to stick to the water and their underwater bases.

ANCIENT SEA GODS OR ANCIENT ALIEN USOS?

Long before visitors from other worlds were named as the likely architects for kingdoms beneath the seas, a number of ancient mariners and high priests declared that certain gods preferred the solitude of the depths of the sea to the lofty heights of Mount Olympus.

Berosus records that the god who gave the Babylonians warning of the coming of the Great Deluge was Chronos, who was associated with a land of plenty somewhere in the Atlantic. The Romans called the Atlantic Ocean "Chronium Mare," the Sea of Chronos; and the Pillars of Hercules were also named the Pillars of Chronos by the ancient inhabitants of the Mediterranean. In other words, the master who spoke warning of coming disaster was identified as a sea god.

Ea, the Chaldean god who brought civilization to the ancestors of the Assyrians, and whose legends are found on the tablets at Nineveh, was represented as half-man and half-fish. Ea was said to have come from a land destroyed by rain and floods, a land now beneath the ocean.

The Indian version of the Deluge tells of Manu, son of Vivasvat, being advised about the coming torrent by a fish that spoke to him from the banks of the Chirini. Later, when Manu and his people had constructed the great ship that would bear them above the catastrophic flood, the great fish, unwearied, draws them over the waters, bringing the vessel eventually to rest on the highest peak of Himavat.

The Orkney and Hebrides islanders sing of the "Silkies," who dwell in the depths of the sea and occasionally rise up to pass on land as humans. According to legend, the Silkies sometimes enter into sexual unions with human partners, and some families on the islands pridefully trace their ancestry back to such sea-spawned seed.

In 1969, when he was chairman of the anthropology department at Drew Uni-

Ea, the Chaldean god of the Assyrians was part human and part fish. He was said to have come from a land under the ocean's surface, one that was destroyed by floods. (*Art by Ricardo Pustanio*)

versity, Madison, New Jersey, Dr. Roger W. Wescott (1925–2000), published his *The Divine Animal: An Exploration of Human Potentiality*, in which he presented a theory that benevolent UFOnauts landed on earth ten thousand years ago with the mission of teaching *Homo sapiens* a better way of life. In Chapter Eleven, "Other Creatures, Other Worlds," Wescott presented his thesis that when Earth's emerging dominant species demonstrated their innate greed and primitive penchant for destruction, their "Cosmic Tutors" gave up in disgust and withdrew to establish undersea bases and await a time when the children of Gaia had advanced to a more receptive intellectual and societal level. Although temporarily thwarted in their attempts to build a better world on Earth, the culturally advanced and scientifically superior species may have emerged from time to time throughout human history to conduct certain spot-checks to see if the hairless apes had improved. Dr. Wescott theorizes that such monitoring might explain the sightings of UFOs—especially those near large bodies of water—which have been reported for thousands of years.

⚔⚔⚔

RESPECTED SCHOLAR SAYS BUDDHA, CHRIST, MUHAMMAD, GENGHIS KHAN, AND ATTILA THE HUN SENT TOPSIDE BY USONAUTS

Further developing his bold thesis, Dr. Roger W. Wescott also suggested that when the UFOnauts withdrew from Earth's surface, they might have taken some humans along with them to train and to tutor according to their advanced principles. Dr. Wescott conjectured that some of these specially tutored humans might have been returned to the surface where they became leaders. Some of these trainees worked to change man for good, while others became corrupted by the combination of their secret knowledge and the malleability of the less-advanced surface humans. Dr. Wescott says that such individuals as Buddha, Christ, Muhammad, Genghis Khan, and Attila the Hun might have been sent up by the USOnauts.

No fanciful thinker, Dr. Wescott held four degrees from Princeton University, which included a bachelor's degree in English and history, a bachelor's degree in general humanities, a master's degree in Oriental studies, and a doctor of philosophy degree in linguistics. He had also acquired a bachelor of literature degree in social anthropology from Oxford University in England. Dr. Wescott was a Rhodes scholar, a Ford Fellow, and a member of Phi Beta Kappa. Dr. Wescott, the author of forty books, including *Predicting the Past: An Exploration of Myth, Science, and Prehistory*, was once quoted at a press interview as saying, "My feeling is that the saucer travelers were pictured as gods by our ancestors. The saucer creatures began teaching man, but, as man gradually began to master his environment, he also developed to the point where he had material goods and he began to wage wars to obtain the goods he didn't have. It's possible this may have disgusted his masters, so they left. The ocean would have been the easiest place for them to go. They could constantly monitor our technology and keep ahead of us."

In Dr. Wescott's opinion, such a theory helps to explain two of the most widespread and persistent legends found among nearly all peoples and all cultures: *one*, that there was a time when gods walked the earth and tutored man; *two*, that there was a land called Atlantis, whose thriving civilization met with catastrophe and sank beneath the sea. Both legends could be distortions of an actual event, which was not a catastrophic annihilation of a continent, but an orderly withdrawal of the "gods," the cosmic teachers, as they transferred their bases from the land to the sea floor.

UNDERSEA COSMIC TUTORS OR ALIEN EXPLOITERS?

Whenever one begins to hypothesize about unidentified underwater objects, or USOs, one cannot help wondering about the true motives of the unknown aquanauts who have been seen piloting such craft at incredible speeds through the depths of the seas. Do these aquanauts really have our best interests at heart, as benign cosmic tutors should have, or might they have become somewhat indifferent to struggling, culturally evolving *Homo sapiens*? If such beings really exist, it would seem unlikely that they are overtly hostile toward man, or we should have been enslaved and conquered long ago. On the other hand, some theorists point out ominously, they may be biding their time until some cosmic time-clock has ticked out an allotted number of hours.

Some ufologists have suggested that something far less than benevolence was displayed by what seemed to be the mysterious ramming of the U.S. nuclear submarine *Thresher* when it went down in the Atlantic Ocean on April 10, 1963. According to official reports, the *Thresher* perished through "instantaneous flooding." A sonar listener stated that he had heard a dull thud of considerable proportions at great depth. In order to destroy a submarine of such dimensions so quickly that there would be no time for a distress call to the surface, the *Thresher* must have been struck by something large enough to have caused a hole of gigantic proportions. Again, can we envision our hypothetical Council of Cosmic Tutors relieving an officer of command for an act of negligence that caused the instantaneous deaths of 129 Earthlings?

Disturbingly enough, our improved metal vessels and more sophisticated navigational equipment have certainly not eliminated mysterious underwater ramming of our vessels by unidentified somethings. Whether or not the

Real Encounters, Different Dimensions, and Otherworldly Beings

An official U.S. Navy photo shows a portion of the sonar dome from the wreck of the nuclear submarine *U.S.S. Thresher.* The sub sank in 1963 from causes about which officials have only speculated.

collisions were accidental, ship owners have been left with enormous repair bills, because the guilty party was not thoughtful enough to leave a card with his name and insurance company.

Ira Pete, owner of the *Ruby E.*, a sixty-seven-foot shrimp boat, had his boat sink under mysterious circumstances in the first week in July in 1961. According to Pete, they were fishing in the Gulf of Mexico, off Port Aransas, when something hooked into the boat and ripped off its stern. Happily for Ira Pete and his two crewmen, there was another fishing vessel close by.

At 3:00 A.M., July 15, 1960, the twenty-four-thousand-ton Panamanian flag tanker *Alkaid*, with a full cargo of crude oil, was struck by an unidentified underwater object as it passed under the Williamsburg Bridge in New York City's East River. The collision tore a massive gash in the starboard side of the big ship, forcing the captain to beach her near the United Nations building. Later, the *Alkaid*, on the verge of capsizing, was towed off to a dock.

After two days of Coast Guard hearings and an investigation by the Army Corps of Engineers, whose job it is to keep the harbor waters swept clean, no explanation could be found for the *Alkaid's* mysterious collision with a USO. Neither could any object be found in the harbor that would have been capable of piercing the tanker's steel hull.

Early in March 1970, the Danish trawler *SE 140* was fishing northeast of the island of Bronhold in the Baltic when an underwater unidentified object started dragging the ship backward. The crewman told journalists and authorities that the trawler was released only when the trawl wire holding the net broke.

In the fall of 1969, a Swedish trawler, the *Silveroe*, collided with a USO off the Baltic coast. The Swedish Navy could only offer the weak explanation that the object "could have been a submarine."

On February 5, 1964, the one-hundred-foot yacht *Hattie D* was rammed by an underwater "something" near Eureka, California. Ten men and one woman were lifted from the fast-sinking yacht in a dramatic Coast Guard helicopter rescue. The survivors agreed that the *Hattie D* had been run into by something big and made of steel. Crewman Carl Johnson, when informed that no submarines were reported in the area and that the yacht had sunk in 7,500 feet of water, replied: "I don't care how deep it was there. What holed us was steel and a long piece. There was no give to it at all."

The *Barbara K.* was a steel-hulled, ninety-foot vessel owned by the National Marine Terminal of San Diego. On October 31, 1965, about 110 miles south of San Diego with 123 tons of tuna aboard, the *Barbara K.* listed sharply to port, rolled over, and sank in one minute.

Skipper Robert C. Newman said later that he was unaware of hitting any submerged object and that they were not loaded to capacity, yet he only had time to flash an SOS, shout an order to abandon ship, and cut away a small power skiff the vessel was towing. Six of the crewmen clung to debris while the other six climbed into the skiff and headed for another vessel, the *Liberty*, four miles away. All hands were saved.

Perhaps it was such a confrontation that accounted for the disappearance of Donald Crowhurst from his yacht late in 1969.

Crowhurst's *trimaran* was found abandoned seven hundred miles southeast of the Azores, nine hundred miles from his final destination, the English port of Teignmouth. Crowhurst was competing in an around-the-world race sponsored by the London *Sunday Times*, and the experienced thirty-six-year-old yachtsman was considered a favorite in the contest. The *trimaran* was found by a British freighter and bore absolutely no clues to indicate why Crowhurst was not aboard.

Real Encounters, Different Dimensions, and Otherworldly Beings

RICARDO PUSTANIO 2012

The Greek myth of the sea sirens tells of women who lured seafarers to their deaths upon the rocky coast by singing magical songs. Perhaps within the myth lies some truth and that Atlanteans used hypno-telepathic abilities against modern-day sailors. (Art by Ricardo Pustanio)

Yachting experts conjectured that the *trimaran* might have been becalmed, encouraging Crowhurst to take advantage of the situation by slipping overboard for a swim. While the yachtsman had paddled about in the ocean, so the explanation went, a small gale may have come up and blown the *trimaran* out of his reach.

Although the sailing experts' explanation certainly seems a sound one, it can do little to solve the mystery turned up by authorities in London when they discovered that four other small sailing craft had been found abandoned in that same area within less than a month. Weather experts in London said that they had not recorded any weather conditions that could account for the disappearances of the crews, and they testified that no gales had been reported in that part of the ocean.

The ancient Greek legend of the sea sirens and their seductive songs can certainly take on new meaning if one regards them as an Atlantean's hypno-telepathic, "Come with us. Come with us." One might do well to follow Ulysses' example of stuffing the ears with beeswax when planning one's next sailing adventure.

During the last week in January 1969, the French submarine *Minerve*, with fifty-two crewmen, and the Israeli sub, *Dakar*, with sixty-nine crewmen, were lost at separate ends of the Mediterranean. Reports were made of an "indecipherable transmission" picked up on the same frequency as the Israeli sub's radio buoy. Mysterious and indecipherable signals were also claimed in the vicinity where the French sub was last contacted. Some reports told of sonar soundings that produced evidence of a metallic object on the sea floor near Toulon.

On December 28, 1955, in the southwest Pacific, the *Arakarimoa* left Tarawa with her sister ship *Aratoba*. The two vessels were in view of one another until midnight, when the *Arakarimoa* suddenly put on speed and went out of sight. The *Aratoba* arrived at Tebikerai anchorage at 5:30 A.M. on December 29, but there was no sign of the *Arakarimoa*. The *Arakarimoa's* engines had been recently overhauled and were in excellent running condition. Although port authorities considered engine trouble unlikely, they computed that, with the maximum current drift of about three knots and the direction WNW and WSW, they should have little difficulty locating the missing ship. But, why, they wondered, hadn't the *Arakarimoa* radioed for help?

The Royal Colony ship Nareau set out at once in search of the *Arakarimoa*. When it returned thirty-six hours later, it had covered 1,700 square miles without finding a clue to the *Arakarimoa's* fate. According to maximum current drift, an engineless vessel should have drifted no more than one hundred miles.

The official explanation was that the *Arakarimoa* had been set upon and completely destroyed by a pirate submarine. Since the ship's only cargo had been 700 empty copra sacks, robbery seemed a weak motive; but at the time, it was as good an official explanation as any.

⸺⚬⚬⸺

FLIGHT 19 AND THE BERMUDA TRIANGLE

Whenever one begins to discuss the theory that extraterrestrial explorers or cosmic tutors might be using the sea floor as a base of operations for their flying saucers, it seems impossible to avoid the topic of the Bermuda Triangle. Indeed, the mysterious sea phenomenon that menaces the Atlantic off the southeastern coast of the United States bears all the signs of becoming as cultish a curiosity as J. R. R. Tolkien's Middle-earth.

The first dramatic mass disappearance in the area occurred on the afternoon of December 5, 1945, when five TBM Avenger propeller-driven torpedo bombers left their base at Fort Lauderdale, Florida, on a routine training flight. All the crewmen were experienced and competent airmen, and they had logged the flight many times before.

It was because this flight was such a routine and familiar one that the men in the control tower exchanged incredulous glances when they received an urgent radio message from the flight commander: "I-I'm not certain where we are. Everything is wrong. We ... we can't be sure of any direction. Even the ocean doesn't look as it should!"

How could it be possible that all five navigators lost their bearings on such an elementary training maneuver on a familiar flight plan? Even if they had run into a magnetic storm that had played havoc with their compasses, they would still be able to see the sun above the western horizon.

When the tower told them to assume their bearing due west, the flight leader replied with mounting fear in his voice that they did not know which way was west. The ocean, it appeared, looked different to them, and they could not see the sun at all.

The tower operators listened in helpless bewilderment as they heard the pilots talking to one another. At first the men cursed their confusion; then their confusion gave way to fear and rising hysteria. Shortly after 4:00 P.M. the flight leader relinquished command to another pilot. At 4:25 P.M. the new flight leader told the tower that they were not certain where they were, but he thought that they must be about 225 miles northeast of the base.

"It looks like we are...." The flight leader's words stopped in mid-sentence, and that incomplete utterance was the last communication ever received from the patrol.

> "It looks like we are...." The flight leader's words stopped in mid-sentence, and that incomplete utterance was the last communication ever received from the patrol.

Immediately upon losing radio contact with the five torpedo bombers, the control tower dispatched a large Martin Mariner flying boat with a crew of thirteen and full rescue equipment. About twenty minutes after it had left Fort Lauderdale, it, too, lost radio contact.

For the next several days, twenty-one vessels and more than three hundred airplanes searched the area for the five bombers and the rescue plane. Twelve land parties patrolled the beaches. The combined efforts of this vast armada of rescue workers produced not a single clue to the disappearances of the six airplanes and the twenty-seven crewmen—not a shred of clothing, not a piece of wreckage, not an oil slick. An officer of the Naval Board of Inquiry pronounced solemnly: "They vanished as completely as if they had flown to Mars." And today, sixty-eight years later, the fate of the pilots and their aircraft remains a well-kept secret of the sea.

It is difficult to chronicle all of the mysterious disappearances that some investigators claim have taken place in that area known as the Bermuda Triangle. According to some, the total is as high as nearly seventy ships, forty-two aircraft, and their passengers and crews, totaling allegedly more than one thousand persons.

Vincent Gaddis, who may have been the first author to bring the Bermuda Triangle to wide public attention in a 1964 article in *Argosy*, briefly hypothesized an atmospheric aberration that opened "a hole in the sky." Gaddis referred to the work of the late Wilbert B. Smith, an electronics expert in Ottawa, Canada, who was in charge of magnetism and gravity studies for a Canadian government project. Smith claimed, in previous investigations, to have discovered regions of "reduced binding" in the atmosphere, which he said had been found at locations of unexplained airplane crashes.

Smith described these areas as roughly circular, up to one thousand feet in diameter, and probably extending upward for great distances. It was Smith's contention that an airplane entering a region of "reduced binding" could experience such a great turbulence that the craft and its passengers and crew could be disintegrated. Smith was uncertain whether the regions moved about or just faded away.

The chilling thought that has occurred to many investigators is whether such areas of "reduced binding" or regions of gravitational and electromagnetic anomalies might be produced and controlled by some unknown intelligence.

There is a great deal of evidence to indicate that magnetic fields can affect the human brain and produce hallucinations, speech changes, and general confusion and disorientation. Not only might an electromagnetic field make a compass needle go berserk, but such a field might very well befuddle seasoned pilots into hysteria and confuse hapless fishermen and yachtsmen into jumping overboard in their mental distress.

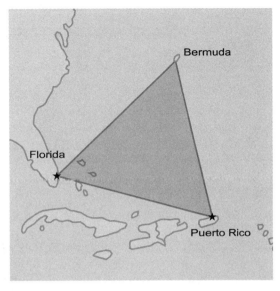

The infamous Bermuda Triangle extends from Miami to Puerto Rico and, of course, Bermuda.

DIRECT ATTACKS OR TRAGIC ACCIDENTS?

Whether done intentionally to destroy innocent interlopers who happened upon something they should not have seen, or to select yet a new batch of *Homo sapiens* for study or retraining purposes, might not the mysterious disappearances of fishermen, seamen, and pilots in such areas as the Bermuda Triangle have been caused by a powerful electromagnetic field produced by an unidentified submarine object?

Two New Zealand commercial fishermen, R. D. Hanning, skipper of the *Eleoneai,* and W. J. Johnson may have had a glimpse of such a mysterious mechanical something and were left both frightened and shaken by the experience.

The strange undersea craft broke surface when the *Eleoneai* was just off New Zealand's Rugged Islands. The fishermen described the USO as having had a tapered structure which rose about fifteen feet above the surface. They estimated that it measured about five feet high at the top and twelve feet at the waterline. They saw no sign of a periscope or a railing, but they did notice a peculiar, box-shaped object about ten feet long and five feet high that surfaced about thirty feet away from the larger craft. Later, in an interview with naval officers who had learned of the sighting, Skipper Hanning expressed his umbrage at the suggestion that two well-seasoned seamen could mistake whales, logs, or floating debris for a mechanical craft.

On January 11, 1967, a four-year-old tugboat, the *Gulf Master*, and her five crewmen disappeared off Sechelt, British Columbia. There had been no more reason for this sixty-six-foot tugboat to have vanished than there had been for the tug that had disappeared in the same area less than a month before. The only clue that investigators had to go on was the reports of extensive UFO activity above the water in that area, both before and after the disappearance of the two tugboats.

FACE TO FACE WITH THE MERMEN

Whether they be cosmic tutors or other forms of alien or native intelligence, some unknown agencies seem to know their way very well along the bottom of our sea beds. What is more, someone, or something, has been leaving tracks.

In 1958, Dr. A. I. Laughton of the National Institute of Oceanography told the British Association for the Advancement of Science, at a meeting in Dublin, Ireland, that he had photographed mysterious footprints with a camera lowered nearly three miles down to the bed of the Atlantic Ocean. "It would be interesting to know what makes them," he said of the tracks. "We have studied the pictures closely for evidence of something at the end of these tracks. So far we have not found it."

In the summer of 1982, the Military Diver Service of the Engineer Forces of the Ministry of Defense, USSR was conducting training of its reconnaissance divers (the Soviet counterpart of the U.S. frogmen) in the Issik Kul Lake in the Transiliysk Ala Tau area. The officers conducting the training were surprised when they were visited by Major-General V. Demyanko, an important official, who had come to advise them of an extraordinary occurrence that he had during similar training exercises in the Trans-Baikal and West Siberian military regions. During their training dives, the frogmen had encountered a group of human-like swimmers almost ten feet in height.

These mysterious swimmers were clothed in tight-fitting, silvery suits and gave no evidence of any scuba diving equipment; only sphere-like helmets had covered their heads.

Alarmed by such encounters with the "mermen," the commander ordered a special team of seven divers to capture one of the creatures with a net. The frogmen pursued one of the "swimmers" to a great depth in the lake, but when they attempted to cover it with a net, the men were blown out of the water.

Although the ejected frogmen were placed as soon as possible in a decompression chamber, three men died and the rest became invalids. The depth of the Issik Kul Lake was not as deep as the Baikal Lake, but Major-General Demyanko had come to warn the frogmen to be wary of any unidentified deep-water swimmers whom they might encounter.

A later bulletin from the Ministry of Defense, USSR listed numerous deepwater lakes where there had been anomalous phenomena and sightings of strange and unidentified discs and spheres surfacing and entering the water. Many encounters with underwater, human-like creatures were also detailed.

UFO researcher-author Paul Stonehill referred to an article published in *XX vek. Khronika neobjasnimogo*, Moscow, which told of a deep sea fisherman named B. Borovikov, who had hunted Black Sea sharks for many years. Then in 1996, while diving in the Anapa area, he saw three giant beings rising up toward him from below. Borovikov described them as milky-white in color with fish-like tails and humanoid faces. The being ascending ahead of the other two suddenly took notice of the human diver and stopped to consider Borovikov. The being had huge bulging eyes covered by some kind of thin glasses. When the other two joined it, the first one, whom Borovikov could now determine was female, waved a hand toward him. Her hand, Borovikov recalled, was web-like, with a membrane that stretched between her fingers. The beings drew closer to their human visitor, then stopped, and suddenly turned around and swam away. Borovikov told reporters that he would no longer dive in that area of the Black Sea.

> These mysterious swimmers were clothed in tight-fitting, silvery suits and gave no evidence of any scuba diving equipment; only sphere-like helmets had covered their heads.

Borovikov's advice might be well heeded by any curious divers who challenge the strangers in our seas without being well prepared.

THE MASTER RACE FROM THE INNER EARTH

The October 24, 2011, issue of Lon Strickler's *Phantoms and Monsters* carries the account of "Jerry," who tells of his encounter with a large reptilian humanoid in a cave in Camden County, Missouri (which was part of a cavern system throughout Missouri and Arkansas). Jerry said that he had finished a twelve-year stint in the military during which he had spent time at the U.S. Army Engineer School in Fort Leonard Wood and received some training in spelunking (cave exploration). After military service, he enjoyed exploring caves for recreation.

On that day in the summer of 1995, Jerry was spelunking solo, checking out a cave that was part of a fairly large system in the area. He had descended a considerable distance into the cave before he found it opening up into a series of chambers. It was then that he heard strange rustling sounds that caught his attention. Dismissing the sounds at first as bats, Jerry was puzzled by what seemed to be the vibrations of a motor and the sounds of someone speaking.

After listening for several minutes, he could no longer resist crawling into a small tunnel to find out what was on its other side. He was astonished to find the chamber well lit and to see that it contained a small vehicle that he thought looked like a golf cart without wheels. A very acrid, vinegar-like odor seemed to permeate the chamber.

Jerry had little time to study the strange vehicle or the well-lighted chamber, for as he watched from his place in the tunnel a reptilian humanoid about seven feet tall suddenly entered the room.

He described the creature as having features and a skull shaped like a human's, but devoid of any hair or ears. The reptilian being had brown scaly skin. "From what I could see," Jerry wrote in his account submitted to *Phantoms and Monsters*, "it had lips and regular-sized eyes. The arms were very long and muscular with human-like hands. It also had a massive four- to five-foot tail that tapered to a point. It was dressed in a gold metallic outfit with long pants and shoes. It also carried an oval pack attached to its back."

As the reptilian was examining something on the vehicle, Jerry tried to take some photographs with his high-speed camera. While he was taking photos, the reptilian creature stopped, turned, and looked in Jerry's direction. "I'm not sure if it heard me," Jerry said, "but it definitely knew of my presence. It then made a terrible 'hissing' sound as it continued to look in my direction. That was enough for me. I quickly started making a beeline out of the cave. When I reached the entrance I was shaking and hyperventilating. I finally reached my vehicle and drove home."

Jerry said that his photographs turned out too blurry to prove his story. When he returned a few years later to attempt to gain more evidence of the strange creature, he was unable to get near because the area is now government property.

Jerry is convinced that he witnessed something that he was not supposed to see. "It pains me to think what secrets are being kept from us," he concluded his report. "To those who say that there are no non-humans living among us, well, think again."

━◅▦◖⫙◗▦▻━

EVIDENCE OF A HIGHLY ADVANCED SUBTERRANEAN CULTURE

Accounts of discovering evidence of a highly advanced subterranean culture and its contemporary inhabitants go back to at least 1770, when a laborer in Staffordshire, England, heard the rumble of heavy machinery coming from behind a large, flat stone in a cave that he had been exploring. Prying the rock aside with his pick, the man was amazed to discover a stone stairway that led deep into the ground. Believing that he had stumbled upon some ancient tomb, the laborer started down the steps with visions of buried treasure awaiting him. Instead, the man swore that he found himself inside a large stone chamber with the sounds of machinery becoming louder, and a hooded figure approaching him menacingly with a baton-like object in a raised hand. The terrified laborer fled back up the stone stairway to the safety of the surface world. Later investigation by others found the entrance to the alleged chamber claimed by the laborer to be blocked with heavy rocks.

Alfred Scadding was one of two survivors of the famous April 12, 1936, Moose River mine disaster in Nova Scotia in which three men were trapped

Accounts by those who have uncovered evidence of an advanced subterranean civilization date back to the eighteenth century. (*Art by Bill Oliver*)

150 feet underground for eleven days. Scadding insisted that just before the roof of the mine caved in, he had seen someone with a flashlight running across the tunnel in which he was trapped with Herman Magill and Dr. David Robertson. The light, Scadding swore, was about two feet off the ground and "swinging as if in someone's hand," moving away from them. Scadding stated that he had "… an absolutely clear and detailed memory of that incident." Later, he was informed by his rescuers that no human being was down in the mine at the time other than the two men who were trapped with him.

Scadding also told investigators that he and the other two survivors of the mine cave-in had heard sounds of people shouting and laughing. He insisted that they were all clear-headed and fully conscious when they heard what they at first thought were children laughing and playing. The sounds brought them hope, because they believed that they were coming from a vent to the surface. Exploration of the area in which they were trapped disclosed no such vent.

Later, before Magill died on the seventh day after the collapse, Scadding said that all of them clearly heard sounds of "laughing and shouting, like people having fun." The sounds of people having a party or a celebration, Scadding said, went on for twenty-four hours without stopping.

Real Encounters, Different Dimensions, and Otherworldly Beings

In 1956, workmen from the Head Well and Pump Company were drilling a 145-foot deep hole on the property of Mr. and Mrs. Earl Meeks, seven miles from Douglas, Georgia, when they stopped their work to listen to an unusual noise coming from the hole. Scott Dinking, with twenty-seven years in the drilling business, said that he had never heard anything like it. As nearly as he and the other men could describe the sound, it seemed very similar to the noise made by an underground railroad. The sounds became so loud and distracting that the Meeks had the hole covered with planks.

In 1963, a Pennsylvania mine cave-in imprisoned miners David Fellin and Henry Throne. While they awaited rescue, the two men claimed that they saw a huge door enveloped in blue light appear before them and swing open to reveal beautiful marble steps with men dressed in "weird outfits" staring at them.

Professor John M. DeLaurier, of the Dominion Observatory in Ottawa, Canada, announced in 1963 that something big and unidentified lay under the remote outpost of Alert, on the northernmost tip of Ellesmere Island. The object, Professor DeLaurier said, was nearly cylindrical, about sixty-five miles long and sixty-five miles thick. The huge something begins approximately fifteen miles below the earth's surface and extends southwest to Alert, to a depth of nearly eighty miles. The object was detected by the same equipment the Alert weather station personnel uses to trace earth tremors and measure fluctuations in the earth's magnetic field. Preliminary studies by Professor DeLaurier show that the object, which appears to straddle the boundary between the earth's crust and its mantle, could possibly cause unusually large distortion in the magnetic field at Alert and induce a strong flow of electricity.

In the spring of 1966, Norman Jensen, an experienced well driller, had been boring for water fifteen miles south of Darwin, Australia, when his drill bit, at 102 feet—having passed through seven layers of limestone, clay, red soil, and sandstone—suddenly struck something soft and dropped to 111 feet. Certain that the bit had bored through to an underground water course, Jensen lowered a pump to make tests. Instead of fresh water, the pump brought up a bucket full of flesh, bone, hide, and hairs.

Constable Roy Harvey agreed with Jensen that he, too, had never seen anything like the gory substance from over a hundred feet down. Dr. W. A. Langsford, Northern Territory Director of Health in Darwin, said that preliminary microscopic examination had revealed the mystery mess to be hair and tissue, just as it had appeared to Jensen and Harvey. Dr. Langsford stated further that there was a possibility that the matter might even be human.

This very interesting puzzle seemed to wither and die when the substance was sent to forensic laboratories in Adelaide.

In the fall of 1968, laborers working on a forty-yard stretch of tunnel under London's Thames River, claimed that they were being harassed by mysterious figures. Big Lou Chambers felt something brush his neck, and when he turned around he saw the figure of a large man with his arms outstretched. Nobby saw the figure as well, and told reporters that he left the tunnel, got a stiff drink, and quit his job.

Some workers thought they were being haunted by the restless spirits of people who had been buried down there centuries ago after the plague swept London. But John Daley, one of the crew, objected, stating that the man he saw was wearing some kind of brown overcoat and a cap. Ghosts from the days of the plague, he conjectured, would not be wearing such modern-type clothing.

⊸⊸⊸⊸

LEGENDS OF THE ELDER GODS

There are persistent legends in nearly every culture that tell of the Old Ones, the Elder Gods, an ancient race who populated the earth millions of years ago. The Old Ones, an immensely intelligent and scientifically advanced race, have chosen to structure their own environment under the surface of the planet and manufacture all their necessities. The Old Ones are hominid, very often described as reptilian in appearance, extremely long-lived, and pre-date *Homo sapiens* by more than a million years. The Old Ones generally remain aloof from the surface peoples, but from time to time, they have been known to offer constructive criticism; and it has been said, they often kidnap human children to tutor and rear as their own. There is scarcely a culture known to humankind that does not have at least one segment of their folklore built around troll-like creatures that live underground and do their best to steal the children of surface folk.

In virtually all the legends, the Old Ones have gone underground to escape natural catastrophes or the hidden death that exists in the life-giving rays of our sun.

An alternate theory, very close to the one set forth by Dr. Roger Wescott concerning undersea cosmic tutors ("Old Gods from the Sea or Visitors from the Stars?"), has it that the Cave Masters are surviving colonies of spacemen, who after walking the earth in god-like demeanor, grew disgusted with their efforts to teach and/or train early humans and retreated to the caves and under-earth bases from which they might watch over the primitive species' intellectual and cultural development.

Buddhists have incorporated Agharta, a subterranean empire, into their theology and fervently believe in its existence and in the reality of underworld supermen who periodically surface to oversee the progress of the human race. According to one source, the underground kingdom of Agharta was created when the ancestors of the present day cave dwellers drove the Serpent People

Could there be an entire world inside the interior of the earth and that, in the event and its access point is at the north pole? Authors such as Dr. Raymond Bernard and Edgar Allan Poe have speculated about it in their works. (*Art by Ricardo Pustanio*)

from the caverns during an ancient war between the reptilian humanoids and the ancient human society.

Among the Amerindians, the Navajo legends teach that the forerunners of *Homo sapiens* came from beneath the earth. The ancient ones were possessed of supernatural powers and were driven from their caverns by a great flood (an echo of the traditional Atlantis myth). Once on the surface, they passed along great knowledge to humans before they once again sought secret sanctuary.

The Pueblo peoples' mythology places their gods' place of origin as an inner world connected to the surface people by a hole in the north. Mesewa, according the Pueblos, was succeeded as leader of the gods by his brother, Oyoyewa, which some researchers have pointed out is quite similar to the Hebrew Yahweh.

HYPOTHESIS OF AN UNCHARTED WORLD IN THE HOLLOW EARTH

In 1823, Captain John Cleve Symmes, a dour, humorless, retired war hero, petitioned the U.S. Congress for funds to conduct an expedition to explore the hollow earth. Captain Symmes and his small band of followers felt somewhat anointed for the task because the great American clergyman Cotton Mather had defended the theory of a hollow earth in his book *The Christian Philosopher*. Mather, in turn, had developed his hypothesis from a little-known essay penned by English astronomer Edmund Halley in 1692.

The theory that there was a vast uncharted world inside our own captured the imagination of Edgar Allan Poe who, in 1835, published his longest tale, "The Narrative of Arthur Gordon Pym," which told of a fantastic land located in the center of our planet, entered by a hole at the south pole. So convincingly did Poe weave the pseudoscientific beginning of his narrative that the great educator Horace Greeley soberly endorsed the Pym adventure as a true account. He obviously did not complete the story and read its later section, which is very evident fantasy. It is likely, however, that young Jules Verne, who would have been nine years old at that time, did finish reading the story and many

An illustration by Édouard Riou for Jules Verne's 1864 novel, *Journey to the Center of the Earth*, imagines an entire world beneath our feet.

years later may have been inspired to base one of his classic novels, *Journey to the Center of the Earth*, on a similar theme.

Dr. Raymond Bernard's (born Walter Siegmeister; 1901–1965) *The Hollow Earth* (1964), originally published by Fieldcrest Publishing Company of New York, has become the classic work in the rather amorphous field of "proving" the existence of an Inner Earth. In his introduction to the book, Dr. Bernard promises to prove that "… the earth is hollow and not a solid sphere … and that its hollow interior communicates with the surface by two polar openings."

Dr. Bernard's *magnum opus* discloses that Rear Admiral Richard E. Byrd flew *beyond* rather than *over* the North Pole and that his later expedition to the South Pole passed 2,300 miles *beyond* it. According to Dr. Bernard, the North and South Poles have never been reached because they do not exist. In his view, the nation whose explorers first find the entrance to the hollow interior of the earth will become the greatest nation in the world. There is no doubt, the reader learns, that "… the mysterious flying saucers come from an advanced civilization in the hollow interior of the earth that, in [the] event of nuclear war ... [would] provide an ideal refuge for the evacuation of survivors of the catastrophe."

⊸◄▥▮◖▯▥►⊸

NAZIS NEARLY DESTROYED THE WORLD IN SEEKING THE MASTER RACE

After Germany's defeat in World War I, a thirty-year-old Army veteran named Adolf Hitler wandered the streets of 1919 Munich in a state of depression and disillusion. Before the war, he had tried to fulfill his dream of being an artist and he had lived the Bohemian life in Vienna, barely surviving by selling an occasional watercolor and by receiving meager support from his mother. The Academy of Fine Arts had rejected him twice, and after his mother died in 1907, he supported himself by small jobs of manual labor. By 1910, he was living in a home for poor working men.

In 1913, Hitler received a small amount of money from his father's estate, and he moved to Munich. In Salzburg, he had been rejected for military service, but in Munich he volunteered to serve in the Bavarian Army as an Austrian citizen. By all accounts he served bravely in the Bavarian Reserve Infantry Regiment. As a dispatch runner on the Western Front in France and Belgium, he received the Iron Cross, Second Class in 1914; the Iron Cross, First Class in 1918; and the Black Wound Badge in 1918. He was wounded in the left thigh during the Battle of the Somme in October 1916 and temporarily blinded by mustard gas in October 1918.

Believing his prospects to be slim in civilian life, Hitler had hoped to stay in the army as long as possible, but he was released from service after the defeat of the Austro-Hungarian army on November 11, 1918. Although he had continued sketching and cartooning while he served in the trenches, his chances of surviving as an artist seemed no more practical or possible than they had before he joined the army.

In July 1919, Hitler managed to be appointed as an intelligence agent of the *Reichswehr,* the Provisional National Defense unit that had been established by the newly formed Weimar Republic. It was Hitler's job to maintain morale among the soldiers and, at the same time, to spy upon the German Workers' Party (DAP). On September 12, 1919, during one of DAP's meetings at the *Sterneckerbräu,* a beer hall in the center of the city, Hitler challenged one of the speakers and began such a violent argument that Anton Drexler, a founder of the DAP, invited him to join the party.

Drexler was a member of the occult Thule Society, and the first members of the DAP were largely made up of fellow members of that secret society.

An associate of Drexler's, Dr. Paul Tafel, also a member of the Thule Society, was a leader of two workers' unions, who wished to form a society that would organize the masses with a strong nationalist fervor. Karl Harrer, a sports journalist and a member of the Thule Society, envisioned a union of German workers under the influence of the Society. Another founder of DAP, Dietrich Eckart, was also a member of the Thule Society, and he became one of Hitler's mentors in the doctrine of the mystical organization. Soon, Hitler was learning about the ancient tradition of the Master of the World, who with his occult powers and his army of a super race would launch an invasion of Earth and subjugate all humans to his will.

German dictator Adolf Hitler was inspired by the occult, which provided him with notions of a "master race" that resulted in such horrors as the Holocaust and World War II. (*Art by Ricardo Pustanio*)

THE THULE SOCIETY AND THE COMING RACE

Of great influence on the Thule Society was *The Coming Race* (1871), a novel by the occultist Edward Bulwer-Lytton, that was set in the Earth's interior, where an advanced civilization of giants thrived. In this story, the giants had built a paradise and discovered a form of energy so powerful that they outlawed its use as a potential weapon. This force, the Vril, was derived from the Black Sun, a large ball of "Prima Materia" that provides light and radiation to the inhabitants of the inner Earth. The Vril was known among the alchemists and magicians as the Chi, the Odic force, the Orgone, or the Astral Light, and they were well aware of its transformative powers to create supermen of ordinary mortals.

The secret society of the Black Sun co-existed with the Vril and the Thule societies in Germany prior to and during World War I and was blended with the other groups in about 1919. While these societies borrowed some concepts and rites from Theosophists, Rosicrucians, and various Hermetic groups, they placed special emphasis on the innate mystical powers of the Aryan race. Others, such as Mme. Helena Blavatsky, had listed the Six Root Races—the Astral, Hyperborean, Lemurian, Atlantean, Aryan, and the coming Master Race. The Germanic/Nordic/Teutonic people were of Aryan origin, and Christianity had destroyed the power of the Teutonic civilization.

The symbol of the Black Sun is suggestive of the plight of the sun when, according to Norse myths, the great wolf Fenrir will swallow the solar orb at the beginning of the Wolf Age. As in many secret groups, there appears to have been more than one order—those who followed the Golden Sun and those who followed the Black Sun. The Black Sun, like the swastika, is a very ancient symbol. While the swastika represents the eternal fountain of creation, the Black Sun is even older, suggesting the very void of creation itself.

THE THULE SUN WHEEL BECOMES THE SWASTIKA

While Hitler was being informed about the master race within the Earth, his fellow party members of DAP were being quickly won over to his political beliefs and the passion with which he preached them. Seeking to make the party more broadly appealing to larger segments of the population, the DAP was renamed on February 24, 1920, to the National Socialist German Workers' Party, the Nazi party. Hitler designed the party's symbol—the Thule *Sonnenrad* (Sun Wheel), a swastika in a white circle on a red background.

The end of World War I had left Germany with its people poor and its morale low. The Vril would be the means of the nation's restoration as a major world power.

Those who learned control of the Vril would become masters of themselves, those around them, and the world itself. Such members of the Lodge as Adolf Hitler, Heinrich Himmler, Hermann Göring, Dr. Theodor Morell (Hitler's personal physician), and other top Nazi leaders became obsessed with preparing German youth to become a Master Race. They wanted desperately to prove themselves worthy of the super humans that lived beneath the surface of the planet.

JOINING SUBTERRANEAN SUPERMEN TO CREATE A HUMAN MUTATION

An important element in the developing Nazi mythos was the belief that representatives of a powerful, underground, secret race emerged from time to time to walk among *Homo sapiens*. Hitler's frenzied desire to breed a select race of Nordic types was inspired by his obsessive hope that it should be the Germanic peoples who would be chosen above all other humans to interbreed with the subterranean supermen in the mutation of a new race of heroes, demigods, and god-men.

Although some authorities on the life of Hitler and the rise of the Nazi party state that the Führer did not maintain his interest in the occult, but soon turned his attention to the promotion of Pan-Germanism, anti-Semitism, anti-communism, and the worldwide establishment of the Third Reich, some who worked closely with him say otherwise. There are a number of reports by witnesses who claim to have heard Hitler screaming in terror, and having rushed to his aid found him cowering in a corner of his office, weeping and shivering in terror that a representative of the Master Race from the Inner Earth had just paid him an unwelcome visit.

In their *The Morning of the Magicians: Secret Societies, Conspiracies, and Vanished Civilizations* (Avon, 1960), Louis Pauwels and Jacques Bergier quote Hermann Rauschning, governor of Danzig during the Third Reich, who repeated a conversation he had once had with Hitler concerning the Führer's plan to assist nature in developing mutants. "The new man is living amongst us, now! He is here! Isn't that enough for you? I will tell you a secret. I have seen the new man. He is intrepid and cruel. I was afraid of him."

> "The new man is living amongst us, now! He is here! Isn't that enough for you? I will tell you a secret. I have seen the new man. He is intrepid and cruel. I was afraid of him."

Rauschning went on to state that he was told by a person very close to Hitler that the Führer often awoke in the night screaming and in convulsions. Always, the frightened dictator would shout that *he* had come for him. That *he* stood there in the corner of the room. That *he* had emerged from his underworld kingdom to invade the Führer's bedroom.

WAS HITLER A SPIRIT MEDIUM?

If, as Hermann Rauschning recalled, Hitler appeared to relate his encounters with the representative of the emergent mutant species in a kind of ecstasy or trancelike state, we can wonder if there is credence to the many rumors and theories that the Führer was mediumistic. In addition to his membership in several occult societies, Hitler's birthplace, the little village of Branau-am-Inn, was for many years a center of spiritualism in Europe. And it has often been said that the infant Adolf shared the same wet-nurse with Willi Schneider, who, along with his brother Rudi, became a world-famous medium.

Whether or not Hitler could be called a true medium, it was while the Vril society—now renamed *Vril Gesellschaft*—was meeting at an old hunting lodge near Berchtesgaden, that they received remarkable news that Maria Orsic (Orsitch) had begun to receive messages from Aryan aliens on Alpha Tauri in the Aldebaran star system. Maria led the *Vrilerinnen*, a group of beautiful young mediums in the society, and she and a sister medium named Sigrun, had learned that a half billion years ago, the Aryans, also known as the Elohim or Elder Race, began to colonize our solar system. On Earth, the Aryans were identified as the Sumerians until they elected to carve out an empire for themselves in the hollow of the planet.

⟨⟨⟨⟨ᛚᚾᛚ⟩⟩⟩⟩

THE VRILERINNEN CHANNEL TRANSMISSIONS
FOR ADVANCED SPACE FLIGHT

Maria, Sigrun, and other members of the *Vrilerinnen*—Traute, Gudrun, and Heike—began to channel transmissions that dictated diagrams and blueprints of advanced flying machines, complete with the mathematics and physics to go with them. The mediums wore their hair long to serve as better receptive antennas for the alien messages.

By 1921, some say that a working model of what would one day be called a "flying saucer" had been built. Working in underground bases with the alien intelligences, the Nazis mastered antigravity space flight, established space stations, accomplished time travel, and developed their spacecraft to warp speeds.

In 1922, members of Thule and Vril claim to have built the *Jenseitsflugmaschine*, the "Other-World Flight Machine," based on the psychic messages received from the Aldebaran aliens. W. O. Schumann of the Technical University of Munich was in charge of the project until it was halted in 1924, and the craft was stored in Messerschmitt's Augsburg facility. In 1937, after Hitler came into power, he authorized the construction of the *Rund flugzeug*, the round, or disc-shaped, vehicle, for military use and for spaceflight. A few years later, the Führer officially abolished all secret societies, but sources indicate that the Vril continued its work unabated.

In 2012, *Iron Sky*, a Finnish science-fiction film about the Nazis' development of flying discs, reignited a debate in Germany about Hitler's development of UFOs. The film centers on real-life SS officer Hans Kammler who was said to have made a significant breakthrough in antigravity experiments toward the end of WWII. The film relates how, from a secret base built in the Antarctic, the first Nazi spaceships were launched in late 1945 to build a military base named *Schwarze Sonne* (Black Sun) on the Moon. This base was to be used to build a powerful invasion fleet and return to Earth in 2018.

According to reports published in German in the magazine *P.M.*, there is "strong evidence" that a Nazi UFO program was well advanced, based on an alien saucer that crashed in Italy. The *P.M.* report quotes eyewitnesses who state that they saw a flying saucer marked with an Iron Cross insignia flying low over the Thames in 1944. Other eyewitnesses claim that they saw a flying saucer-type craft produced in Prague in 1945 actually become airborne. Records state that the best known of the Nazi UFO projects was the Schriever-Habermohl scheme, named for Rudolf Schriever and Otto Habermohl.

According to *P.M.* magazine, Joseph Andreas Epp, an engineer, said, "Fifteen disc prototypes were built in all, with a central cockpit surrounded by rotating adjustable wing-vanes forming a circle. The pitch of the vanes could be adjusted so that during takeoff more lift was generated by increasing their angle from a more horizontal setting. In level flight the angle would be adjusted to a smaller angle, similar to the way helicopter rotors operate. The wing-vanes were to be set in rotation by small rockets placed around the rim like a pinwheel. Once rotational speed was sufficient, lift-off was achieved."

THE NAZI EXPEDITION TO THE HOLLOW EARTH

Subscribing to another popular pseudo-scientific theory, Hitler had come to believe that Earth was concave and that humankind lived on the *inside* of the globe. According to the theory advanced by a number of the Führer's like-minded scientists, if the Nazis were to station their most accomplished radar experts in the correct geometric position they would be able to determine the precise position of the British fleet and the Allied bomber squadrons, because the concave curvature of the globe would enable infrared rays to accomplish long-distance monitoring.

In April 1942, Hitler, [Nazi party leaders] Hermann Göring and Heinrich Himmler, and their fellow exponents of the Hollow Earth belief construct, sent an expedition to the island of Rügen in the Baltic Sea to establish the radar base. Based on the teachings of the Vril Society, they had complete confidence in their application of the ancient vision of the concave planet. At the same time, there were certain very old traditions that insisted that the Knights Templar had hidden the Holy Grail and the Ark of the Covenant somewhere on one of the Baltic islands.

Far from a fanciful plot device created for the "Indiana Jones" motion picture series, Hitler did authorize a number of expeditions formed by Himmler to acquire as many holy relics as possible.

Far from being a fanciful plot device created for the "Indiana Jones" motion picture series, Hitler did authorize a number of expeditions formed by Himmler to acquire as many holy relics as possible. The Führer and his inner circle believed that such a grand accomplishment as possessing such legendary artifacts of power and majesty, as well as discovering an entrance to the Inner

Empire, would convince the ancient Masters who lived there that the Nazis were truly worthy of mixing their blood with them in the hybridization of a master race.

❖❖❖

WORLD LEADERS WHO RECEIVED VISITS FROM THE OLD ONES

Adolf Hitler was not the only world leader who was said to have received visitations from mysterious counselors from the Old Ones in the Hollow Earth.

The Red Man first appeared to Napoleon during the ambitious military leader's Egyptian campaign. The strange little visitor claimed to have warned the rulers of France in the past and declared that he had now come to warn Napoleon. When Napoleon protested the Red Man's admonition that the people of France were growing to fear his ambition, the mysterious adviser told the military genius that he had been at his side since he was but a schoolboy. "I know you better than you know yourself," he chided him.

The Red Man told Napoleon that his orders to the French fleet had not been obeyed. Even though the Egyptian campaign had begun on a note of triumph after the bloody Battle of the Pyramids, the enterprise would fail and Napoleon would return to France to find her closed in by England, Russia, Turkey, and an allied Europe. Domestically, the Red Man warned, Napoleon would be confronted by the mobs of Paris.

True to the Red Man's prediction, the Egyptian campaign failed. In 1809, after the Battle of Wagram, Napoleon made his headquarters at Schönbrunn where, one lonely midnight, he again received his mysterious adviser.

The Red Man made his third and final appearance on the morning of January 1, 1814, shortly before the Emperor was forced to abdicate. The stranger appeared first to Councillor (and future French prime minister) Louis-Mathieu Molé, and demanded that he be allowed to see the Emperor on

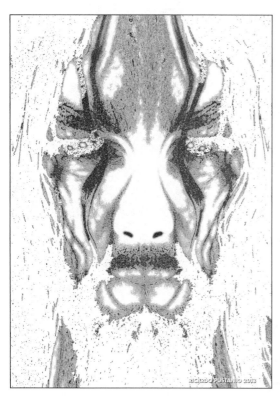

The Old Ones have had their otherworldly hands in human events for centuries, influencing rulers from King Charles XII of Sweden to Napoleon Bonaparte. (*Art by Ricardo Pustanio*)

matters of urgent importance. Molé had been given strict orders that the Emperor was not to be disturbed, but when he went with the message that the Red Man was there, the mysterious stranger was granted immediate entrance.

It is said that Napoleon beseeched the Red Man for time to complete the execution of certain proposals, but the prophetic messenger gave him only three months to achieve a general peace or it would be all over for him. In a futile effort to gain more time, Napoleon desperately tried to launch a new eastern campaign. Such a move left Paris to fall into the hands of the Allies, and on April 1, three months after the Red Man's final appearance, Talleyrand and the Senate called for Napoleon's abdication.

King Charles XII of Sweden sought the counsel of a Little Gray Man with ruddy complexion, who gave him a ring that would not vanish until the day of the ruler's death. King Charles cut a mighty swath across Europe, Russia, and Turkey, and his feats became legendary. As did Napoleon, Charles resisted his mysterious counselor's entreaties to make peace. In 1718, as the Swedes were besieging Fredrikshald, one of Charles's officers noticed that the ring was no longer on his leader's finger. Moments later, Charles fell dead with a head wound.

RACIAL MEMORIES OF AN UNDERGROUND ADVANCED CIVILIZATION

In the March 1945 issue of *Amazing Stories*, editor Ray Palmer introduced the Shaver Mystery, a purported "racial memory" of a young welder named Richard Shaver (1907–1975), who first claimed to have remembered a life in the caves, then later maintained that he had recently been in the vast underground civilization of cave dwellers. *Life* magazine (May 21, 1951) called the Shaver Mystery "… the most celebrated rumpus that ever racked the science fiction world." Richard Shaver, however, never called his accounts anything other than factual reportage.

It was Richard Shaver's contention that in prehistoric times, when our solar system was young, Earth was inhabited by a race of cosmic super-beings who had come here from another solar system. Although the Elder Race were not truly immortals, they had discovered secrets of incredible longevity. This, together with their highly developed scientific technology, caused them to be regarded as gods by the primitive and unsophisticated humans. The Elder Race possessed fantastic mechanical devices, which Shaver calls "mech," capable of projecting three-dimensional images, extracting or implanting thoughts into others' minds, scanning over great distances, curing diseases, producing food and clothing, and killing and destroying life when necessary.

Real Encounters, Different Dimensions, and Otherworldly Beings   **117**

In Shaver's version of the Hollow Earth Masters, after a time, the Titans began to notice that the once beneficent sun now contained detrimental rays that were shortening their life-span by causing premature aging. To escape the harmful rays of the sun, the Elder Race entered deep underground caverns and began carving a fantastic subterranean kingdom, using their ray guns to disintegrate rock. Soon they had constructed powerful machines that could duplicate the health-giving rays of the sun while excluding the detrimental radioactivity. *Homo sapiens* continued to evolve in the sun, ignorant of the rays which shortened their life span, and puzzled by the withdrawal of their gods.

Shaver warned his readers that the Elder Race was not without its sensualists, and certain of its members, particularly the lesser ones, varied greatly in morality and intelligence. Perhaps the majority of the Elder Race regarded their lesser-evolved human cousins with the superiority and ill-concealed contempt that a pompous research scientist might feel walking amongst Stone Age aborigines. Others may have exploited the females of the human tribes and may even have set the more barbaric tribes against each other for the perverse pleasure of the Elder Race, who may have openly rooted for, and secretly assisted, their favorite tribes and warriors. The more humane among the Elder Race did their best to assist the primitive humans to develop a more functional culture and technology. According to Shaver, the ancient myths and legends are the unsophisticated surface dwellers' version of the myriad activities of the Elder Race.

<hr>

A Warning to Future Humankind

Shaver's "warning" to future humankind was that the dero (see page 119) are becoming more numerous and have scattered the benign tero with their constant attacks. The greatest threat to humanity lies in the grim fact that the dero have access to all the machines of the Atlan technology, but they don't have the intelligence or the highly developed moral sense of the ancients to use these machines responsibly.

The dero have possession of "vision ray machines" that can penetrate solid rock and pick up scenes all over Earth. In order to accomplish instant transport from one point to another, they have access to the Atlans' teleportation units. Frighteningly, the dero long ago gained control of the mental machinery that can induce "solid" illusions, dreams, and compulsions in topsiders. In addition to the aerial craft that we call UFOs, the dero possess death rays that can wreak terrible havoc.

According to Shaver, the dero are notorious for their sexual orgies, and they apply "stim" machines that revitalize sexual virility and "ben" rays that heal and restore the physical body. These mechanisms were created by the ancient Atlans thousands of years ago and are still in perfect working perfect working order because of the high degree the high degree of technical perfection with which they were constructed.

We surface dwellers are the descendants of the Abandondero who were unable to gain access to the caves at the time of the great exodus of the Titans from Earth. Most of our early ancestors died off; some degenerated into such lumbering hominids as Neanderthal; others, the hardy ones, survived, and through the centuries our species has developed a greater tolerance for the sun, which allows us to live even longer than the subsurface tero with their machines of rejuvenation. At the same time, the beneficent rays of the sun have prevented in our kind the mental and physical deterioration that perverts the dero and weakens the tero.

Although we have a common heritage with the tero and the dero, the passage of time has prevented the great mass of surface dwellers from possessing more than dim memories of the glory days of Atlantis, Lemuria, Mu, and the epochs when there were "giants in the Earth." However, Shaver cautions us, by no means have the dero forgotten us. These sadistic monsters take enormous delight in creating terrible accidents, confusing the goals of our political leaders, provoking surface wars between nations, and even in causing nightmares by focusing "dream mech" on us while we sleep.

In later years, Ray Palmer left the pressures of working for Ziff-Davis and its string of magazines and chose to establish a publishing company in his native Wisconsin. When Brad Steiger met with him in the late 1960s, Ray lived on a heavily wooded, 124-acre farm near Amherst, Wisconsin, just a few miles from the converted school building that housed his Amherst Press and from where he issued such magazines as *Flying Saucers*, *Space World*, *Rocket Exchange*, *Forum*, and *Search*.

"Perhaps I made a grave mistake," Palmer said, "but I altered what Shaver stated were his 'thought-records' into 'racial memory.' I felt certain that the concept of racial memory would be far more believable to the readers, and offer a reasonable and perhaps actual explanation of what was really going on in Shaver's mind—which is where I felt it really was going on, and not in any caves or via any 'telaug rays' or 'telesolidograph' projections of illusions from the cavern ray operators."

On the other hand....

Real Encounters, Different Dimensions, and Otherworldly Beings

THE WEE PEOPLE: GUARDIANS OF THE EARTH MOTHER

Brandie wrote to tell of an incident that has always stood out in her mind even though it occurred some years ago. She was doing dishes, washing and rinsing, and cleaning counters in the downstairs kitchen, when the following occurred:

"I was at the end of the kitchen counter moving things around," she said, "when something caught my attention. It was like a quick spark of light, and it flashed before disappearing. I looked at the kitchen table, and under it I saw movement. I looked from where I was to see someone, a small female being, crawling under the table.

"She sat there with her knees bent and head hunched peaking out at me. At first we stared at each other.

"As she blended in with the morning sunlight, it seemed as if she wasn't fully corporeal. She shifted as if agitated, as if she had not expected me to see her. She wasn't wearing any clothes, it seemed, and her hair was messy and ragged going all over the place. She had wide eyes that looked sort of scared.

"We continued just to stare at one another until I decided maybe I could extend an olive branch and talk. I tried saying hello in the most non-threatening way I could, but she just freaked out with a sharp breath and vanished.

"Later on I went to look at the book *Fairies* by Brian Froud, and there on the cover was a being similar to the female being that I had seen under the kitchen table. The resemblance shocked me, because here was this girl on the cover of a book of beings that I never would have thought to actually exist. Yet there she was."

Real Encounters, Different Dimensions, and Otherworldly Beings

If you should ever meet one of the wee folk in your life, never ask for its name and never call it a fairy. (**Art by Ricardo Pustanio**)

MEETING WEE FOLK UNAWARE

Many readers of this book will agree with Brandie that they, too, have encountered numerous beings that they never would have thought actually existed. In this chapter, we will hear from those individuals who had their reality altered forever by meeting fairies unawares.

A word of advice from the annals of encountering the wee folk: If you should ever meet an entity that appears very much like the beings portrayed in your old children's book of fairy tales and if you wish to survive the meeting without any nastiness, there are two rules you must remember—don't you dare ask its name and don't you dare call it a fairy.

According to those who speak the Gaelic tongue of Scotland and Ireland, the wee folk prefer to be known as *sidhe* (also spelled *sidh*, *sith*, *sithche*, and pronounced "shee"). There is disagreement as to the exact meaning of "sidhe." Some say that it refers to the mounds or hills in which the supernatural folk abide. Others say that it means "the people of peace," and that is how the sidhe generally behave toward humans except for two seemingly incurable elfin traits: 1) kidnapping human children to rear as their own and leaving one of their own (a "changeling") to be reared by unsuspecting human parents; and 2) shape-shifting into a seemingly endless variety of forms in order to work mischief (usually for the good), for baffled humans.

A SMALL VOICE CALLED TO GRETCHEN IN A WISCONSIN FOREST

Gretchen from Milwaukee writes that one day as she was relaxing in a lovely Wisconsin forest, admiring the beauty of nature's handiwork, she heard a small voice calling out to her.

As she looked down to the spot from which the voice had echoed, she saw a little elf-like creature sitting on the trunk of a tree. She returned his greeting and asked his name.

"He said I could call him 'Pumpkin,'" Gretchen told us. "He appeared at first to be less than two feet tall, but then, suddenly, he grew much larger for a moment, then shrank back down."

"I did that with the expansion and contraction of my breathing," he told Gretchen. "I knew you would like to see it."

Pumpkin explained that he worked with the vegetable kingdom, the plants and the shrubs. He and his kind energized the etheric bodies of the plant kingdom, so that all life can be maintained and strengthened.

After they had spoken for a moment or two, Pumpkin suddenly looked up from his work with the shrubs as though he heard someone call.

"I must go now." He smiled at Gretchen, then disappeared.

Gretchen told us that after her encounter with the wee, loving, happy nature spirit, she was even more deeply in awe of God's kingdoms and his creations on our beautiful Earth.

⎯⎯⎯⎯

ENCOUNTERING NATURE SPIRITS IN SEDONA

Charmaine Yarune Boericke moved from Los Angeles to Sedona, Arizona, and soon began to feel as though she was walking with one foot in earth-bound reality and the other foot in another dimension. She laughingly conceded that she doesn't always know just which side she's on, but said, "It is all magic and it is all so beautiful."

Charmaine was working on a book about nature spirits, and she said that she had seen quite a number of the etheric entities in the Sedona area. According to her analysis of the beings, she has found them to be quite different from the ones that she has met before in other places. "I don't always see elementals," she said. "I wish I could. Nor can I tell others how to see them. It is just when I'm particularly filled with an exquisite joy and love that they just suddenly appear—and they are as solid as you and I."

The energies that Charmaine discovered in Sedona were very strong and sometimes quite capricious. On one occasion, she said, she had been walking on rocks downhill when she suddenly stumbled.

"I turned a somersault in the air and landed on my face," she said. "I could have been badly hurt, but I was not injured in the slightest. At first I couldn't believe what had happened: A nature spirit had grabbed hold of me and taken care of me so I would not be hurt. The being had turned me over in the air, then set me down gently."

Whether or not it was Charmaine's intense interest in researching the nature spirits that attracted the entities to her energy, she believes that their intercession during what could have been a very nasty fall indicates their essential benign feelings toward humans.

⏤⫷⫸⏤

GINGER HAS INTERACTED WITH WEE PEOPLE SINCE CHILDHOOD

We were surprised when a friend of long standing admitted to us that she had interacted with the "wee people" since her early childhood.

"I think they come from another dimension," Ginger said. "I may be sitting just kind of staring at the floor, and suddenly little specks will seem to appear and to move about and form a picture of one of these beings—and then there he is beside me. Sometimes there will be two, three, or more of these wonderful characters manifesting before me. A smile always crosses my lips, because these little beings are my friends. They've been with me for many years, since my early childhood.

Ginger, a woman who has been in contact with the wee folk much of her life, believes they may be coming to our world from another dimension. (*Art by Ricardo Pustanio*)

"I don't feel it is a psychic thing," Ginger explained. "I don't go into a trance or somehow 'will' the beings to appear. To me, these beings are more real than the so-called natural world around me.

"Sometimes these little beings talk to me, but their voices seem to come from inside my head. It's more often like a thought than a sound. Besides relaxing me and entertaining me, these entities help me in many ways.

"For instance," Ginger continued, "several days ago I was sitting quietly watching these little people as they danced for me. Suddenly one of them said, 'Why are you sad today?' Another one spoke up and said, 'Instead of worrying about your problems, why don't you help somebody?' As he danced away, he spoke again, 'Remember, you can't help someone else without helping yourself, too.' With that final comment, they all vanished."

Later that day, Ginger did have an opportunity to help someone and while she didn't expect things to turn out the way they did, the eventual results opened a door that brought more help to her than anything else had done for a long time.

"I am always grateful to the Little People for their good advice," Ginger said.

⚬⚍⚏⚍⚬

AMONG STEIGER QUESTIONNAIRE RESPONDENTS, NEARLY THIRTY PERCENT REPORT SEEING WEE FOLK

Among the more than thirty thousand men and women who have returned The Steiger Questionnaire of Mystical, Paranormal, and UFO Experiences, a remarkable 29 percent claim to have seen elves, fairies, or some form of nature spirit.

Betty Kirkland, who now lives in a suburb of Chicago, wrote in her response to the Steiger Questionnaire that she had acquired fairy helpers when she was just a child of three. "I am now 33, married, with two little girls, eight and six—and I think they, too, have received fairy guardians, for I have seen little sparkles of light above their heads when they are sleeping."

Betty recalled how, when she was three years old, she first saw the Wee People on the farm in central Illinois where she spent her childhood. "I saw a little man and little woman picking apples that had fallen from the trees in our orchard. They were taller than I was at that age, so I thought at first they were just some very short people that my mother had allowed to enter our orchard. What really caught my attention is the way they were dressed. With their conical hats and bright green and red costumes, I thought they wore very strange clothing for farmers."

When Betty approached them they just smiled at her and went on picking certain apples and placing them in colorful cloth bags. "But when in my childish curiosity and bluntness I asked them what their names were, they looked shocked," she recalled. "The little man's mouth dropped, and the woman gasped in a shrill, tiny voice, 'Oh, no! She can see us! She's not supposed to be able to see us!'"

And then, Betty said, the man began to laugh in a high-pitched giggle. "Sure she can see us," he told his companion, "she's got the gift. See the glow around her wee head?"

Betty remembered that the woman asked the man if "the child is a changeling." Although that term meant nothing to her at the time, Betty later learned that a "changeling," according to fairy lore, is a hybrid fairy-human child that the fairies sometimes leave in place of a newborn infant that they "borrow" to take with them to their underworld kingdom.

Real Encounters, Different Dimensions, and Otherworldly Beings

The male fairy introduced themselves as fairies, himself as Acorn, his companion as Fluff.

"She made a little curtsy when Acorn introduced her," Betty said. "I thought it was so cute when she did. I had never seen a woman do that before. Later that night, when my mother asked me to wash my hands and face for supper, I curtsied. Mom laughed and wondered where I had learned to do that. I told her that a fairy named Miss Fluff had shown me how, and Mom just laughed harder."

Betty enjoyed the company of Fluff and Acorn throughout her child-hood. "They would usually just appear seemingly out of nowhere," she said, "so it didn't take me long to figure out that they were invisible to human eyes most of the time. Some evenings I would look out the window of my bedroom and see the 'fairy lights' of Acorn, Miss Fluff, and other fairies mixed in with the fireflies and dancing and swirling around in the darkness."

On one dramatic occasion, her two fairy guardians distracted an angry bull from butting eight-year-old Betty when she inadvertently crossed the pasture during a bovine mating event. Another time when she was ten, Acorn and Fluff chased off a stray dog that had invaded their farm and was likely rabid. It had approached Betty, growling, foaming at the mouth, about to charge, when sparkling lights swirled around its head and pulled it away by its floppy ears.

"Less than a year later, they saved me from drowning in the creek that ran near our farm," Betty said. "I had seen some older neighbor kids jumping off the banks into the water, and I had incorrectly assumed the depth as being much less than it truly was. And to make matters worse, I was alone that afternoon."

She was soon sputtering, threshing about in the water, panicked that she could not touch the muddy bottom with her toes. "I would surely have drowned if Acorn and Fluff had not hovered over me and pulled me to the bank. There was no one else to help me, but my fairy guardians were there."

As she grew into her teenaged years, Betty saw her fairy friends less and less. "But when I was ill or sad or depressed, I would first see sparkling lights swirling around me … and then I would hear their delightful laughter and know that everything would be all right," she said. "And so it has been throughout my adult years, as well."

WHO ARE THE WEE FOLK?

For many people today, the image of an elf is firmly established in the characters of either the handsome Legolas Greenleaf or the lovely, ethereal Arwen as depicted in the Sir Peter Jackson films of J.R.R. Tolkien's *Ring* saga

Are wee folk supernatural beings or survivors of an ancient civilization far predating any human culture? (*Art by Bill Oliver*)

(as portrayed by actors Orlando Bloom and Liv Tyler). While the elves in Tolkien's vision are tall and stately beings, tradition has most often portrayed elves and their fellow citizens from the unseen realm as diminutive, hence, "the wee people." Small in stature though they may be, elves, the "Hidden Folk," are not beings with whom to trifle.

In most traditions, especially in the British Isles and Scandinavia, the wee people, the fairy folk, were thought to be supernormal beings who inhabited magical kingdoms beneath the surface of the earth. Fairies have always been considered to be very much akin to humans, but they have also been known to be something more than mere mortals and to possess powers that humankind would consider to be magical.

Some theorists have suggested that the fairy folk may actually have been the surviving remnants of a past civilization populated by a species of early humans who were of diminutive stature compared to modern *Homo sapiens*. These little people may have been quite advanced and possessed a technology that seemed to be magical compared to the primitive tools of the migrating, primitive, hunter-gatherer humans who later became the established residents of the area. The little people may have died out, they may have been assimilated into the encroaching culture by interbreeding, or they may largely have gone underground, emerging topside just often enough to be perpetuated in folklore and legend.

Other scholars and researchers of the considerable body of fairy lore that exists worldwide maintain that fairies are entities that belong solely to the realm of spirit. Many of the ancient texts declare that the fairies are paraphysical beings, somehow of a "middle nature betwixt Man and Angel."

> In most traditions, the fairies are a race of beings, the counterparts of humankind in person, but at the same time, nonphysical or multidimensional.

Some biblically inspired authorities have sought to cast fairies as an earthly incarnation assumed by the rebellious angels who were driven out of Heaven during the celestial uprising led by Lucifer. These fallen angels, cast from their heavenly abode, took up new residences in the forests, mountains, and lakes of Earth. As fallen angels, they now existed in a much-diminished capacity, but still possessed more than enough power to be deemed supernatural by the human inhabitants of the planet.

In a variation on that account of the fairies' origin, other scholars contend that after the war in Heaven, the dispossessed angels materialized on Earth and assumed physical bodies very much like those of humans—those beings declared "a little lower than the angels." Eventually, these paraphysical beings took humans as mates, thereby breeding a hybrid species of entities "betwixt Man and Angel."

Medieval theologians seemed to favor three possible theories to explain the origin of fairies:

1. They are a special class of demoted angels

2. They are the dead or a special class of the dead

3. They are fallen angels.

Most of the ancient texts declare that the fairies are of a middle nature, "betwixt Man and Angel," and because they are of a nature between spirits and humans, they can intermarry and bear children. This belief echoes the passages in Genesis which tell that the "sons of God," the fallen angels, intermarried with the "fair daughters of men" and produced people of great abilities on Earth.

In most traditions, the fairies are a race of beings, the counterparts of humankind in person, but at the same time, nonphysical or multidimensional. Unlike angels or other multidimensional beings, fairies are thought to be mortal in existence, even though they lead much longer lives than their human cousins.

Shakespeare made fairies famous in a number of his masterworks, such as *A Midsummer Night's Dream*. He is largely responsible for the concept of the wee folk as being mostly benign—mischievous, perhaps, but never evil. Sir

Walter Scott emphasized the beauty of the fairy realm and the struggle of the fairies to achieve humanlike souls. The famed poet W. B. Yeats had a nearly obsessive interest in the paranormal and believed strongly in fairies.

C. S. Lewis, author of many classic books on spiritual matters, including *Mere Christianity* and *The Chronicles of Narnia: The Lion, the Witch and the Wardrobe*, once wrote that the wee folk are a third rational species. The angels are the highest, having perfect goodness and whatever knowledge is necessary for them to do God's will; humans, somewhat less perfect, are the second; fairies, having certain powers of the angels but no souls, are the third.

Since the beginning of time, it seems that the human race and the ultra-dimensional race of fairies have shared this planet, experiencing a strange, symbiotic relationship. In all traditions, the fairy folk are depicted as possessing many more powers and abilities than *Homo sapiens*, but for some inexplicable reason, they are strongly dependent on human beings—and from time to time they seek to reinforce their own kind by kidnapping both children and adults. (Tales of folk being abducted by smallish beings did not begin in the last few decades with the stories of UFO abductions by small, bug-eyed aliens.)

Through the centuries, many people have noted the clear parallels between the actions and deeds of the fairies and the angels. Throughout the long history of interaction between humans and fairies, there have been those mortal men and women who have somehow managed to win the favor of the fairies through a process beyond the ken of mortal men. If the fairies see fit to do so, they will even assist at the birth of a special mortal couple's child, and they will tutor and protect that child throughout his or her lifetime—just as guardian angels would. On behalf of such favored humans, the wee ones can materialize to help a poor farmer harvest a crop and have it in the bins before a storm hits, or they can clean a kitchen in the twinkling of an eye to ease the stress of an exhausted housemaid. With the advent of the UFO Age, there now appear to be clear parallels between the actions of the fairies and the claims of the actions of extraterrestrial visitors.

One factor has been consistent in fairy lore: The "middle folk" continually meddle in the affairs of humans—sometimes to work good, sometimes to do harm; sometimes to elevate human consciousness, sometimes to seduce humans into following the ways of the Darkside.

The fairies are said to be able to enchant humans and take advantage of them. It is often related that they can marry humans or—if they wish no lasting relationship—they can cast a spell on an unlucky lad or lass and have their way with them against the mortal's will. The Wee Folk seem too often intent on kidnapping human children and rearing them as their own. They also seem to delight in abducting adults and whisking them off to the underground kingdom to trifle with them.

Real Encounters, Different Dimensions, and Otherworldly Beings

Smallish beings from UFOs also have been reported to hypnotize contactees and abductees in order to employ some kind of mind control in order to make Earthlings more malleable. There have been reported cases in which humans claimed that they were whisked inside space ships and experienced missing time upon return. It has been suggested that hundreds of thousands of men and women have been abducted and probed sexually in what has been argued is an attempt to create a hybrid species.

On the positive side, certain contactees have claimed beneficial interactions with aliens that have permitted them to make major scientific discoveries, accomplish medical breakthroughs, and to achieve great material success. Many individuals claim to have been healed after their contact with extraterrestrials, and they have expressed their belief that the aliens are generally benevolent in their intentions toward humans.

WEE FOLK IN NATIVE AMERICAN TRADITIONS

The authors have spent a great deal of time studying tribal legends and folklore with many Native American medicine priests, so we were not at all surprised to discover that there doesn't appear to be a single tribe that does not acknowledge the existence of the wee people. And the generic Native American name for fairies, puckwudjini, is so similar to the ones used to identify the wee people in other parts of the world that one might actually entertain the thesis that such uniformity may suggest that the fairies themselves have given the name as their own personal identification.

Puckwudjini is an Algonquin word, commonly used among many Native American tribes, which signifies "little vanishing people." *Puckwudjini*—the name brings immediately to mind Shakespeare's "sweet Puck," who in *A Midsummer Night's Dream* chuckles about how foolish mortals be. From Puck in England we cross the waters to find *Puke*, a generic name for minor spirits in all the Teutonic and Scandinavian dialects. Puke is cognate with the German *spuk*, a goblin; and the Dutch, *spook*, a frightening ghost. There is also, of course, the Irish *pooka*, of Elwood P. Dowd and Harvey fame, as well as the Cornish pixie. Separate the suffix of Puckwudjini and we are left with jini, the Arab's magical denison of wondrous lamps and other domiciles.

Twylah Nitsch, a great Native American medicine teacher of the Seneca tribe, told us that one day as she was sitting at the edge of a river, she glanced up to see a "little vanishing person" coming toward her. When their eyes made contact, the little person scowled and asked: "Can you see me?" And then he answered his own question: "You *can* see me!"

Certain landmarks and other natural areas are apparently sacred to the wee folk. Woe to the human who violates these important places. (*Art by Bill Oliver*)

"Of course I can see you," she said, laughing. "I'm a medicine teacher, a shaman, one who strives always to be at one with nature. I can always see you and your kind."

The wee person was persistent. "But only when we allow you to do so. I wasn't allowing you to see me, so you shouldn't have been able to."

The medicine teacher shrugged. "Don't worry. I won't tell the people over there at the picnic table that you are here. But you better quickly be about your business, because I know those children at the swings have already spotted you."

RESPECT THE LANDS SACRED TO WEE FOLK

Careless or disrespectful humans who trespass on forest glens, rivers, or lakes considered sacred to elves may suffer terrible consequences. Entrepreneurs who wish to desecrate land whereon lie fairy circles or mounds in order to build a road or construct a commercial building may find themselves combating an unseen enemy who will accept only their unconditional surrender—or at least an acceptable compromise.

⊸⊸ᶆᶅ⋔⋔ᶅᶆ⊷

CONSEQUENCES OF DISRESPECTING
THE RULES OF THE HIDDEN FOLK

In 1962, the new owners of a herring-processing plant in Iceland decided to enlarge the work area of the building. According to Icelandic tradition, landowners must not fail to reserve a small area of their property for the Hidden Folk, and a number of the established residents earnestly pointed out to the recent arrivals that any addition to the processing plant would encroach upon the plot of ground that the original owners had respectfully set aside for the elves who lived under the ground.

In a condescending manner, the businessmen explained that they didn't harbor those old superstitions and neither did their highly qualified construction crew who had modern, unbreakable drill bits and plenty of explosives.

But the bits of the "unbreakable" drills began to shatter one after another.

An old farmer came forward to repeat the warning that the crew was trespassing on land that belonged to the Hidden Folk.

The workmen laughed when the old man walked away—but the drill bits kept breaking.

Finally, the manager of the plant, although professing disbelief in such nonsense, agreed to the local residents' recommendation that he consult a local elf seer to establish contact with the Hidden Folk and attempt to make peace with them. The seer informed the manager that there was a very powerful member of the Hidden Folk who had selected the plot near the herring-processing plant as his personal dwelling place. He was not an unreasonable being, however. Elves really do try to get along with humans and compromise whenever they can to avoid violence. If the processing plant really needed the plot for its expansion, the elf seer said, the Hidden One would agree to find another place to live. He asked only for five days without any drilling, so that he could make his arrangements to move.

The manager felt a bit strange bargaining with a being that was invisible—and as far as he was concerned, imaginary. But he looked over at the pile of broken drill bits and told the seer that the Hidden One had a deal.

Work on the site was shut down for five days to give the elf a chance to move. When five days had passed and the workmen resumed drilling, the work went smoothly and efficiently until the addition to the plant was completed. There were no more shattered bits on the unbreakable drill.

Because the incident cited above occurred in 1962—practically back in medieval times in some young people's minds—many readers will no doubt assume that Icelanders of the twenty-first century no longer cherish such quaint beliefs. Those readers would be wrong.

MISCHIEF BEFALLS THOSE WHO
DO NOT RECOGNIZE THE ELVES' DOMAIN

In the *Boston Herald*, December 25, 2005, Ric Bourie wrote that highway engineers and construction crews still regard the Hidden Folk very seriously: "Mischief befalls Icelandic road builders who can't recognize good elf domain, including breakdowns of heavy equipment and even worker mishaps and injuries. It is said to have happened on more than one job site, enough to take the mythology seriously. Consequently, road planners here consult with an elf expert before routing a road or highway through rock piles that may be elf habitat."

> Since ancient times, it seems that the Irish have understood that there are certain areas that the wee ones consider sacrosanct

Bourie interviewed elf seer Erla Stefánsdóttir, who named elves, gnomes, dwarves, angels, light-fairies, and "the hidden people" as all belonging to classes of what she called elfin beings. Any of the above-named entities, Ms. Stefánsdóttir said, "... can get quite upset if we ruin their houses or go against their wishes. They get very upset and we have to face the consequences. They can put a spell on us."

While some people may be surprised that the stereotypically stoic Scandinavians believe in elves and other beings from the hidden world, it seems that the whole world embraces the stereotype of the country folk of Ireland taking their wee people seriously. According to popular leprechaun and elf stories, the Irish know that to disturb the mounds or raths in which they dwell is to invite severe supernatural consequences. Since ancient times, it seems that the Irish have understood that there are certain areas that the wee ones consider sacrosanct, or special to them. Certain mounds, caves, creek areas, and forest clearings have been staked out by the Hidden Ones as their very own, and the wise human, sensitively in touch with the natural environment, knows better than to trespass on such ground.

TROUBLE AT THE FAIRY MOUND AT WEXFORD

The trouble at the fairy mound outside the village of Wexford began when workmen from the state electricity board began digging a hole for the erection of a light pole within the parameters of a rath. The villagers warned the workmen that the pole would never stay put, because no self-respecting community of fairy folk could abide a disturbance on their mound.

The big-city electrical workmen had a coarse laugh and made uncomplimentary remarks about the level of intelligence of the townsfolk of Wexford. The workmen finished digging the hole to the depth that experience had taught them was adequate; then they placed the post within the freshly dug opening and stamped the black earth firmly around its base. The satisfied foreman pronounced for all within earshot that no fairy would move the pole from where it had been anchored.

However, the next morning the pole tilted askew in loose earth.

The villagers shrugged that the wee folk had done it, but the foreman of the crew voiced his suspicions that the fairies had received some help from some humans bent on mischief. Glaring his resentment at any villagers who would meet his narrowed, accusative eyes, the foreman ordered his men to reset the pole.

The next morning that one particular pole was once again conspicuous in the long line of newly placed electrical posts by its weird tilt in the loose soil at its base. While the other poles in the line stood straight and proud like soldiers on parade inspection, that one woebegone post reeled like a trooper who had had one pint too many.

The foreman had endured enough of such rural humor at his expense. He ordered the crew to dig a hole six feet wide, place the pole precisely in the middle, and pack the earth so firmly around the base that nothing short of an atomic bomb could budge it.

Apparently fairies have their own brand of nuclear fission, for the next morning the intrusive pole had once again been pushed loose of the little people's rath.

The foreman and his crew from the electricity board finally knew when they were licked. Without another word to the grinning villagers, the workmen dug a second hole four feet outside of the fairy mound and dropped the pole in there. And that was where it stood, untouched and untroubled—exactly where the wee folk permitted it to stand.

⊸⊸⊸⊸⊸

THE ROCK IN ST. FILLANS BELONGED TO THE WEE FOLK

In *The Times*, November 21, 2005, Will Pavai and Chris Windle tell how a small colony of wee folk living beneath a rock in St. Fillans, Perthshire, cost developer Marcus Salter, head of Genesis Properties, nearly $40,000 when community pressure forced him to scrap his building plans and start again.

A group of his workmen had been about to move a large rock from the center of a field to make way for the new housing development.

According to Salter, one of the residents of St. Fillans came running, shouting that they couldn't move the rock or they would kill the fairies. At first Salter thought the man was joking. Then came the series of angry telephone calls.

Salter attended a meeting of the community council where he learned that the council was considering lodging a complaint with the planning authority, which was likely "to be the kiss of death for a housing development in a national park."

Although the Planning Inspectorate has no specific guidelines on how to deal with fairies, a spokesman told Salter that "Planning guidance states that local customs and beliefs must be taken into account when a developer applies for planning permission."

Salter was forced to redesign the new estate so that the wee people's rock would be in the center of a small park nicely situated within the new community.

AN AMERICAN IN IRELAND
LEARNS NEVER TO CROSS THE WEE PEOPLE

When we were discussing some recent accounts of wee people activity receiving media attention, author, researcher, and journalist Patricia Ress recalled her stay with an Irish family when she visited Ireland some years ago.

"They owned a large hotel that dated back to before the Easter Uprising (1916) and had housed lots of IRA [Irish Republican Army] activity," Patty said. "The owner of this place, Mr. Conroy, told me that there are fairy rings all around the area outside of Dublin—especially in St. Kevin's Bed. There is a story of a truck driver who made fun of the villagers for their superstition about the 'fairy circles' and to prove how stupid he felt they were, he drove his truck through one of them! Then he got out of the truck, laughed at the crowd watching him, and promptly died of a heart attack! Conroy swore that this man was a big fellow in perfect health."

Patty heard another story while she was in Ireland about some construction workers who wanted to remove a stump near a fairy ring. They felt that since it wasn't actually *in* the fairy ring, the coast was clear. They tried to dynamite the stump three or four times and nothing happened. They checked the dynamite, the wiring, and so forth, and *nothing*. Finally, they all saw a little man dressed in green climb out of the stump and run. Just as he ran off, the stump exploded into a million pieces! As crazy as this sounds, there was a photographer there from the local newspaper who had heard about all the problems and was going to take a picture of them trying to blow up the stump. He did actually get a picture of the leprechaun. However, Patty was told, the photograph is locked away somewhere in Trinity College.

Patty recalled many conversations with the maid at the hotel where she stayed, and the maid said that she had heard many stories of people who had seen the "wee folks." And on one thing all the stories agreed, Patty said, "You *never* want to cross one! Not ever!"

—◉—

WE ARE PART OF A LARGER COMMUNITY OF INTELLIGENCES

Our many years of research have led us to theorize that there may exist, throughout the world, pockets of energy in which another order of intelligence abides. And we should make clear that we agree wholeheartedly with elf seer Erla Stefánsdóttir, who includes elves, gnomes, dwarves, angels, light-fairies, nisse, brownies, skaramooshes, and Devas as a single shape-shifting intelligence that we have come to call "The Hidden People." In some instances, these pockets of intelligent energy may be influenced by human intelligence and manifest in a physical form as a variation on the theme of a human image. In other circumstances, this energy may direct and control—even possess—human beings.

In essence, these "nature spirits" may be the "Elder Race" or "The Old Ones" referred to in so many myths and legends. These vortexes of intelligence may constitute a companion species to our own and may well have maintained a strange kind of symbiotic relationship with us throughout the centuries of mutual evolution.

American David Spangler of Findhorn Foundation community in Scotland claimed that he was told by such an intelligence that these entities recognize humankind as a necessary and vital part of the synergistic state of the planet; thus these entities are essentially benignly concerned with human survival because it bears directly upon the survival of Earth. Spangler's understanding of humankind's relationship to these entities is that we were "first cousins," and that we somehow had a common ancestor.

We perceive The Other, whether of terrestrial or extraterrestrial origin, as communicating with us essentially through the subconscious mind. That is why experiences with these entities seem to happen more often, and most effectively, when the percipient is in an altered state of consciousness, and that is why UFO experiences, fairyland adventures, angelic visitations, and so forth, sound so much like dreams. They are really occurring when the percipient is in a dreamlike state. The conscious mind of the percipient remembers certain highlights of the experience—or interprets the symbols and lessons in a consciously acceptable manner—but the actual teaching mechanism and the important information have been indelibly etched upon the experiencer's subconscious.

What such seemingly disparate phenomena as the appearance of wee people and the visitations of angels throughout the world means to us is that we humans are part of a larger community of intelligences, a much more complex hierarchy of powers and principalities, a potentially richer kingdom of interrelated species—both physical and nonphysical—than most people are bold enough to believe in. As we have previously declared, once we have correctly fathomed the meaning of The Other and its total relevance to our lives, we will perceive an evolved Intelligence, whose manifestations we have been mistakenly labeling as our gods, our angels, or our demons, and who has been challenging us, teaching us, and preparing us to recognize our true place in the cosmic scheme of things.

MEETING STRANGE CREATURES IN DARK FORESTS

Humankind has been aware of strange creatures, both seen and unseen, physical and nonphysical, since at least the Paleolithic Age (c. 50,000 B.C.E.), when primitive artists painted images of supernatural beings on the walls of their caves. As early as the third millennium B.C.E., the written records of ancient Egypt and Mesopotamia recognized a hierarchy of supernatural beings that ruled over various parts of the Earth, the universe, and the lives of human beings. These ancient people also believed in lower levels of entities that might be either hostile or benign in their actions toward them. Every known culture on Earth has its accounts of benevolent and malevolent beings who manifest from an unseen world, and in recent years there has been a tremendous surge of interest in ghosts, demons, and creatures of darkness, as well as guardian angels and guiding spirits, who transcend everyday existence

⊶⊷

A VICIOUS ATTACK ON A YOUNG COUPLE BY A "DAMNED THING"

Together with the return of her questionnaire, Lorrie Jastrow sent us an account of an experience that happened to her and her fiancé, Karl, shortly before their marriage. They had gone to a movie, then decided to drive out to the tiny house in the country where they would live after they had celebrated their nuptials.

Lorrie thought it was fun to go out there and plan their future. The house was on land that was too heavily wooded to be good farmland, but they didn't intend to farm the acreage, only to plant a small garden for vegetables. Karl would continue his job in town.

Real Encounters, Different Dimensions, and Otherworldly Beings

RICARDO PUSTANIO 2012

Karl was attacked by a malevolent presence, but one that was invisible to his fiancé, Lorrie. (*Art by Ricardo Pustanio*)

"Our only light that night were our flashlights," Lorrie wrote in her account. "Since we wouldn't be moving in for another month or so, the landlord had yet to switch on the electricity. He had given us keys to the place, though, and he didn't mind that we would drive out there to dream about our future life together."

That night when they walked into the house, Lorrie had an eerie feeling that something was wrong, that they were not alone. "Karl must have felt the same way as I did," she said, "because he kept looking over his shoulder, like he expected to catch sight of someone spying on us.

"Then we heard a strange chattering, like some giant squirrel or chipmunk, coming from a dark corner in the room," Lorrie continued. "It suddenly seemed so unreal, unearthly, and a strange coldness passed over my body. I told Karl that I wanted to leave, that I was frightened."

But before they could move toward the door, Karl suddenly threw his hands up over his head as if he were trying to grab at something behind him. His head seemed pulled back and to one side. His mouth froze in a grimace of pain and fear, and his eyes rolled wildly. He lost his balance, fell to his knees, then to his side. He rolled madly on the floor, fighting and clawing the air around his neck.

Lorrie stood stunned with fear and bewilderment. Karl managed to struggle to his feet. His eyes bulged, and he gasped fiercely for each breath. Some unseen thing seemed to be strangling him. He gasped that they must run to the car, that Lorrie must drive.

Somehow, they got out of the house with Karl stumbling, staggering as if something heavy and strong were perched atop his shoulders with a death grip about his throat.

"I … can't get the damned thing off of me!" he gasped.

At last they got to the car. Lorrie got behind the wheel, and Karl told her to drive … fast. He was still trying to pry the invisible thing's hands from his throat.

Lorrie drove for about two miles down the road—and suddenly there was a blinding flash inside the car. A brilliant ball of light about the size of a basketball shot ahead of their car, then veered sharply to the left and disappeared into a clump of trees.

"I did not stop until we were back in town," Lorrie said. "Karl lay gasping beside me, his head rolling limply on the back of the seat. He did not speak until we were well inside the city limits, then he said that some inhuman thing had jumped on him from the shadows of the house. He was certain that it could have killed him if it had really wanted to do so."

Lorrie Jastrow concluded her account by writing that although they returned to their small home in the country with some trepidation, they never again encountered that monstrous, invisible strangler that chattered like a giant rodent. Once the nature spirit had time to calm down and come to terms with the fact that humans were reclaiming the empty house, it moved on to another more appropriate dwelling. But it certainly did give Karl and Lorrie a piece of its mind before it did so.

⏤⏤⏤

THE UNINTENDED CONSEQUENCES OF LEAVING A VACATION HOME UNOCCUPIED

People who leave their vacation homes empty for the major portion of the year also frequently suffer from a nature spirit or some woodland being developing a proprietary interest in what appears to be vacant property, free for the taking.

Scott Halstead said that he and his family had vacationed in the same cabin in the northeast for the past twenty-two years. "We started vacationing in this cabin when Allan was two years old, and we always take the last two weeks in August," he stated in his account. "And for twenty-two years, we've had to share the cabin with something else."

Scott and his wife, Lynette, made a point to emphasize their contention that although the "something else" sometimes frightened them, their sense of the entity was that it was extremely protective of the cabin and the grounds on which their cabin and others like it had been built.

"The cabin and nine or ten others are situated on a beautiful lake," Halstead said. "And old Charlie the caretaker knows that there is something kind of spooky going on around there, but he usually just shrugs and says that it doesn't bother him. It sometimes bothers his dogs, though. He's got two big German shepherds, and I've seen them cower and whine when neither Charlie nor anyone else was near them."

Lynette said that when their son Allan was about four years old he would say that he had an invisible friend named Mo-Ko who lived in the woods. "If we were afraid that he might wander off in the woods, he would say, 'Mo-Ko won't let me. He says that I have to stay near the cabins.' Who could complain if his invisible playmate was also a good babysitter?"

> "**H**e's got two big German shepherds, and I've seen them cower and whine when neither Charlie nor anyone else was near them."

Lynette and Scott agreed that the most dramatic evidence of a guardian spirit looking over the cabin came in 1985 when Allan was eleven and their daughter Tonya was seven.

"Scott and I had gone swimming," Lynette said. "The kids knew that we would be chilled when we got out of the lake and a fire would feel good to us. Allan had watched his father building a fire for years, so he knew the basics, but he just kept piling on kindling. Tonya tossed newspapers and magazines onto the fire, and pretty soon they had a huge blaze roaring in that fireplace."

Shivering, clutching towels to their chilled bodies, Scott and Lynette returned to the cabin to see the colonial-style rag rugs in front of the fireplace on fire, the curtains to the side of the chimney ablaze, and another finger of flame moving across scattered newspapers toward the living room carpet.

"There was that moment of panic, when you just kind of scream and shout before your brain kicks in," Lynette said. "Allan and Tonya were standing against a wall, crying their heads off in fear."

And then, as weird at it may seem—as strange as it is for Scott and Lynette to attest to—something started to beat out the flames.

"I'm standing there barefooted and soaked in my swimming suit with a towel wrapped around me," Scott said. "I don't even have time to react, really, when I see something snuffing out the fire. More than beating out the flames, it's like something is smothering it, as if it is covering the fire with a big wet blanket. In minutes, what looked like it would be a major disaster has become a smoke-filled cabin, a couple of burned and scorched throw rugs, a blitzed curtain, and two crying kids."

Lynette said that she hugged Allan and Tonya and gave thanks to God "… and to whatever protective spirit looks out for the cabins."

Over the years Lynette and Scott said that there were numerous signs to indicate that some spirit entity was protective of the cabin. All of the family said that from time to time they felt someone was watching them. Items would disappear and reappear in bizarre places. And an eerie kind of scratching noise would often be heard issuing from within the walls.

Out of curiosity, they once wrote to the Wagners, a family they knew rented the cabin in July, and asked if they had ever noticed anything "peculiar" during their occupancy.

"Beverly Wagner wrote right back and said, 'I imagine you're referring to the invisible live-in maid?'" Lynette laughed at the memory. "The Wagners had noticed some of the same numerous little things that we had, but once when they left a messy table after a party at the cabin, they woke up the next morning to discover that someone or something had stacked the dirty dishes in the sink and cleaned the table top. Jim Wagner jokingly said that it must be elves, so he left a bowl of oatmeal on the front step that night. In the next morning it was gone, but, of course, birds or some critter could have eaten it."

Scott and Lynette speculated that it could be the spirit of some Native American who cherished the environment around the lake and who kept a vigil over the cabins and their inhabitants, but they added that they had come to believe that the force, the energy, that loved the place so much was something more primeval.

"It's almost as if nature itself is somehow protective of the few remaining areas that we humans haven't covered over with concrete and erected shopping malls and gas stations," Scott said. "Sometimes I would visualize some kind of elf or nature spirit sitting outside near the lake, looking across the beauty of this area toward the city and sighing, 'What fools these mortals be.'"

THE "MANLIKE THING" AT THE SIDE OF THE ROAD

She thought it was a man walking along the side of the road ... until it sprouted wings and flew into the night sky. (*Art by Ricardo Pustanio*)

Josephine wrote to us to report a real encounter with a man-like thing that occurred at approximately 1:30 A.M. on June 21, 2011. "My niece experienced a frightful event which has her rethinking about her lifestyle and changing it," Josephine said. "She was driving on the highway when she came upon what she thought was a man walking on the road. As she got closer, the creature spread its wings and flew up and she almost hit the 'thing.' When she looked in the rear view mirror, she saw that there was a vehicle behind her. She saw the vehicle swerve, as if it had almost hit the creature, too. My niece was terrified and didn't entertain the thought of whether she should stop and ask the other vehicle behind her to confirm what she had seen. She was traveling with family in different cars that night, and she stopped at the next town at a gas station with good lighting to wait for her mom to catch up. Then she asked for her sister to ride home with her that night."

Josephine's specific question was whether her niece's frightening encounter could possibly be linked to the date being the beginning of the summer solstice and various activities associated with conjuration of entities. Could such entities be summoned to manifest in physical form to roam the earth and to be seen at this time? Or was this a common creature sighting that could appear any time of the year?

"I do know one thing," she said, "this is a first for our family." Then she added, "Besides the sightings of the lights in the sky that have been seen in our area that the military claims are unexplainable."

ENCOUNTER IN A DARK WOODS

By Noe Torres

Noe Torres, UFO investigator, is the author of Ultimate Guide to the Roswell UFO Crash *and* Fallen Angel: UFO Crash Near Laredo, Texas. *Noe holds a bachelor's degree in English and a master's degree in library science from the University of Texas at Austin. With California UFO researcher Ruben Uriarte, he has written three books:* Mexico's Roswell: The Chihuahua UFO Crash, The Other Roswell: UFO Crash on the Texas-Mexico Border, *and* Aliens in the Forest: The Cisco Grove UFO Encounter. *With Roswell historian John LeMay, Noe wrote* The Real Cowboys & Aliens: UFO Encounters of the Old West. *He also served as editor and publisher of the books* Roswell USA *by John LeMay,* Roswell Alien Autopsy *by Philip Mantle, and* Russia's Roswell Incident *by Paul Stonehill and Philip Mantle.*

In the 1940s, my parents owned a small frame home surrounded by four acres of orange and grapefruit trees in a very isolated corner of South Texas, about twenty miles from the border with Mexico. The home and surrounding groves of trees were incredibly dark at night, as there were no sources of artificial light and the nearest town was ten miles away. I vividly remember as a child staring nervously out the window of my bedroom at the dark, shadowy trees at night and wondering what things might lurk there.

I also remember a story my mom told me several times about the night she had a close encounter with an "entity" amidst the trees surrounding our home. This was not the type of tale that mothers tell their children to keep

Noe Torres is a UFO investigator and author. (*photo courtesy Noe Torres*)

"I vividly remember as a child staring nervously out the window of my bedroom at the dark, shadowy trees at night and wondering what things might lurk there." (*Art by Ricardo Pustanio*)

them from wandering out of the house at night. In fact, I was already around ten or twelve years old when she first told me about it, and her tone was deathly serious. I believe she told me the story as a means of getting a very distressing incident off her chest.

It happened in the dead of night when my dad was out of town on construction work and my mom was home alone with three sleeping children. She was awakened by noises and commotion coming from the backyard. The various barnyard animals that my parents kept penned in the backyard, including goats and chickens, were highly agitated. The family dog was barking and whimpering.

Into the middle of this commotion stepped my mother, eager to determine what was stirring up the animals. In order to reach the animal pens, she had to walk about a hundred feet from the rear door of the house and into the midst of a grove of closely-planted citrus trees. She was essentially surrounded on all sides by the trees. As she walked toward the pens, she was joined by the family dog, which still seemed to be frightened and agitated.

The front of the wood frame house near **Mission, Texas**, where Torres and his parents lived. (*Photo courtesy Noe Torres*)

Suddenly, my mom felt what she described as a "presence" and she heard a "commotion" directly overhead. Simultaneously, the dog began barking very loudly, leaping high into the air, and snapping its jaws at some unseen thing. Mom was unable to lift her head up to see what was above her. She felt a "force" or "will" that denied her the ability to lift her head up. A circle of light seemed to suddenly spring up around her, and she continued hearing strange whining or whirring noises from above.

A devoted evangelical, my mom immediately assumed an attitude of prayer and began requesting God's help with the situation. Around her, the chaos persisted as her dog continued leaping wildly into the air as if trying to reach something.

The situation seemed to reach a "stasis," during which time seemed to be frozen. She did not know exactly how long this state persisted.

Then, in an instant, the light around her "blinked off," the dog became quiet, the penned animals were still, and the presence that she had felt in the sky above her was gone. Somewhat dazed by the experience, she stumbled back to the house and took some time to sit and recover from her ordeal before returning to bed.

She told me this story several times and always seemed to be struggling to understand it ... to puzzle it out. The incident troubled her deeply, and left her feeling confused and unsettled. She thought about it all the rest of her life and tried in vain to make sense of it. Unfortunately, I did not know enough

Real Encounters, Different Dimensions, and Otherworldly Beings

about UFOs at the time to check into whether she might have experienced "missing time" as a result of the encounter.

⊰═◍〜◍═⊱

DARK FOREST ENCOUNTERS MAY PRODUCE LIFE-ALTERING INSIGHTS AND NEW TEACHINGS FOR HUMANKIND

On a hot fall day in 1979, Brad answered the doorbell in the Steiger home in Scottsdale, Arizona, to find an attractive, well-dressed, young Hispanic man on the front porch. The unexpected caller identified himself as a Peruvian gems dealer who was calling on clients in the United States. When he had stopped for gas at a truck stop outside of Phoenix, he saw a long-haired man dressed in a robe being harassed by a group of young men. He intervened, took the robed fellow into his car, and asked if he could help him in some way. The man, who was dressed like an Old Testament prophet, reached into his robe, and handed the salesman a piece of paper with an address on it. The address was that of Brad Steiger.

"Do you know this man?" the Peruvian gentleman asked Brad, a quizzical smile and frown betraying his skepticism.

As Brad drew closer to the automobile, the robed, bearded man slid out of the passenger's seat and stepped out onto the hot pavement. He smiled broadly and waved.

The jewelry salesman soon had Brad's answer. "Yes," he replied. "He is a good friend of mine, Dr. Wolf Weilgart. He is a genius, a professor of linguistics and psychology. We used to teach at the same midwestern college."

In 1966, after Brad had written his first book on UFOs, *Strangers from the Skies*, many of his fellow faculty members had great fun making "little green men from Mars" jokes at Brad's expense. When Dr. Wolfgang John Weilgart was asked his opinion of such matters as space creatures, the questioners no doubt expected the psychotherapist with doctoral degrees in linguistics and psychology from universities in Vienna and Heidelberg to diagnose Steiger as a bona fide crackpot. Instead, Dr. Weilgart replied that when he was a child, he had met beings from elsewhere who wished to teach him and guide him in helping others toward the ways of peace and understanding. What was more, in a single mystic moment, he was given aUI (see page 149), a new language for a new brotherhood of man.

The two men had become friends, and in 1967, Dr. Weilgart had written the "Afterword" to Brad's book, *The Mass Murderer*, a study of serial killers. After Brad had left the faculty and obtained an office in the city, Dr. Weilgart would come often to discuss matters psychic, psychological, and literary.

Brad invited Wolf and the Peruvian Good Samaritan inside for a cool drink and an escape from the blistering Arizona sun. After accepting a few minutes of hospitality, the salesman excused himself and said that he must be attending to business and appointments that he had made in Phoenix. Wolf thanked him for delivering him to the Steigers, then blessed the young man for his good heart and kindness.

Wolf told Brad that he would not stay long; he had only come to give Brad a message.

"I will not live much longer," Wolf said. "From here, I will go to Berlin where they will honor the memory of my mother, who was a poet laureate. I have only come to tell you that soon you will be alone to share the message of peace from space."

Brad protested such talk of Wolf's death, and he insisted that Wolf stay with him for a few days before he resumed his pilgrimage.

Wolf would accept only a bowl of soup, which Brad prepared for him, and he asked only if he might take the spoon with him for future meals on the road.

After he had eaten the soup and placed the spoon in a small purse attached to the cloth belt that bound his robe, Wolf asked Brad to take him to a place outside the city where he would continue his journey by relying on the kindness of open-minded motorists to pick up a hitch-hiker dressed like a prophet from the Bible.

As loudly and as strenuously as Brad protested against letting his friend off on the highway to fend for himself, Wolf calmly assured him that he would be protected. He had been traveling in such a manner for quite some time.

Since Wolf would have it no other way, Brad did as his friend wished and brought him to a truck stop where he prayed a righteous truck driver would take Wolf safely to a destination that only his inner-guidance would determine.

Dr. Wolfgang John Weilgart died in January 1981, and Brad has thought often of his friend and his remarkable life of mission and service.

He was a child of five in his native Austria when Dr. Weilgart had his first cosmic experience in a forest. A stranger in a star-strewn mantle appeared to him and said: "Thou must die, Wolfgang."

The young Wolfgang answered firmly and without hesitation: "I am ready." From that moment on he felt that a new cosmic life-stream had entered him, as if his former life had been dissolved, as if his former self had died.

After his childhood visitation, Wolfgang dictated to his older sister a drama *SaradUris* (which, in the Language of Space, means that "good light" which comes "through the Spirit"). SaradUris is a spaceman savior who comes

oliver

Dr. Weilgart had his first cosmic experience in an Austrian forest when he was only five years old. It was at that time that he "died" and was reborn with cosmic energy. (*Art by Bill Oliver*)

to the earth to guide humankind away from its wars and to bring peace through understanding. The rules of peace revealed in this drama are not only derived from sentimental love, but also from a justice which is based on the status quo as well as on a program of survival for those who are worthy to survive and can survive. "Creative Spirit, lives on still! Destroyers perish, while they kill."

Dr. Weilgart related his most crucial cosmic experience in poetic form as an introduction to his book *aUI: The Language of Space—Pentecostal Logos of Love & Peace.* The boy "Johnny," seated at a mountain creek, is alerted to an alien presence by a strange, flute-like sound. There is a mysterious being, a butterfly with green, leafy wings and root-like legs. Johnny says:

> It circled and sat down on my knee.
>
> The sounds it made were piped through its flute-like body, and yet they wafted from far away.
>
> And then I knew that this thing must have come from somewhere else.
>
> And I began to understand that it was talking to me. Could we be friends?

Real Encounters, Different Dimensions, and Otherworldly Beings

It showed strange signs, and put them together, and they made sense.

And what I heard was from another place. I learnt

The language of Space.

Johnny learns that the Being has come from a distant star, from where his kind had watched Earthmen fight against the dragons and monsters of the ancient sagas. "But now when nature's foes lie defeated at his feet, man turns his weapons against his brethren, and his rallying cry is still the slogan of hate, the word of conventional language."

Your words give murder a beautiful name, and call a killer a hero.

So if I gave you the gold of my wisdom wrapped in the burlap bags of your words,

You would use it to club each other to death....

When Wolfgang told his parents of his experience, they sent him to a psychiatrist, who, however, found the six-year-old child's only abnormality to be the fact that he could solve the problems of a thirteen-year-old. His Binet IQ tested above 200. (Dr. Weilgart was made a member of American Mensa, the world's highest IQ society.) The psychiatrist warned the child that in Western society, uncommon experiences may be told only as dreams or in poems.

Dr. Weilgart wrote his first doctoral dissertation on "Creation and Contemplation." It was one of the few outspoken pacifist statements against Hitler and the whole Nazi ideology of aggressive action.

His father, Dr. Hofrat Weilgartner, had worked for the *Anschluss* (the annexation of Austria by Germany), and so the Nazis expected similar cooperation from the son. But Wolfgang John had another of his cosmic communications. He spent an afternoon and evening wrapped in contemplation. In a cosmic insight of peace, his father's dreams of the glory of the German Reich and his mother's entreaties faded into nothingness.

The Nazis had offered Wolf a high position in their secret service because of his fluency in a dozen languages, his knowledge of psychology, and his friendship with the underground, against whom they wished him to be an informer. Although this "intelligence" position would have been the only way to rehabilitate himself in the eyes of the Nazis, whom he had offended by his dissertation, Dr. Weilgart refused.

His cosmic voice told him to flee to Holland. He had few friends whom he could trust, and no connections with practical helpers. Following his inner voice, he set out for the border. He was stopped by a patrol, but the inner voice took over, and to his surprise Dr. Weilgart heard himself command the patrol to another mission. Strangely, the patrol obeyed, as if Wolf had been in the uniform of a higher officer.

Soon Holland was being rapidly invaded by the Nazis, who would have executed Weilgart as a deserter. The young mystic's inner voice brought him to the Dutch Governor of Java, who happened to be in the Hague, and he wrote an American visa for Weilgart and gave him a ship ticket. In the meantime somebody had sent Weilgart's poems to Thomas Mann, a Nobel Prize and Goethe Prize winner, who gave him a postdoctoral research fellowship there to write his book *Shakespeare Psychognostic*.

From 1945 to 1950, Weilgart served as professor at Xavier University for Tropians and Caucasians. ("Tropians," for the race originating in tropic climates, and "Caucasians" are terms he preferred to "blacks" and "whites," which make the contrast too harsh. Also, "black" in Western languages has a negative connotation. In *aUI*, the Language of Space, a Negro is called *iau*, "sun-space man"—a man adapted to sunny regions.) Then he received a United Nations' (U.N.) research grant, finished his second doctoral degree in psychology and psychotherapy at the Universities of Heidelberg and Zurich, became a psychotherapist for the U.N., and invented the WERT (Weilgart-Ethos- Rhyme-Test), not only for crime and suicide prevention, but for personality development. Chand & Company of New Delhi, India, published Weilgart's *Language of Space*. The "Language of Space" makes man immune against the slavery of slogans and the idolatry of ideologies, for it makes language a communication of transparent truth.

In 1971, Brad Steiger was contacted by Melanie, a housewife in Colorado, who suddenly began to recall a life on another world. At the same time, she began to go into trances to predict coming Earth changes. Brad was sent a tape on which Melanie uttered brief snatches of her "native tongue" during a trance session. Brad was told by other researchers that linguists at a number of universities in Canada and the United States had been unable to determine the root of the supposed language.

> **B**rad Steiger was contacted by Melanie, a housewife in Colorado, who suddenly began to recall a life on another world. At the same time, she began to go into trances to predict coming Earth changes.

Brad asked Dr. Weilgart if he would listen to the tape and see if he could offer any clues to the origins of the strange language. Dr. Weilgart found Melanie's dialect unknown to him in any language other than in the logos of *aUI*.

Once before, when he was a young psychotherapist, Dr. Weilgart received a shock when he had encountered a young boy in a mental hospital who addressed him in *aUI*. Dr. Weilgart learned that the lad had been placed in the hospital because he insisted on speaking only in this language, which was unintelligible to his parents, teachers, and physicians. The young psychotherapist went to the director of the hospital and told him that the boy was not sick, that his language made sense. The director ignored Dr. Weilgart and ordered electroshock treatment for the boy.

The boy resisted the electroshock as much as he could. He told Dr. Weilgart that he feared the treatments would make him forget what he had learned on the "other star." In his struggle the boy died, but with his dying words he said to the psychotherapist: "You believe in me. You tell others about the Language of Space!"

Now Dr. Weilgart was listening to a woman from Colorado who one day was a busy housewife and mother, the next, after touching the Cosmos, a revelator who spoke often in an unidentified language.

The psychotherapist in Wolf was cautious. He pointed out to Brad that the woman's unconscious might have retained bits and pieces of overheard Amerindian dialects, and now, years later, was reassembling them and uttering them as a language from another world. But he wrote down *aUI* symbols as Melanie's voice uttered the sounds again and again from the tape recorder.

Because Melanie spoke very rapidly, Dr. Weilgart was not able to hear all of her words, but he transcribed the following phrases which he plucked from the strange speech: "way of movement around space." … "from life above space" … "to move for a light-existence" … "a good existence in a dimension above space."

Had Melanie somehow received a mental infusion of knowledge and awareness in the language of a multidimensional being on an otherworldly plane of existence?

——◁▥◁∫▥▷——

His Psyche Traveled to the Moon and Beyond

Another great mystic who had unusual "playmates" from other dimensions as a child was our friend the remarkable sensitive Olof Jonsson. In *The Psychic Feats of Olof Jonsson*, Brad Steiger was able to relate Jonsson's adult impressions of these entities:

"They may have been the same entities that so often represent themselves to small children as fairies and wood sprites.… But, somehow, on occasion, I believe that I was able to see them as they really were. They were taller than I, but not nearly as tall as my parents. They were, perhaps, just under—or just over—five feet tall. They had much larger heads and proportionally much smaller bodies than an adult human. Their skin color varied from bluish-green to golden brown to a shade of gray. It was they who began to tell me wonderful things about the universe and Cosmic harmony.… I felt that they were friends, that they wanted to teach me and to help me.… I am still convinced that they are friendly and intend to help man as much as they can without interfering in humankind's own development and free will."

Some may recognize the name Olof Jonsson as the psychic sensitive who was chosen by astronaut Edgar Mitchell for the Apollo 14 Moon to Earth ESP experiment in February 1971. Several months before launch-off, Mitchell had asked a select group of parapsychologists to locate a sensitive subject for an experiment across a million miles of space. Jonsson, a Swedish-born Chicago drafting engineer, and one of the most laboratory-tested psychics in the United States, was selected for this history-making experiment.

As a witness to literally hundreds of tests and experiments with Olof—from PK (psychokinesis, mind-over-matter) to endless card-guessing tests with the Zener deck (star, circle, square, wavy lines, and cross)—and as the author of his biography, Brad was hardly surprised when it was revealed that the psychic involved in the tests with Mitchell was Olof Jonsson.

Once when the two of them were discussing the possibility of intelligences on other planes of existence, Olof said that he believed there to be forces in the universe, minds that can help us gain information about the true meaning of life. He believed that there is a dynamic force and that intelligences are associated with it.

Who are these intelligences?

They could be entities from other places in the universe. Perhaps they are the souls of those who have died on highly evolved planets, who have left their radiation in the universe; and their intelligence remains as a force for good and for spiritual evolution.

These intelligences may cloak themselves as holy figures, as wise old Tibetan monks, as astral teachers, but they are bodiless forms of benign intelligence. They may cloak themselves because the human brain will more readily accept an entity that looks like a human being, rather than a shapeless, shimmering intelligence.

These beings have the ability to absorb our actions and our thoughts so that they may know better how to direct us toward cosmic harmony. These beings avoid language and work with us on an unconscious level. The phenomenon of telepathy affords us proof that language means nothing to the unconscious. We do not think in words, but in ideas and feelings. What language does God speak? The feelings and the harmony communicated between the unconscious levels of self constitute the one "language" that all humans understand. That is God's language.

Olof became one with the Great Mystery on May 11, 1998.

Real Encounters, Different Dimensions, and Otherworldly Beings

UNKNOWN BEINGS OF TERROR AND THE DARKSIDE

From time to time throughout history, unknown beings arise from the dark side of human consciousness to begin a campaign of terror that becomes contagious and spreads like a phantom virus across an entire nation. Such seems to be the case with Slenderman, a contemporary Boogie Man that rages unfettered throughout the United States. Our friend and colleague the Paranormal Pastor Robin Swope has been monitoring the mental monster gone amuck since the beginning of this viral epidemic.

SLENDERMAN—SOMETHING AWFUL THIS WAY COMES

By Pastor Robin Swope

He was officially created in an Internet contest when the readers of the "Something Awful" forums were asked to create a paranormal entity in a thread named "Create Paranormal Images." The scheme was to create eerie images and use them to trick people on paranormal forums into thinking they were genuine. Users started photoshopping images by adding fake ghosts and other bizarre figures, usually accompanied by an imaginary back story to make them seem authentic.

On June 10, 2009, a user named Victor Surge posted to the thread with two photos and a claim that the entity stalked children. The explanation that Surge included with the photos was the haunting detail that the photographs were taken on a day on which fourteen children disappeared. He then further explained that the library where the photo was found burned down a week after the pictures were taken. The entity was a shadow creature, overly tall and thin. It had long arms that stretched to inhuman lengths to ensnare its prey. To add to its unearthliness, the fiend had no face. His primary motivation was to kidnap and kill children. Supposedly, he was always seen just before the disappearance of a child or even a mass kidnapping of multiple children. He seemed to prefer silently stalking in fog-enshrouded streets and wooded areas so he could obscure himself from the casual eye. However, children have been able to see him when adults in the vicinity could not. The mythos also stated that children have dreams or nightmares concerning a tall, slender man before their disappearance. The meme of Slenderman was born.

Quickly the mythos was expanded. Once Slenderman was seen, he would stalk you for the rest of your life. His goal was to slowly drive you insane by appearing in your periphery, eventually threatening you with death.

> Some say the Slenderman myth is inspired by archaic archetypes of folklore, like death stalking the plague riddled inhabitants of Medieval Europe....

Soon his victims no longer were limited to children. Teenagers and adults were soon to become stalked by the tall, faceless man. The mythos quickly gained some trappings similar to ufology's Men in Black phenomenon as he appeared in a dark modern suit with white shirt and black tie. He also gained added appendages, which sprout from his side like tree limbs.

One UFO site adds: "Once his arms are outstretched, Slenderman's victims are put into something of a hypnotized state, where they are utterly helpless to stop themselves from walking into them. Slenderman is also able to create tendrils from his fingers and back that he uses to walk. Whether Slenderman absorbs, kills, or merely takes his victims to an undisclosed location or dimension is also unknown as there are never any bodies or evidence left behind in his wake to deduce a definite conclusion."

Soon image boards across the Web contained threads including original Slenderman art as well as stories. Blogs were dedicated to the mythos and YouTube videos chronicled the diabolical entity's torment of a few ill-fated individuals. In short order, there was an alternate-reality game built around the monster: "Marble Hornets," which combines YouTube and twitter accounts to build a narrative surrounding a film student's discovery of horrifying film footage his friend had taken.

Some say the Slenderman myth is inspired by archaic archetypes of folklore, like death stalking the plague-riddled inhabitants of Medieval Europe as depicted in Hans Holbein's sixteenth century woodcuts of the Dance of Death. But recently the mythos and folklore have begun to manifest into real life.

On November 6, 2009, a young man called *Coast to Coast* A.M., the popular late night radio program, to report an encounter his girlfriend had with an entity resembling Slenderman, prompting a flurry of listeners to call to relate their own stories of Slenderman-type encounters.

I, too, have received stories of various encounters of Slenderman. The first came in August of 2009, from a woman named "JoAnne": "… from childhood I have seen this demonic figure. He is a tall shadow. He has no face, but he has long arms. Out of the corner of my eye on certain nights I see him and his arms seem to be reaching out to me, and when I turn to look at him, the thing is gone. I have the real feeling that if I don't turn around to look at him his arms will catch me up and I will die."

JoAnne then described some personal details of her life that accompanied the "Slenderman" appearance, which included child abuse and neglect at a young age. Close to the end of her letter she made the chilling announcement: "I am afraid that he is stalking me, and that one day I will not be able to catch him trying to snatch me up. This fills me with such fear, words can't describe. Sometimes I think I am going nuts. I feel like he is going to get me when I don't expect it. Some nights I can't sleep, noises outside make me jump. When the wind cranks up and things start to rattle, I am so scared. I need help!"

I responded to "JoAnne," and gave her some simple prayers and commands for the entity to leave her alone. I have tried to contact her numerous times, but I never get a reply. One part of me feels it might be a psychotic incident with prolonged effects on her mental state, but when I started to receive other similar letters, I began to think twice.

I received an anonymous comment on my blog dated January 12, 2010, that in part reads: "My name is_____. I am being hunted by a shadow creature. It is tall and thin and tries to catch me in its long arms. I saw it in a dream, and now it is real. All I see in the face are two eyes, and when I look in them those arms try to get me."

And a few more recent ones:

I am now 16 years old, and I had never heard of Slenderman until now … what really freaks me out is that I had one of these dream experiences about Slenderman. I was 5 or 6 and I was having a dream of people I never knew or saw, playing a prank on me at a cemetery. There was one person up in a tree, recording everything, while I was walking. They buried a jack-in-a-box, so I couldn't see it; but when I did, a hand came out of the box. The scary thing about the hand was it had long, unnatural, slender fingers that were trying to get a grip on my whole leg. It scared me, so much that I fought back and ran, searching my way out of the cemetery to the gates.

Before I could reach the gates, I saw to my left a moving shadow. I stopped before the gate to watch it slowly moving to stand in front of me. When I looked up, the shadow had become a man wearing a suit, but he had no face, just a large grin. To me it looked like he had a cloak on, but on a second look the folds of the cloak actually looked like arms. He tried reaching for me, but before he could, I woke up, screamed, then ran to my parents' room.

I slept in my parents' room for about three weeks until I didn't have the dreams anymore. In those three weeks, I had that dream over and over. It would continue where it left off, showing me more of the suited man. I stopped having the dreams, but I never forgot them. Even now, I have a feeling that I am being watched and when I do, I automatically think about that dream. I don't know why, but I just do. Was that man the Slenderman the so-called myths say? I only learned of the Slenderman today from a friend. Now I'm afraid if that man in my dreams was the Slenderman truly trying to get me—or if he just loves to scare the hell out of people.

Here is another from a thirteen-year-old girl:

I'd rather leave myself nameless, but here it goes: I've been seeing this thing ever since I was about eight years old. Just last night I remember I was having a nightmare about Slenderman. The only thing I remember, was waking up after his arms started coming after me.

When I read about the other girl who got abused when she was young, I can relate. I still am somewhat abused, but it doesn't happen as often.

I was taking a picture outside today, and Slenderman appeared. He was just so casually standing in the background. I soon felt really sick after seeing him, so I went inside.

Around 4, my Mom told me to look outside to see if my brother's girlfriend's car was pulling in. Slenderman was there, and he snapped his head in my direction.

At 5, my brother, his girlfriend, and some of his friends went for a walk, and said they saw somewhat of a tall man standing next to my window. When they looked at him again, he was gone. I'm not sure if I should take this as an attempt to come after me or simple paranoia.

Is this some sort of fiction become reality because of the overworking of imagination and the psychosomatic power of a projected entity, such as a tulpa? Or is it a demonic entity that has taken on the guise of an Internet mythos to feed on fear and destroy the minds of those that fall into its deception?

I was about to go with the latter until recently when I heard a few stories that place the Slenderman in paranormal experiences before the mythos was ever created.

The first came from a coworker who told me that around 2002, at a previous place of employment, she had made friends with a woman who had paranormal encounters. One of the most chilling was in the mid-1990s, when she awakened in the middle of the might to see a tall, dark, and thin humanoid figure at the end of her bed. As it reached out its arms, its fingers elongated to an inhuman length and reached toward her head. She was paralyzed. Even though she tried to scream and move, she could not. As the tendril fingers wrapped around her head, she lost consciousness.

She awakened that morning feeling very sluggish. Shortly after that terrible night, she became ill, had frequent headaches and nausea, and could not sleep. So she sought medical help, and as a consequence, she had an X-ray done of her head

Stories of the Slenderman tell of a creepy, preternaturally thin, human-like entity that pursues children. (*Art by Ricardo Pustanio*)

and upper torso. The doctors found that a small, metallic object had been implanted into the base of her skull. When the doctors tried to remove the foreign object, they found that it had become entangled into the central nervous system at the spinal cord, and it was too risky to remove.

The woman showed the operation scar to my coworker as proof. But my coworker still did not believe the story, which irritated her friend very much.

The friend then brought her X-ray to work and showed my coworker the proof. A small metallic object had been implanted at the base of her skull in such a location that made it inoperable.

Was this woman an alien abduction and implant survivor? At first look that seems the conclusion, but the appearance and aftereffects of the encounter matches the Slenderman mythos so closely that it makes one ponder. In fact, after telling my coworker about Slenderman, she was shocked and a bit unnerved. It fit perfectly. But why the implant? Perhaps to follow a victim the rest of his or her life?

A few months ago I put a request out on my blog for any readers who had a Slenderman experience to write in and tell me about it. It so happens that some of the responses predate the invention of the mythos.

Real Encounters, Different Dimensions, and Otherworldly Beings

First, from a man in the midwestern United States who wishes to be anonymous because of his position in society:

Dear Pastor:

I stumbled onto your website much by accident and was intrigued by the "slenderman" story. I have vivid memories from childhood regarding a throng of these people emerging from the woods near our house, which was about a quarter mile from the edge of a large state forest in _____. As a child growing up in the 1950s, my mom always warned me about "gypsies" who occasionally made their way through our neighborhood. Even so, I was intrigued nevertheless. I recall one occasion quite vividly. I was about 4 or 5 years old, playing in the back yard. I recall going into the garage, which was separate from our house. I became aware of a swishing sound, like someone walking through tall grass. I glanced out the garage window and saw an entire line of these 'slender people' coming out of the woods just beyond our neighbor's house. They were heading our way.

I was momentarily frozen. What did I do now? Fearful the "gypsies" might carry me away, I retreated into a corner of the garage and watched the procession through a crack in the wall. This was something out of storybook land! They were all slender, but some were taller than others. A few wore scarves, but their garb appeared drab with colors faded. There were a few 'slenders' of small stature, whom I took to be children. They were holding the hands of the ones wearing scarves. I could not see their faces, but I recall their fingers were exceedingly long.

When they crossed into our backyard, they continued walking single file in zombie-like fashion. When they reached the coal shed (which was behind the house, but about 10 feet from the garage) they divided into two lines. One line went between the coal shed and the house. The other passed between the coal shed and the garage. They continued in their slow, relentless pace, walking past the side of our house, down the road and up the hill in their slow, plodding fashion.

As soon as they were out of sight, I rushed into the house. My mother immediately locked all the doors and drew all the window shades until my dad came home from work.

Over the intervening years, I have often wondered about that day. Who were those strange people? Where did they come from? Where were they going? Your photo triggered recollections of that afternoon in the garage, but I saw more than just a shadow person. I saw the whole clan!

And another from "Jason" in Ohio:

My 22-year-old brother used to have dreams about Slenderman as a 7-year-old, and he doesn't even know about the Slenderman myth. We were talking about weird experiences in our old house, and he started telling me about his dreams about a tall guy without a face.

He also said that once when he was in that house by himself, he was at the other end of the hallway, and he saw a creature similar to that description lean out the door of his bedroom and look at him.

And a final short remark from another individual who chooses to remain anonymous:

At times I think I see him out in the streets. But it's happened way too many times for it to be a coincidence.

So what is happening? Encounters of a being similar to Slenderman have been happening for decades. What shall we make of this?

I first read about Slenderman in his full mythical glory about two years ago before piecing together the jigsaw pieces. And even then I was unnerved as I have not been in many years.

Is there something in the dark?

I hope it is not the stalking Slenderman.

⚊⚊⚊⚊

SIGHTINGS OF "STICK MAN" IN MIDDLE TENNESSEE

By Sandy Nichols

"That is strange!" I thought to myself as I read the email reply from Cathy Brockway. I was sure I had included Cathy's name on the list of people when I sent out two previous emails describing my other two sightings of the creature I had recently begun calling "Stick Man." Oh, well! It didn't matter. I would simply reply back to her and share what I had told the others. Little did I know when I hit the Send button that Cathy would write back and inform me that she had also seen this creature not far from my home, but nearly two years before.

Cathy had received the previous emails I had sent out, but in those emails I never referred to the creature as "Stick Man." In my email describing my third sighting, I simply got tired of not having a name for the creature, so I simply nicknamed it "Stick Man." Such a name seemed appropriate because to me he looked like a cross between a walking stick and a skeleton. Cathy then put two and two together and knew that I was describing a similar creature to the one that she had seen.

Cathy had contacted me through my research site, Alien Research Group, in late 2009 because of her interest in various aspects of the paranormal. She was looking for someone she could trust enough to share some of her strange experiences. Several emails back and forth and numerous phone conversations in the ensuing months that followed assured Cathy that I was someone whom she could trust. In order to help her understand some of her experiences better, I believed that Cathy also needed to hear perspectives other than mine. Cathy shared with me that she had also had some ghostly encounters, so I arranged a get-together at my home for her to meet two of my very good friends, Bret and Gina Oldham of Halo Paranormal.

Not too long after meeting Bret and Gina for the first time, they introduced me to a new spirit communication method that they had devised using the Ghost Box. I had heard about the Ghost Box being used in ghost investigations for years, but frankly I was never impressed with the results that other groups were getting. But after agreeing to participate in several Ghost Box sessions with Bret and Gina, I came away convinced that the method that they employed was second to none. By using this new method, I believed that Cathy would come away from the session with a better understanding of her ghostly experiences. In time I would also introduce Cathy to Brent and Joan Raynes, as well as Chandra Harrison. Soon, Cathy would become a permanent member of our special group conducting Spirit Box sessions and investigations.

This first Ghost Box session with Cathy was scheduled for a Saturday evening, and everything went according to plan. Cathy bonded well with Bret and Gina, and during and after the session she was amazed and excited that such a process to communicate with the Other Side could work so well. It was late by the time the session was over, and soon Bret and Gina headed home. Shortly thereafter, Cathy departed. It would not be until March 2013 that I would learn of Cathy's sighting of Stick Man on this May 2010 night.

The part of my description that caught Cathy's attention the most was where I had described how part of the creature seemed to glow in a mixture of three different colors. In subsequent emails, then by phone, I learned the full details of her sighting and she used some of the same words to describe the creature that I had thought of but not yet used.

Within a few seconds after Cathy had left my driveway, she reached the end of the cul-de-sac that I lived on and turned right onto Saddle Springs Boulevard. She had barely turned right when her thoughts changed from the

Ghost Box session to that of planned events with her family the next day. Another hundred yards or so down the road, these thoughts faded as the headlights from her van illuminated what she believed to be at first a severely malnourished, over-sized deer. This deer was standing just off the road next to a driveway. As she drew even closer she began to wonder if she was seeing a deer at all or something entirely different.

"When I first saw him, he was down on all fours. His head was shaped something like a Chihuahua's, but without any type of a protruding muzzle or snout," she recalled. "It was more flat looking. As I got a closer look, I could see no skin or hair covering the creature's body. Its arms, legs, and trunk looked more skeleton-like than anything else. The bone structure was no more round than the cardboard core on Christmas wrapping paper. And the whole body had this really strange yellow, red, and orange glow that was like a cross between translucent, neon, and opaque. The glow was really hard to describe. I could not tell if the creature was self-illuminating or its body was just reflecting my car headlights."

She was also concerned that whatever this was it would suddenly bolt across the road, so she quickly applied her brakes and slowed her vehicle down to a crawl. This was a very wise decision for suddenly this creature reared itself up on two legs and ran not more than a foot in front of her vehicle across the road. But using the word "ran" is rather understated, based on Cathy's experience.

"He moved so quickly that it was almost like a blur," she explained. "And there was something else. Even though he was a blur, I could still see his form, but I could not see the upper half of his head. It had not disappeared, but was just hidden from my line of sight because it was above where the roof and front window converge.

"During the rest of my drive home, I was having this back and forth battle going through my thoughts. My logic was trying to convince me that it was only a deer, but at the same time my logic was also telling me I had witnessed something amazing and very strange, something unknown."

After hearing the full details of Cathy's experience, I was convinced that she and I had witnessed the same creature with only the slightest of physical variations.

An illustration by Sarah McKinney and Phillip Sajovic, copyright © Sandy Nichols.

The First Sighting

It was a mild night in late summer of 2012 as I stood in the parking area of my driveway. As I waited for the arrival of Bret and Gina to conduct an impromptu Ghost Box session, I gazed westward as the last rays of the waning sun were setting on the horizon. I had always been fascinated with the time of dusk. It is that magical time when the light of day and the darkness of the night are equal in their opposite brilliance. And so it was during this momentary truce between the safety of the light and the eerie sounds and shadows of the dark that I saw the creature for the first time.

He appeared suddenly, standing upright, a mere two feet off the side of the road, facing the road and not more than 150 feet in front of me. It was as if he had just materialized out of thin air, which, in fact, is exactly what he did.

He was well over seven feet tall. His arms and legs looked more like the bones of a skeleton than anything else, and their size matched Cathy's description to a tee. They were jet black in color. His arms and legs were long and jointed about half-way down, with his arms appearing to be slightly longer than his legs. While standing upright and still, with his arms hanging straight down, the end of his long, slender fingers reached down to the halfway point of what seemed like the knee joint and the foot. His feet were long and slender, as were what seemed to be his toes. His legs were attached to the side of the torso at the very bottom, while the arms were attached to the side at the top of the torso, much in the same way as human arms are attached.

His torso was just a smidge bigger than his arms and legs, but unlike the full body illumination that Cathy experienced, only the torso of the creature was glowing with that same neon/translucent/opaque mixture of color. Since no headlights were shining on the creature during this sighting, it was apparent that the creature somehow had the ability to self-illuminate various body parts.

As I stood there and soaked up the characteristic details of this creature, I was hoping that Bret and Gina would turn down my street to witness what I was witnessing. But after about five to six seconds of standing upright and still, the creature began to move, but in a slow-motion sort of way. He raised his right leg and moved it forward, and his foot came to rest halfway across the road. He then moved his left foot and it came to rest two feet on the other side of the road. As soon as the right leg caught up with the left leg, the creature simply disappeared.

I was more than just astonished at what I had just seen. The creature needed only two steps to cross a twenty-eight foot distance. This meant that the stride of each step was fourteen feet long.

Bret and Gina arrived at my home just minutes later, and I shared with them what I had just witnessed. Bret's response was serious but whimsical at the same time, "With what we have witnessed here at the Paranormal Palace, there is no telling what hangs around here."

What I figured was the last of the strange sightings for the night, wasn't … kind of. As it turned out, my two black labradors witnessed what we assumed to be the same creature.

After the Spirit Box session, I walked the Oldhams to their vehicle. Gina was already sitting in the car on the passenger side, while Bret was standing in front of the open door of the driver's side. They had parked on the left side of the parking area with their car facing up the street. I was standing on the back, right side of the car, sharing one more thing with Bret before they left. My younger lab, Carolina, was sitting on the driveway some ten feet behind and to the left of the car. Savannah, the older lab, was standing in between me and the right side passenger door, looking into the car. At first I thought she was looking at Gina moving around, but instead her stare was fixated through the front window at something in front of the car. I wondered what had caught her attention, but I could see nothing.

Suddenly, she bolted around me to the left side of the car, stopped, and assumed a defensive position just to the left of the open driver's door. Her front end was down. Her back end was up. Her hackles were raised back to her tail, and she was growling and barking at the exact same time at something in the side yard. We looked and could see nothing.

In the eight years we have had her from puppy stage, she had never, ever once shown this type of aggressive behavior. She and Carolina are two of the most gentle and loving dogs we have ever owned. Everybody just loves them, but on this night there was no mistaking her intent. She was totally pissed at something.

She stayed in this posture for about thirty seconds, when suddenly she jumped back about a foot as if something had lunged at her, but then she immediately reset herself back into her aggressive, defensive posture. Bret and I sensed that she was not going to jump back again. But then she did something else totally unexpected. She moved to her right, beside Bret and a little in front of him. She then began to back Bret up toward the back of the car. It was so obvious that she was now trying to protect Bret, since he was the closest to whatever she was upset with. Also around this time, Carolina had moved up just to the left of Savannah.

Then, just as unexpected as before, both dogs shot through the small but thick bushes that lined the mulch bed in front of the car and into the side yard. About half way across they both turned to the right and headed toward the back yard, with Savannah continuing to bark and growl. They stopped at the back property line where it merges with the woods behind my home. Several minutes later they both returned to the car.

While we tried to figure out what they were after, Savannah and Carolina suddenly bolted again, but this time into the front yard to the left of the car, and straight through a thick cluster of rose bushes in the side mulch bed. They crossed the street, stopped, began sniffing the air, and after a minute or so returned to the car. Nothing else occurred for ten minutes, and Bret and Gina finally departed.

One reason we do so many Ghost Box sessions at my home is because the ghosts and spirits (and apparently other entities) are attracted to me, as well as to the history of the area. The ghosts and spirits also seem to enjoy us communicating with them. Throughout the years, Savannah and Carolina have gotten used to the regular spirit manifestations that roam my home, and they only bark at any new ones that show up. But then they get used to them as well.

It made no sense to me, Bret, or Gina, why my dogs would get that upset at one of the entities. Their normal reaction to the ghosts and spirits was not Savannah's reaction that night. Our best guess is that the Stick Man returned and my dogs just did not like him.

The Second Sighting

I was just taking it slow and easy down Arno Road, heading home while taking an alternate route and avoiding the construction work on Interstate 65 just south of Franklin, Tennessee. The cool air seeping into my car from the driver's side open window felt refreshing after being on my feet all day volunteering at the church that my wife attends. This volunteerism was an annual October event for me to help the church prepare for its biggest fund-raiser of the year. I enjoyed helping out, and I liked the people with whom I worked. Never once throughout the years had any of these folks criticized me or thought me evil for doing my paranormal research and investigations. As a matter of fact, some would even send me emails every once in a while, sharing information that they thought I might find interesting and/or useful to my writings.

But my focus was not on these thoughts as I continued down the road. Instead, I was remembering the amazing UFO sighting that my wife and I had witnessed almost a year before to the day on this same road, and by coincidence, driving home from the church after the completion of the fund-raiser. Little did I know that just a couple of miles down the road from the area of that UFO experience I would have my second sighting of "Stick Man."

I was a bit surprised at the lack of cars on this country road. Usually there is residual traffic at 7:30 P.M. heading home from the mall area located just north of Franklin. The only car to be seen was one about a mile in front of me. As it turned out the driver of this vehicle was driving even slower than I, and within several minutes I had caught up with this car. Since this was a country road with farm land and scattered homes, I did not want to make the driver nervous by tailgating, so I kept about a fifty-yard distance between us. We soon passed the location of my UFO sighting, and we were approaching the crossroad of Peytonsville-Trinity, when the driver clicked on his right-hand turn signal.

Believing that the driver was getting ready to turn on this crossroad (west), I slowed down—but then I had to slow down even more. Instead of turning at the crossroad, the driver began a very slow turn into a side driveway off of Arno at the home on the corner that faced the cross road. As soon as the driver had fully entered the driveway, I turned on the high-beams of my car and that is when I saw "Stick Man" for the second time.

He was standing in a vacant field that was located on the left, facing Arno. He was almost in line with the driveway that the car had turned into. Unlike my first sighting, he was not glowing on any parts of his body. His entire body color was jet black except for his head, which was a shade lighter than the rest. A few seconds later, he began to move toward Arno Road, and his forward progress indicated that he was moving a bit faster than the first time I saw him. Though he was not moving as fast as Cathy Brockway had described, he seemed to be jogging in slow motion.

Little did I know that just a couple of miles down the road from the area of that UFO experience I would have my second sighting of "Stick Man."

He crossed Arno in two steps, not more than fifty feet in front of me. My car is a newer model with the new headlights, so he was illuminated as if he were standing in the middle of a spotlight without the blurring effect. Once across Arno he continued to move west in front of a three-railed black fence-line that was a property separation boundary from the house on the corner and the one right before it. Even though the creature and the fence were close to the same black color, I could still see the creature fairly well, even though he was now a full hundred yards or so from my car.... Then he suddenly just vanished right before my eyes just as before.

After Stick Man had vanished, I looked to see if the driver of the other car had possibly seen the creature. Even though the car was at the end of the driveway and its tail lights indicated it was in park, the driver had not emerged from the car. I considered, for the briefest moment, turning into the driveway and talking to the driver, but since it was night I thought it best not to.

There was no doubt that this was the exact same creature that I had seen a few months earlier, and probably the same creature that Cathy had witnessed.

Third Sighting

In the ensuing months I began an intensive search of the Internet, looking for any reported sightings, photos, or illustrations of this creature. I found no photos or illustrations, except for drawings of the typical "cartoon" type "Stick Man," but I did find a couple of videos on YouTube. With the headings of "Stick Man" and "Unknown Creatures," these videos supposedly showed two strange creatures captured at night on infrared by CCTV systems. After viewing the videos, I came to the conclusion that the supposed creatures were no more than a couple of people walking on stilts covered by white sheets. Serious researchers and investigators are all too aware that such videos only add fire to the skeptics and debunkers who claim that anything reported as paranormal is the result of trickery, lies, or someone's imagination. But there is no doubt in either Cathy's or my mind that what we witnessed was a real and unknown creature rarely reported and seen. We both considered ourselves lucky to have seen him, but I was to have one more sighting.

> When he reached the corner of my pool house, the top of his head was several inches above the height of the gutter, which is just inches shy of twelve feet above the ground.

As I relaxed in the warmth of the bubbling water of my hot tub, I could see that the nighttime sky was crystal clear and afforded me the opportunity to do a little sky-watching. I looked in all directions, hoping to catch another glance of the mysterious lights that would suddenly appear from time to time in the sky or in the farm fields, vacant lots, and woods that surrounded my home. But on this particular night it was "Stick Man" that caught my attention.

When I first saw him he was less than fifty feet away from me, motionless, and not more than ten feet away from the side pool gate. I could not discern much detail of his body in the darkness, but his form was unmistakable, with the light colored background of the night sky illuminating the ground behind him. He seemed to be several feet taller than in my first two sightings, but within a second or two I knew the reason why. He began moving slowly toward the back right corner of my pool house/office some twenty feet from where I first spotted him. When he reached the corner of my pool house, the top of his head was several inches above the height of the gutter, which is just inches shy of twelve feet above the ground. At this point I had a clear view of him through the pool fence gate. He was gliding effortlessly through the air some four feet above the ground, and eventually I lost sight of him as he moved totally behind the pool house.

In most of my alien-type abduction experiences, it was nothing for the aliens to float me through the air from one location to another. Apparently, this creature had this same ability. I also got to thinking of how strange it was that he also had the ability to change his color.

But after thinking about this further, it did not seem that strange after all. There are several animal species here on earth, both on land and in the sea, that have this ability. So I guess in nature, wherever nature happens to be, that there is nothing to prohibit an unknown species from having similar abilities.

A side note: As I was in the process of writing this account, I was contacted by someone who lives fifty miles away from me who was in search of answers for his/her abduction experiences. As we chatted on the phone, this person just happened to mention seeing this strange creature that he/she had never seen before. From the description given, it seems very possible that this person had also encountered "Stick Man."

⏤⏤⏤

THE MENACING THREE MEN IN BLACK

While the Internet blogs and the Blogtalk radio programs are currently dispensing frightening tales of the Black-Eyed Kids and Slenderman, it remains to be seen whether these contemporary memes of terror will approach the longevity of UFO research's most persistent menace, the Three Men in Black (MIB).

Ever since organized flying saucer research began in the early 1950s, a large number of UFO investigators have claimed to have suffered personal harassment and unusual accidents. Some researchers have even attributed mysterious deaths of their fellow investigators to the ominous trio. At the very least, UFO researchers have said that sinister voices have whispered threats over the telephone and warned certain researchers to discontinue all inquiries into the UFO mystery.

The template for the appearance of the MIB occurred in September 1953, when three agents of an alleged silence group made their first in-person visit to Albert K. Bender, who had organized an international flying saucer bureau. According to ufologist Gray Barker, Bender had received certain data that he felt provided the missing pieces for a theory concerning the origin of flying saucers. Bender wrote down his thesis and sent it off to a friend he felt he could trust. When the three men appeared at Bender's door, one of them held that letter in his hand.

The MIB told Bender that he was the only one among many researchers who had been able to stumble upon the correct answer to the flying saucer enigma. Then they filled him in on the details. Bender became ill. He was unable to eat for three days.

UFO investigators Dominick Lucchesi and August C. Roberts, two men whom Brad Steiger came to know well, called on Bender and encouraged him to break his silence concerning the mysterious Men in Black. But Bender told them that the MIB had been "pretty rough" with him: "Two men did all the talking, and the other kept watching me all the time they were here. He didn't take his eyes off me."

Bender went on to say that when people found out the truth about flying saucers there would be dramatic changes in all things. Science, especially, would suffer a major blow. Political structures would topple. Mass confusion would reign.

Roberts and Lucchesi kept chipping away at Bender's wall of silence, but to most of their queries they received only a noncommittal, "I can't answer that."

In 1962, Bender declared that he would at last tell his story to the world in *Flying Saucers and the Three Men*. This perplexing volume served only to confuse serious researchers as it told of Bender's astral projection to a secret underground saucer base in Antarctica that was manned by male, female, and bisexual creatures.

The questions that have remained to plague UFO investigators ever since were many: Were Bender's experiences really of a psychic nature? Was his book deliberately contrived to hide the true nature of his silencing? Had the whole experience been clothed in an extended metaphor that might yield certain dues to the perceptive researcher? Had Bender created the incident out of whole cloth to gain publicity for books and lectures?

On June 24, 1967, Dominick Lucchesi told Steiger that Bender seemed to be a changed man after the three Men in Black had visited him. "It was as if he had been lobotomized," Lucchesi said. "He was scared and he later suffered from tremendous headaches which he said were controlled by ' them'! Whenever he would think of breaking his silence, one of these terrific headaches would just about knock him out."

"The three Men in Black shut him up and he's stayed shut up," August C. Roberts added. "Today Bender manages a motel in California. We still correspond, but he refuses to discuss flying saucers."

"In my opinion," Lucchesi said, "the Men in Black are representatives of an organization on this planet, but they are not from any known bureau in our government. I believe both these men and the UFOs come from some civilization which has flourished in a remote area of Earth, such as the Amazon, the North Gobi Desert, or the Himalaya Mountains. It is possible that these are underground civilizations."

"I have a feeling that some day there will come a slow knocking at my own door," Gray Barker wrote in *They Knew Too Much about Flying Saucers*. "They will be at your door, too, unless we all get wise and find out who the three men really are."

Howard Menger, a personable contactee who claimed to have been taken inside a flying saucer and to have talked with aliens, said that when he was living in High Bridge, New Jersey, in 1957, two men in dark business suits came to call on him. "They flashed authentic-looking credentials and claimed to be agents from a government bureau," Menger told Steiger. "They looked like ordinary people. They warned me to quit talking about flying saucers and to drop my research. We had quite an argument, and they claimed to have considerable power. Whether this was power of influence or over ordinary people, I don't know."

In an "Open Letter to All UFO Researchers," which was published in a 1966 issue of *Saucer Scoop*, by the late Joan Whritneour (later O'Connell), Steiger's coauthor of *Flying Saucers Are Hostile* and *New UFO New UFO Breakthrough: Allende Letters*, researcher John A. Keel set forth his opinion that the Men in Black are the "intelligence arm of a large and possibly hostile group." After discussing various types of contact, Keel went on to say that he considered the Men in Black to be professional terrorists "and among their many duties is the harassment of the UFO researchers who become involved in cases which might reveal too much of the truth."

> John A. Keel set forth his opinion that the Men in Black are the "intelligence arm of a large and possibly hostile group."

Keel's pursuit of the silencers led him to uncover some extreme cases of personal abuse in which certain contactees or investigators have been kidnapped by three men in a black car. The researcher notes that "it is nearly always three men who subject the victim to some sort of 'brainwashing technique' that leaves him in a state of nausea, mental confusion, or even amnesia lasting for several days."

Keel's "Open Letter" in *Saucer Scoop* concluded with words of admonition and warning:

> We are now on a vicious merry-go-round and we are caught in the middle of this bizarre conflict. Contacts are being made … then suppressed … on a dizzying scale. Information is being gained … and lost … at an ever increasing pace. One of the ironies of all this is that no policeman in his right mind associates black cars, kidnappers, amnesia victims, and black eyes with the UFO phenomena. Many of these cases never get beyond local police departments. Neither the FBI nor any other central government agency is engaged in collecting information on these aspects. Even local newspapers seldom take notice of these cases…. [S]ince the victims are often children and teenagers … most newspapers make an effort to protect young people by suppressing 'crime news' involving them.

> Because the official law enforcement agencies are unwilling, or unable, to cope with this growing situation, it becomes the responsibility of the private civilian investigator to collect and collate the full details on these incidents. The hazards of such investigations are obvious, but the job must be done. And it must be done fast, with courage and intelligence.

All of this has been brought upon us because we have wasted twenty years chasing lights in the sky and fussing with the Air Force. We have allowed a serious and volatile situation to develop under our noses while we played with aimless speculations about the origin and nature of those rather insignificant vehicles overhead. We must switch our attention from the vehicles to the occupants. The menace is not in our skies. It is on the ground—and at this moment it is spreading like a disease across the country and the world.

In his address to the 1967 Congress of Scientific Ufologists, Keel told of his personal mission to track down the silencers. He said that dark-complected mystery men had sometimes silenced saucer sighters *before* the witnesses had had time to report the sighting. On occasion, Keel said, he had arrived on the scene within moments after the mysterious silencers had departed.

According to Keel, the Men in Black visited and silenced eight communities in Washington state in May 1967. Several homes in Long Island were unwilling hosts to the silencers in June.

"The UFOs don't want us to know where they are from," Keel stated. "They have been lying to contactees since 1897!" (Keel explained this reference by stating that the first Man in Black may have appeared in Texas in 1897, when, according to newspaper accounts, some "pottery" had fallen from a mysterious airship. The next day, a dark-suited man of "Oriental complexion" arrived in town and bought up the strange fragments.)

How did representatives of the U.S. government feel about the silencers circa 1967?

"We have checked a number of these cases," Colonel George P. Freeman, Pentagon spokesman for Project Blue Book was quoted as saying, "and these men are not connected with the Air Force in any way." Colonel Freeman went on to say that by posing as Air Force officers and government agents the silencers are committing a federal offense.

No other U.S. security group claimed the MIB in 1967 nor will they in 2013. It has never been within the line of duty of any government agency to threaten a private citizen or to enter his home without a search warrant. No government agent is empowered to demand surrender of private property by any law-abiding citizen.

As visitations of the MIB have occurred to most serious UFO researchers, so, too, the Steigers have received a number of peculiar interactions that seem related to this phenomenon:

- Individuals who discussed UFOs with them or reported sightings of aerial phenomena claim to have received telephone calls from unpleasant individuals who warned them not to contact the Steigers again.

- A friend touring in London, England, suddenly found his path on the sidewalk blocked by three dark-suited men of Asian appearance who inquired if he knew the Steigers; then, when he recovered from shock and admitted he did, he was told to inform them that they would soon receive a visit from them.

- An associate of the Steigers, a former detective with numerous law enforcement contacts, said that an automobile seen following their car was not recognizable as any known make of automobile and had bogus license plates.

- Upon several occasions after checking into hotels and picking up the room telephone to check with the front desk, voices have been heard discussing the Steigers' arrival. The voices fall immediately silent when challenged as to who is on the line.

- Angry communication from individuals claiming that Brad Steiger had engaged in crude and rude behavior at lecture appearances have been silenced when Brad proved that he had not been in those particular cities and had given no lectures on the dates at which those events were alleged to have occurred.

Sometimes, the Steigers wonder if the UFO silencers are really from a secret branch of government. Prior to the Steigers' lecture near a major U.S. Air Force base, the sponsoring group proudly showed the Steigers their new state-of-the-art sound and recording equipment, worth in excess of a million dollars. They assured the speakers that audience members would have access to tapes of the lectures within minutes after the evening's events concluded. Then, in panic and complete confusion, the sound engineers discovered that Sherry's lecture was completely blank, even though sound engineers swore that they constantly monitored the recording process while she spoke. Perhaps the tape was blank because Sherry had disclosed some aspects of her research that had never been publicly revealed.

Once, over dinner at a Chinese restaurant in New York City in 1966, John A. Keel gave Brad several accounts about the kind of paranormal harassment that he had undergone since beginning his investigation of the Mothman near Point Pleasant. Most unsettling were his accounts of the infamous "three Men in Black" who had visited him, threatened him, and given him a remarkable display of their abilities. Keel confided that he had observed a repertoire of preternatural talents that had profoundly demonstrated that those particular MIB were beings "beyond the ken of mortal men."

Just exactly what is the "silence group" that seems determined to make a sinister battleground of flying saucer research? Are they, in spite of official denials, agents from a top-secret U.S. government agency, which knows the answer to the flying saucer enigma and has been commissioned to keep the truth from the American public? Could they be agents from another terrestrial political system that endeavors to guard its secret just a bit longer? Or, as some researchers have theorized, could the silencers and the UFOs be coming from an older terrestrial race that has survived and become more technically advanced as it thrives in some remote region of Earth? Whoever composes this persistent silence group either know—or give the impression of knowing—a great deal more about the universe than we at our present level of scientific knowledge have been able to guess.

THE THING ON JOHN'S BED

By Pastor Robin Swope

As a late baby boomer, I experienced much of the '60s counterculture. Free love and free drugs were the motto of the times in which I grew from childhood to adolescence. I had many a friend who never made it to adulthood; and if they did, by the time of this writing, they are more than likely consigned to the care of a nursing home or an adult care facility. Observing the negative effects and the inevitable consequences suffered by many of those who abandoned themselves to the Age of Aquarius served as a warning for me.

Johnny was a friend of mine who loved getting high. One night after a long evening of partying, he went home to his basement bedroom to listen to some relaxing music in the dark.

He did not know how long it was before a loud sound roused him from his half slumber. With a quick flip of a switch, his night light came on, and he sat up to see what had caused the commotion.

That was when he saw the thing scurry across the floor.

It had quickly made its way from the bathroom to duck behind a pile of clothes to the left of his bed. He could barely discern what exactly it was but it was small, short, and bipedal. It ran faster than his cat, and it had made the four-foot run in a split second. It was also very dark in color.

It was not a squirrel. This was the northeastern United States, so it could not have been any kind of monkey. The odd thing was that that was what it looked like—a miniature human scuttling across the floor. It did not slump its back as it ran from the restroom to the pile of clothes in the corner. No, it looked like a husky little man in the dark as it passed into the pile of soiled apparel.

Panicked, Johnny was unsure as to what to do next. He decided to stay in the safety of his bed, and he pulled the covers up a bit to hide in the safe and warm, self-made cocoon.

As he sat there looking into the dark recesses of the basement for any sign of movement near the laundry pile, he was sure he saw something in the back of the room. It darted to and fro, as if it were trapped in the semi-darkness of the room. It appeared to stay in the safety of the shadows so it could not be fully seen by the young teen in his bed. However, its frantic movement betrayed Johnny's observation that it was clearly seeking escape.

Soon the movement abruptly stopped.

The shadow grew larger as the thing came closer in the darkness, slowly making its way to the edge of the bed.

In the seconds when it disappeared at the bed's edge, Johnny did not know whether to feel relief or panic. Had it retreated to his worst nightmare to plague him no more, or was it lurking under his bed waiting for him to come out from under the covers so that it might do its diabolical deeds upon his soft, pink flesh?

Johnny saw something scurry across the floor in his bedroom. It looked to be small, short, and bipedal. (*Art by Ricardo Pustanio*)

The seconds seemed to span an eternity as Johnny waited for a movement from above the bed or under it. Then as the horror of the reality that was to befall him permeated his mind, his spine became as a frozen icicle hanging down from a lonely, woebegone ledge.

He felt a tug on the comforter that he had so desperately pulled tight to his body, and a single, lone hand of impish size came over the edge of the bed. It was soon followed by its equally unwelcome twin.

The comforter was pulled down from Johnny's clutching hands as the weight of the thing bore down at its edge.

Soon the full body of the being came into sight.

It had a face circled in dark, oily hair, and its dark skin glistened in the ambient lighting. It almost looked human—if a human face could have been forged in the depths of hell by a creator who had no pattern with which to form it. The thing had the basics of twin eyes and ears, but they were both disproportionate and at odd angles. The mouth twisted in a grotesque grin and opened to reveal teeth that made no sense for the small confines from which they had emerged.

As it made its way with dire purpose up the sheet, Johnny was still frozen in fear with the sight he beheld before him. That the grotesque little being meant him ill will, there could be no doubt. But as to what he could to protect himself from such a creature, that was left to his own small wit. Finally as he felt the small feet cross the sensitive skin of his stomach, he knew for a certainty that this was no mere illusion—and he finally decided to act.

In a blur of motion, he flipped the comforter over onto the small beast that dared assault him, and with a twist he enclosed it in the billowing cover of the comforter. He then began to hammer the snare that held the creature against the bare cement floor of the basement.

After a few minutes of ceaseless pounding on the floor, Johnny caved into the fatigue of his overworked muscles and let go of the wadded up comforter. Breathing heavily he fell heavy on the bedside and examined the balled up mass that lay before him.

The twisted comforter containing the creature did not move. It was a motionless wad of fabric on the cold cement floor. Warily he prodded it with his extended foot, but still there was no movement that he could see. With apprehension and a dread that he had never before experienced in his short life, the teen began to unwind the fabric of the comforter to find....

Absolutely nothing.

The comforter was empty. He was certain as he had repeatedly hurled it against the floor that the comforter had contained some considerable mass. But there was simply nothing there.

He breathed a heavy sigh, and in an unspoken oath, he vowed never to mix again the concoction that he had ingested that night—if he could remember what it was.

Through a fitful night of half-sleep, he tried to forget the hallucination that had seemed so real. But whenever he closed his eyes, he saw the creature climb up the bed, and he felt the small, clawed feet dig into his abdomen.

He awoke in the morning feeling worse for the wear, and with heavy limbs, he forced himself into the bathroom to take his shower and to make himself somewhat presentable for the day of work that lay before him.

As he stepped into the shower, he slipped and fell, hitting his head against the thin Plexiglas of the cheap basement shower in his room. The shower floor was slick from an oily residue, and as he regained his balance he saw the thick, dark red ochre of drying blood that covered the floor.

Then, as he strained his head in horror, he saw his gutted and disemboweled cat lying at the head of the shower, with half of its internal organs missing and its body torn apart as if from some savage attack of a primordial creature from the blackness of hell.

His beloved pet had fallen victim to the same creature that had climbed up his bed that very night to assault him.

If it were not for the grisly slaying of his cat, Johnny's experience could be easily dismissed as a psychotic delusion caused by the overindulgence of various mind-altering drugs.

But something tore that poor creature apart that night and made off with various organs. Was it Johnny himself in a panic-induced, drug-induced rage? Or was it the creature he had seen in his altered state of consciousness? People who dabble in various mind-altering substances perceive things that people in a normal state of consciousness have no perception of.

> If it were not for the grisly slaying of his cat, Johnny's experience could be easily dismissed as a psychotic delusion caused by the overindulgence of various mind-altering drugs.

The use of pharmaceuticals to attain spiritual epiphanies can be traced to ancient shamanistic practices by numerous worldwide cultures. Experiential knowledge achieved by these individuals would tend to suggest that the use of psychoactive drugs may tend to open the perception of those participating in cultic drug rituals to attain an altered state of consciousness that cannot be perceived by the most ordinary beings. It is a supplement to the God-ordained spiritual gift of discernment of spirits that can often attract beings of a malicious nature. Some shamans, like many we encounter in our modern society, are gifted by God to perceive a different world around them. They can actually see entities and judge their purpose and nature. In aboriginal societies, such persons who had the gift to sense when oppressive forces were at work also had the power to overcome them. Their role was that of healer, guide, and spiritual leader for the group. But many such roles were hereditary. While many shamans did not rely upon pharmaceutical enhancements of their gifts, many of their offspring, who were not as spiritually gifted, tended to rely upon artificial means to enhance their abilities. Such an abominable practice tends to draw the darkness.

In brief, that is why the Bible classifies witchcraft and sorcery through the words Pharmakeia and Pharmakeus. Drugs provide an unnatural way to attain spiritual enlightenment that can often lead to spiritual oppression. In altered states of consciousness, one can often perceive beings that dwell in the twilight of reality. And some of these twilight beings can cling onto the person for a lifetime, draining their soul and ruining their life.

Real Encounters, Different Dimensions, and Otherworldly Beings

On occasion, Johnny is afraid of the dark. He fears the flashbacks during which he will once again see the little dark man that scurried across the floor. He fears seeing the being that disemboweled and partially ate his cat in the bathtub. He has seen it three times since, but only that one time long ago did it attack anything dear to him or cause any harm. Even clean and sober he feels helpless against the dark forces that he unwittingly unleashed that night long ago in the late 1970s.

Was it all a drug-induced illusion? Perhaps. Or did Johnny really see a dark creature from beyond our realm of the senses that lurks in dark places which we cannot perceive? I dare not guess.

Now well into his forties with a lifetime of experiences behind him, nothing Johnny has ever experienced has been so real and surreal at the same time. All he knows is that the cat was dead, and the horror from beyond the pit of hell that he saw in that abysmally dark basement years ago was real.

To him that is enough.

THE GHASTLY ATTACK IN THE CABIN

By Dan Wolfman Allen

Fall 1996

At the time, I was employed as an auto body repairman/painter in northwestern Washington state and renting a cabin in a rural area. I was living there alone, with my two wolf dogs, Bear and Cub. It was a small house, the type you see throughout rural areas in the North and North Midwest, and not in the best condition inside or out, but plenty for the budget of a bachelor and his two dogs. Because the house had been built in the 1940s, there were always creaks and groans, and I'd never paid much attention to them, especially in an area where heavy rains and storms were normal and frequent.

Anyone who has owned dogs that are 90 percent wolf blood, as both of mine are, knows that they have near human-level intelligence, and by the age of six months, both of them had learned how to open cabinets and doors with their jaws and paws. You also know if you keep them in the house with you at night, owning brand new furniture is not a good idea.

The evening ritual around the house was that Bear would go to sleep at the foot of my bed as the guardian, and Cub, who had a case of separation anxiety, would start the night by lying at the side of the bed, keeping an ever-lasting eye on me as I read myself to sleep. Some time after I had turned off the reading lamp and had gone to sleep, Cub would climb up on the bed and sleep by my side. Every morning I'd wake up to his cheery face welcoming me to another day.

There was a third wolf in my life—my totem and spirit guardian, a white and charcoal tundra wolf named Stardancer. Now and then, my two material wolf dogs would stop and stare at something phantom-like moving around the floor of the house, and I'd always expected they had caught glimpse of her. Anyone with a cat or dog has suspected that animals can see things that we cannot. Through many cases that I have investigated since, I have come to the firm belief that some dogs and cats can see into the spirit world.

Back then, I'd sometimes catch Bear and Cub both looking at something far above the floor. There was a distinct difference when they would watch the low-slung phantom, which I suspected was Stardancer. Her presence would cause them to have playful and quizzical expressions and body postures. When they would watch what appeared to be taller phantoms, their body postures became cautious and on guard. Hindsight being 20/20, I should have paid more attention to this, but being tired from my daily routine, at the time I never gave it much of a thought until that one particular night in the fall.

RICARDO PUSTANIO 2012

His attacker was invisible at first, but then he saw what looked like an old man whose face was contorted in rage. (*Art by Ricardo Pustanio*)

I hate to use the old cliché of "It was a dark and stormy night," but indeed it was. Should you live in northwestern Washington, you would know the type of evening of which I speak—one of those post-summer evenings where the temperature drops, a low, level fog begins to envelope the fields, and a heavy rain hammers the windows. At first nothing out of the ordinary had taken place, just the evening ritual of letting the boys out of the day kennel, feeding and playing with them for a few hours, then cooling down by watching WWF wrestling. I ended the night by reading myself to sleep while listening to Art Bell's guests describe UFO encounters on the radio program *Coast to Coast*.

Shortly after 2:00 A.M. I was jolted from my sleep. Something was putting tremendous pressure on my chest, forcing me nearly four inches into the mattress and keeping me from breathing!

I began flailing my arms about and kicking the sheets off the top of me, trying to fight off whatever it was that was pressing against me. All I could manage was shallow breaths.

At this point in my life, I was used to heavy labor, combined with lifting weights for two hours, four days of the week. I had studied Karate and Aikido, and had trained in medieval swordsmanship. I wasn't an Arnold Schwarzenegger, but along with my Old Norse genetics, I was certainly menacing enough to make a would-be assailant think twice. But here I was, completely helpless to defend myself against an invisible attacker … a feeling to which few can relate!

What was seconds seemed like hours as I continued flailing. At first all I could feel on my chest was a tremendous weight, but gradually, I began to feel what I can only describe as a pair of hands. Continuing to struggle, trying desperately and in vain to wrestle whatever it was atop of me, I managed to lift my head to try and spot whatever it was.

At first, I could see both my wolf dogs, cowering in the doorway, both whining and intensely staring at whatever it was on top of me. I looked upward, in the direction of where my dogs stared. At first I could see nothing, but slowly, wavering air, like the disturbance you would see above a paved roadway in the desert on a very hot afternoon.

Gradually, the fog took form, and above me, I could see my spirit guardian, Stardancer, standing over me.

Continuing to struggle and gain a full breath, I kept my eye on the disturbed air, and an apparition gradually appeared—an image, which under the circumstances, would be etched into my mind forever. I saw the face and shoulders of an old man. His eyes were black as night. His face, though containing the expression of all the pent-up anger of Hell, seemed wrinkled and leathery from years of toil in the outdoors. His short, patchy hair seemed almost a cartoonish representation of a balding man in his late sixties. I had never seen this man before, and I had no idea why he would wish upon me any ill will.

In almost a fraction of an instant, his expression turned from rage to that of one who had seen a ghost himself. Just as instantaneously as it had materialized, the apparition vanished. The pressure on my chest was released so quickly that my chest vaulted upward. As I tried to fill my lungs with the air which they had been deprived for so long, I began to feel a new depression on each side of me on the mattress. It was as though a very large dog were standing vigil over me. As I looked upward, a faint, shapeless fog began to form over my body. I could hear a low growling just above me.

Gradually, the fog took form, and above me, I could see my spirit guardian, Stardancer, standing over me. Her face was pointed toward the window, and she continued to growl toward something I could no longer see.

In the doorway, my wolf dogs gradually ceased their whining, and their expressions tuned from fear to inquisitiveness. Stardancer ceased her growling and turned her attention toward me.

"I'm sorry, Beloved. He's gone now," she communicated to me in what I believe to be a form of telepathy, as I've never noticed her mouth moving when she speaks to me. "I'll make sure he doesn't return."

With that, she turned into a wisp. All the weight disappeared from the mattress, and her spirit form floated toward the window until it dissipated. As I sat upright, breathing heavily, both my wolf dogs tentatively entered the room. Bear, the big bad alpha, sat on his haunches in the center of the room, trading his gaze between the window and myself. Cub walked to the center of the room, first staring at the window, then seconds later, jumped up on the bed and started licking my face. Needless to say, I couldn't get back to sleep for the rest of the night.

A week later, when my landlady came by to collect the rent, I began to question her about any strange goings-on in the house previous to my stay.

She claimed that she hadn't heard of anything. The two former renters had only stayed for four months at a time, but they had not mentioned anything.

I inquired if there had been any deaths in the house. All she knew was that before she bought the house a retired shipbuilder had lived there and had hanged himself in the shed three months after his wife had died.

I remained living in that house for another eleven months with no further occurrences.

ENCOUNTERS WITH A MENAGERIE OF MONSTERS

On November 16, 2011, around 9:00 P.M., a fisherman named Bob saw something unusual along the embankments of the Sacramento River and called the Paranormal Hotline, conducted by Paul Dale Roberts, to report an encounter with a "Wetlash."

Paul Dale Roberts, an experienced paranormal researcher and Director of Haunted and Paranormal Investigations International who has investigated everything from haunted houses, UFO sightings, and vampires to demon possession, asked Bob to explain what a "Wetlash" was.

Bob: My Indian friend calls it a Wetlash. It was the damnedest thing I ever saw. This watery creature came out of the river. It had long ears, must of been about 3 1/2 feet high. It wore knee-high boots, a strange shirt with an open collar, and the longest tail ever. At the end of his tail, he was holding a fish. The Wetlash caught my eye and looked at me with a strange look and went back into the water immediately.

Paul: This is a very strange sighting. Could the sighting be of something else, something natural? Could it have been a glop of water ascending into the air, from the movement of your boat?

Bob: No, it was a creature, it looked like one of those elf-type of creatures from *Lord of the Rings*.

Paul: So your Indian friend calls it a Wetlash? What did he say it was?

Bob: He thinks it was a water elemental and that it came from Europe.

Paul: Water elementals are essentially etheric matter. There are a variety of nature spirits. People know these nature spirits as fairies, ondines, etc. They don't have to always come from Europe.

Bob: If not Europe, then where are they from?

Paul: From all over. The Jews call them Shedim. The Egyptians called them Afries. Africans named them Yowahoos. Persians called them Devs. If this was an elemental entity, it may have been here in America for a long, long time.

Paul: Bob, tell us something about yourself.

Bob: I was born and raised in Sacramento, lived in Carmichael for about seven years now. I am married with three children. I work for the state government. I am an avid fisherman. I love taking my boat out and seeing what I can catch.

Paul: Were you drinking?

Bob: No, I never drink when I am on the waterways!

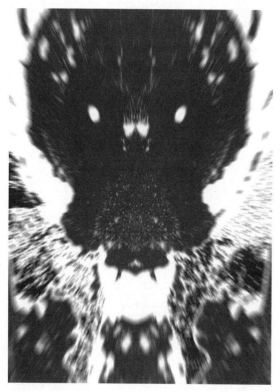

Greg Posada and Eugene Pointer saw werewolves in their home state of Wisconsin. They saw them drinking from a lake before running off. The encounter was followed by a UFO sighting. Are werewolves actually astral beings? (*Art by Ricardo Pustanio*)

WEREWOLVES OF SHAWANO COUNTY, WISCONSIN

We are grateful to Paul Dale Roberts for the details of another intriguing call to his paranormal hotline.

Greg Posada and Eugene Pointer of Shawano County, Wisconsin, called the paranormal hotline with their report of two werewolves seen near Grass Lake on January 9, 2013. They claimed that these two creatures that appeared to be werewolves were definitely bipedal.

One of the creatures had grayish hair, while the other had brownish hair. Both creatures had snouts.

When the creatures were observed, they both seemed to be bent down drinking water from the lake. Eugene and Greg both claim that the creatures sniffed the air and then turned and looked at them. They let off a howl that sounded like that of a regular wolf, then ran off into the nearby thicket.

The encounter occurred around 14:00 hours, and Eugene and Greg were both shaken by this encounter. Greg says that the brown-coated creature was at least seven feet tall, while the gray-coated creature was perhaps six feet tall.

Eugene said that this was not the end of the story. After their encounter with the werewolves, no more than ten minutes had passed when they spied a silver disc in the surrounding forest. The silver disc was hovering and then shot up into the sky.

The sighting of the disc lasted only about three minutes, but during the time of the sighting, everything felt surreal. Everything moved in slow motion.

Eugene and Greg felt relaxed and at ease while they watched the disc in the sky. Eugene does not understand how they could have two paranormal encounters in one day.

[Special Note from Paul Dale Roberts: Bigfoot on many occasions has been associated with the sightings of UFOs. Could Wisconsin werewolves also have a connection to UFOs? I would definitely say it's possible. The surreal effect that Eugene describes sounds like the "Oz Factor," a.k.a. the "Oz Effect."]

Sightings of Bigfoot have been connected with nearby sightings of UFOs, so some speculate there is a connection. (*Art by Ricardo Pustanio*)

The "Oz Factor," Roberts explains, is a term invented by author/researcher Jenny Randles in 1983 to describe the strange, seemingly altered-state-of-consciousness experienced by some witnesses of unidentified flying objects. Randles has noted the strange calmness and lack of panic described by the witnesses, relative to the bizarre circumstances that they experienced, and says that they define the Oz Factor as "the sensation of being isolated, or transported from the real world into a different environmental framework … where reality is but slightly different." The Oz Factor is associated with the fairy tale land of Oz (as in *The Wonderful Wizard of Oz*.)

⊰⊱

WE'VE BEEN SEEING MONSTERS SINCE AT LEAST THE STONE AGE

There is no known culture on this planet that has not, at one time or another, cowered in fear because of the savage attacks of a nocturnal predator known as a therianthrope, a human-animal hybrid such as a werewolf, or a werebear or a werelion or a weresomething. Such creatures were painted by Stone Age artists more than ten thousand years ago and represent some of the world's oldest cave art—and they probably precipitated some of the world's first nightmares.

What could be more ghastly and repulsive to the human psyche than half-human, half-animal monsters that wait unseen in the dark to bite the throats and drink the blood of men, women, and children? Vampires rose from their dank graves by night to sustain their spark of life through the drinking of blood. Werewolves devoured the flesh and blood of their victims by night or day. How could people defend themselves against these blood-hungry creatures when they also had the ability to shape-shift into bats, wolves, and luminous fogs? And then there were the supernatural beings, such as the incubus and the succubus, who were more interested in seizing human souls than in sucking human blood.

It is difficult for those of us who live in the modern world to imagine the night terrors of our ancestors as they prepared to face the demon- and monster-riddled world after sundown. Such researchers as Brent Raynes are always ready to pursue any trace of the age-old monsters that are still reported to haunt the citizens of our modern world.

BIGFOOTS, ELEMENTALS, AND GHOSTS—*OH, MY!*

By Brent Raynes

Brent Raynes has been investigating and researching UFOs since 1967. He is the author of Visitors from Hidden Realms *and the editor of* Alternate Perceptions *magazine. Brent has traveled extensively across the United States and into Canada interviewing numerous witnesses and researchers. He has taken a comprehensive global and historical perspective on the ufological landscape. He has also participated in Native American rituals and ceremonies, gaining valuable insights and information from his interactions with these wisdom keepers. Brent is able to make revealing comparisons between the interrelated experiences and disciplines of parapsychology, shamanism, Jungian archetypes, and ufology.*

On a recent field investigation in which I was called in as a UFO consultant in the rural setting of Deer Lodge, Tennessee, not only did I have fresh leads to probe and ponder with regard to a family who reported both recent UFO and paranormal phenomena, but I was also able to engage in some friendly shop talk with experienced paranormal investigators who would be assisting on this case. I learned of some truly puzzling, potentially revealing, and at times quite disturbing, personal incidents that had occurred to them while they were involved in other paranormal case investigations.

The date was Saturday, July 7, 2012. Chandra Harrison, my daughter and co-host of "Alternate Perceptions" online radio (www.liveparanormal.com), was the driver and I was the navigator. Chandra is also a field investigator for Tennessee Spirits Paranormal Investigations, which is the organization that had extended an invitation for me to accompany them on this particular assignment.

For several years, up to the present, family members at this location have reported experiencing a variety of ongoing paranormal disturbances (i.e., sounds of footsteps where no one can be seen, unexplained voices that sometimes would call their names); the apparition of a tall, dark, broad-shouldered, shadowy figure; a woman who appeared to be from the antebellum period, with a parasol and wearing a bustle dress; as well as the spirit of a little girl who had blond hair and pigtails and wore a blue dress who identified herself as Pearl). On Christmas Eve, the mother and her son, who was twenty-two, reportedly observed a luminous capital H-shaped object moving through the night sky.

[Author's note: With minimal effort you can Google details on H-shaped UFOs being reported by others at other locations. For example, Pittsburgh, Pennsylvania, 2009; Fayetteville, Arkansas, 2011; near Musquodoboit Harbour, Nova Scotia, 1997; and Mount Vernon, New York, 2007 (complete with photographs). The Mount Vernon sighting was in the daytime and suggested by some to have been a mylar balloon. Some are in daytime and some are at night (at which time they are reported to be illuminated).]

Interestingly, when we did a "ghost box" session (an electronic device with which to record ghostly voices) with the family later that night, my daughter Chandra asked the spirits, "They (members of the family) reported some lights in the sky. Do you know anything about this?"

Immediately a male voice stated (and I recorded this) "Yes, we do. During Christmas."

Coincidence? We also asked the spirits to say hello and to give their first names to different family members present. We recorded immediate, interactive-type responses such as, in one instance, "Hi" (and then the mother's first name, just as I had requested). A male spirit who almost always comes through to help with our sessions is named Bishop, and he came through a lot during this session as well.

Bigfoot at Dixon Springs, Tennessee

"It was easily 6 to 7 feet tall," Melissa Argo, lead investigator with Tennessee Spirits, explained to me.

Some reports of Bigfoot do suggest that they're apparitional or at least temporary transmogrifications of matter, more than being simply a straightforward, regular, biological critter from our own sphere of existence. (*Art by Dan Allen*)

"I know what I saw, and it was big, tall and hairy," Michelle Phelps, investigator with Tennessee Spirits, agreed. "It walked out into the open at a nearby clearing, then stopped behind a bush and seemed to watch us for awhile."

"What was weird, was there was a deer or a big dog that walked out first," Melissa recalled. "It did not run. It walked, and when it hit the treeline the other thing followed."

Melissa mentioned that there was a light nearby, plus they had flashlights.

I was told that the eyes reflected light from the flashlight beams. I asked if Bigfoot had been part of the activity reported at the haunted site they were investigating, and Melissa replied that it hadn't been, adding, "That was just an added perk."

The Bigfoot sighting happened at Dixon Springs, Tennessee, a couple of months earlier. Melissa has lived in the country all her life and is very familiar with all kinds of wildlife, but she had never seen anything like this before. She is now a little reluctant to go into the woods alone anymore.

Some reports of Bigfoot do suggest that they're apparitional or at least temporary transmogrifications of matter, more than being simply a straightforward, regular, biological critter from our own sphere of existence. The late psychoanalyst Nandor Fodor's *Encyclopaedia of Psychic Science* has accounts of birds and various animal forms materializing in séances, including an "anthropoidal ape" that appeared several times to witnesses at the famed Polish medium Franek Kluski's séances from 1919 to 1922.

Of course, as my late friend Dr. Berthold Schwarz, a distinguished psychiatrist who delved in-depth into both parapsychology and UFO research, once mentioned to me, addressing these matters and searching for a "unifying theory" for any of it certainly "rouses our deepest resistances." Objectivity is truly a most challenging and difficult course to plot and follow in such strange waters.

A Haunted Bed and Breakfast in New Orleans

Marge Bernstein, a co-director and case manager for Tennessee Spirits Paranormal Investigations recalled how she was once investigating a haunted bed and breakfast site in New Orleans when she had a frightening encounter with what she believes was an elemental being. The house had been the scene of a very violent murder of a mother and her child, and during the investigation one of the team members had been psychically attacked, wherein an invisible presence was strangling this person.

"You could see the hand marks on her throat," Marge told me.

Later, as they were attempting to re-enter the bed and breakfast, Marge saw what a psychic later told her was an "elemental."

"The creature I saw outside the B&B—I hate using movies to describe things—but, I'd have to say its stature and outward appearance was equal to 'Dobby' in the Harry Potter movies. It stood on two legs, had two arms, and its face was like ours except for the mouth area. The mouth was protruding out about two-three inches with irregular teeth. Yellow for the white of the eye. Skin is brown (dirty), and it stood two, maybe two and a half feet tall. I care to never encounter that creature again."

An Elemental Sighting at Stones River National Battlefield

Marge Bernstein described another elemental being sighting, this one a fairy-type entity. She recalled:

This happened at Stones River Battlefield. Two years ago, on the anniversary of the Battle, January 1, three team members and their families joined us to 'investigate' the Slaughter Pen area. Within this area is a walking trail on which I started walking. About half a mile in, on my right, I felt multiple spirit presences. I walked off the path into a wooded area approximately 100 feet from the walking path. I stopped and sat down to see if any of the spirits would talk with me. I always talk to the earth when I'm out in the woods. I feel respect and a connection to these energies that help me to communicate with them at times.

While sitting quietly, I saw a whitish blue light, no larger than a ping pong ball. My feeling was that it wasn't a spirit orb, which I had witnessed at Mt. Olivet Cemetery. When the orb was approximately 15–20 feet away, it looked as though it burst. When the burst happened, a little, very thin woman appeared. Although looking human, I knew it wasn't human nor spirit. She was about two feet tall, white-skinned and wearing a greenish

Marge sensed multiple spirits one January day. She was drawn off a path and into the woods where she encountered fairy spirits. (*Art by Bill Oliver*)

brown gossamer 'dress.' Seeing her was like picking out a person in camouflage amongst the wooded background.

Her eyes were dark-colored. From the distance between us, I couldn't tell you the actual color. She just smiled at me, touched a cedar tree and disappeared. I got up, walked over to the tree that she had touched and touched it myself. My guide then said: "Knock on wood." So I knocked on the tree and said thank you to the being for showing itself to me. The total experience lasted but 45 seconds tops.

"I went home and looked up the myths of fairies and the saying 'Knock on wood,'" Marge added. "To my astonishment, the saying comes from the Irish myth that advises people when entering a forest to knock on the trees before entering to ask for protection and the guidance to catch prey to feed their families.

"Some things I've experienced were beautiful, yet others have given me gray hairs," Marge reflected.

Shortly after Marge had shared with me her elemental fairy incident, I came across this sentence in *Alien Impact* by Michael Craft: "... malevolent evil fairies were said to drain blood from both men and cattle. These spirits were said to flock around battlefields to partake of the lost essence from hordes of dying men."

John Keel wrote in *Operation Trojan Horse*, "Flying lights and spheres are said to accompany some fairies and little people. Witnesses were paralyzed in their presence, just as the unfortunate people who reportedly encountered vampires in central Europe were supposedly frozen in their tracks by some mysterious force or power radiating from the entities."

A Wee Brown Man in Taft, Tennessee

"I have ten acres, a creek and a spring," a lady from Taft, Tennessee, told me recently. "I was out by my creek, and I picked up this really pretty pink rock. I love rocks."

She tossed it down in the grass nearby with the intention of coming back to it later, but when she returned it was gone.

"I said that if there were any spirits there that could help me find my rock [she says she has had psychic ability since childhood], I want my rock. Then I looked, and there it was, right where I had been looking. Then I looked again, and there was this little, little guy. He was a monochrome brown. He had a hat and shoes.

"I've read about the fairy stuff, so I asked, 'Can I have this rock? No strings attached?'

"He said yes, so I picked it up. Later, I felt the urge to put this rock in a tree next to my spring. I went back about a month later and it wasn't there anymore. Tradition has it that elementals often hang out around springs, creeks, swamps, and lakes."

Trying Her Hand at Demonology

Marge has certainly had her share of frightful, gray-hair-inducing experiences, it would seem. A while back she was working on a case in the area of Lewisburg, Tennessee, after which she decided to become a "demonologist." She was with a researcher named Tommy, who utilized rituals of exorcism of the old orthodox Catholic Church, and a psychic named Julia, when suddenly a "black mass" about five feet tall came out of a nearby wall.

"I started screaming, because I got a pressure on my head that felt like my brain was going to crack in half," Marge told me. "I said to Julia, 'What is this pain in my head?! Why is this hurting?' she said, 'It's a psychic attack.'"

Tommy then sprinkled some holy water on the "black mass."

RICARDO PUSTANIO 2013

When Marge decided to become a demonologist she had no real appreciation for the soul-wrenching terrors she was about to face. (*Art by Ricardo Pustanio*)

Marge said, "There was a loud growling sound. I was recording. I had the headphones on and everything. The growl did not show up on my recorder, even though we had all heard it!"

This has happened to Marge and others with her on other investigations— a voice is heard, but it will not record.

Marge recalled an investigation near Franklin, Tennessee, when an investigator asked a spirit for its name. Both investigators immediately heard "Jacob" loud and clear.

"Even though we heard it with our ears," Marge said, "neither of us had it recorded on our recorders."

Raynes' Correspondence with John A. Keel on Alien Entities, Elementals, and Hauntings

How does one explain such contradictory events? More than one person hears a noise, and yet it fails to register on any recorders that were running at the time? Objectively real physical events are supposed to consistently register on such recording instruments. Yet, alas, psychic events seem time and again to contradict the normal laws of physics that operate in the physical world of our everyday senses and science.

In the early 1970s, I corresponded with noted author John A. Keel about such anomalies. He recommended I study the works of a brilliant parapsychologist named G.N. Tyrrell, who had come across the enigma of supernatural voices that sometimes wouldn't record and apparitions that wouldn't photograph.

"I have had experience with this sort of phenomenon myself," he confided in a letter. In *Operation Trojan Horse*, Keel described how he had developed a network of UFO "silent contactees" in his investigative travels through some twenty states. In addition, he wrote how he had actually entered into communication with the entities themselves. He wrote: "When a UFO would land on an isolated farm and the Ufonaut would visit a contactee, he or she would call me immediately, and I would actually converse with the entity by telephone, sometimes for hours. It all sounds ridiculous now, but it happened. My notes, tapes, and other materials testify to the fact."

In our correspondence, Keel shared how some of his anomalous phone calls "failed to record (tape came out blank) or nothing but heavy static was recorded."

Keel was able to speak regularly to an entity named Apol. Sometimes Keel talked with Apol on the phone for up to two or three hours at a time. "I could ask him any kind of obscure question and receive an instant and accurate answer," Keel wrote in *The Mothman Prophecies*. "Where was my mother's father born? Cameron Mills, New York, of course. Where had I misplaced my stopwatch? Look in the shoebox in the upper right-hand corner of the bedroom closet (it was there)."

As he noted the increasing accuracy of other predictions that he had been given, one major prediction really had Keel concerned. The entity had predicted that during an upcoming Middle East peace tour, Pope Paul VI would be knifed at an airport by a man dressed in a black suit wielding a black knife.

"Late that May, UFO entities also declared that the Pope would visit Turkey in the coming months and would be bloodily assassinated," Keel wrote in *Operation Trojan Horse*. "Weeks later the Vatican suddenly announced that the Pope was, indeed, planning to visit Turkey in July."

Fortunately that prediction seemed to sizzle out. But then, in a lengthy letter from Keel dated November 23, 1970, he wrote me: "… the elementals are busy again in my area and I have again been warned about the coming assassination of the Pope (discussed in *Operation Trojan Horse*). The Pope is leaving shortly for a visit to the Philippines, Indonesia, etc. He will be visiting areas where there is considerable political unrest and he could be in serious danger."

Four days later, on November 27, 1970, Pope Paul VI landed at the Manila International Airport and, as Keel later wrote in *Mothman Prophecies* that "the scene described to me in 1967 suddenly became a reality. A man dressed in the black garments of a priest came out of the crowd and sprang at the pope with a long black knife in his hands." Luckily, security guards intervened and the attempted assassination plot was nixed. "The would-be assassin was a Bolivian painter named Benjamín Mendoza, who allegedly practiced black magic and witchcraft," Keel added. "Witnesses said that he had glassy eyes and seemed to be in some kind of trance during the attack."

"Many hauntings are ascribed to elemental beings," Keel also wrote in *Operation Trojan Horse*. From little people to "indescribable monsters" to more normal-looking human beings, the occult literature on such apparitions extends back many centuries.

"The most interesting elemental type is the humanlike being who materializes at séances," Keel added. "Such beings have actually been photographed and examined by medical doctors. The spiritualists have developed their own jargon to describe and explain these unbelievable materializations, but it does seem that these entities are identical to the Ufonauts. ... In the majority of cases, the entity resembles an Indian or an Oriental, with high cheekbones, slanted eyes, and reddish or olive skin. ... Sir William Crookes, the famed physicist, attended no less than forty-five materializations of this kind, photographing and physically examining the entities."

⊸◌◌◌〢◌◌◌⊷

THE MOTHMAN, WINGED MONSTER, HARBINGER OF TERROR AND DEATH

On November 15, 1966, two young married couples—Stephen Mallette, Roger Scarberry, and their wives—were driving through the marshy area near the Ohio River outside of Point Pleasant, West Viriginia, when a winged monster, at least seven feet tall with glowing red eyes, loomed up in front of them. Later, they told Deputy Sheriff Millard Halstead that the creature followed them toward Point Pleasant on Route 62 even when their speed approached one hundred miles per hour.

When the story of the red-eyed, winged monster achieved local circulation, Mr. and Mrs. Raymond Wamsley, Marcella Bennett, and Ricky Thomas stepped forward and said that they had seen the giant birdlike creature near the same abandoned TNT plant a few miles north of Point Pleasant. A few days later, Thomas Ury said that an enormous flying creature with a wingspan of ten feet had chased his convertible into Point Pleasant at seventy miles per hour.

Some said that excited, suggestible witnesses had seen Sandhill Cranes, a large bird indigenous to the area that can reach heights of six feet and achieve wingspans of ten feet. UFO researchers made correlations between bright lights seen in the sky and the appearances of Mothman, suggesting that the winged creature was of extraterrestrial origin. Others theorized that toxic chemicals dumped at the TNT site during World War II may have caused bizarre mutations in wild birds.

More witnesses came forward with accounts of their sightings, and the legend of Mothman was born. Although the majority of witnesses compared the tall, red-eyed monster to a bird the media dubbed the creature "Mothman," because, as writer John A. Keel noted, the *Batman* television series was very popular at the time. "Birdman" didn't seem to carry the same sinister quality as "Mothman," a winged being that comes out at night, a being that might be angelic or demonic, a being that could warn certain individuals of impeding danger—or cause bad things to happen to others.

RICARDO PUSYANIO 2012

The Mothman is a monster with red eyes that stand some seven feet tall. Several who have witnessed the Mothman have later committed suicide or died other unnatural deaths. (*Art by Ricardo Pustanio*)

Intrigued by the stories, Keel visited Point Pleasant on numerous occasions and learned about the bizarre occurrences associated with Mothman's appearance, including the eerie forecast that the Silver Bridge in Point Pleasant would collapse and many people would be killed as a result. It is with Keel that the Mothman mystique began to acquire an existence of its own. In 1975, Keel wrote in *The Mothman Prophecies* that "there would be many changes in the lives of those touched by Mothman," and a "few would even commit suicide."

Mary Hyre, the Point Pleasant correspondent for the Athens, Ohio, newspaper *The Messenger*, became a friend of Keel's and assisted him in a number of his investigations concerning the Mothman. Twenty-six months later, Mary Hyre died on February 15, 1970, at the age of fifty-four, after a four-week illness.

Cryptozoologist Loren Coleman, author of *Mothman and Other Curious Encounters* (2002), has been keeping tabs on the deaths that appear to be associated with the entity on his website www.cryptomundo.com. Coleman lists the demises of at least eighty-five men and women who had some association with Mothman from the 1960s to the present day. A cautionary note here: many of the individuals on the Mothman Death List may have been elderly or ill already.

Coleman's first recorded victims were those forty-six unfortunates who became the Silver Bridge victims, when at 5:04 P.M., on December 15, 1967, the bridge at Point Pleasant collapsed during rush hour. Forty-six lives were lost, and forty-four bodies were recovered.

Coleman lists the demises of at least eighty-five men and women who had some association with Mothman from the 1960s to the present day.

A naturalist, cryptozoologist, and animal expert who appeared on numerous television programs, Ivan T. Sanderson served as Keel's main consultant on the natural history behind the reports of Mothman. Sanderson, aged sixty-two, died on February 19, 1973, of a rapidly spreading cancer.

In addition to John Keel, from 1966 to 1967 no other person was on the scene in Mason County, West Virginia, as often as Gray Barker, a theatrical film booker based in Clarksburg, West Virginia, who became interested in UFOs in 1952. In 1956, Barker wrote *They Knew Too Much about Flying Saucers*, the first book dealing with the Men in Black, mysterious figures who menace UFO researchers. Barker was fifty-nine when he died on December 6, 1984, "after a long series of illnesses" in a Charleston, West Virginia, hospital.

Donald I. North, a Point Pleasant native who saw Mothman in the TNT area in the 1990s, died in an automobile crash in 1997.

On October 24, 2001, Marcella Bennett, who was an eyewitness to Mothman on November 16, 1966, lost her daughter, Robin Pilkington, who was only forty-four. Robin's death would be the first of a wave of witnesses' relatives' deaths during the time leading up to and during *The Mothman Prophecies* motion picture release.

As the movie based on John A. Keel's book began screening on January 25, 2002, Stephen Mallette, one of the first four witnesses of Mothman, was mourning the passing of his brother, Charlie, who had a brain tumor.

On February 15, 2002, soon after the town was bustling with Mothman promotions and attention, one of Point Pleasant's better-known Mothman eyewitnesses, Tom Ury, suddenly lost his fifty-two-year-old brother, Gary.

Ted Tannebaum, sixty-eight, the executive producer of *The Mothman Prophecies*, died of cancer, on March 7, 2002, in Chicago, Illinois.

British actor Sir Alan Bates, sixty-nine, died the night of December 27, 2003, at a hospital in London after a long battle with cancer. Bates played "Alexander Leek" in the *The Mothman Prophecies*. "Leek" was Keel spelled backward.

On August 3, 2004, Jennifer Barrett-Pellington, forty-two, wife of *The Mothman Prophecies* director Mark Pellington, died in Los Angeles. Her husband had included a "Special Thanks" credit to his wife for her support of him on that film.

John A. Keel passed away on July 3, 2009, after a long illness.

⚯

A Late Night Encounter of the Werewolf Kind
By Nick Redfern

Nick Redfern is the author of many books, including The Real Men in Black, Monster Diary, *and* There's something in the Woods.

For the most part, the supernatural, paranormal, ufological, cryptozoological, and conspiratorial things that I write about occur to other people. Just occasionally, however, they have happened to me. And when they have done so, it has been a jarring experience, to say the absolute very least. One particularly memorable and monstrous event took place in the early hours of a morning in August 2002—right during the period of time when I was deeply involved in the writing of my Gonzo-inspired book, *Three Men Seeking Monsters.*

It was around 4.00 A.M. and I was awake and yet not awake. And I couldn't move. I was utterly frozen in bed. I suddenly became aware, however, of something awful: a terrible and infernal thing was slowly heading down the darkened corridor that linked my bedroom to the living room. That something, which I could see in some strange and unclear fashion, was a man-sized figure with the head of a wolf and dressed in a long black cape. It emitted strange and rapid growling noises that seemed to be a language—even though I couldn't understand it— and the creature, whatever its origin was, seemed mightily ticked off about something. As it closed in on the door, I made a supreme effort to move my rigid form and finally succeeded, just as the man-beast entered the bedroom. In an instant it was gone, and I was wide-awake.

Skeptically minded souls might say that because I was so immersed in the writing of *Three Men Seeking Monsters* at that very time, I had a particularly vivid dream which was experienced in a somewhat altered state of mind. Such a scenario is not impossible. Hypnagogia is a term that was coined in the 1800s by a French scholar named Alfred Maury. However, it has a history that extends long before Maury came on the scene. References to this strange condition can be found in the writings of the Greek philosopher Aristotle; in the works of the English Elizabethan occultist, astrologer, and herbalist Simon Forman; and in the written output of the Italian renaissance mathematician and physician Gerolamo Cardano. So, with that said, precisely what is hypnagogia?

Basically, it's a term that describes the stage between wakefulness and sleep—a stage in the sleep process that may be dominated by a wide and infinitely varied body of sensory experiences. For example, those in states of hypnagogia have reported hearing voices ranging from barely audible whispers to wild screams. Others have heard random snatches of speech—largely nonsensical, but occasionally containing unusual fictional names—and others have seen disembodied heads, or what appear to be fully-formed entities in their bedrooms. Humming, roaring, hissing, rushing, and buzzing noises are also frequently reported by people experiencing hypnagogia.

It is not out of the question that this is what I experienced. But, as is the case with so many aspects of paranormal activity, the matter is not so clear-cut. A solid and sound argument can be made that the phenomenon responsible for encounters of the seemingly supernatural kind has the ability to induce radically altered states of mind, perception, and awareness, including hypnagogia. The big question, however, is why?

It may do so to ensure that the witness perceives the phenomenon in a fashion that accords with a pre-planned agenda based around communication, manipulation of the mind, and control of the audio-visual senses. In other words, even if hypnagogia does play a role in the type of experience in which I was immersed, it may be an induced and externally prompted role, rather than one that always occurs purely at random and wholly internally to the person undergoing the experience. And, with that thought fixed firmly in mind, here's where things get really interesting.

The Dream Machine is a stroboscopic, flickering device that can produce startling visual stimuli and which was the brainchild of artist Brion Gysin and Beat Generation-author William Burroughs's "systems adviser," Ian Sommerville. Essentially, the device is constructed from a cylinder with slits cut in the sides, and which is placed on a record turntable and rotated at seventy-eight or forty-five revolutions per-minute. A light-bulb is suspended in the center of the cylinder, and the rotation speed allows the light to escape from the slits at a constant, regular frequency, of between eight and thirteen pulses per second. This frequency range corresponds to alpha-waves, the electrical oscillations that are generally present in the human brain while in a relaxed state.

Studies of those who have used Dream Machines suggest the pulsating light stimulates the optic nerve and alters the brain's electrical oscillations—to the extent that increasingly bright, complex patterns of color begin to form behind their closed eyelids. Invariably, those same patterns turn into symbols and shapes that both capture and transfix the "viewer." In a number of cases, such actions have resulted in the participant suddenly entering into a state of hypnagogia. If such a condition can be achieved via the use of mere light-bulbs and turntables, then the idea that a far more advanced phenomenon—but one that is also definitively light-dominated in nature—could achieve something very similar seems not so strange or unbelievable.

And, still staying on this specific train of thought, there's something else to ponder with regard to this matter of lights being used to provoke hypnagogia and—as a direct result— create startling images of fantastic, non-human entities. In many profound cases of a UFO nature, the object in question is brightly lit. In bizarre creatures cases, such as those involving Bigfoot or werewolves, the "animals" are often described as having self-illuminating, or highly reflective, eyes of a blazing red nature.

An example of a Dream Machine, a simple device in which a barrel with slits cut into it rotates around a light source such as a light bulb. The resulting flickering light is meant to transfix the viewer and cause him or her to enter a state of hypnagogia.

If a Dream Machine and its bright lights can place a person in a state of hypnagogia, which then provokes extraordinary imagery of, well, just about anything, then maybe those brightly lit saucers of the sky and glowing-eyed monsters of the woods are doing exactly the same. Perhaps their very own paranormal luminosity allows them to appear for us in whatever guise they choose—aliens, Bigfoot, fairies, demons, goblins, even the menacing Men in Black—via deliberately created, hypnagogia-style states in the poor witness. Maybe there was more to my early-hours encounter in 2002 than, ahem, meets the eye. And, yes, that was a case of pun-intended!

LOOKING BEHIND THE CURTAIN WHERE MONSTERS EXIST

It was about 1970 when, after almost perpetually traveling hither and yon for nearly twelve years, it finally occurred to us that all these various and ostensibly dissimilar phenomena which we were chasing around the planet to examine might be, in reality, manifestations of a single source, one Great Mystery, as our American Indian Medicine friends would state it.

Could angels, spirit guides, Bigfoot, aliens, fairies, and gods or goddesses actually be a multidimensional intelligence presenting itself in whatever humanoid form would be more acceptable to the percipient than the incomprehensible true face of the Other?

Could there be some as yet unknown physical law that could at times activate (or be activated by) our unconscious minds? In some instances, that

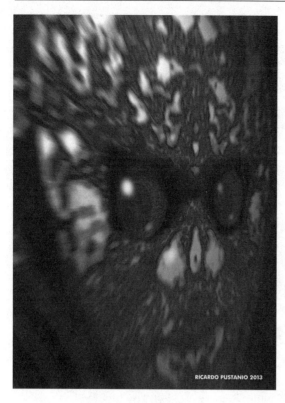

RICARDO PUSTANIO 2013

Could all the strange and unusual creatures that people have come across be manifestations of multidimensional intelligences attempting to assume some form that can be comprehended by human beings? (*Art by Ricardo Pustanio*)

law—or energy—might not itself be intelligent, but it would be able to absorb, reflect, and imitate human intelligence.

At the same time that we pondered these questions, we were aware of the argument that many such entities might be dramatic products of our collective unconscious, with an independent life-force which could sustain itself on our beliefs.

Our late friend Michael Talbot conjectured that it is the subjective and paraphysical aspect of UFOs that shed most light on their nature. If UFOs appeared to be totally a physical phenomenon, Talbot pointed out, it would be easier to deal with them as extraterrestrial or even ultra-terrestrial manifestations. The fact that we have not been able to resolve the conflict between their subjective and objective natures indicates that perhaps the only conflict is in our assumptions concerning experience. Not only must UFOs be considered in both their subjective and objective lights, but the categories of "real" and "unreal" become meaningless.

It may be that one day humankind will be able to see the UFO intelligences, angels, fairies, goblins, and the menagerie of bizarre monsters as they really are, free of all psychological mechanisms and telepathic projections. That day, though, will not come until we have learned to manage our own affairs and until we have realized the liberating truth that we, too, can literally become as gods under God.

After Dorothy, the Tin Woodsman, the Scarecrow, and the Cowardly Lion had endured the tribulations and torments along the Yellow Brick Road and in the Wicked Witch's castle and had learned to manage their own affairs, they saw at last the Wizard of Oz as he really was, a kindly charlatan. Not a bad man, just a bad wizard.

ANGELIC HELPERS AND MESSENGERS

Marianne, who lives in Wisconsin, believes that we each have a guardian angel, but also when we need them most, God sends us special angels. She recalled the cold and sleeting mid-December afternoon in 1988 when she and her fifteen-year-old son left the surgeon's office.

"My son had a growth on his spine that needed to be removed and the surgery was scheduled for January 6, 1989," she said. "I was so consumed with worry that I almost didn't see her standing there—a tiny, elderly nun, maybe five feet tall and 90 pounds, if that much. She had a very concerned look on her face as she peered out the glass doors at the cold December weather. I asked her if I could help, and she told me she couldn't find a ride home to the convent."

Marianne thought this was a little odd. She understood from her years attending Catholic schools that nuns always traveled together. Who would leave a small, elderly nun stranded anywhere alone by herself?

"I offered her a ride back to the convent and she readily agreed," Marianne said. "We talked about many things during the drive, everything from my grade school memories to where I was presently attending church. She had a way of always turning the conversation back to me and my upbringing and faith. She was even able to pull my son into the conversation. This was no small feat as he was in the midst of trying to be the world's worst teenager."

When they arrived at the convent, the tiny nun placed her hand on Marianne's shoulder. "As she did, I felt this wonderful feeling of peace, and she told me in this soft, soothing voice, 'Be close to God, because you never know when you will need Him. Believe … He will not fail you.'"

With that statement she quickly left the car, said her thanks, and disappeared inside the convent's side door. Marianne wasn't sure what she had felt or if it was real, but she did know that she felt stronger and more at ease about her son's surgery.

Six days into the new year, Marianne's son had his surgery, and it was successful. However, the turbulence at home became worse between them, and on the first of March, he and his best friend ran away from home.

For three days, Marianne prayed that the two boys would be safe. "Once again I thought of the little nun who told me to remain close to God because I might need Him," Marianne said. "I really needed Him then."

On the third night after the boys had run away from home, Marianne received a call from the Tennessee state police informing her that they had picked up the teenagers and they were all right. Tennessee was a long way from Wisconsin for two teenagers roaming on their own.

When Marianne's son came home and seemed repentant for having caused her so much worry, she hoped that life would settle down.

"I ended up having major surgery on March 28," she said. "It all turned out well. Six weeks later, I was recovered and turned 40. I was feeling wonderful and thanking God for the miracle He had given me because I could have lost my life if the surgery had not been done quickly."

Marianne said that she was slowly settling into a quiet life when once again everything shattered around them. "On June 21, my mother-in-law passed away unexpectedly and just as we tried to stop reeling from that tragedy, my father was admitted to the hospital on July 25 with a diagnosis of terminal cancer. Life was a blur of hospital visits and radiation treatments and bringing him home just to have to readmit him. We lost him just 35 days later, on August 29."

"I always say that 1989 was the worst year of my life," Marianne commented, "and I don't know how I would have survived it all if it were not for the tiny nun and the warmth that passed through me from her touch."

"I truly believe that God sent her to prepare me for the year ahead. I am not sure if she really was a nun and God used her as His vehicle of grace—or if she had come directly from heaven to that spot near the doors of the medical clinic on that cold December afternoon. But I do know that she was *my* angel, and that I will always believe."

—⫸⫷—

THEIR ANGEL DROVE A WHITE TRUCK

Patricia Ress is a newspaper reporter, magazine writer, novelist, and radio host who has explored the paranormal for many years. She, too, has had her own encounter with an angel:

A man in a truck came out of nowhere and pulled the couple's broken-down car all the way back to their home ... and then disappeared. (*Art by Ricardo Pustanio*)

Several years ago my husband and I were going through a spate of financial hard luck. Nothing dire, just hard on us.

One night we had both been working extra hours. My husband picked me up after work and we were heading home in one of our older unreliable cars. About half-way home, our car engine went out at a stop sign, and we had no idea how we could get help at that hour.

I was beside myself when out of nowhere a huge white pickup pulled up behind us with a hook and chain and offered to pull us home! We agreed and he did.

When we got home, we told the man to wait a moment as we had to open the house and make sure everything was all right. But when we went back out into the driveway, he and his huge white truck were gone!

He couldn't possibly have left that quickly or manipulated his large truck out of the area where he had pulled us in front of our kitchen door! To this day, we believe that this was somehow an angel and it was a message that God was indeed watching over us!

And as a kicker to this angel incident, I turned on the radio to get ready for bed, and they were playing a song called "Angels Among Us"!

⌁∿⌁

AN ANGEL GAVE HIM HOPE
AFTER THE DEATH OF HIS WIFE AND CHILD

Brian was twenty-three years old and on top of the world when Kristi, his bride of three months, came home early from work and told him that they were having a baby. Brian remembered thinking that he had to be the luckiest, happiest man in the world.

Unfortunately, Brian continued with his account, the story doesn't have a "and they lived happily ever after" ending.

About four weeks later Kristi became ill—very ill. At first, her doctor told her that she just had a very bad case of morning sickness. The young couple went along with that diagnosis for about a month until Kristi got worse. She could hardly get out of bed.

After another trip to the doctor's office, the doctor diagnosed Kristi's illness as pneumonia, and he immediately admitted her to the hospital.

Two weeks passed, and Kristi was getting no better. Brian sought a second opinion, and was shocked to be told that his loving wife of barely four months had cancer.

Kristi's suffering was brief, and she and their child—and part of Brian—died three days later.

"Needless to say, my life fell apart," Brian said. "I couldn't work. I couldn't sleep. I couldn't eat. I couldn't function at all. I knew my life was over."

Brian went to a local park that he and Kristi went to often for walks when they talked about their future together.

"I sat there on a park bench for a couple of hours and, to be honest," Brian admitted, "I was strongly considering leaving the Earth and all its suffering behind me."

Just about that time a middle-aged man, a complete stranger to Brian, sat down next to him, and put his arm around him. "He said only a few words to me," Brian said, "words that I repeat every day that help me get through life's hard times. The stranger said, 'You know, He doesn't give you anything that you can't handle.'"

Brian recalled that he literally fell apart and wept openly for several minutes. "I have never cried so hard in all my life," he said. "I felt like the biggest weight had been lifted off of my shoulders. I stood back up and felt just a little bit taller and stronger than just a few minutes before. The man gave me a reassuring embrace before leaving, without so much as an introduction."

"These words were given to me in my darkest hour, and I gladly lend them to whoever might be in need of them at any time. Please don't forget them. Write them down if need be and set them on your desk at work (your boss might even think the sign is referring to him)."

As Brian looks back on the situation twelve years later, he knows that was the turning point of his life. "I now am married to a wonderful woman whom I love very much," he said. "I have two wonderful children who are a blessing, to say the least."

Does Brian believe that the man in the park was an angel sent to him in his time of need?

"I have no doubt whatsoever!" Brian answered emphatically.

ANGELS—MULTIDIMENSIONAL BEINGS WHO REALLY SEEM TO CARE

For centuries now popular traditions have perpetuated the belief that good people become angels when they die. However, in the three Abrahamic religions of Christianity, Judaism, and Islam, angels are a species apart from us who are directed to a particular human or humans for the purpose of delivering a message of guidance, offering spiritual counsel, or in some extreme instances, providing miraculous healing of physical illness or accomplishing rescue from threatening circumstances. If we strictly adhere to the traditional definition of an angel as interpreted by the three monotheistic religions, we humans do not die and become angels. Judeo-Christian scriptures declare that we mortals were created a "little lower than the angels," and we are two very different energy forms.

Although angels are frequently called spirits, it is understood in the Judeo-Christian tradition that they may possess corporeal bodies when seen on Earth. Angels throughout history have often been mistaken for ordinary humans when judged by their appearance alone; those individuals who have confronted them have often felt the physical effects of the beings' otherworldly powers.

In the teachings of Islam, there are three distinct species of intelligent beings in the universe. There are first the angels (*malakah* in Arabic), a high order of beings created of Light; second are ethereal, perhaps even multidimensional, entities known as al-jinn; and third are human beings, fashioned of the stuff of Earth and born into physical bodies.

When people speak of their "guardian angels," they are referring to those unseen, benevolent entities who, according to many traditions, have been assigned to individual humans at birth to guide, direct them, and on occasion, to protect them.

Some recipients of angelic phenomena have come to believe that they were visited by benevolent beings from another dimension of time and space. Perhaps, some have theorized, these Spirit Teachers manifest from another plane of reality, another dimension of being. They may be members of an ancient teaching order from the past, a spiritual brotherhood/sisterhood from the future, or a fellowship that exists in the Eternal Now.

In recent years, the theory that it may have been the angels who created humankind has become increasingly popular. These paraphysical entities, or beings of pure mind, these "angels," continue to shepherd the planet and monitor its progress. Some scholars of the apocryphal texts, as well as those of the accepted books of the Bible, point out that the mysterious beings known as "The Watchers," or the "Holy Ones," have as their mission the observation of humankind.

If you believe that you have made contact with a heavenly being, remember the admonition of scripture to test the spirits. Astral masqueraders take great delight in deceiving humans. The malevolent beings, the so-called Fallen Angels, are always out there, waiting patiently to ensnare the innocent, the unwary, and the unprepared.

Some individuals have been deceived into believing that angels can be made to reveal winning lottery tickets and the names of the fastest horses at the race track. Some who claim angelic encounters imply that these supposed beings can even be commanded to carry out acts of personal revenge.

Those men and women who make such claims have been seduced into accepting the dangers and hazards of bargaining with Darkside entities. A true angelic being would never permit itself to be transformed into a money machine or a thug, but there are malevolent entities that would gleefully appear to obey such commands just long enough to ensnare such greedy and savage souls.

VISUALLY IMPAIRED, SHELLY FELT A STRANGER TAKE HER ARM AND LEAD HER THROUGH THE DARK

Shelly always makes a point of reminding people that they should not place angels above God, but she firmly believes that angels are an unforgettable reminder that God truly cares about every detail of our lives.

The kind stranger helped the visually impaired Shelly to the pharmacy, treating her in such a way that it seemed as if he knew her well. (*Art by Ricardo Pustanio*)

Shelly is visually impaired. "I do have some sight," she explained, "but many factors affect it, such as the time of day, how bright the sun is, how much contrast is in the environment, and so on."

She recalled the "incredibly rainy day in mid-winter" when she was out on the street. "Although it was only 3:30 P.M., it was getting dark," she said. "I fear dusk more than anything. I can see far better at night than when it is dusk."

Shelly was trying to get to a pharmacy where she would be able to turn in her utility bill. It was past due, and she really had to get it taken care of that day—but even though she had been to that pharmacy a hundred times, she had become disoriented in the dusk and the heavy rain.

"The manner in which the area was paved made it hard for me to distinguish between the sidewalk and the street," she said. "When I was nearly mowed down by a car, I stopped to pray. I was soaked to the skin, confused, and on the verge of tears."

Shelly declared that she is quite an independent person, but she realized that there was no getting herself out of this fix.

Real Encounters, Different Dimensions, and Otherworldly Beings

"Lord," she prayed. "I need your help. Please help me."

She wasn't even finished with the prayer when she heard a robust man's voice asking if he could help her.

"I looked up at him, and he appeared to be in his early sixties or late fifties," she said. "He was wearing a blue raincoat and a blue baseball cap. I think he had a patch on one shoulder. It looked like a postman's uniform. He had a ruddy bronze complexion with a shock of white hair just above the roll of flesh on the back of his neck."

> "He knew me better than anyone else I know.... There was no doubt that he seemed to know everything about me."

Shelly explained that she really hated to ask people for help, "because people get carried away with the good deed of helping me until I'm overwhelmed. And they usually ask a lot of irrelevant questions about my condition."

She told the man that she was trying to get to B's pharmacy and that she had to get there before it closed.

"Oh, I know where that is," he said in a cheerful voice.

"Here it comes!" Shelly thought. "Now I'll never get rid of him."

Then, according to Shelly, he did the most amazing thing. "He turned away from me and offered me his elbow. I about fell over. My own parents still try to push me ahead of them if they think I need guidance. Even my boyfriend doesn't know how to guide me."

Shelly took his arm, and found that it was warm and surprisingly dry. As they walked, she became the one who started rattling away about how she got herself into this predicament and that she had almost given up and thought she was going to have to sit somewhere until it got dark in order to find her way home.

"I needed to vent," she said. "I needed to just be heard without being told what to do or what I should have done or having to answer the question, 'How many fingers am I holding up?'"

The man never said another word. He just listened.

Shelly had a profound and growing sense that this man knew her very well. "He knew me better than anyone else I know," she said. "There was no doubt that he seemed to know everything about me."

When they rounded a particular corner, Shelly recognized where they were.

"Oh thanks!" she told her benefactor. "I know where I am now."

But as she let go of his arm and turned to thank him, "There was no one there," she said. "No one. Just the rain. There were no footsteps walking away. Not even a shadow."

Shelly remembered that she seemed to stand on that corner in the rain "… for the longest time, trying to comprehend what had just happened. It just couldn't be, but it was as real as everything else around me. When I thought about it, I hadn't heard any footsteps coming toward me when I was praying. I had been a little startled, in fact, because the nice person seemed to just appear out of nowhere."

Tears welled up in her eyes as she felt the reality of what had just occurred. For a moment, she feared the powerful emotions might pull her to the ground.

"Oh, God," she asked, turning her face up to meet the rain. "Do you think so much of me that you would send me an angel?"

Shelly thinks she's seen her angel possibly two other times. "I'm pretty certain about the second time," she said. "He was walking with a lady. I had a guide dog by this time, but I still on occasion got disoriented. He gave me the directions I asked for, then vanished."

In evaluating her supernatural experiences, Shelly thinks that God really wants people to be mostly unaware when they are interacting with an angel.

"God doesn't want us seeking after angels instead of Him," she said. "I don't think all angels are alike, and I definitely think they very often assume a very ordinary appearance in order to not draw attention away from what is more important.

"After all, it was not really about my meeting an angel. It was about God sending me exactly what His child needed. He just did it in a more tangible way than usual."

—⊸◌◖∫◗◌⊶—

REAL ANGELS DO APPEAR TO BE MORE THAN MYSTICAL EXPERIENCES

Some contemporary scientists suggest that such mystical experiences can be explained in terms of neural transmitters, neural networks, and brain chemistry. Perhaps the feeling of transcendence that mystics describe could be the result of decreased activity in the brain's parietal lobe, which helps regulate the sense of self and physical orientation. Perhaps the human brain is wired for mystical experiences.

While the physical activity of the brain and its psychological state may sometimes serve as a conduit to a transcendent world, we believe that the appearance of the benevolent beings that we most often recognize as angels is far more than a manifestation of a belief in the unknown, a blending of brain chemistry, or a personification of our hope in a spiritual comforter. Angels may truly demonstrate that there is some spiritual reality that exists outside of us, that is interested in our human condition, and with which we may somehow communicate.

While in many instances there is little or no physical evidence to demonstrate any kind of proof of the encounter to the skeptical materialist, the individuals who received visitations from benevolent beings are left with an unyielding conviction that their lives have been forever changed. For some reason which they may never fully understand, they were selected to undergo a mystical experience with a guardian angel, a spirit guide, an emissary of dimensions beyond the known. These ordinary men and women were invited to participate in a very personal, very subjective, extremely illuminating experience that is as intimate, as life-altering, as revelatory, and as unifying as the human psyche can apprehend.

A SKEPTIC UNTIL AN ANGEL SAVED HIS LIFE

"**I** live in the United Kingdom and work in mobile satellite communications," Michael told us. "On this particular day my colleague and I were assigned to work from a farmyard next to the air force base at RAF Fairford in Gloucestershire. I was on the evening shift from 6 P.M. 'till 6 A.M. We were there to provide live transatlantic television feeds of the aircraft taking off during the Iraq War."

At about 3 A.M. in the morning on our second day at the site, I received a call from our clients to tell me to stop the transmissions and take a rest break for about two hours. Our satellite truck has revolving seats and the passenger seat in which I was sitting was reclined and facing into the middle of the truck towards the operations area instead of facing forwards towards the windscreen. The vehicle was completely locked, all doors secured, all windows fully closed. I set my alarm to wake me at about 4.30 A.M., and I soon fell asleep in the reclined position with my right shoulder and head leaning against the side door window.

I have no explanation for what happened next. Suddenly I felt what I can only describe as the fingers of someone's hand prodding me hard on my right shoulder, as if telling to wake me up quickly. In my immediate panic, I realized that I was hard up against a closed window and that this couldn't be possible. Jolting upright, my instinct was to use both hands to push the "fingers" away, but as I did, my hands immediately connected with the closed window. A second or two later, taking a deep breath, I realized that the operations area was full of hydrogen sulphide gas, the smell of which I recognized straightaway, and that the cause must be the generator's battery having overcharged. I immediately flung the door open to clear the air so I could breath properly again, after which I was fine.

I am not a devout or religious person, and perhaps in some ways, I am skeptical of such things. But this experience has left me in no doubt whatsoever that on the particular evening in question, it could only have been my guardian angel who saw my predicament and came to my aid. I can find no other explanation, no matter how I look at the circumstances of what happened.

HIS GUARDIAN ANGEL SAVED HIM FROM DROWNING

General Manager/Ghost Hunter Paul Dale Roberts of Haunted and Paranormal Investigations International told us of an encounter with an angel that saved his life:

> During the hot summer of 1996, I was with my ex-wife, Patricia, and her niece at the Sacramento River. We were lying out in the sun and enjoying the water.
>
> At some point of time, I took the rubber air mattress we had with us and placed it on the calm waters of the river. I was lying on top of the mattress, feeling the warmth of the sun, when a speedboat raced by. The speedboat created high waves, and I found myself falling off the air mattress.
>
> I was in deep water and found myself sinking quickly. I started panicking. I am not the best swimmer in the world, and before I knew it, I hit bottom.
>
> Then all of a sudden I felt hands pushing me, grabbing me and pulling me forward towards the shore. As I

Roberts was not a very good swimmer, but when he fell off his floating mattress and began to sink in the Sacramento River he felt hands pulling him to shore, but neither he nor his wife saw anyone come to his aid. (**Art by Ricardo Pustanio**)

popped my head out of water, I thought for sure it was my ex-wife who had saved me. Then I looked at the beach area and there was my ex-wife talking with her niece.

I was shocked. Who was it who had saved me? I looked around to see who my savior was, so I could properly thank my hero. There was no one around to take credit for saving my life. After a while, I was able to swim the rest of the way to shore safely.

When I got on the beach, I continued to look around for my rescuer. My ex-wife asked what I was looking for. I told her I felt hands and arms grabbing me, pulling me to the shore. When I told her this, she laughed.

> My ex-wife asked what I was looking for. I told her I felt hands and arms grabbing me, pulling me to the shore.

Now, when I think back to this moment, there is only one other logical explanation—it was an angel who saved me. I was saved because it wasn't my time to go. I am to serve another purpose, whatever that purpose may be.

I believe that we all have guardian angels. They are here to watch us, to observe us, to advise us, to shelter us, to protect us. Embrace your angel, because one day you may need its help.

An Angel Brought Her a Miracle Healing from Cancer

Beverly Hale Watson has written thirty inspirational books and prefers to be identified as a minister who has been in service to God for the past forty-three years. She is the founder and director of the Sevenfold Peace Foundation, which has published and distributed spiritually inspired books worldwide for the past twenty-five years. The Foundation, located in Grapevine, Texas, offers intuitive counseling, educational materials, classes, and support services to individuals on their path to enlightenment. The Foundation also works with local community service agencies in providing various types of assistance to people coping with serious life challenges. Beverly sent us the story of her encounter with an angel that resulted in a dramatic miracle healing:

> Hospitalized at the age of 24 for possible breast cancer, I was scheduled for surgery early the next morning. In order to divert my mind from the surgery, I was preparing a Sunday school lesson at approximately 11:15 P.M. All of a sudden I realized that my life was totally in God's hands.

I started to pray and said, "Thy will be done!" Instantly an angel appeared at the foot of my bed. It was a brilliant Light Being (like the sun) that went from the floor to ceiling and the width of the bed. As it faced me, great love poured forth from the angel. At the same time a surge of heat entered the crown of my head, shot through my body, and exited my feet, leaving me with a peace that passes all understanding.

I was wheeled into surgery at 8:00 A.M. the next morning. When the doctors opened me up they found *nothing*—not even what had appeared on the X-rays. All tumors and cysts were gone. I had received a miracle healing.

Three weeks later, I realized that I had been blessed with unexplainable spiritual "gifts" to be used to help mankind. Thus began my life's journey in service to God.

BEFORE HE DISAPPEARED, THE "DOCTOR" SAVED THE LIFE OF HER NEWBORN BABY

Pastor Robin Swope shared the angelic encounter of one of his parishioners when he was pastoring a Christian and Missionary Alliance church in New Castle, Pennsylvania, in his blog article, "Angels of Mercy":

Debbie was almost to term with her baby when she was called out to work. It was time for rush hour traffic, and she took small side roads through the mountains to get to the city. On a narrow curve, she lost control of her car and it tumbled down the small hill off the side of the road.

Luckily the crash was buffered by landing on the limbs of the trees that littered the side of the hill, but still it was bad enough. Debbie had broken her leg in the crash. But she took a deep breath, regained her composure, and fashioned a makeshift tourniquet to stop the bleeding. She flipped open her cell phone and called 911.

When asked by the operator where exactly she was, Debbie had no clue. Unfortunately, this was the early 1990s and at that time they did not have our modern GPS equipment that we use to find stranded motorists. Back then many crash victims would call 911 to ask for help only to let the operator hear them slowly die from their injuries. Having friends in the health care field she knew these stories all too well.

> **S**he knew the search parties sent to look for her could pass by on the road above and not even know she was there.

That was when the panic set in. She knew the search parties sent to look for her could pass by on the road above and not even know she was there.

She tried to drag herself from the wreckage so she could make it to the road above. But in the struggle her water broke.

Lying there in pain and panic, a man appeared, rummaging through the brush. He had a medical bag in his hand and immediately got to work in silence.

Once the baby was delivered and Debbie's wounds were set, they made their way up the cliff to the road above.

Resting at the top on the guardrail Debbie saw the oncoming lights of the sheriff's van come across the turn.

She turned to thank her rescuer, but he had vanished into nowhere.

———

AN INTERNATIONALLY KNOWN DOCTOR DECLARES HIS ANGELIC CONTACT

Who says that scientists cannot be touched by angels? This medical researcher admits that he has received contact with angelic teachers for more than sixty years.

Dr. C. Norman Shealy, M.D., Ph.D., is well known worldwide as an innovative healer and teacher. He is professor of energy medicine, president emeritus, Holos University Graduate Seminary in Bolivar, Missouri, and this is his story:

> For over sixty years I have had sudden important "knowings," sometimes as a vision, sometimes as an abstract understanding. Twenty-four years ago I experienced the first of a few dozen audible contacts with angelic guides. One of the most important took place about 16 years ago, while I was jogging in the woods in Holland. I suddenly had a vision of a copper pyramid with crystals at the top. I made a sketch of this when I returned to my room. The following night my angelic teacher spoke to me: "Where do you think that image came from yesterday?"
>
> I replied: "I thought it was mine."
>
> My guide said: "I put it there. You need to work with that."
>
> I returned home and received permission to work with 75 patients in such a pyramid, activated by a Tesla coil. I treated

them daily for one hour, five days a week, for two weeks, 25 patients each with rheumatoid arthritis, back pain or depression. Seventy percent were markedly improved within two weeks.

But I felt there was no way to get this device approved by the FDA. So for the next 12 years I worked with five other circuits in the human body, developed a specific stimulator, the SheLi TENS, which could reduce pain, as well as selectively raise DHEA (dehydroepiandrosterone), aldosterone, neurotensin, or calcitonin, or reduce free radicals.

The guide gave me the physical locations of points; I had to figure out the proper acupuncture points and the neurochemistry. That done, I came to the conclusion that life could be extended to an average of 140 years if people would just activate at least the three energetic rings to rejuvenate DHEA and calcitonin as well as reduce free radicals. I presented this work in my book *Life Beyond 100—Secrets of the Fountain of Youth*.

As I spoke in over 42 cities about this approach, I learned that a majority of people were not willing to spend 20 minutes a day required for the work. And, in fact, a majority of people were not interested in living even to 100 years!

In January 2007, I awoke at 4 A.M. with the image of that copper pyramid, and knew I had not finished the work given to me years earlier! I then tested the effect of the pyramid on telomere rejuvenation in six volunteers. Telomeres are the tail of DNA and are an accurate reflection of longevity. Ordinarily, telomeres shrink an average of one percent each year. Within three months telomeres had regrown an average of one percent.

As I talked about this, I learned that most people would not put a pyramid in their house. After careful meditation, I realized that the only way this finding might be useful is to convert it to a mattress pad.

Integrating another message from 20 years ago—"If you placed crushed sapphire over the heart, it would bypass the need for bypass surgery"—I created the mattress pad with copper and sapphire, connected to a Tesla coil. This can then be plugged into a timer, so that the entire solar homeopathic treatment (a term given me by the angelic guide) can be done while you sleep.

Within an additional seven months on this device, the six subjects had had telomeres grow an average of 2.9 percent. This means that rejuvenation of telomeres is proceeding at an average of 3.4 percent each year, instead of declining at 1 percent per year.

I have applied for a patent on this approach. It will be my 11th patent. All have been the result of angelic guidance!

Indeed, I consider my entire career guided by angelic wisdom.

I have documented much of my 85 percent successful therapeutic approach in over 30,000 patients in a DVD, *Medical Renaissance: The Secret Code.*

⸺◦⟨⟨⟨⟩⟩⟩◦⸻

THE AMAZING BUTTERFLY PEOPLE WHO BROUGHT COMFORT TO THE TORNADO-RAVAGED CITY OF JOPLIN, MISSOURI

Astonishing stories of the Butterfly People began to rise out of the horror and devastation of the tornado that ravaged Joplin, Missouri, on May 22, 2011. The tornado killed 161 people, shattered and shredded more than nine hundred homes, and collapsed large business buildings. Small children, some two and three years old, described their rescues from the deadly winds and attributed their safety to the Butterfly People. Some adults who heard the strange descriptions of the beings as "butterflies" made an insightful answer to the seeming theological confusion. Very young children may not have known what angels were or how they were supposed to appear to humans, but they did know about butterflies.

There were many accounts of miracles in Joplin during the terror wrought by the tornado. A four-year-old boy was snatched up by the strong winds and carried away to be deposited without a scratch in a field six miles from his home. His answer to the deputies who recovered him was that beautiful angels held on to him all during his flight.

A little girl, not yet three years old, told how the Butterfly People kept her father and her safe in their airborne automobile. When she was corrected by a well-intentioned listener who told her that she and her father were alone in their car when the wind lifted them aloft, the girl insisted that Butterfly People were with them all the way.

Some of the older children identified their rescuers and protectors as angels, but described their beautiful wings as those of huge butterflies. In the parlance of the day, nearly all the children said that the butterfly-like wings were "awesome."

In the December 19, 2011, issue of the *St. Louis Post-Dispatch*, Todd C. Frankel reviewed the stories of the Butterfly People that had circulated in the chaotic first days after the tornado: "The stories were shared in hospital wait-

The devastation of Joplin, Missouri, by a tornado in 2011 was nearly total. The Butterfly People came to the aid of the victims of this tragedy.

ing rooms and in lines for donated food.... The stories about Butterfly People coursed through Joplin, passing one by one and then by the many, tales describing what children reported seeing on that Sunday night in May as the tornado bore down. The children said the Butterfly People protected them. These stories, tales of guardian angels, could be dismissed as a child's fanciful imagination. But the stories have taken hold here."

CLARISA BERNHARDT'S MESSAGE FROM THE ARCHANGEL RAPHAEL

Clarisa Bernhardt is one of today's leading psychics who first came to national attention because of the accuracy of her predictions regarding earthquakes. The "Earthquake Lady" soon became popular as a psychic to many Hollywood stars and celebrities, and in one dramatic instance, may have been instrumental in saving the life of President Gerald Ford. Clarisa also writes a regular astrological column for Shirley MacLaine's website. Clarisa is widely recognized for her mediumistic abilities and her regular angelic communications.

> In one of my angelic communications, they expressed to me the importance for people to be aware that they are *not* limited to Christmas time of the year and can appear with a message any-where or at any moment.

Real Encounters, Different Dimensions, and Otherworldly Beings

RICARDO PUSTANIO 2012

Psychic Clarisa Bernhardt is known not only for her ability to predict earthquakes but also for her communications with angels, including the Archangel Raphael. (*Art by Ricardo Pustanio*)

In a beautiful vision, the angels also told me they so want to help people, but they must be asked. Usually, after a brief message, they are gone. However, on this one occasion they lingered and then stepped forward to me and said that they were so surprised that more people did not ask for help.

From that moment on I have tried to let people know that the angels truly want to help, but there seems to be an important divine rule that they must be asked.

You are helping angels to fulfill their destiny by *asking* them for that help. You can help the angels by communicating to them, simply by speaking softly as you see them in your heart. Have no doubt, they will try to help you as they are allowed.

I feel blessed to have received several communications on numerous occasions from the Archangel Raphael. Earlier this year the Archangel gave me a message that just might be encouraging to others in seemingly difficult times such as the world is currently experiencing. He usually speaks to me of Hope, and I always try to share his thoughts in my column when he communicates to me and I would like to share this one now with you.

A Message from the Archangel Raphael, Given to Clarisa Bernhardt—© May 2008

When you find Hope; embrace it with the inner

Starlight of your heart....

As you walk towards the dawn of a new day.

For Hope carries one through the darkest of nights and times to the

Brightness of a morning filled with shining new possibilities!

If you are looking for something beautiful to give another,

Then simply try giving them hope, and you will find that you

Have also given it to yourself.

ENCOUNTERING SPIRIT GUIDES AND TEACHERS

When spirit mediums or channelers speak of their guide, they are referring to an entity from the Other Side who assists them in establishing contact with the spiritual essence of deceased humans. The spirit guides of mediums usually claim to have lived as humans on Earth before the time of their physical death and their graduation to higher realms of being.

In shamanic traditions, the spirit guide serves as an ambassador from the world of spirits to the world of humans and often manifests to the shaman to serve as a chaperone during visits to other dimensions of reality. It seems quite likely that today's mediums and channels are contemporary expressions of ancient shamanic traditions.

For the more contemporary spirit mediums, who often prefer to call themselves "channels," the guide may represent itself as a being who once lived as a human on Earth or as a Light Being, an extraterrestrial, or even an angel. Regardless of the semantics involved, today's mediums and channels follow the basic procedures of ancient shamanic traditions.

Native American traditionalists and others who follow the old ways go on vision quests to learn the identity of their spirit guide and their symbolic totem animal manifestation. These men and women trust that their guides are concerned about them and observe their earthly activities. While mediums and most shamanic traditions believe spirit guides may be summoned during altered states of consciousness and that one may pray for their intervention or assistance, there is general agreement that one must never pray to spirits guides or worship them.

Many contemporary spiritual seekers have begun to wonder if the differences between a spirit guide and a guardian angel are just a matter of semantics. As New Age thought began to spread, many wondered whether a differentiation was necessary. Guardian angels and spirit guides are both nonphysical, multidimensional beings whose mission it is to provide important guidance, direction, and protection for their human wards on the physical plane. Nearly all traditions assign the guardian angel or guide to watch over their human from the time of the soul's birth into the physical Earth body until the soul leaves its corporeal shell for the Other Side. Today, more and more spiritual seekers prefer avoiding issues of religious, shamanic, or spiritualist dogma and have begun to refer to any benevolent, compassionate, otherworldly entity as a Light Being.

While mediums and many shamanic traditions believe spirit guides may be summoned during altered states of consciousness, orthodox religious traditions insist that angelic missions originate from a higher power and therefore lie beyond a human's desire to initiate contact. One may pray *for* angelic intervention, but one must never pray *to* an angel. A consistent dogma in all traditions warns against worshipping either angels or spirit guides.

> A consistent dogma in all traditions warns against worshipping either angels or spirit guides.

According to these delineations, we may be making some progress toward drawing a distinction between spirit guides and angels. But when we speak of the concept of a *guardian* angel, the boundaries that are supposed to separate the two categories of ethereal entities truly become blurred.

And when the UFO contactees came on the scene in the 1950s and began to channel messages from the Space Brothers, clear-cut distinctions between angels, guides, Light Beings, and the new missionaries from Outer Space once again became rather murky.

In the 1960s, when we first began seriously investigating the claims of the UFO contactees, those men and women who proclaimed that they were in contact with beautiful, benevolent beings who piloted the flying saucers arriving on Earth from other physical worlds in the universe, we drew immediate parallels between those who channeled Outer Space beings and the spirit mediums who provided inspirational messages from their guides. After we had listened to a good number of sermons relayed by the contactees from the "Orthons," the "Zumahs," and the "Mokas" from Venus and beyond, we saw how similar these messages were to the inspirational words communicated by spirit mediums from the "Katie Kings," the "Shooting Stars," and the "Professor Gillespes" from the Other Side and beyond.

And when many of the contactees told us that the UFOnaut had appeared to them in a "light and vaporous form" because of the different frequencies between our dimensions, we were again reminded of the "light and vaporous forms" that had long been associated with the séance room and the spirit circle.

HAROLD'S SPIRIT GUIDE TOLD HIM
THAT ONE DAY HE'D BE A SCIENTIST

Harold, a biologist from California, indicated in his addendum to our questionnaire that he met the entity who became his guide when he was five years old.

"At the time," he explained, "I thought she was a real, physical person. But then I noticed that she glided, rather than walked; and when she seemed finished with the delivery of her message to me, she simply disappeared. In addition to some rather advanced spiritual concepts, I remember that she also scolded me for playing in the mud on a cold day. After she was gone, I experienced the realization that I had heard her in my head many times before she appeared that day."

When he was eleven, Harold stated that he received a vision of a being that he at first believed to be Jesus. "I later realized that the entity, who said that he would now become my permanent guide, was actually a spirit being who only appeared to me as a figure resembling my concept of Jesus, which was based on a popular painting of Christ. At the time, I was very religious in a strict orthodox sense, and the being understood that I would only accept a spiritual guide in the form of Jesus.

"My spirit guide used some awfully big words which I could not understand at that time, but I was able to remember them until I could comprehend them. Basically, the gist of what he said was that I was to grow to become aware of many things related to the physical sciences and help others achieve a balance between the scientific and spiritual worlds. I have tried my very best to achieve that mission."

CREATING MUSIC THAT TRANSFORMS,
AS WELL AS UPLIFTS, THE SPIRIT

In 1975 two young musicians, Steven Halpern and Iasos, burst into public consciousness, pioneering what came to be known as "New Age Music." We have always referred to these two brilliant and marvelously talented individuals—both of them friends of ours—as the men who brought music of the angels to Earth.

"I've always been strongly attracted to music, although my parents never played any music around the house," Steven said. "My early career as a

RICARDO PUSTANIO 2012

New Age artist Steven Halpern is inspired by the ancient cultures written about by such authors as Edgar Cayce and Manly P. Hall. He also feels a connection to angels, who he feels have on occasion become co-composers. (*Art by Ricardo Pustanio*)

jazz/rock/R&B trumpet and guitar player was transformed literally in an instant, when I was initiated into the ministry of healing music in late November 1969."

In 1971, Steven began to research the healing power of sound in earnest. His studies of brainwave biofeedback demonstrated how music could be a perfect adjunct in yoga, massage, meditation, and all kinds of healing practices.

"Through reading Edgar Cayce, Manly P. Hall and others, I was aware of the secret history of music in ancient cultures. I prayed to discover what healing music would sound like in the late twentieth century," he said.

Steven's prayers were answered in a deep meditation in a majestic redwood grove near Santa Cruz, California. "In that transformative peak experience," he told us, "I received the vision of what this 'healing music for the New Age' would sound like. More dramatically, I suddenly became able to play this music on piano, which was an instrument I had never formally studied.

"I also learned that my process of 'composing,' of tuning in to my Muse, was really a co-creative act," he continued. "Almost simultaneously, I recognized that there was 'a band of Angels' that assisted me when I sat down at the keyboard to play. These beings played through me."

Over the years, Steven has found that this direct inspiration has taken various forms. "Sometimes my physical fingers are placed on the keys," he explained. "Other times I'll hear the upcoming phrases in my head, and then play what I hear. At other times, I won't even be aware of playing music; the boundary dissolves, and I become 'the music.' I become an instrument of the instrument. In other situations, the inspiration comes when I am editing, and listening back to what I believe is the completed master tape. I'll suddenly receive a very clear thought-form, of a specific tone that needs to be added, or deleted, or an entire song re-sequenced in the album's order."

Perhaps most dramatic, Steven said (and was backed up by his studio engineer), are the many inspiring occasions that have occurred while he is recording his albums. (In fact, many of these are brought together in his album *Gifts of the Angels*, which openly acknowledged the source of Steven's inspiration.) At least once in the course of recording every album, the studio would suddenly be filled with a bright, luminous light. On one occasion, Steven almost levitated off his seat, as the sublime energy transported him instantly into divine bliss.

"At first, my engineer thought the electrical equipment had gone haywire," Steven recalled. "I shared my metaphysical perspective with him, and we agreed to refer to these experiences as a 'CVS' (celestial voltage surge)."

Steven's unique use of musical tone, time, and space have inspired millions of men and women who agree with Dr. Larry Dossey, author of *Reinventing Medicine* and *Healing Words*, who declared Halpern "… a musical magician, a healer with sound … Music is one of the most powerful healing forces available, and Halpern wields this medium with immense skill." Marianne Williamson, bestselling author of *A Return to Love*, has observed that Steven's music "has uplifted a generation of seekers. He has created a soundtrack for our evolutionary journey."

In many of his public concerts, psychics and aura readers come up to Steven afterwards to tell him of the angelic beings that they see with him on stage. "I don't see them myself," Steven said, "but I certainly have always felt them."

Steven said that his "band of angels" also has a sense of humor. "On the 30th anniversary of my first recording date, January 4, 1975, for *Chakra Suite*, I was in the studio working on my latest meditative soundscape, *Tonal Alchemy*. Shortly after beginning, I felt a tremendous inrushing of energy, and a total shift in my being. Although I didn't hear voices as such, I was told, 'You didn't think we would forget what day this is, did you? Here's how we want to update the recording of *Chakra Suite*.' In the next instant, I received specific instructions on how to create a new key track and how to resequence in the album.

"I love surprises," Steven said, "and I love how their angelic love continues to inspire and support my work of creating more peace on the planet, and more peace within each of us."

Iasos' family moved to the United States from Greece in 1951 when he was four. He began taking piano lessons when he was eight and flute lessons when he was ten, but by the time he went to college at Cornell University, he found that he preferred pursuing his musical studies on his own, analyzing music from many different cultures.

"Then, around 1968, I began spontaneously and surprisingly to hear music in my mind, as if I were wearing headphones," he said. "This was a most unusual music. Emotionally, it felt much more heavenly and loving than normal earthly music. And it also included many unusual sounds not at all typical

Real Encounters, Different Dimensions, and Otherworldly Beings

of earthly musical instruments. Since this was before the era of electronic musical synthesizers, I had no frame of reference at all for these unusual sounds."

After graduating from Cornell in 1968 with a degree in anthropology, Iasos decided to move to California to dedicate his life to manifesting for others the "heavenly music" that he heard in his mind.

> In 1972, Iasos had a profound mystical experience wherein he experienced a kind of "flash-memory-recognition."

"I didn't think everyone would like it," he said, "but I believed that many on the planet would love it—and that they would find it as uplifting, healing, spiritually invigorating, and harmonizing as I did. But then my logical mind would kick in and say, 'You don't even have the foggiest idea of how to create sounds like those, much less the music itself!' Then to my amazement, I heard a voice inside my mind—very male, very powerful, and with infinite conviction—say to me, 'You can do this!'"

In 1972, Iasos had a profound mystical experience wherein he experienced a kind of "flash-memory-recognition." Although the "flash" may have lasted only one second in linear time, after the extraordinary experience Iasos *knew* beyond any doubt what his life's mission was to be. He also received the knowledge that he was in contact with a one-dimensional being named Vista who would transmit musical visions into his mind so that he could manifest them and make them available to all who would be responsive to such music.

Iasos believes that the whole point of inter-dimensional music is not to gain fame and fortune for its performers, but to create music that would help men and women to make the leap into higher vibratory rates as our entire planet continues to raise all its frequencies to higher and higher realms.

To more completely explain the purpose behind his agreement with the being Vista, Iasos said that their spiritual collaboration was to create and make available:

1. Music that can help Souls achieve an enhanced resonance-connection with the grander part of who they are

2. Music that can function as a vibrational gateway into celestial dimensions of Light and Love and Awareness

3. Music that can facilitate body energies fine-tuning themselves into a higher and more refined resonant coherency

4. Music that can help bridge the connection and merging with one's Light Body

5. Music that can directly nourish the Soul through a continuous stream of concentrated beauty patterns

In the years since Vista first made his identity known to him, Iasos has maintained a connection with the inter-dimensional being. "When a musical vision is transmitted to me, I simultaneously receive three things," Iasos said. "First, what the music is to be, that is, the chords, melodies, composition, and so forth. Second, how to create that music, such as technical tips on how to create special sound effects or sounds for that particular piece of music. Third, what effects that musical composition will have on those people who respond to it. And Vista's read-out on these effects is always perfectly accurate."

Iasos has emphasized that the manner in which he works with Vista is not trance channeling. He maintains that he is always in a normal consciousness state when he is working with the being.

"Perhaps it is more accurate to say that it is an overlapping of our consciousnesses which allows musical ideas to get transferred," Iasos speculated. "Another way of looking at this would be to say that Vista 'superimposes' certain musical concepts over my consciousness. I then experience those concepts as artistic inspiration."

Iasos knows that Vista always and fully honors his free will. "This even includes the possibility that I might at any time decide to no longer work with him. He has never interacted with me to keep me on course—although I am certain that he wishes me to do so. Such beings as Vista have something called 'infinite patience'—a quality I suspect is easier to attain when one is functioning outside the realms of time and space."

If Vista always and fully honors Iasos' free will, how does the being prompt the musician to produce a particular piece of music that he wishes to be created? "To attain his goal, while simultaneously honoring my free will, he transmits a musical vision into my mind that is so beautiful, so endearing, so awesome, so overwhelmingly divine that it melts my heart," Iasos said. "Once I have entered that surrendered state of a totally melted heart, I acquiesce. I say to Vista, 'Yes, I do commit to manifesting this music—no matter what! I will manifest it!' And so far I have always kept my promise, no matter what was happening in my personal life."

Millions of appreciative individuals have found the combined visions of Vista and Iasos to be "overwhelmingly divine." R. Buckminster Fuller remarked that to listen to Iasos' music was "to enter a new and profoundly beautiful world." Philosopher Alan Watts proclaimed that Iasos was "doing the classical music of the New Age." *Keyboard* magazine acknowledged Iasos as "one of the most authentic masters of meditative music."

After years of collaboration with Vista, Iasos met Crystal, the interdimensional being's feminine counterpart, who sends him emotional support in the form of a unique energy called "Liquid Crystalline Essence." Iasos describes these showers of energy as feeling effervescent.

"These showers are like champagne or ginger ale," he said. "They sparkle in a manner that makes me feel very lightheaded and exhilarated. Imagine millions of tiny bubbles of light, all exploding with the happy desire of raising your vibratory rate. However, unlike liquid, this energy totally passes *through* me, filling the mostly empty spaces between all the electrons of my being."

Iasos greatly enjoys feeling the loving and caring energy of Crystal around him. "To have such an immensely evolved being sending me her loving radiation feels just sublime," he said.

───❧ ✿ ❧───

ALL PEOPLE MAY BE POTENTIAL MYSTICS

The great philosopher William James once observed that the Mother Sea, the fountainhead of all religions, lies in the mystical experience of the individual. All theologies, all ecclesiastical establishments are but secondary growths superimposed.

The power of mystical experience lies within each human individual. Although many Western cultures discourage such beliefs, it is our own spiritual connections and experiences that have inspired the religions of the world. (*Art by Ricardo Pustanio*)

Although the Western world has not greatly encouraged the individual mystical experience for the past couple of centuries, it is becoming quite clear to many serious-minded theologians, sociologists, philosophers, and other observers of the contemporary scene that all people may be potential mystics, just as they may be potential poets, artists, and musicians. If mysticism is but another facet of creativity, then it may be set in motion by some singularly significant activating experience, such as when one glimpses an angel, a spirit, a ghost, or a hooded Spirit Teacher. The manifestation of this psychic/spiritual catalyst somehow activates the percipient into receiving his or her first glimpse of a much greater reality that appears to stretch to the farthermost reaches of the universe.

───❧ ✿ ❧───

ENCOUNTERING MY SPIRIT GUIDE AND THE OTHER HALF OF MY SOUL
By Brad Steiger

I shall never forget that night in the summer of 1970 when I was awakened by a strange sound that I can only describe as the buzzing of a metallic bee. Our bedroom seemed suffused by a very soft greenish light. I propped myself up on one elbow and was jolted into full wakefulness when I saw what appeared to be a hooded man in a striped coat leaning over my late wife, Marilyn (1938–1982), moving his arms in a fluid, undulating motion. Shifting instantly to primitive defense modality, I reared back to deliver a roundhouse left. The blow never landed.

The adrenalin was pumping. I was fully awake. But in the next few seconds I crumpled to the bed. I began to weep, not "I would like to think" out of fear, but in awe or confusion. I heard an androgynous voice speaking, telling me not to be afraid. "He won't hurt you," I was told. "You will not be harmed. Listen. Listen."

I have always been a very light sleeper. If I am disturbed during my rest period, it may take me hours to fall back into slumber. For another thing, I have always functioned on very little sleep. I will often lie in bed most of the night thinking through a writing problem or actually plotting out my next day's output. But in this instance, I fell instantly back to sleep and I awakened with no conscious memory of what it was that I was supposed to hear.

When I described my hazy recollection of what I considered a bizarre dream and wondered if Marilyn had experienced anything unusual during the night, she said that she had a strange memory of hearing a voice, but thought that it might have been one of the children talking in his or her sleep.

The next evening I was once again awakened by the buzzing of that metallic bee. This time I could see an orb of green light moving down the hall and turning into our bedroom. I felt a momentary jab of fear. I was lying on my stomach. I slid both elbows under me, banishing primal fear with an effort of will.

The peculiar buzzing sound was coming closer, becoming louder. The bedroom was once again suffused by a greenish light. A tiny orb seemed to be telling me to listen, listen, listen.

I remember hearing nothing, but this time some part of my consciousness must have listened, for I awakened with the outline of a book in my mind.

As soon as I got to the office that morning, I called Tam Mossman, my editor at Prentice Hall, and told him that I wanted to do a book on the spiritual mechanism involved in the revelatory experience. He simply whistled, and told me to go for it. That book was to become one of my most popular and most important, *Revelation: The Divine Fire* (1973).

An interesting and unexplainable footnote to the story of how the book came to be has always intrigued me. Just a few days after I received an advance copy of my published book from Prentice Hall, I received a very strange letter

Real Encounters, Different Dimensions, and Otherworldly Beings

from a musician in Chicago who said that he had received a package with no return address in his mail box. The mysterious package contained a copy of *Revelation: The Divine Fire*. As he glanced through the book, he was startled to see that it was the very book that he had been inspired to write after a hooded figure had appeared in his bedroom the summer before.

As the musician explained to me, he had awakened from this strange encounter feeling excited about writing a book about the revelatory experience that he would title *The Fire of Revelation*. He was so inspired by the mission that he had received from the vision of the hooded being that he began to research the subject. He had even gone so far as draw up a list of interviewees that almost completely matched the individuals that I had included in *Divine Fire*.

Then reality set in, he wrote. He was a music maker, not a book writer. He just didn't have the mental tools to write a book. And he wouldn't know the first thing about getting one published. But, he concluded, he was glad that I had carried out the mission and the message that a very persistent "someone" wanted to get out to the world. One can only wonder how many others had received a similar vision of the hooded entity and were told to write their own version of "the Divine Fire."

Pondering this very interesting letter, I smiled with a gentle shock of recognition. All of my life, since early childhood, I have heard etheric music … beautiful, inspirational music … sometimes complete with vocal choruses. And all of my life, I have been frustrated because I have absolutely no musical talent—even after taking lessons for more than four years.

But, as my friend Iasos told me when I was complaining about my musical frustration, "Isn't writing nearly 200 books enough for you?"

The Spirit Teacher's Second Visit in 1982

In 1982, a little more than ten years after transmitting The Divine Fire to me, the Spirit Teacher manifested in my office in Phoenix when I was working late one evening. At this time I was the editor of a small publishing company and manager of a recording studio, producing other people's books and cassette tapes while striving to maintain my own career as an author, lecturer, and paranormal researcher.

Most evenings, after having worked on my duties for the company from ten to five, I would start work on my own writing projects. On many nights, I would often fall asleep at my typewriter—the same faithful 1923 Underwood that had tapped out *The Divine Fire* and, by 1982, eighty other books—and spend what remained of the night asleep on the floor beside my desk. Every day I was forced to deal with the stresses arising from the financial problems of the company, the individual temperaments of the staff, the eccentricity of one of our principal backers, and the fickle demands of the marketplace.

My Spirit Teacher's materialization on this occasion was in sharp contrast to his prior dramatic arrival in a glowing green orb. I simply looked up from my work and a hooded being was seated across from me on the other side of my desk.

He still wore the cowl, but I could distinguish shadowed male features, a rather prominent nose of the type commonly called "Roman," and a salt-and-pepper beard. During his prior appearances, his voice (or the voice I heard) seemed rather androgynous. On this visit, his voice issued in pleasant, rather deep, male tones.

> The purpose of this visit seemed entirely focused on helping me to decide what my next move should be in terms of furthering my career.

The purpose of this visit seemed entirely focused on helping me to decide what my next move should be in terms of furthering my career. He had come to help me evaluate my options.

While the session had begun in my office, we were suddenly transported to a large room with heavily laden book shelves set against stone walls. I was now seated across from his "desk," a large, coarse, wooden table.

It seemed as though we spoke for many hours, but I cannot be certain if our meeting occurred in linear or other dimensional time. Neither can I recall exactly any nuggets of wisdom to share with others. It was very much like being caught in a memory pattern in which one recalls the essence of what was said, rather than exact words.

During the course of our discussion, I was given to understand that he was a member of an ancient order of Spirit Teachers who manifested from time to time to oversee the fulfillment of certain projects. Since we humans liked to have names for our acquaintances, I sensed that he would be comfortable with "Elijah."

Sometime before the first light of dawn reached through the window shades of my office, he had gone, but he had left me with concepts and information that were acutely necessary to make an intelligent decision regarding the dilemma that had faced me prior to his visit.

Elijah seemed a fitting name for the entity. The parentage of the biblical prophet Elijah is unknown, as if he had just somehow materialized in a time of need. It was said that Elijah could travel from place to place with such speed that it was as if he traveled in a whirlwind. And Elijah was said not to have died: He ascended by fiery chariot. In my cosmology, I could very much accept the proposition that the Elijah of the Old Testament was a multidimensional being.

It is clear from an examination of many biblical references and certain passages from the Dead Sea Scrolls that Elijah was regarded as a helper, a guide

Real Encounters, Different Dimensions, and Otherworldly Beings

who would manifest in times of need. In Matthew 11, Jesus says that John the Baptist was more than a prophet, he was Elijah. In Mark 9:11, after Jesus, Peter, James, and John returned from the Mount after Jesus' transfiguration, the other disciples asked if it was true that Elijah must return again. Jesus answered that Elijah would return to restore all things. As he hung on the cross during his crucifixion, observers stated that they heard Jesus cry out to Elijah.

When I confided to a rabbi acquaintance of mine that I had interacted with a being that I considered my Spirit Teacher and whose name was Elijah, I initiated a great burst of excitement. He exchanged confidences and said that his teacher was also named Elijah.

I want to make it very clear that I am in no way suggesting that the expression of the Other that took the form of my Spirit Teacher was *the* Elijah of the Old Testament, but I do feel that his energy does manifest in the Elijah vibration.

In 1984 Elijah Appears in Order to Heal

A little more than a year later, in 1984, the image of the cowled being came to me at a time when I was truly undergoing a dark night of the soul and

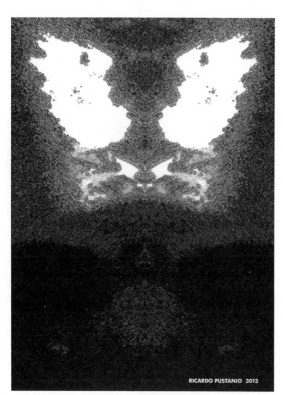

Elijah appeared this time to help Brad heal his own body with special foods. (*Art by Ricardo Pustanio*)

suffering from an extremely painful blight on my physical body. I had become covered with painful boils and swellings, and I had no idea what their origin could have been.

When Elijah appeared that night, he gave me specific instructions to ingest a certain combinations of foods, which I protested would be liable to make me feel even worse.

Rather than scold me for my ingratitude and ignorance, the entity spoke soothingly and assured me that I would get well immediately if I but followed his instructions.

Lying on my bed, unable to bear even the touch of a sheet on my painful sores and boils, it seemed unlikely to me that I would get well immediately, regardless of who told me to eat whatever concoction.

That, however, is exactly what happened. I struggled to my feet, managed to mix the bizarre combination of ordinary food items, ingest it, and within two or three hours all traces of the swellings had vanished from my body. Never to return, I am delighted to add.

Although he did not manifest in any guise that I was able to recognize in the next few years, it would later become clear to me that Elijah had been working earnestly behind the scenes of my life.

Elijah Brought Greetings from a Very Special Person

In October of 1986, I received an invitation from my friend Stan Kalson, the director of a holistic research group in Phoenix, to attend an evening lecture. I hadn't given him a firm commitment about whether or not I would attend the event, but since the metaphysical center was only a short distance from my apartment, I decided at the last minute to go.

Just before the evening's proceedings were to begin, an attractive blond lady asked if the seat next to me was taken. I told her that she was welcome to sit down. She introduced herself as Mary-Caroline Meadows.

After only a few moments, Mary-Caroline turned to me and told me that she brought me greetings from our very dear mutual friend, Sherry Hansen.

I had met Sherry only once five years before, but even in our brief meeting, I had thought her a beautiful and fascinating woman. My curiosity aroused, I asked if Sherry was in Phoenix.

Mary-Caroline said that indeed she was. According to her, she and Sherry took a class together, and when she mentioned that she would be seeing me that night at a lecture, Sherry had said to be certain to say hello to me and to give me her love.

I was suddenly so intrigued to learn that Sherry was in Phoenix that my normally rational journalist's mind did not pause to wonder how Mary-Caroline, who was meeting me for the first time, could possibly have known that she would see me at the lecture that evening, especially since I myself had not known until minutes before the presentation began that I would be there.

What I did not yet realize is that when benevolent beings really want to bring someone together with that special person, they will make it happen.

After the lecture, I returned to my apartment, paged through the Phoenix telephone book, and found the listing for Rev. Sherry Hansen. It took me two weeks to muster the courage to call her, and another three months of remarkable telephone conversations before I asked her out on a late-night coffee date.

As we grew to know each other more and began to share confidences, I told her of my mystical experience with writing *Revelation: The Divine Fire* and my encounters with the Elijah entity. Astonished, Sherry shared her own experience in 1972 with an entity who identified itself as Elijah, which, we ascertained, would have been precisely when I was working most intensely on the book.

Real Encounters, Different Dimensions, and Otherworldly Beings   **231**

Sherry had been meditating during a prayer-healing meeting that she led in her home when she was startled by a voice and vision that was so three-dimensional that she was momentarily confused. In her vision, two sandaled feet began walking toward her, and the closer they came the more distinctly she could see the edge of a brown, monk-like robe. Then she heard a voice cry out, "Elijah!" Silence. Then another call, this time louder: "Elijah!" And a third call, louder still, a shout: "Elijah!"

> It seemed clear to her that people needed to perceive the Oneness and the interconnectedness of all life.

The third shout was so audible to her inner self that it brought her out of meditation. She noticed that everyone else in the prayer circle of about fifteen people had their eyes open and were staring directly at her. Startled that she was suddenly the center of attention, Sherry asked if anyone else had heard a voice call out three times. All indicated that they had heard nothing, but had observed from her countenance that she had experienced something out of the ordinary.

When asked if she wanted to share, which was the usual procedure for anyone in the group when someone has had a vision, a message, or even if restlessness had occurred during their meditation, Sherry proceeded to tell the group that the vision and the voice were so real that when she opened her eyes she had fully expected to see a robed, biblical-type figure standing in their midst. She had thought that the voice calling out "Elijah" had been meant for the whole group.

The next day, as if it were a continuation of the Elijah experience, it was shown to Sherry how she might combine her interests and backgrounds in nursing, healing, the ministry, and counseling. She saw herself establishing a place of education where one could understand how the body, mind, and spirit functioned and interacted. It seemed clear to her that people needed to perceive the Oneness and the interconnectedness of all life, whether it was the relationship of our minds and bodies to the environment, the planet, or to the universe.

It was as if the entire vision of her mission was set forth as she feverishly wrote down what she could recall from an experience that at first seemed ineffable. Over the next many months, the vision began to come together first in words. In 1972 a form of a school and retreat center for families began to emerge. With a great deal of continued research and development, it emerged in the early 1980s as the Butterfly Center for Transformation in Virginia Beach—a holistic school for body, mind, and spirit in which truths might be explored and shared without dogma or labels.

In the spring of 1987, Sherry and I established a business and research association. One afternoon, I received a call from Mary-Caroline, who in the interim months since our initial meeting, had been away from Phoenix, conducting insightful research with dolphins. As we chatted, I thanked her for connecting me with a good friend of hers.

Naturally curious, Mary-Caroline asked who.

When I told her Sherry Hansen, there were several moments of silence. Finally, Mary-Caroline said that she didn't think she knew anyone named Sherry Hansen.

I was stunned. "Of course you do. The night that we met, you told me that you were bringing me greetings from our mutual dear friend, Sherry Hansen."

Mary-Caroline politely repeated that she was certain that she didn't know anyone by that name.

I persisted, "You told me that the two of you were taking a class together. Sherry asked you to say hello to me, to give me her love."

Keeping her voice pleasant, Mary-Caroline said, "Brad, I really do not know anyone named Sherry Hansen, so I could not have promised her that I would bring you greetings from her. Secondly, I have *taught* classes in the Phoenix area, but I have never *taken* a class from anyone in Phoenix."

After I said good-bye to Mary-Caroline, I decided that I would solve the mystery of why she had denied knowing Sherry, and I called Sherry at her office.

"I just had a call from your friend Mary-Caroline," I told her.

"My friend, *who?*" she asked.

"Mary-Caroline. Don't tell me you don't remember. An attractive, tall, blond lady. You took a class with her in Phoenix just a few months ago."

Sherry was firm in her response. "I haven't taken a class *with* anyone or *from* anyone since I've been in Phoenix."

"Sherry," I said, deciding to admit something that I never before revealed, "it was because you asked Mary-Caroline to greet me at the lecture that I even knew you were in Phoenix. It was because of her relaying your message and your wishes of love that I called you."

"That is most interesting, Brad," Sherry responded, "because I do *not* know *anyone* by the name of Mary-Caroline—and I know nothing about her meeting you at any lecture!"

And then, for the first time, it became clear to me. My Spirit Teacher had temporarily "borrowed" Mary-Caroline's body and her consciousness in order to bring Sherry and me together.

The third time that Elijah appeared to me was in my apartment in Scottsdale, Arizona, in May of 1987. On this occasion, our meeting was very brief. He stood looking down at a photograph of Sherry on my nightstand, then smiled at me and nodded. With a final gesture of blessing, he disappeared. He had confirmed that Sherry Hansen was the one with whom I was to carry out the fruition of my mission on Earth.

It is my conviction that I should never directly call upon Elijah, nor should I ask him for help or request his intercession. I heed the admonitions given in numerous sacred works that advise against seeking to summon one's spirit guide as inadvertently creating the risk of worshipping the being or encouraging undue reliance upon one's celestial companion. I am, after all, supposed to learn how to accomplish my mission on Earth with as little help as possible from other dimensional allies. Then, too, there is the danger that if I should seek to summon him, I could be opening the portal to an astral masquerader to pose deceptively as Elijah.

On the other hand, on many occasions, I have been aware of Elijah's subtle influence and inspiration in my life and in my work. And who knows, I may even have met him again in one of his many guises as I have continued on my quest. He may have been the strong hand that reached out from the crowd at an intersection and pulled me back just in time to avoid being struck by a speeding taxi. Or he may have been the stranger who claimed to have been the victim of a pickpocket and needed just the exact amount of money that I had in my wallet to buy a bus ticket home to see his wife and kids.

COMMUNICATING WITH ANIMAL TOTEMS AND NATURE SPIRITS

Understanding the sanctity of nature and having a reverence for life begins with the recognition that we humans are but one species of living beings on the Earth Mother. All living beings are the Great Mystery's sacred creations, endowed with spirit, consciousness, and intelligence. One of the quickest and most effective ways to understand that it is the very same Spirit that flows through you and through all other beings is to learn the proper use of animal symbology in the creation of your own personal totem.

Among the Medicine teachings of the traditional Native Americans, the totem represents the physical form of one's spirit helper. While the Great Mystery lives in everything animate and inanimate, according to the shamans, it also exists as itself. It is above us and at the same time is us. It is not a "God" in the common religious sense of God. Neither are the totems "godlings," separate pantheistic deities. However, there may be a comparison to the concept of guardian angels. The totem entity may in some ways be compared to a spirit guide or guardian angel that presents itself on the earth plane in the form of an animal.

However one wishes to identify and name the animal form that represents one's spirit helper, we suggest that to do so may create a spiritual-psychological mechanism that can bring about great personal transformation and manifest an extended sphere of awareness in an ever-expanding reality construct.

As Grandmother Twylah Nitsch, Repositor of Wisdom for the Seneca Wolf Clan, taught us, the traditional Native American sees the work of the Great Mystery in every expression of life on the Earth Mother. Regrettably, for far too long, such a belief was misinterpreted by the invading Europeans, who in the early days of conquest and mission work saw the native people interact-

Brad and Sherry with Grandmother Twylah, Seneca Repositor of Wisdom.

ing with totem animals and became convinced that they worshipped idols and a hierarchy of man gods. Few of the invaders were able to perceive that to see the expression of the Deity in everything is not the same as seeing everything as Deity.

Dallas Chief Eagle, a shaman of the Teton Sioux, once told us, "The Great Mystery created nature for us to use and preserve, but this gift also imposes obligations upon us. We are only passing through life on the way to the spirit worlds. Always remember that you have to know what you are in order to feel the Great Mystery in nature—and it is only through nature that you can gain communion with the Holy Mystery."

The spirit helper is very often received during the vision quest. Tribal elders and Medicine priests tutor the young initiates for many weeks on what to expect and what is expected of them. Most important, they are made to understand that they are to fast, exhaust their physical bodies, and pray to the Great Mystery at least three times a day, asking that their totem guide appear to them.

Fay Clark, one of Brad's mentors, who was reared in the Winnebago tradition, told us that the shaman advised his group of supplicants that after a few days on the quest, a forest creature would be likely to approach them, as if to offer itself as a guide. The elders warned the young men that the temptation to accept the first animal that approached them as one's spirit helper would be great; but if they were able to endure the continued hunger and exposure, the Great Mystery would be certain to send them a more powerful spirit helper, one especially destined for the individual. The supplicants were told to thank each animal for its coming and to tell it of its beauty, strength, and intelligence, but to also inform it that they sought one even greater. If one endured, the initiates were told, their true spirit helper would appear as if it were glowing, as though it were composed primarily of light.

"One important thing we were taught," Fay said, "we must never call upon our guide until we had exhausted every bit of physical energy and mental resource possible."

Brad received his principal totem animal in August of 1974, when Twylah Nitsch, who had worked with him on the book, *Medicine Power: The American Indian's Revival of His Spiritual Heritage and Its Relevance for Modern*

Man, did him the great honor of adopting him as a son into the Wolf Clan of the Seneca and initiating him into the Wolf Clan Medicine Lodge. His adoptive name is *Hat-yas-swas* (He Who Testifies), and he was charged with seeking out and sharing universal truths. Brad felt comfortable with the wolf as his personal totem and spirit helper. Canids, particularly wolves and dogs, have often appeared in significant dreams that have aided him in solving troublesome problems.

In the early 1990s, we visited Twylah at her home in the Cattaraugus Indian Reservation, thirty miles south of Buffalo, New York. Twylah was a direct descendent of the great Seneca chief Red Jacket, a staunch defender of his people's traditions and a brilliant orator.

Twylah and her family lived in her ancestral home that had been built in 1858 by her great-grandfather, Two Guns. She had preserved the original Seneca longhouse from the old Buffalo Creek Reservation, and this was where the teaching lodge meetings were conducted.

We discussed at length the tribal legends that tell of other worlds before our own having been destroyed and of people emerging from the destruction that had been visited upon a former civilization on the North American continent. The Seneca prophets say that the world has undergone the traumatic experiences of birth, death, and rebirth six times before—and they predict that all of humanity now stands on the brink of destruction prior to entering the final world in our evolutionary cycle.

Grandmother Twylah told us that she foresaw dramatic changes coming to the Earth Mother, who is presently very much out-of-balance, and Twylah envisioned great cosmic beings gathering to assist humankind through this terrible time of transition.

"Thunder Beings are truth beings," she said, referring to these powerful entities who offer humans their assistance. "Their teachings are of truth, and they are filled with love. In these final days, it is important to think of unconditional love and not to permit anything to interfere."

Thunder Beings, according to Grandmother Twylah, have come to assist humanity in the upcoming difficult transitionary period coming to our planet. (*Art by Ricardo Pustanio*)

Real Encounters, Different Dimensions, and Otherworldly Beings

Twylah believed that the Thunder Beings are now speaking to everyone, "but only the awakened Thunder People are listening."

In order to hear the Thunder Beings, she gave firm advice: "Go within … go within … go within. Go within to your vital core."

On August 21, 2007, we received word from Twylah's son Bob Nitsch of the Wolf Clan Teaching Lodge that "our beloved Grandmother Twylah Hurd Nitsch sang her song and made her Skywalk back to the world beyond the Skydome. The way made clear by Skywoman for all humankind to follow."

THE NIGHT I MET MY TOTEM

By Dan Wolfman Allen

Winter 1992

I have been many things in this lifetime—comic book artist, animator, hot rod builder, champion race car driver, painter, mechanic … but things were not always thus. Once upon a time, there was a shy boy who had a hard time saying "no." Serious problems may arise when you combine a malleable age with meekness, and the inability to say "no"— mainly in the form of not being able to tell when you are falling in with the wrong crowd until it's too late.

Picking the wrong school is one of the worst choices I made, for at the time, I not only picked one with a mediocre graphic arts program (one that would not push me and vastly improve my abilities), but it happened to be the Number One party school in the country. I got involved with the wrong crowd right off the bat, and my inability to focus on a single career goal started pulling me away from studies, thereby resulting in my dropping out of college before I could complete a bachelor's degree.

So it was back home and searching for a job. I had a number of low-paying jobs, but I also managed once again to get in with the wrong crowd. I had hit rock bottom.

Although it is difficult to admit now, one night I found myself out on the porch with the barrel of my 8mm Mauser World War II sniper rifle stuffed under my jaw and my finger on the trigger. I had always considered myself a good person; but because of my own actions, I had allowed myself to spiral so far downward I didn't want to live any more.

As I began to put pressure on the trigger, there came a counterforce that began to press my thumb upwards. I couldn't explain it other than some external force, something outside of me, wouldn't allow me to go through with this act. Finally, disgusted that I was even a failure at this, I unchambered the round, flung the rifle into the closet, and tossed the unspent round into the woods behind the apartment complex. I went inside, and it didn't take but five minutes before I fell asleep.

That night, I had a very vivid dream. I found myself in the middle of the woods. It was a dark as darkness could possibly be. I could see the outline of tall, mighty trees against the night sky, but as far as ground level, total darkness.

It wasn't long before I had the feeling that I was being watched. After scanning the darkness, I spotted a pair of glowing, amber eyes staring back at me. After several seconds of locking eyes with whatever was lurking in the darkness, a voice pierced the stillness: "What you were about to do was wrong. Everybody that chooses to take on a physical body has been given a task to perform, and yours is far from accomplished."

Immediately, I shot up, wide-awake. The voice was female—and one of the most beautiful that I had ever heard—speaking to me in a motherly tone. Being rather skeptical, I began making excuses and believing that it was all a psychological manifestation. I had no idea this was the beginning of something that would drastically change my life.

The following four nights, I had the same dream. The fifth night, the dream took a turn. This time whatever was in the forest did not speak. Whatever it was, blinked, and the eyes disappeared.

The next thing I knew, something with powerful jaws and sharp teeth latched onto my wrist. The bite was not so harsh as to break skin, but powerful enough to hold on and begin tugging. I allowed whatever had hold of my wrist to begin leading me to its will. For several minutes we walked through the dark forest, until I could begin to see light in the distance. As I continued to be led, the darkness began to diminish. I could begin to see the lush, moss-covered, old growth forest around me. It was like being in a part of the earth that had escaped the ravages of our current civilization, as pure and pristine as things must have been at the dawn of time.

Finally, we were at the shore of a mist-covered lake. As the jaws released my arm, I came to rest, seated upon a fallen log. As the sweet, calming, motherly voice broke the stillness, I saw her.

At first, in his dreams, he heard the beautiful voice of a woman talking to him, but days later his dream became dark and fangs gripped his wrist, leading him into a forest.... (**Art by Ricardo Pustanio**)

Real Encounters, Different Dimensions, and Otherworldly Beings

Seated on her haunches was a charcoal and white tundra wolfess. Her coat was mostly a radiant white, with a band of charcoal fur beginning at her nose, running atop her muzzle to her forehead, covering the top of her head, extending down the back of her mane to her back, and covering the top quarter and tip of her tail. The charcoal accent also covered all four of her paws and faded halfway up her front and rear lower legs.

I stared deeply into her bright amber eyes and asked, "Are you my guardian angel?"

"We are all merely spirits created by God ... all in different forms that please him, each with a different purpose," she sternly answered. "We have been soul mates since creation. Some, like myself, choose to stay in the spirit world and watch over and guide the ones we love. Others have chosen to take the challenge of flesh together and are overseen by friends and family."

"What is this purpose? Why I am here, and what is it exactly I am supposed to do?" I asked.

"That is part of the great mystery," she replied, "I cannot tell you. You have to find it for yourself. Those are the rules of the game of the flesh. The Master has given you free will for a purpose. I can only guide you; you will have to discover your purpose yourself. When you come home, all will be revealed."

Things did not immediately improve. I had many rough years after this, where I began to improve myself, before things got better. Some things did change immediately, though—things within myself. That shy, easily manipulated boy began to have confidence in himself and would no longer allow other people to push him around. Six years later, I would become a model employee, known never to be late, and someone who worked tirelessly to get things done, no matter what the obstacle. Ever since that first meeting with Stardancer, she has always been at my side in spirit. Meetings by that lake in my dreams are continuous. Sometimes I see her a couple times a week, and then I will not see her for over a year. But she still calls me to our spot for consultation, and there have been times she has even manifested in life-endangering situations.

From 2000 to 2008, my hopes of becoming an auto-racing star were on the rise, and I became a very popular driver, helping kids to achieve their dreams while winning multiple championships and emphasizing safety and many new class packages.

One of the most influential partnerships came in 1998, when I met Brad and Sherry Steiger. Since then, I have devoted my life to the search for truth. Five years ago, I became an ordained Christian minister (non-denominational) and have volunteered countless hours to help people come to terms with paranormal difficulties and other problems in their lives. There has never been a greater reward than helping others, and now I truly believe I have found my true purpose and path in this lifetime.

On more than one occasion, Stardancer, my totem/spirit guide, has saved my life. One time I was driving around a 1991 Chevy S-10, called by auto mechanics a "Beer Can" truck, because of the thin sheet metal used in the modern era of vehicles (now they are even thinner or just made out of plastic). I had pulled up to the intersection right outside of my apartment building (it was a red light). As soon as the light turned green, and I was ready to proceed through the intersection, I heard Stardancer shout, "STOP!" I turned to see her sitting on her haunches on the passenger seat, and she quickly motioned with her eyes and muzzle for me to look forward. As I did, a large, mid-1980s Impala (four-door, full-sized passenger car) came screaming through an open lane, running the red light, and sped through the intersection at over eighty mph! If she hadn't called out, the car would have struck me directly in the driver's door, and with its mass and speed, most likely would have killed me!

> On more than one occasion, Stardancer, my totem/spirit guide, has saved my life.

In the winter of 2008, I was on my way back from work on a cold, icy day. I was in that same Chevy truck, but I had it ninety percent restored. Halfway home, I was stopped at an intersection, three cars behind a red light. In my right ear, I heard Stardancer say, "Put on your top harness." At the time, unless I was traveling on a freeway or on a road with a speed limit over thirty mph, I just wore my lap belts. I looked over in the passenger seat, and there she was, once again, sitting on her haunches, staring at me. After the previously mentioned incident, I knew to pay attention. While the light was still red, I undid my lap belt and slid into the full racing harness, latching up the entire safety belt assembly.

As the light turned green, she whispered in my ear, "Keep it slow, and be ready to hit the brakes." I did so, keeping plenty of space between myself and the car in front of me, expecting the car in front of me to lock up its brakes. She then whispered, "Remember your racing crash training." I had had more than fifteen years of Kart-racing experience.

Just as she finished whispering to me, a late 1960s Ford truck (the era where they still built trucks like tanks) with bald tires, going well over the safe speed limit, started spinning on an ice patch in the oncoming lane, crossed the median and hit me dead in the left front. I had just enough time to do what Stardancer suggested before the impact. My truck was slightly lowered, and the other truck, being slightly lifted, cleared my front bumper and hit nothing but sheet metal. The impact was such that it completely mashed my hood and left front fender, swung the driver's side door open, shattering the glass, bent the radiator back at a 45-degree angle several inches above the base, and shoved the engine back off its mounts.

As the impact ended, I had the presence of mind to kill all the electrics in the truck. I undid my harness, and to the amazement of everyone at the scene, I climbed out the driver's side window (it was shattered out) with no more than a couple minor scratches to my arm! When the police officers arrived, they were amazed to see (from the condition of my truck, which was obviously totaled) that I was up and walking around without injuries, calm and collected. After taking the reports that I was driving well under the speed limit and quite safely, they attributed my condition to the safety equipment I had installed and my racing survival training, though I know it was a bit more than that (of course I didn't tell them about Stardancer and her warning).

Interestingly enough, after the reports were filed and the cleanup was going on, the lady who was behind me in the accident quietly asked me where my dog had gone. "Didn't you have a big white and grey dog sitting in the passenger seat? I thought I saw one while we were stopped at the light."

His Spirit Guide Took the Form of a Bird to Let Him Know Things Were All Right with His Father in Heaven

James, in Edmonton, Alberta, Canada, said that it had been almost eight years since his father had died when he decided to take a walk along the North Saskatchewan River in one of Edmonton's parks. James regretted that he and his father had never been particularly close, and he suddenly found himself missing him dearly.

"I began to remember the lighter moments we had together during my childhood years," James said. "I recalled the Christmases when we shared searching for the perfect yuletide tree in waist-deep snow, the warm summer evenings when he would take me and my three sisters to the movies in his old 1947 Dodge, his laughter when we sat down for breakfast and how he and I would challenge each other to see who could eat the most eggs.

"Now, I stood in the drizzling autumn rain overlooking the river, yearning for those happier times we had spent together. I looked up at the gray sky and began to pray. I prayed that Dad was in a better place. I prayed for his forgiveness for the mistakes I had made in life, as his son. I prayed that he would know that I forgave him for the sometimes harsh ways he treated us. And I cried. I cried because I finally came to realize how much he really meant to me. I cried because I deeply missed him. I cried because, in my heart of hearts, I knew I really loved him."

It was then that James noticed a flock of small birds soaring toward him from across the river. They landed on the leafless branches of willow trees all around him.

Real Encounters, Different Dimensions, and Otherworldly Beings

"Then one of them gave me the surprise of my life," James said. "It flew directly at me and perched, unafraid, upon my shoulder. It chirped and chirped as it actually peered straight into my face. I didn't move. In fact, I was in awe of its candor. It remained on my shoulder for at least a full minute. Then it lifted its wings and rejoined its buddies. Immediately, the birds flew away. Back across the river."

Was it a sign?

James said that he has always believed in angels. "I believe my angel was telling me, through nature, that everything is all right. That my father had received my prayers and was pleased.

> "I believe my angel was telling me, through nature, that everything is all right. That my father had received my prayers and was pleased."

"I believe on that chilly autumn day, when I opened my heart in truthful prayer, God's love shone down on both my father and me. And I was granted a small miracle of acknowledgement from above.

"Today, I am much closer to my dad than I ever was. And I must thank an angel whose sole purpose, I believe, is to watch over me and guide me—in some cases with a miracle—to our Lord's universal home. And my father's waiting arms."

THE INCREDIBLE GIGANTIC BUTTERFLY

Paul from California sent us an astonishing report of what may be among the more unusual sightings of a kind of spiritual totem ever recorded. While we quite often receive reports of individuals having sighted huge birds, larger than condors or eagles, in the skies, we have never received a report of a gigantic, red-orange colored butterfly flying at about ten to twelve thousand feet.

According to Paul's remarkable report:

It was a partly cloudy/partly sunny day where I live in Montrose, California, Los Angeles County, just north of the Glendale/Burbank area. The sky was clear. It was approximately between 2:30 and 3:00 P.M. on October 15, 2010, that I walked to the back of our apartment complex to feed our small group of squirrels and birds. I also went back there to check on one small baby squirrel that was always in the tall elderberry tree. I just stood back there, quietly scanning the tree for "Little Sam" the squirrel, when I noticed above the tree line coming from my right, way out in the sky, a sizeable object that was moving at a steady to moderate pace. It was not soaring fast. Just passing from right to left in the sky.

As I said, it was a clear sky, partly cloudy/partly sunny, and it didn't take long to realize that this object was something quite unique. It was too large to have been a regular bird, and it did not look like an airplane or anything mechanical.

The reason why it was so odd is that, although seeing this from my angle looking up at it, I could not make out any real definition, but I did see what looked like wings above this mass—wings that flapped like those of a butterfly. It looked like how a gigantic butterfly would appear at a great distance in the sky. It was not streamlined nor did it have wings open like a bird soaring. As it kept passing over, I looked at this object that I then considered to be some kind of very large bird because of the wings that I saw flapping— but in the motion that a butterfly would flap its wings.

I first thought that it had to be a huge bird because of the many sightings of enormous birds that have been recorded. And the thought of a gigantic butterfly was, to me, outlandish.

Lastly, I do remember some color in this mass, and to the best of my memory, it had shades of red-orange, possibly reddish-yellow. It flew like it was in no rush at all. I went around the apartment building to see if I could see more of it, but I couldn't. I had not been able to see any real definition like a head or tail, but the butterfly-type wings and motion were standouts in my memory.

Then about a week later, on October 24 or 25, Imelda, a woman in Lake Havasu City, Arizona, provided a much more detailed account of a gigantic butterfly which she reported to Stan Gordon (a writer and researcher on UFOs and the paranormal), who sent it on to me. Here it is below:

> I do not normally do this (reporting what I see) … but I just saw a huge butterfly/bird today! It is now 4:08 as I am writing this, but it happened an hour ago as I went out to take a video of the jet fighter exercises that they always do around this time of the year … [I was] scanning the sky … for the jets with my digital camcorder. I slowly turned around … and lo & behold there it [the gigantic butterfly] was, around 10,000 ft above our house … I was able to take a few pictures, but they are just specks.…

> At first I said to myself: what the heck is that? It had a wingspan of 15–20 feet across. I thought it was an over-sized butterfly with the color of burnt orange or gray-orange, and it was sooo huge! It wasn't there when I came out of the house to scan the skies for the jets, but it just suddenly appeared right above our house some 10,000 ft or higher.

> Under each wing I could see from below … a black circle in a yellowish circle; yellow being thin & the black being the center, and the wings surrounding it were burnt orange. It flapped lightly away from our house (but I did not *hear* it flapping) then

turned around as it reached a group of clouds. Then it just glided so fast back towards our house/above me then glided up so fast … I can't keep up of the other details of how it looked. However, I cannot see any … body on it, just some dark thing in the middle. I cannot say I saw a beak for a bird or an antennae/proboscis for butterfly. I guess because it was too far away to see the "body" or owner of the huge wings.

You be the judge of what it was. If you have seen a [flying eagle with outstretched wings], then that is how the wings would look from below. But since there was the burnt orange color and the circles on its wings, you would think it was a giant butterfly.

I had not heard of a Thunderbird until I searched the net for answers for what I saw. It can't be the Mothman [a legendary birdlike creature sighted in New Jersey] since it wasn't black at all, and I didn't see any glowing red eyes. How it disappeared was more amazing: it passed above me then just glided up so fast then … came zooming down, down, down, but I wasn't able to see where it landed since the roofs of our neighbors' house blocked my view. But I am sure it came zooming down somewhere in the hills.… What was it?

Paul established contact with the woman and received the following from her:

"I believe it manifested to me as a Thunderbird with the markings of the owl butterfly … As I said before in my report, the wings were "out-stretched like an eagle's."

In March 2013, Paul sent us an update of his thoughts regarding the strange sightings of the gigantic butterfly:

It's been two years since Imelda's and my sightings. The Japan quake in Fukushima hit after the sighting. I had a loss in the family that began manifesting two months after the sighting in December 2010. There is a lot more to the Butterfly sighting than meets the eye. I believe it appears to warn, to guide, to prepare and to acknowledge those who are transforming spiritually in their lives, and to those who are doing things to help, assist, and nurture animals and people alike. This has been proven to me over the past two years from what we have received out of the sighting.

Very briefly, my wife and I nurture and take in rescued animals … even wildlife … among them, abandoned and injured squirrels. Shortly after the sighting in November of 2010, I was given an abandoned baby squirrel that was missing one arm up to the shoulder. "Little Joe" is not releasable and we kept him. He's doing fine.

Real Encounters, Different Dimensions, and Otherworldly Beings

The praying mantis visited Paul for a week, staying with him until his loved one passed away, and then, apparently, leaving him a gift. (*Art by Ricardo Pustanio*)

About one week after we got one-armed Little Joe, I was watering my garden. From my pine tree, a praying mantis walked down and jumped very gently onto my arm. It stood up on its hind legs. It had only one arm. I placed it gently on my step. It stood up on its hind legs again and raised its one arm to the sky, as though like a champion boxer would after winning a fight. The mantis stayed about a month, then it left after my loved one passed. Shortly thereafter, I received a very special gift—a weaving of a butterfly-heart. Where it appeared and how is not so amazing to me, because I know where it came from and why. I have it here with me now.

DEVAS, HUGE VEGETABLES, AND THE FINDHORN COMMUNITY

In 1962, three spiritually disciplined individuals—Peter and Eileen Caddy and Dorothy Maclean—established a unique community near the seaside village of Findhorn in northeast Scotland. Attempting desperately to raise vegetables in the sandy and dry soil in order to provide food for their table, Dorothy discovered that she was able to contact the nature spirits of plants. She was informed by the intelligences that they might be considered *Devas* (from the Sanskrit, meaning "shining ones"). She was further told by the Devas that they were of an order of evolution existing parallel to humankind and that these entities wielded vast, archetypal, formative forces that could energize the processes of nature. The "shining ones" also warned that far too many modern-day humans had lost their contact with the nature spirits and with their sense of oneness with nature. Such a separation on the part of a major part of humanity had greatly increased the very real danger of destroying the world.

The Devas provided Dorothy with instructions on how to make the most of the scruffy garden outside of Findhorn, and the three adults and the Caddys' three sons, began to grow huge vegetables, herbs, and flowers of dozens of varieties. Word spread among horticultural experts of such phenomenal produce as forty-pound cabbages, and the Findhorn gardens soon became world famous.

Metaphysically minded men and women came to visit the community and to marvel at the accounts of human interaction with Devas that had resulted in extraordinarily large vegetables and fruits being produced from the rocky, barren soil of northern Scotland. In the 1970s and early 1980s, the population of those who served the Findhorn garden grew from six to approximately three hundred members, all of whom wished to live a conscious, ecologically and holistically balanced existence.

Eileen Caddy published a bestseller, *Opening Doors Within,* a collection of daily inspirations, and in 1980, Dorothy Maclean released her autobiography, *To Hear the Angels Sing.* Eileen's autobiography, *Flight into Freedom,* was published in 1989. Peter Caddy left Findhorn in 1979 to travel internationally and relay accounts of their marvelous adventures with the Devas. He returned regularly to visit the gardens in Scotland until his death in Germany in 1994. Peter's autobiography was published posthumously in 1997.

In 1970, David Spangler, a young American arrived at the seaside village to become a director of the Findhorn Foundation and its community and to serve as principal of the Findhorn Foundation College. He authored *Revelation: The Birth Of a New Age* as well as a number of booklets published by the Findhorn Foundation.

Spangler returned to the United States in 1973, and we arranged to meet for a conversation about Findhorn and the extraordinary Devas who worked with the community.

Brad and Sherry asked Spangler why the entities at Findhorn seemed benignly concerned with helping people to exist. Was it because the woodland or nature spirits are generally concerned about growing vegetables and helping humans to obtain greater balance, or was it that the people at Findhorn had somehow learned to control or channel the energy of these entities in a positive way?

David Spangler: I would say that they [the entities at Findhorn] are benignly concerned about our welfare, at least the majority of them are. But, by the same token, there's an impersonality about that concern, too. I would say that what they are concerned about is the maintenance of harmony and wholeness, a synergistic state within the Earth, and they recognize that humanity as a species is a necessary and vital part of that synergistic state. Therefore, the health of humanity is their concern because it reflects the health of the planet. Also, humanity wields forces at the moment which bear directly on the health of the planet.

In some sense, there's concern for us along the line of self-enlightenment, coupled with an awareness that if their kingdoms are going to prosper, humanity has to prosper in relationship to those kingdoms. At the same time, there's a definite impression given that humanity is important, but not indispensable.

Real Encounters, Different Dimensions, and Otherworldly Beings

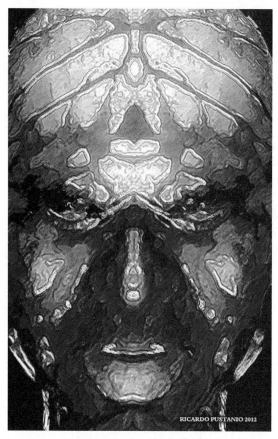

Devas and human beings share a distant ancestral past, but Devas remain more connected to the natural world than humans do. (*Art by Ricardo Pustanio*)

Sometimes we get the feeling they're saying that if humanity doesn't get it together, a whole different evolutionary cycle may take over—which will move us out of the picture, at least in our present state. I would say that there is this concern; and on an individual level, as far as personal contact went, it certainly was interpreted as a benign, personal concern.

But as the entities often pointed out, they weren't as concerned about Findhorn raising vegetables as much as they were concerned with getting across the point of their existence. They felt it was a real necessity that humanity alter its conception of reality so as to include their [the entities'] existence.

Brad and Sherry: Are we humans on the evolutionary cycle of becoming nature spirits—or are the Devas on the evolutionary cycle of becoming human?

Spangler: Actually, it doesn't have to be either one. It can be parallel evolutionary cycles. With the nature spirits, that seems to me to be the case.

Apparently in human evolution, at least on the physical level and to some extent the psychological level, the Devas extend out of a common source with certain elements of the nature kingdom. We're first cousins to each other, sort of like humanity and the ape. We seem to have a common ancestor or, in some cases, we have sprung out of the nature kingdom itself, and we are individualized Devas. But even that isn't exactly true; humanity itself has other antecedents, which are not of this planet.

It is my understanding that elements of what now constitute human nature and human potential—ingredients that went into the mix out of which we are now emerging—are not derived from this planet, either spiritually or otherwise, but come from other sources. In a way, humanity is an evolutionary cycle unto itself, which has overlapped to some extent with Devic evolution or nature spirit evolution—and to some extent, evolution of a transplanetary nature.

The Devas themselves are not all one kind of being. There are Devas that are cosmic in nature; there are also Devas that seem to be planetary in nature. The distinction that I make between the two, between Deva and nature spirit, is more a distinction in terms of the focusing of energy.

What Findhorn calls a nature spirit—the elemental beings, fairies, what not—deals with each specific form of plant or animal entity on a level that could be considered to represent the personality aspect, whereas the Deva represents the soul aspect.

That could also be true for human beings. The soul aspect, to me, is the cosmic aspect and could be equated in some ways with an extraterrestrial source.

I would even divide Deva again to say that there are those Devas which are extraterrestrial in their source, but which are working on Earth energy, terrestrial energy, and non-terrestrial energy. And there are Devas which are working with the nature of our plant and animal kingdom. Now these beings may have come from non-planetary sources at the time Earth came into being, but they have now identified pretty completely with Earth purposes.

Brad and Sherry: Were the people at Findhorn ever concerned about the problem of contacting negative entities?

Spangler: I don't believe in any absolute sense that there are either good or evil entities. What you have are beings who are part of some cycle of ecology. But situations arise wherein ecologies get disrupted for one reason or another, and in that disruption they find themselves part of ecologies they weren't meant for. Or they may find some kind of rebalancing is taking place, and within that framework polarizations arise.

Then I do see the emergence of entities which are anti-ecological, or, to put it another way, attempting to create and impose a different ecological system than the system for which their work was designed. In that sense, one of the most prevalent evil entities on Earth is man!

I view humanity as a species, and I view each of us as a god, as far as that goes. I certainly believe in beings who are more expressive of a creative principle or who can embody a creative principle with greater impact and results than we can at the moment. They would seem, relative to us, to be gods, but we would appear to be gods relative to lesser forms of evolution. I do believe there are definite connections between us and whatever we would look to and say, "These are gods."

Real Encounters, Different Dimensions, and Otherworldly Beings

—◁〜〜▷—

CONTACTING DEVAS

Instruction by Dr. P. M. H. Atwater

Totally relax the body mind and enter into The Silence of meditation, contemplation, or deep peace. Surround yourself with the radiance of protection or simply state in prayer that you are completely protected and only that which is of God and in accordance with God's Truth can ever come to you. It is helpful to do this in a quiet and supportive environment where you feel at ease.

Desire to contact the devic level, and have the clear image in your mind of who you want to reach and why (who in the sense of what deva; the deva of carrots, the deva of mice, the deva of marriage, or whomever—as near as I can tell there is a deva for every element and relationship in the earth plane).

Relax even more and just wait, listen without expectations. Initial contact may simply be a burst of light or a feeling that a powerful presence has entered your awareness.

For most people, more than one try is necessary before contact is made. Seldom do devas communicate in words. Usually their form of communication is to envelop you in the real truth behind your experience. They help you to see and feel what is really at the heart of any issue or situation. Emotions seem not to interest them.

Contact with devas is not always pleasant for they are direct in what they would impart and are not necessarily "courteous" by human standards. Their concerns seem to be based more on your willingness to actively co-participate with them in maintaining the perfection of creation than in the mere "mouthing" of words which make them appear "holy."

The goal of contacting a deva, as I see it, is to gain clear, insightful direction and guidance.

GHOSTS, POLTERGEISTS, AND RECORDING SPIRIT VOICES

Angela Thomas told us that she is a firm believer that spirits are around us more often than not. "Some people can sense them, others can hear them, and still more can see them," she said. "As for the latter, in my opinion, I feel that most of us see them and have no idea that what we are seeing are spirits. Spirits can come across as the living, and unless one is engaging with them, they may appear as people walking among us. The average person may think that only psychics can see spirits in human form; however, most of the professed psychics I have come to know claim they hear them more than see them.

"We are all psychic with degrees of abilities that range from minor to full-blown awareness." Angela said, "but even the very best of psychics don't stop and question each and every image in front of them as one of this world or the world beyond."

As a professional psychic-clairvoyant, Angela has dealt with many spirits; in the mid-1980s, she was gradually and reluctantly coming into her own abilities.

Especially for this book, Angela explained for us what it is like to be able to communicate with spirits.

It wasn't something I'd speak about too often as living in the Bible Belt would almost guarantee accusations of being evil or psychotic. I learned to suppress as much of my abilities as possible by ignoring the truth and denying anything perceived as a psychic ability. And, many times, I had no idea that what I knew was unique. It would take several years to recognize what abilities

I truly had through a series of events. One such event came quite unexpectedly through old friends.

Having moved back to the Mississippi Gulf Coast, I was eager to visit with old friends. I felt especially close to the Russells with whom I had attended school. Shortly after arriving at their home, they led me next door to visit with their grandmother, Olga, who was a charming woman from Panama. I hadn't seen her for many years. Olga was married to Bill, a retired American G.I., who quickly dominated the entire conversation. Bill told joke after joke and between the laughter, he inquired about the car I was driving.

"What kind of deal did you get for that car?" he asked. "How many miles are on it?"

"I haven't the slightest idea," I answered, trying to avoid giving out any financial information. "As for the miles, I never keep up with that sort of thing."

He was quite surprised at how little I knew about cars and proceeded to give me a lecture on how important it is to know about one's transportation. I would learn throughout several visits with him that he was a car fanatic. He would describe the size of motors and schematic detail regarding any car he brought to my attention. While listening to him, I couldn't help but feel he had missed his true calling.

Several months following my last visit with Bill, I received a phone call announcing that he had passed. I attended the funeral mass and followed the procession to the funeral home for the wake where additional friends were gathered. It was there that an event would take place that I will never forget.

All of a sudden I saw Bill walking in the parking lot. He was checking out the cars as if he was a buyer on a used car lot. I couldn't believe what I was seeing.

The main door of the funeral home opened into a large foyer decorated with elaborate drapes, large vases, and floral paintings, a sad attempt to imitate a stately, southern home. I was led to the receiving room for the viewing. Bill's family and friends were seated in folded chairs, which appeared out of place compared to the fixed décor of antique furnishings. Sprays of flowers were spread throughout the room and Bill's open casket lay prominently centered in the room. This was my first wake, and as strange as this sounds, the worst part of my experience was having to bear the weight of the awful silence that seemed to penetrate the entire funeral home. After I paid my respects, I walked to a break room in the back of the funeral home.

Bill's stepdaughter, Dee, was already seated at a table in the break room. She had flown in from Arizona for the funeral. We chatted briefly and promised to catch up before she flew back home. While we were both in the break room, I walked over to a window that looked out over the funeral home's parking lot and stood there admiring the nice, sunny day. All of a sudden I saw Bill walking in the parking lot. He was checking out the cars as if he was a buyer on a used car lot. I couldn't believe what I was seeing.

"Oh my God," I found myself saying aloud. Imagine my shock to see Bill waltzing around the parking lot when earlier I had seen him lying in an open casket. I couldn't take my eyes off of Bill. He continued on to the next car, and this time, he stooped over to look at a license plate! I was about to turn around to Dee when I heard her speak up.

"Don't worry, Angie. That's his twin brother," Dee said in her Panamanian accent. I felt relieved that she was acknowledging the person in the parking lot, and more relieved that I wasn't losing my mind. I wasn't quite prepared to think I was looking at a spirit walking around. I stood at the window for the longest time trying to rid myself of the feeling that sat in the pit of my stomach. Dee left the room long before I decided to leave on my own.

A couple of years following Bill's passing, I flew to Arizona and stayed with Dee. For the first time in years, she and I were able to catch up with one another's lives. Dee spoke about her early adult years, her marriage to a U.S. citizen, and her fast introduction to American culture. The conversation led to her mother, Olga, and her stepfather, Bill. As she spoke his name, I remembered that she had mentioned that he had a twin brother. I was curious how Bill's twin was doing.

"How's Bill's twin brother?" I asked assuming Dee would answer with a simple word such as "fine." Instead she just looked at me as if I had asked something wrong.

"Bill doesn't have a twin brother. He has a twin sister, though. How did you know he had a twin?"

I thought she was joking around, so I inquired again. This time, I recounted what she had told me in the break room. "Don't you remember the day we were in the break room at the funeral home and I saw someone that looked just like Bill walking around in the parking lot, and you said that's his twin brother?"

"No. I never said that. You never mentioned that to me," Dee said matter-of-factly.

Believe me when I say, I was dumbfounded. It was right then and there that I realized that it was Bill and no one else walking around the parking lot. I explained to Dee that he was whole and walking with the same stride he normally walked with. He looked the same as he did when alive: light-skinned, tall, and bald, wearing dark-rimmed eyeglasses. The voice I heard behind me telling me it was Bill's twin was her voice; accent and all. It took me a few minutes to grasp the idea that a spirit, not Dee had spoken to me. I realized that my first experience of hearing a spirit had taken place. What I found a bit hard to fathom was its ability to mimic Dee's voice, and my capability of hearing it. Regardless, it had happened. Dee wasn't surprised. She accepted my account of the story and went on to say, "That's just like him to check the cars out on the day of his funeral." We had a good laugh about that.

Since that day, I have learned about spirits and their abilities to communicate with us. Whether they appear to us as whole, living people, or we merely hear their voices, spirits do wish to let us know they are there. It is their way of comforting us, to let us know they are alive on another plane of existence. I realize their consciousness lives on, and their life on the other side and our ability to communicate with them is but one thought away.

<hr/>

A Beautiful Ghost Brought Her Cheer at the Art Show

Priscilla Garduno Wolf of Tijeras, New Mexico, has won several awards for her art, poetry, and photography. She has served as vice president of the New Mexico Art League and Gallery, and president (later vice president) of Nor Este Arts Association. She is a member of the Arizona Artists Guild, "Spirit" (Native American Arts and Pow Wows), and an advisor to the Hispanic Education and Media Group. Priscilla—"Little Butterfly" is her Jicarilla Apache name—is accomplished in watercolors, pastels, and sketching with colored pencils.

Priscilla's interest in art began in the first grade, and she remembers that her first painting brought laughter from her classmates, for she had colored her impression of a horse with purple crayon. "I didn't win any award for that painting," she reflected, "but I was proud of my horse."

She considers herself largely self-taught and credits the skills of her craft to her grandparents. She also acknowledges them for believing in her and teaching her the lasting values of life. In 1999, Priscilla had an article published in *Fate* magazine that featured her grandfather, Antonio Trujillo, and in 2003, she told the story of her Apache grandmother, Matilde Fernandez Trujillo, in *La Herencia del Norte*. The story of Matilde, an orphaned Apache girl, as well as the accomplishments of her granddaughter, Priscilla, are part of The Women of the West History Trail in New Mexico.

In the summer of 2000, Priscilla was sitting in the New Mexico Art League and Gallery in Albuqerque, where she often serves as receptionist, as well as exhibitor. "It had been a slow day," Priscilla said, "when suddenly the door opened and a beautiful young girl came in. She was so friendly and seemed to glow with her beauty."

Priscilla told the young woman that she should check the art work, but she said, "I came to see you."

"She grabbed a chair and sat close to me," Priscilla said. "She spoke about my recent depression and reminded me that life was beautiful and that I had so much to live for. She also encouraged me to share my life stories and my artwork with others."

Priscilla could not help reacting with surprise. This lovely girl was a total stranger and Priscilla had certainly conveyed nothing of her personal life to her. "And yet, she seemed to know everything about me," Priscilla said. "I felt so relaxed and calm in her presence. We talked about so many things, and she made me laugh and count my blessings."

One of Priscilla's fellow artists walked into the gallery and assumed that she was speaking with a long-time friend.

Priscilla Wolf. (**Photo courtesy Priscilla Wolf**)

Priscilla experienced a moment of awkwardness, because she had not learned the lovely girl's name and she realized the artist was standing there, waiting to be introduced.

But at that moment, the girl excused herself, saying she had someone else to visit. As she was walking out the door, she vanished before the eyes of Priscilla and the other artist.

"So I said goodbye, as she disappeared," Priscilla said. "I call her my visiting artist Angel, and once again I asked God, what have I done to deserve all your good?"

In 2003, Priscilla and her family bought their first large home in Tijeras, and she now has her own art studio, which she calls "South Dakota." In addition, she has made one of the rooms into a chapel dedicated to her mother, Claudia Trujillo Garduno, in memory of her devotion to the Virgin Mary.

<hr>

APPEARANCE OF GHOSTLY FOOTPRINTS AFTER A SPIRIT BOX SESSION

Our friend Sandy Nichols is an indefatigable researcher of the UFO mystery and all things paranormal. As we were writing this book, he sent us an account of enigmatic footprints that appeared on the floor after everyone had gone home after working a Spirit Box, a device used by some psychical researchers to contact spirits through the use of radio frequency.

As I shared in my previous email we had a Spirit Box session in my home on Saturday, July 14, 2012. The first and second floors of my home, except for the master bedroom, all have hardwood floors. We conducted the Spirit Box session in my entry foyer, and I set up a card table for our equipment and some chairs to sit in. Before and after the session we walked all around the entry foyer and around other areas of my home. I left the table and some of my equipment in the entry foyer until Sunday morning to finish the cleanup.

The first thing I noticed that morning was what appeared to be three narrow footprints to the left of where we were sitting and right before a colored, laser-type device someone had set up just inside the study. Wide-open archways on three sides of the foyer lead into the dining room, the study, the main hallway, and the den area. I walked the entire house and did not find another footprint on any other part of the hardwood floors, first or second floors. Neither did any of us see these footprints while walking around in the entry foyer, before or after the session. We would have noticed these prints because they were dusty prints. The two prints together measured a little less than eight inches long, the single one a little less than ten inches long.

Back in 1999 or 2000, during the winter season in another house I had built, I got into my hot tub about 3:00 A.M. one morning. While relaxing in the hot tub, it began to lightly snow outside. Twenty minutes later, I was out of the hot tub and had gone to bed.

About 8:30 A.M. I awakened to go to the bathroom, and after, I went out on the deck to smoke a cigarette. It had snowed about three inches and right dab in the middle of the back of my three-quarters of an acre yard was an open area where there was a perfectly circular area of melted snow, twenty to thirty feet in diameter. There were two sets of narrow, footprint-type tracks beginning on the backside of the melted area of snow and basically walking side by side further back into my back yard to the left.

The footsteps continued on to almost the back of my property line. Once they had reached this point, one set of footprints turned and traveled back toward the middle of my yard and stopped some fifty feet left of the melted area of snow. This set of footprints then returned back to the left

Sandy Nichols. (*Photo courtesy Sandy Nichols*)

A session in which a Spirit Box (also sometimes called a Ghost Box) uses radio frequencies as a method for contacting the dead and other spirits. (*Photo by Sandy Nichols*)

corner of my yard, and then both sets of footprints traveled back to the back area of the melted snow from where they had started. Never once did they walk over or on top of their footprints in either direction. I took photos from the deck, then went and measured the prints.

Each of the prints in the snow was about eight inches long. One of the things that really caught my attention was the shape of the prints. They looked as if they were something akin to ballerina shoe prints. The prints in the foyer look very similar to the ones in the snow.

As for July 14, my wife went to bed as soon as my friends left. I locked up the main house, went to my home office (which is part of the pool house), and turned on the alarm system for the main house from there. When my wife returned from church early the next afternoon, I asked her if she had gone into the entry foyer. She had not.

I know, and my friends know, that the footprints in the foyer were not there when we all left for the last time the night before. So these prints were

The black rectangular line in this photograph highlights the small footprints the author found left on his porch. No one knows who made them, but they appear to be left behind by little ballerina slippers. *(Photo by Sandy Nichols.)*

made after I had already locked up and turned on the alarm to the main house. P.S.... My friends call my home "The Paranormal Palace" because of all the ghosts that live here and the other strange stuff that happens here.... kind of cool living here.

A HAUNTED OFFICE: THE TAPPING CABINETS

By Paul Dale Roberts

I have been working a lot of overtime in my real job. I have a friend, who also works a lot of overtime in his real job. My friend knows I am a writer and ghost hunter. I will not be disclosing the name of my friend, nor where he works, because he could find himself in a lot of trouble for letting me go into his building after working hours—plus, I could probably get into trouble.

About 9:00 P.M., I got a call from my friend: "Paul, are you working overtime, or are you at home?" Paul: (deep sigh) "Working overtime." Friend:

"Then Paul, get over here, it's happening now!" Paul: "Okay, I just have a couple things to get out and I will zip over there!"

My friend claims that the office building where he works is haunted. Some of the employees have claimed that trays that are supposed to go in a certain way are moved backwards in the morning.

My friend, a workaholic, puts in late hours at this establishment and says at times the cabinets in four cubicles will make a distinct, loud tapping sound. It only happens every so often, but when it does happen, it will last for up to a couple of hours.

My friend sneaks me into his office area, and lo and behold, I hear the tapping sounds on one of the cabinets in a cubicle. I enter the cubicle where the tapping sounds are originating and the tapping sounds switch over to the next cubicle's cabinet. I run over to the next cubicle and it moves again into another cubicle and then another cubicle.

The tapping sounds on the cabinets go around four cubicles. So when you reach one cubicle cabinet where the tapping sounds are heard, it moves to the next cubicle's cabinet and so on and so on.

It was the weirdest thing I have ever witnessed. You could even see the cabinets shake. It sounded like a person with long fingernails was actually tapping the cabinets.

I was in this office for a period of twenty minutes, and I chased the tapping sounds during that whole time, trying to catch up with it. I could peek into the next cubicle and see the cabinets shake from the tapping, but as soon as I arrived in that cubicle, it had already shifted into the next cubicle.

My friend said that most of the employees think it's the ghost of a former female employee who died by sitting in her parked, running car in her garage. She died of inhaling hydrogen sulfide gas. She committed suicide because she found out her husband was having an affair with one of her coworkers at this building.

The tapping of the cabinets happens every so often. I was fortunate and I was able to witness the paranormal by actually hearing the tapping and seeing the cabinets shake. I believe that for the tapping sounds to move away from me, from cabinet to cabinet, shows some kind of intelligence at work.

⟨⟨⟨⟩⟩⟩

POLTERGEISTS AND OUR PLASTIC REALITY

Paul Dale Roberts' account of the tapping, shaking cabinets sounds very much like a haunting that strays into poltergeist territory.

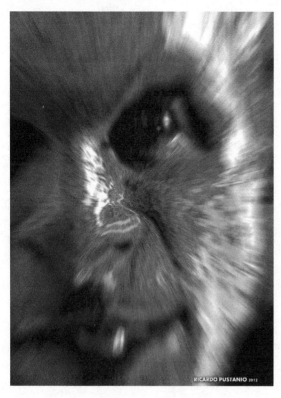

Poltergeists are "noisy ghosts" that are somehow born when a human is being denied the ability to express him- or herself in more acceptable ways. (Art by Ricardo Pustanio)

The temptation is to personify the poltergeist force and to endow it with attributes of intelligence. Traditionally, the poltergeist was thought to be a rather nasty, disembodied spirit. The word itself is German for "noisy ghost," or "throwing ghost." But it seems that the poltergeist is most often "born" when some aspect of the human personality is being denied more accepted avenues of expression.

The raw energy of the sex changes that occur during puberty and the sexual adjustments of the marital state have often been identified as having somehow provided the impetus for the peculiar psychokinetic discharge responsible for poltergeist activity. Many "psi" researchers have observed that more often a girl than a boy is at the center of poltergeistic disturbances, and that the sexual changes of puberty are associated with either the beginning or the termination of the phenomena.

Brad Receives a "Priceless" Inheritance from a British Seer

Harry Price, the British journalist-psychical researcher, devoted much of his life to an examination of the poltergeist phenomenon. His book *Poltergeist Over England* is a classic study of the wide range of poltergeist activity, and many of his articles have served as references for other writers in the field of paranormal inquiry, including Brad.

As might be expected, Price received accounts of poltergeist activity from all over the world, and it appears that he was in the process of writing a much larger work on the poltergeist subject at the time of his death on April 24, 1948. Price's letters and notes regarding this particular phenomenon went to the well-known British clairvoyant John Pendragon, who had assisted in the research at Borley Rectory (once called the most haunted house in England) and who would later serve as the subject of one of Brad Steiger's books (*Pendragon*, 1968). When Pendragon passed on in January 1970, Brad learned that he had made him his heir and that his solicitors had bundled up stacks of Harry Price's research papers and posted them to his office in the States.

Brad felt incredibly honored by such an inheritance, for the "ghost hunter" heroes of his early days of research were Hereward Carrington, Dr. Nandor Fodor, Sir William Crookes, William James, Sir Oliver Lodge, Fredric W. H. Myers, and Harry Price.

We are pleased to share herewith a few selections from the dozens of letters Harry Price received in regard to his inquiries regarding psychokinetic and haunting manifestations:

From Kuala Lumpur, Selangor, British Malaya [Malaysia]:

Some European girls whom we know rang us up one evening to say that peculiar things were happening in their house—knives and spoons wouldn't stay on the table; potatoes and onions kept leaping out of their box; wooden clogs were thrown at people. We all went down to investigate that evening, and after a number of days, we are all entirely convinced that there is no hoax, but that this is a genuine poltergeist case.

I have myself seen with my own eyes and am prepared to swear on any oath, that the following occurred: 1) A round stone about an inch in diameter dropped from a completely bare ceiling; 2) a piece of glazed tile fell out of a tiled roof; 3) a knife flew past my face when I was the only person in the room; 4) several potatoes and onions leapt out of a wooden box and rolled across the floor.

The medium, or whatever you wish to call it, of all the manifestations seems to be the Malay maid, as she is always around when these things happen. She has only recently been engaged, and before she came, nothing was reported. All the skeptical policemen who have investigated, and myself, are quite convinced that this is not a put-up job. I have so often read of these things that it is fascinating to have first-hand acquaintance with them, and to be convinced, as I am, that such things do happen by some agency or power that one cannot at present explain.

From a woman in Stalbridge, Dorset, England, who had been beset by ghostly phenomena since, as a child of eleven, she would awaken to become aware of a small child lying beside her:

Early in February 1940, I awoke to the sounds of the most terrific bangs on my bedroom door. I called out, "Who is there?" A short silence, then another set of dreadful bangs. I quite thought the door would give way.

I opened it expecting to face a burly ruffian. Instead, all was calm and serene, and not a soul to be seen. I am not particularly nervous, but that did upset me, and in fact, made me ill. For some time afterward I slept downstairs, but eventually returned to my old quarters....

One day last year, five of my windowpanes were badly cracked at about the same time, with nothing whatever to account for it.

Real Encounters, Different Dimensions, and Otherworldly Beings

On another occasion, I took a ring off my finger whilst in the kitchen, dropped it, heard it run over the linoleum, and after giving a spin, come to rest behind the door. But when I went to pick it up, I could not find it. Many weeks later, on going to my dresser cupboard to get a tall tin from an inner corner of the lower part, I found my ring reposing behind it.

That cupboard was closed when I dropped the ring. Even if it had been open, there is a deep ledge along the bottom of it which the ring would have had to jump over and then get into that far corner behind the big tin, which nearly reached the shelf above it. And even now I can distinctly recollect hearing the ring roll across the floor and give a spin before coming to rest behind the door.

From Worcester, England, the recollections of a woman who had lived with an aunt and her family while they were under siege by a poltergeist:

When I was about thirteen the whole household became disturbed as a result of extraordinary rappings on the windows of the house. Queer noises, shufflings, etc., were the terror of my young life.

The rappings on the windows and showers of stones apparently hurled in handsful from without never seemed to have been connected by the family with myself. The young daughter of the house seemed to be favored by these attentions, as they usually happened in a room where she was present and usually when she was alone.

We all heard the rappings; indeed, they were so violent one could not have failed to hear them, even though one might not actually be in the particular room where the demonstration was taking place.

For many years I did not experience anything of the same character, until, in 1913, I went to live in a large house near the station in Mayfield, Sussex. There we were worried by sounds like deep breathing under door frames, doors constantly being slammed, a barking dog we could never trace, and sounds suggesting the upheaval of large pieces of furniture in the attics, which were devoid of any furniture.

The letters go on, stacks of them, from men and women in all walks of life. There is an extremely long report from MacKinlay Kantor, who would one day win a Pulitzer Prize in literature, telling of a baffling poltergeist case in his home town of Webster City, Iowa.

⚺

THE PERVERSE TALENTS OF THE POLTERGEIST

One of the questions that we are most interested in answering is whether these breaches of our physical laws can be accomplished through *mental effort*—either conscious or unconscious—or if the physical organism is no more active in its participation in the process than are the chunks of ice, stones, and crockery that appear to drop from the sky.

This frustrated desire to more fully express one's self, combined with the chemical changes taking place in marital or sexual adjustment, may literally explode into violent, unrestrained psychokinetic activity.

It may be startling to consider the mind capable of bursting free of its three-dimensional bonds and utilizing specialized talents that know virtually no limits. The poltergeist seems to offer measurable proof of the mind's limitless creative capacity, but the tragedy is that the poltergeist phenomena represent a perverted, uncontrolled aspect of this ability.

> Poltergeists throw things, break windows, and can even cause fires.

The perverse talents of the poltergeist range from the tossing of pebbles to the manufacturing of disagreeable odors. Poltergeists throw things, break windows, and can even cause fires. But, as one investigator commented, "The phenomena are exactly such as would occur to the mind of a child or an ignorant person."

If the poltergeist is provided with enough psychic energy to develop a voice or the ability to communicate by raps or automatic writing, its communications are usually nonsensical, ribald, or downright obscene.

Author Sacheverell Sitwell observed that the poltergeist appeared always to direct its power toward "the secret or concealed weaknesses of the spirit ... the obscene or erotic recesses of the soul. The mysteries of puberty, that trance or dozing of the psyche before it awakes into adult life, is a favorite playground for the poltergeist."

Why the *baser* elements of the human subconscious should find their expression in the poltergeist has been a matter of great speculation among psi researchers. Why shouldn't our noblest instincts be projected too? Physical violence is often directed toward the unconscious energy center of the phenomena, and a parent, a spouse, or a sibling may come in for his or her share of the abuse as well.

Because of the poltergeist's general low-level activities, the unconscious energy center, as well as his or her family, will generally declare the manifestations to be the work of some demonic, external agent. On the other hand, the question of external intelligence somehow interacting with the unconscious agent of poltergeist activity is difficult to resolve. Many percipients of poltergeist phenomena have reported seeing grotesque, gargoyle-like entities that they felt were in some way associated with the haunting. Whether these beings are externalized projections of the agent's unconscious may be debated extensively—and, at present, inconclusively.

It may be well within the creative power of the human psyche to materialize other voices, other personalities, and junior psyches. (Isn't this what novelists and playwrights do quite "normally"?) If a poltergeist can manifest voices and forms, as well as pebble-throwing and crockery-smashing, then we are still talking about the human mind shaping a lively piece of our "plastic" reality. But *if* a poltergeist is an entity possessing an intelligence independent of the agent, then the noisy ghost is indeed "feeding" upon its medium's psychic and sexual energies and using a human agency to implement whatever purpose it may have.

THE IMMORTALITY QUESTION

One of the main reasons neither science nor society at large has seriously considered the immortality question is the lack of tangible, physical evidence proving that there is anything other than a void waiting for us when we die. Skeptical scientists will remain untouched by the most moving and heart-warming inspirational anecdotes of personal experience, and even the most open-minded of contemporary scientists are reluctant to get involved in the abstract and esoteric elements of faith and religion for fear of tarnishing their shields of objectivity.

> For quite a few years now, a number of serious-minded psychical researchers have been recording spirit voices on tape and even communicating with these remarkable vocal manifestations.

All this may one day change, thanks to breakthroughs into the hidden reaches of immortality that have been made by modern technological instrumentation—most frequently by simple audiotape recorders. For quite a few years now, a number of serious-minded psychical researchers have been recording spirit voices on tape and even communicating with these remarkable vocal manifestations. Perhaps for the first time in history, even the most materialistic of scientists will have something tangible with which to work to prove the reality of life after death. A great deal of work must be done in this area of research to produce a universally acceptable demonstration of the survival question that will fit the criteria of absolute proof, but many researchers feel that their experiments are accumulating such evidence.

EDISON BELIEVED THAT THE DEAD COULD BE CONTACTED VIA ELECTRONIC MEANS

The concept of contacting the dead through electronic means goes back to Thomas Alva Edison, the Genius of Menlo Park, who believed that the soul of a human being is composed of "swarms of billions of highly charged energies which live in the cells." Edison further maintained that when a person dies, "this swarm deserts the body and goes into space, but keeps on and enters another cycle of life and is immortal."

In the October 1920 issue of *Scientific American*, Edison revealed that he was, in fact, working on a device that would facilitate communication with the deceased. It was his intention to fashion an electronic instrument so sensitive that it would be able to detect even the slightest movements of discarnate entities. His fellow pioneers in electronic achievements, Charles Proteus Steinmetz and Nikola Tesla, agreed that it should be theoretically possible to communicate with other dimensions.

Notes in Thomas Edison's personal diary reveal such observations as the following:

> I believe [our bodies] are composed of myriads and myriads of infinitesimally small individuals, each in itself a unit of life, and that these units work in squads—or swarms as I prefer to call them—and that these infinitesimally small units live forever. When we "die" these swarms of units, like swarms of bees, so to speak, betake themselves elsewhere, and go on functioning in some other form of environment.

> I cannot believe ... that life in the first instance originated on this insignificant little ball which we call Earth. The particles which combined to evolve living creatures on this planet of ours probably came from some other body elsewhere in the universe.

Every schoolchild knows that Edison's legacy to his fellow humans includes the electric light, the gramophone, motion pictures, and scores of other inventions which have made life easier, more productive, and more enjoyable in the twentieth century and beyond. But few know that among the diagrams of unachieved creations lay the plans for a machine that would enable its user to speak to the dead.

And those who knew Edison best stated that he was reluctant to take any credit for any of his remarkable achievements. In his opinion, he was simply a vehicle or a channel for information from a higher source.

"I proclaim," Edison said, "that it is possible to construct an apparatus that will be so delicate that there if are personalities in another existence or sphere who wish to get in touch with us, this apparatus will give them the opportunity. Why should personalities in another existence spend their time working a triangular piece of wood over a board with lettering on it [referring to the common Ouija Board] when something much better can be devised?"

During a period of six or seven months, Edison is said to have worked full-time on his project of building a "dead man's gramophone," and he allowed few people entrance to his laboratory. Nobody knows for certain if his

Real Encounters, Different Dimensions, and Otherworldly Beings

device for speaking with the deceased was ever completed or if it was ever a successful application, but it was the genius of Thomas Edison that lay the groundwork for the research in electronic voice communication that is being conducted today.

⊸◍◍◖ƒ◗◍◍⊷

DR. KONSTANTĪN RAUDIVE'S PIONEERING WORK IN ELECTRONIC COMMUNICATION WITH THE DEAD

In 1971, Taplinger Publishing Company sent Brad a review copy of *Breakthrough: An Amazing Experiment in Electronic Communication with the Dead* by Dr. Konstantīn Raudive, a book that had created a sensation in Europe. The Latvian-born Raudive, a noted psychologist and philosopher, had lived in Sweden and Germany since the close of World War II and had become well known in both the literary and scientific communities.

Sometime in the mid-1960s, Dr. Raudive discovered the work of Swedish author Friedrich Jurgenson, who had encountered the phenomenon of spirit voices quite by accident when he was out in the woods attempting to capture bird songs on his tape recorder. Jurgenson knew that the voices had somehow appeared on his recordings without the intervention of any human agency.

Further experiments demonstrated that the spirit voices did not appear at random, but seemed to respond to invitations to manifest themselves. The voices always identified themselves as specific deceased personalities, but all spoke much faster than normal speech.

⊸◍◍◖ƒ◗◍◍⊷

DISCOVERING SPIRIT VOICES AMONG THE RECORDINGS OF BIRD SONGS

In her book *A Psychic Explores the Unseen World*, Kay Sterner recounts a visit to Jurgenson in Sweden in 1972. During an experiment, Jurgenson invited his spirit guide and any other entities who wished to communicate to speak to them on the tape recorder. An hour and a half later, they replayed the recording. Kay writes that all this may have been a matter of routine to Jurgenson, who listened to a number of voices in Swedish responding to specific questions that he had asked, but she was excited and filled with anticipation.

"Then," she writes, "to my total amazement, we heard a female voice clearly singing a Negro spiritual in English. Mr. Jurgenson called out excitedly, "It is unmistakably Mahalia Jackson's voice." Mahalia Jackson died in 1972.

Dr. Konstantín Raudive had been investigating postmortem phenomena for twenty-five years before he learned of Jurgenson's experiments, and he embarked on a research program of his own, employing the strictest of professional standards and establishing firm documentation of his results. It wasn't long before Dr. Raudive was joined in his research by eminent European scientists, physicists, and theologians.

━═⏣⎰∿⎱⏣═━

THE PHENOMENON OF RECORDING SPIRIT VOICES

What is meant by the phenomenon of recording spirit voices? Those who make such claims define the phenomenon as the unexplained manifestation of human voice-like sounds on recording tape. These sounds are in fact vocal sounds, and human language is employed, but it must be understood that the voices cannot be heard during the recording period. They can only be heard during the playback.

Once one becomes accustomed to the voices and has learned how to screen out any interference, anyone can understand what is being said. When the recordings have been made by serious researchers, one may assume that the voices are genuine and have been verified by respected scientists.

Where the voices originate and how they get onto the recording tape, however, remain open questions.

> Where the voices originate and how they get onto the recording tape, however, remain open questions.

When one is initially exposed to the electronic voice phenomenon, the thought which comes first to mind is that they might be random voices somehow picked up from a radio station or some other type of sound transmission. That objection leads to the most mystifying characteristic of the paranormal voices on tape: The operator of the tape recorder may actually enter into an intelligent conversation with the mysterious voices.

The spirit voices may be heard not only responding to specific questions, but in some instances, they volunteer information—and the unseen intelligences appear to be aware of all that is occurring at the site of the recording. In certain cases, the information volunteered by the spirits of the dead has been precognitive.

It does take some diligence and determination to work with the electronic voice phenomenon. For one thing, it is hard on the ears. The voices are often faint, and the sentences and phrases may often be brief, rapid, and barely audible, even with maximum amplification. And sometimes background noise and interference may be extremely difficult to penetrate.

When listening to tapes containing successfully recorded paranormal voices, one is immediately aware of their eerie nature. Some voices are mechanical sounding; others are whispered and echoing. Yet there can be no mistake—they are voices speaking in a human language. The voices captured by Dr. Raudive issue forth in German, Russian, English, Latvian, and many other languages.

─────◦◦◦◦◦ ◦◦◦◦◦─────

PROFESSOR WALTER UPHOFF BRINGS ELECTRONIC VOICE RESEARCH TO THE UNITED STATES

Shortly after the publication of Raudive's *Breakthrough* in the United States, Brad met the very serious-minded Professor Walter Uphoff, who had taken as his mission the tracking of electronic voice phenomena in this country. Uphoff had first learned of Dr. Konstantin Raudive's experiments during one of his frequent trips to Europe, where he had contacts with psychical researchers all over the continent.

Skeptical at first, he was invited to Dr. Raudive's laboratory at Bad Krozingen, Germany, to hear the voices for himself. The initial exposure to the experiments being conducted by the respected scientist motivated Uphoff to explore the electronic phenomenon as thoroughly as possible.

At the time of Brad's first meeting with Walter Uphoff and his wife, Mary Jo, Professor Uphoff was working mostly independently (and occasionally under the auspices of the internationally known psychic Harold Sherman and his ESP Research Associates Foundation of Little Rock, Arkansas) to check out the validity of spirit voices recorded on tape by the Lamoreaux family in White Salmon, Washington.

The first thing that Brad noticed about Uphoff was that he was a realist, a man of science and education. He was also a man accustomed to the tough infighting of labor and management. His book *Kohler on Strike* was cited by Robert F. Kennedy as being an extremely important study in the field of labor relations.

Later, Brad learned that Uphoff had found Michael Lamoreaux, a former teacher who had been doing graduate work at a college in the Northwest. Like so many others, Lamoreaux had become interested in the paranormal voice phenomenon after reading Dr. Raudive's book. He had tried unsuccessfully for two months to capture spirit voices on tape by following the procedures in *Breakthrough*; then, during a visit to his two brothers, success was achieved on their first night of experimentation.

─────◦◦◦◦◦ ◦◦◦◦◦─────

THE REMARKABLE LAMOREAUX BROTHERS

By June of 1973, the Lamoreaux brothers had accumulated hundreds of pages of transcribed paranormal voices that they had captured on tape.

Their technique was simplicity itself. They would turn on the tape recorder and ask whatever spirit might be listening some specific questions. They next allowed the machine to record for fifteen seconds. After that brief time had elapsed, they would rewind the tape and play it back to see if they had picked up any spirit voices.

Professor Uphoff soon ascertained that the Lamoreaux brothers were especially interested in gaining information about life after death, and they had interrogated the spirits for specific details about the world that lies beyond the grave. The paranormal voices that came through on their tape recorder described the ethereal region from which they communicated as a frequency or vibrational level, a dimension, rather than a physical location.

> **Professor Uphoff soon ascertained that the Lamoreaux brothers were especially interested in gaining information about life after death.**

Pareenah (phonetic spelling) was the name spirit voices gave the Lamoreaux brothers for the earth-plane of existence. *Deenah* was the designation applied to the main place or state where one goes after physical death. According to the spirit voices, although this state appears to be largely a subjective reality, it has some rather stringent rules. Most of the spirits coming through the tape recorder said they now existed in *Deenah* and referred to themselves in that state as *Moozla*. Those who disobeyed the rules and laws of *Deenah* are sent to *Nillow*, an apparent region of conditioning. Once one has been made more fit for spirit progress, he or she may return to *Deenah*. Those entities that must remain for a longer period of time are called *Nillowins*. There was also described an area of therapeutic environment wherein the spirits are permitted limited movement.

NO MEDIUMISTIC ABILITIES ARE REQUIRED TO RECORD SPIRITS

Tracking down spirit voices is not an esoteric science reserved for initiates or those with special training in electronics. Anyone with a tape recorder can take part in this form of psychical research. It may be that there is an element of extrasensory perception or mediumistic ability involved, but this has not been determined as a necessary requirement for a successful recording of spirit voices.

Some researchers have suggested that Dr. Konstantín Raudive had some abilities as a medium, but there are no published reports of his being aware of such talents before he seriously began to record paranormal voices. It is also known that Michael Lamoreaux once slipped into a trance state during a taping session. He had never done this before, and he did not at first realize that his "nap" of three or four minutes had actually lasted for well over half an hour.

A general consensus among electronic voice researchers indicated that they spent an average of two months before they got really impressive results. On the other hand, many researchers state that they were successful on their very first effort.

A point on which all electronic voice researchers agree is that it is very necessary to go back over early tapes and review them. They have discovered that as their ability to hear and to understand paranormal voices improved with experience, they are able to hear voices that they had initially missed.

Walter Uphoff prepared some guidelines for people who wish to conduct experiments in capturing spirit voices with their own tape recorders. There is no guarantee that anyone can duplicate the successful experiments that have been carried out around the world, but if a person is serious about recording the spirit voice phenomenon, he or she should resolve not to become discouraged if early attempts are unproductive.

There is no absolute rule as to when and where recordings should be attempted. Professor Uphoff advised experimenters to select a place that is as free as possible from all extraneous noises. The best time appears to be in the evening, especially around midnight.

Since the weather is always a factor in radio transmissions, it is advisable to avoid times when there are large amounts of static electricity in the air.

Very often, the spirit voices are heard in the pauses between words and sentences, so Professor Uphoff advised novice experimenters always to speak slowly and clearly.

"What must be guarded against is becoming an uncritical believer," he warned. "Everyone I know who has devoted time to listening to the spirit tapes grants that something paranormal is happening. Some feel more comfortable if they can somehow credit the voices to the work of the experimenter's subconscious. But no one has come forward with an explanation of the dynamics or the forms of energy involved in producing the phenomenon.

"Tape recorders have become one more instrument to push the frontiers of the unknown back and to bring us closer to the awareness that man is more than a mere combination of chemicals and electrical energy—and that what we know as human personality may not cease at death."

SARAH WILSON ESTEP AND THE AMERICAN ASSOCIATION OF ELECTRONIC VOICE PHENOMENA

Over the nearly twenty years that we knew of Sarah Wilson Estep (1926–2008) and her fine work with the American Association of Electronic

Voice Phenomena, we were impressed with her tireless efforts to compile recordings of spirit voices that were of high quality and bound to impress the professional skeptics. And Sarah was the first to admit that she completely understands the position of those who doubt the validity of spirit recordings. As a long-time psychical researcher, Sarah recalled that her initial reaction to someone who claimed that he or she had recorded voices of the dead on tape was utter disbelief.

Before her death in 2008, Sarah had recorded spirit voices from other dimensions, and after amassing well over twenty-four thousand messages from beyond, she felt that she might safely say that she learned a great deal about life on the Other Side.

In her book, *Voices of Eternity*, she writes that those spirits who have spoken to her via tape have expressed feelings of both joy and sadness. "Most have been surprised at what they found. They contribute, on their own, totally unexpected yet meaningful comments. My direct questions are frequently answered.... Musical chords and notes have been played at my request.... I have been assured of their support, their protection, their help. They have asked me for help."

Sarah stated that one of the greatest rewards of her work had been her ability to assist those who are grief-stricken with the loss of a loved one and to give them hope and comfort in the knowledge that people they loved are continuing to live on the Other Side.

In her advice to novice experimenters, she suggested that it is better to make one five-minute recording each day than to sit down once or twice week to record for half an hour: "Those on the Other Side soon learn when and where you will record, and if you are persistent, they will start to speak to you. Each experimenter must work out his own way to record. I always start each recording with the date, time, and a welcome for those who come in love and peace. During a five-minute recording session I will ask three or four questions, allowing at a minute between questions for the answer."

Sarah Estep was always frank in admitting that she had searched since she was a child for evidence that we survive death. She persevered, she said, until she finally found the answers in the "voices of eternity."

The paranormal voices recorded on tape and other electronic means affirm that they are the surviving personalities of human beings who once lived on Earth. Whether these voices truly represent who they say they are has yet to be proved to the satisfaction of our material sciences.

The fact does remain, however, that the voices do exist and have been captured on tape. For those who are convinced that research with electronic

> The paranormal voices recorded on tape and other electronic means affirm that they are the surviving personalities of human beings who once lived on Earth.

spirit communication fulfills its promise, it is no longer necessary to seek out a medium in order to establish contact.

Those who wish, and who have the patience, may be able to work with their own electronic equipment in order to establish the truth of personal survival and solve the age-old question about life after death to their own satisfaction.

PEOPLE AND PLACES FROM OTHER DIMENSIONS

In pondering the subject of Other Dimensional entities, Brandie replied that her experiences with the Shadow People would certainly seem to fit the bill. "I'm not sure what they are," Brandie said, "but I remember first seeing them when I was a little girl."

⟨⟨⟨ ⟩⟩⟩

BRANDIE'S MEMORIES OF HER ENCOUNTERS WITH THE SHADOW PEOPLE

During the early- to mid-1990s my family was living in a two-story, light green house in Dorchester, Massachusetts. When I was around six or seven, I was given my own room. It didn't have a real door, only the leftover remnant of beads that often served as a door in the '70s.

My first night sleeping in the room, I lay watching the unicorn night-light that was shining dimly in the room. I couldn't sleep and was feeling uneasy. The nightlight had cast a few shadows, and I began matching up every shadow in the room with its proper object. To the right of the nightlight, across from me on the wall, was this odd shadow. It didn't fit anywhere. It had a tall presence that felt completely unnatural. To my surprise, it stepped off of the wall and walked/glided forward.

I stared at it, and then I looked towards my closet. There I saw three more dark and dense shadows. The illumination from the nightlight was slowly being swallowed by shapes of human-looking entities. There were about four of them, and they varied in shape and size.

The shadow on the wall "stepped off of the wall and walked/glided forward." (*Art by Ricardo Pustanio*)

The ringleader, it seems, was in front of my bed, and I couldn't help staring at him in shock. He seemed much like a tall, human male, with tousled hair, and it seemed as if he wore glasses.

All of the shadow beings had red or an orangey-red eyes. I was extremely frightened and scared to leave my bed. I was so absorbed by him that when I finally broke the gaze to look around, I saw a huge shadow slowly spreading along the wall of my room. It was spreading fast and was touching the ceiling just blotting out all the light in the room. It was the darkest thing I had ever seen. I felt like screaming and crying, but I couldn't do anything.

I believed my life to be in danger, and I went into a fight-or-flight mode. The open doorway was my only hope, but these shadow people had surrounded my bed.

I spotted a slight opening near the door. So, frightened beyond belief, I jumped off of that bed and ran for my life across the hall to my grandmother's bedroom.

All I remember is screaming and shrieking for them to let me in. I scratched, banged, and clawed at the door, nearly losing my mind.

I remember looking back and seeing these Shadow People still looking at me. The one with the glasses bent down a bit to look at me through the doorway, but they hadn't moved. It just freaked me out more that they were still there and I was crying in despair. I fell through my grandma's doorway and don't remember much after that. I think I passed out.

Over the years, especially in my teens, I used to see them spying on me. Sometimes I'd catch them in the living room moving behind the couch in the dark. They seemed to be much shorter than the male-like beings I saw when I was around seven years old. They didn't like to be seen, and they would run from me and disappear.

THE MYSTERIOUS SHADOW PEOPLE

In the United States and Canada, the discussion about real encounters with Shadow People has become one of the hottest topics in the paranormal field. Late night radio programs and the Internet are flooded with reports of encounters with shadowy figures that startled individuals have glimpsed moving quickly about their bedrooms, living rooms, or backyards. In most instances, the experiencers view the figures with their peripheral vision, but nonetheless, they are convinced that "something" has been there.

In 2009, Jason Offutt had collected enough stories of Shadow People encounters to write *Darkness Walks: The Shadow People Among Us*, and the book provoked even greater response from those people who had encountered the entities in their own homes. Lively debates over whether these beings are spirits of the dead, aliens from another world, or energy-seeking vampires from other dimensions continue to keep listeners and readers up until the wee hours of morning.

Entities of the Shadow have been with humankind for centuries. As beings from another level of our multidimensional universe, they are often summoned by human emotions, especially fear, self-doubt, and greed.

While many witnesses believe the Shadow People to be spirits of the dead, the entities may have nothing to do with the question of life after death. They may not be ghosts trapped somehow in the environment of a room, a home, an office, or an eerie forest. Some witnesses have become convinced that their encounter with a Shadow Person was precipitated by their sighting of a UFO and that the dark being was closely associated with the glowing object that they first sighted in the night sky.

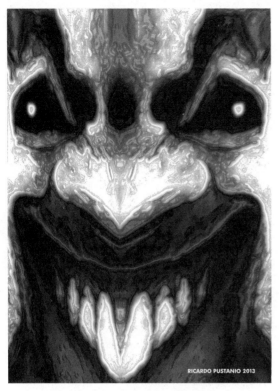

The Shadow People can be summoned into our presence by baser human emotions such as greed and fear. (*Art by Ricardo Pustanio*)

A good number of percipients of the phenomenon believe the Shadow Person with whom they interacted was benign, benevolent, and/or angelic in character. Perhaps, they suggested, the Shadow People have really begun to manifest in great numbers because they seek to bring us to a higher awareness of the complex universe in which we reside.

It seems, though, in evaluating a vast number of reports that we have received, most of the Shadow People appear to fit the category of cosmic tricksters and entities who intend to work mischief upon their witnesses. And, regretfully, there are some of the beings who do not appear to have our best interests at heart. They may have trespassed into our world with the intention of possessing our bodies or capturing our souls.

Very often, the Shadow People appear to have been invited into a human's space by someone dabbling in the occult. Curious and previously innocent minds can offer a wide-open portal to this world when some individuals begin "playing" with such devices as the Ouija Board.

<hr />

DABBLING IN THE OCCULT COULD INVITE A SHADOW PERSON

Virginia told us that a few years back she and her sister were working a Ouija Board when weird occurrences began to happen. At first, it was like footsteps in the hall and on the ceiling. Then there would be loud thuds, like someone wearing boots or heavy shoes.

Then things began to get stranger.

One night while Virginia was in bed, she began to stare into a dark corner of her room. She was about to close her eyes when she noticed that the shadow began to get darker and darker. She couldn't quite understand what was happening, so she just continued to stare.

Then the shadow took up almost the entire corner, and she could see a silhouette of a person.

Fear sunk in at this point, and she could feel him staring right through her.

Virginia then saw this "shadow" man step out into the light and everything was visible except for the features of his face. He then walked right past her bed and out into the hallway. He seemed like an intelligent sort of Shadow Person or spirit. Virginia was extremely scared, and she didn't tell anyone about the incident for quite a while. She is not certain whether it is the same "shadow" person or not, but since then Virginia has seen the entity quite often.

Virginia said that she has had her hair lifted up while she was in the shower. The action caught her off guard, but by the time this incident occurred, she was becoming used to such manifestations and had accepted that she lived alongside spirits.

But there are things that are harder to accept.

The darker things began only a couple years ago, Virginia said:

When I would be out in public places, I would see people with no whites in their eyes. Their eyes would be totally black.

I tried to ignore all these things, and I decided that my imagination had gotten the better of me. One night when I was in the shower, I thought that enough was enough and I declared that such creatures did not exist.

All of a sudden, I began choking. I became extremely afraid. It felt as though I was being choked from the inside out.

Whatever it was, I sensed that it would not stop until I said that "demons do exist; Shadow People do exist!

Some time after Virginia thought that she had made peace with the entities by conceding their existence, she was sitting alone in the house by herself when "… out of nowhere it felt like something reached into my chest and began to squeeze my heart. I thought I was having a heart attack. It felt like something was trying to pull my heart out of my chest. I honestly thought that this was it, and I asked for God/the Great Spirit to spare me. I begged Him—and as soon as I asked for spiritual help, the pain started to subside."

Since that time, Virginia has been repeatedly awakened by a loud, hissing growl coming from the middle of her room. She has also heard scratching on the wall at the head of her bed.

HER DEEP FAITH SEEMED TO KEEP THE SHADOW PEOPLE AT BAY

Endowed with a high degree of spiritual and psychic sensitivity, Kari was much better equipped to deal with shadow entities than are many who suddenly find themselves faced with the unknown.

Kari witnessed the Shadow People several times at her home and in one encounter she became paralyzed, but she realized later that their intent was not to harm. (*Art by Ricardo Pustanio*)

In Kari's words: "At a young age, I watched humanoid shadows cross the hallway in my home, moving from one room to another. Often I could catch the movement out of my peripheral vision and would be staring directly at them when they moved across open space. My brother and mother also witnessed them.

"I ruled out natural causes that may have created a movement of shadows in many of these instances. The shadows moved independently of any backdrop and passed across open space without any distortion of distance or angle."

One night Kari was awakened in the middle of the night by two shadows passing over the bed. She *felt* two presences in the room and looked in the direction from which she had felt the movements. She saw two, solid-looking, dark, human-shaped shadows standing at the end of the bed.

The moment she saw them, she became paralyzed and felt a weight pressing down on her chest. She emphasized in the recounting of her experience that there was no sense of suffocation, just a weight that would not allow her to get up.

When she realized that she couldn't move, she became frightened and began to pray.

"I couldn't speak," Kari said, "so I prayed loudly in my head. The figures seemed unaffected by my prayer for protection and lingered a few moments before moving toward the back door of the house and disappearing. The pressure and paralysis had left the moment they turned away, but I remained still until they were gone."

Looking back on the event, Kari sensed no maliciousness or evil from the shadow men, or shadow walkers, as she began to call them. The experience was terrifying only while she was experiencing paralysis, a sense of inability to act.

"I actually wanted to *ask* questions of the visitors," she said, "but when I discovered I was unable to move, I became fearful of their intentions. Now, I consider it an instructional experience, made forceful because a point was being made, a lesson given that I would not forget: Remain aware of the potential dangers of wandering spirits/entities, and not to leave myself unguarded. Since then, I have taken personal steps toward spiritual protection (primarily deep faith in a higher power, and in my own force of will)."

—⊸∏∪∏⊷—

BEWARE THE LOST BOYS WITH THE BLACK EYES

The Shadow People seem closely related to another meme that, since 2003, has had people all over the world reporting encounters with the Lost Boys with the Black Eyes. At this point, no one knows for certain who these beings are, but we will once again champion their place of origin in some multidimensional corner of the universe.

The modus operandi of the entities is basically the same whenever they manifest.

1. They knock on the door and appear as boys in their early teens. There are two, sometimes four, beings who are dressed as typical teenagers. The leader, usually the taller of the boys, asks to use the telephone or the restroom.

2. The homeowner senses that these are not ordinary children, and the sight of the black eyes fills him or her with fear.

3. When the homeowner refuses to allow them admittance, they continue to speak politely, but they plead that it is too cold or too hot or some other matter of great urgency.

4. When the homeowner continues to refuse their requests, the boys began to plead that they must come in, they need to come in.

5. The homeowner is increasingly overwhelmed by feelings of fear. After absolutely refusing to let them enter the home, the black-eyed boys walk away—and disappear.

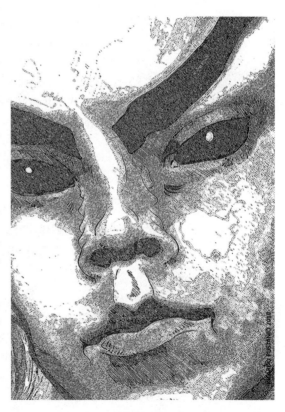

Another form of the Shadow People is that of youthful-looking boys with black eyes. (*Art by Ricardo Pustanio*)

In his article "Are Black-Eyed Beings Walking Among Us?" on www.rense.com, May 5, 2008, Ted Twietmeyer listed some common characteristics of black-eyed beings that he had discovered.

1. The black-eyed beings sometimes dress in inconspicuous clothing that will fit in with the general population, but they are often reported wearing clothing that appears out of sync with contemporary times. Sometimes they seem to favor odd color combinations.

2. Black-eyed children approach adults quite forcefully, and they do not act with the shyness expected of most normal children. While they may be verbally forceful in demanding entry into a home or an automobile, they seldom become physical.

3. Evil is the most common characteristic that eyewitnesses report feeling after encounters with both black-eyed children and adults.

4. The fact that the black-eyed adults and children alike ask permission to enter a home or a vehicle suggests the ancient spiritual law that forbids Evil to enter a person's domain without that individual granting it permission to do so.

5. The black-eyed entities appear to be solid beings. They are not ghosts or other disembodied creatures.

6. The great majority of encounters with the black-eyed ones occur after dark. Some researchers have suggested that these beings may not be able to tolerate direct sunlight.

DID THE MILITARY DISCOVER PROOF OF A MULTIDIMENSIONAL VORTEX IN MISSOURI?

Recently we received a report from Ethan, who, being familiar with our theories concerning the multidimensionality of various entities, provided us with powerful circumstantial evidence to support our claims.

Between 2004 and 2006, Ethan was stationed at Whiteman Air Force Base in Missouri. According to his account:

[E]very 23 days exactly, you could set your clock to it, between 0100–0200, we would get a thermal hit of a man-sized image inside the tree line of our perimeter. By the time we were able to respond to the location (within 3–5 minutes), the image would be gone.

I saw this image several times, and each time it would appear behind a tree, walk to the side, then move back behind the tree and vanish. Each appearance of a man-sized image lasted about 30 seconds.

One evening, we had a soldier stand at the spot where the image would appear. The trooper was 6" 7' and weighed 225 pounds. We did a side-by-side comparison and an overlay image with this particular solider. My guess is that the mysterious image was about one foot to a foot and a half taller than he, but was easily twice as wide. These incidents continued until the base removed the trees, then the images stopped.

At the time I lived off base around the same general area and exactly every 24 days, my dog would start growling and barking at the patio door that overlooked a field. She would refuse to go out and generally acted scared. We also had reports of our military working dogs, weighing upwards of 100 pounds, refuse to go into those woods around the same time, on some occasions dragging their handlers back out of the woods.

I know about your theory that Bigfoot is an extradimensional creature that every once in a while appears in our dimension. This theory may hold fact, because I do not see how something that size could have evaded all of the sensors and cameras that we had set up. I also believe that we were monitoring a creature that had some kind of territorial claim to that area.

Had the soldiers at Whiteman Air Force Base detected some kind of multidimensional vortex area where entities could arrive in our frequency and disperse to other areas of the planet?

⋘〰〰〰〰⋙

A MOST UNUSUAL MOTEL

Sometimes one can wander into a dimensional vortex quite by accident. Joan, a broadcast journalist, told us of her stay in a most unusual motel.

As she told the story, her resume had been received with enthusiasm by a large radio station in the southwest, and she had been asked to come in for an interview. Since she was presently employed at a station in a smaller city nearly two hundred miles from the possible new position, she asked her friend Elaine to accompany her on what would be an overnight trip.

Joan said that they arrived in the city quite late and were sorry that they had not made reservations before their departure, for the choices for comfortable accommodations were rather slim.

They were about to resign themselves to spending the night in a run-down motel on the edge of town when they turned a corner and noticed a small, but very attractive, motel directly behind a soft-serve dairy drive-in. The motel had very few rooms, but the place appeared to be clean and well-kept, and Joan and Elaine reasoned that the traffic from the drive-in would be minimal at that late hour and would not disturb them.

A quiet, white-haired, rather distinguished-looking night clerk handed them their room key after they had registered and pleasantly wished them a good night's sleep. The crisply clean room had two queen-sized beds, and Joan remarked that she and her friend enjoyed one of the most restful night's sleep that either had had for months.

Joan's interview was set for eight o' clock sharp, so the two women were up early to turn in their key and grab a couple of doughnuts and coffee from the continental breakfast offered by the motel.

The interview went well, and Joan accepted the job offer from the station manager. The man said that he loved her voice and promised her an afternoon talk show, in addition to covering special features and doing the early evening news.

Joan was exuberant. She was moving up in her career to a much larger radio station and with a considerable increase in pay over her present position.

On the way out of town, Joan and Elaine decided to drive past the motel where they had enjoyed such a good night's sleep. Joan had paid cash for the room, and the manager had neglected to give her a receipt. She should have one for her business records, she reasoned, and besides, neither one of them had seen the name of the motel.

"We drove around and around that corner again and again," Joan said. "but there was no motel to be seen. We knew it was directly behind this dairy drive-in, but now there was nothing but a vacant lot there. We thought we were going crazy. We stopped and asked people about the motel behind the Dairy Freeze, but no one knew what we were talking about. They definitely thought we were crazy."

At the time Joan told us her story, she had been with the radio station in the city with the vanishing motel for fifteen years.

"Every once in a while," she admitted, "I will still drive around behind the dairy bar and try to sneak up on the motel. It is never there. And according to people in the community, there never has been a motel, inn, hotel, or hostel on that site. Ever. But it was certainly solid and real wherever it really exists.

"Elaine and I know that we didn't sleep on the ground behind that drive-in, and we didn't sleep in the car," Joan sighed, ending her unusual account. "But where did we spend the night? What dimension did two tired women enter that evening and enjoy a wonderful, restful sleep in? Believe me, there have been many stressful times since when I have wished that I could hide away under the covers of one of the beds in that motel in the middle of nowhere."

~∙∙∙∙∙∙∙~

GETTING LOST IN ANOTHER DIMENSIONAL REALITY

Perhaps one of the most confusing of all circumstances concerning getting lost for a time in another dimensional reality is when it happens to you on what should be very familiar territory. Witness this account from Emmet, who on Mother's Day, May 11, 2008, had a very disconcerting trip on what should have been a non-eventful drive.

"I live in Iowa City, Iowa. I am fifty-four years old, in great health, college-educated (biochem major), do not and have not used drugs. Alcohol consumption is minimal to not at all. I have seen and experienced many of things that you write about, and I had no fear of anything until Mothers Day, 2008."

Here is Emmet's account of that very strange day:

We were invited to our oldest daughter's for Mother's Day dinner in Marion, Iowa. My wife went on ahead. Not liking lots of traffic and realizing that it was now 6:40 P.M., I asked for the quickest route back to 1-380 to get to Iowa City. Having received directions, I was proceeding nicely and got to 1-380 in approximately fifteen minutes, as opposed to the half-hour-plus that it took on Collins road and going across town.

Once on 1-380/218, I called my wife and let her know that I was on my way. The interchange was about ten minutes north of the Collins road exit. The call lasted about two minutes.

Five minutes later, I called another friend who lived in Iowa City and talked for about ten minutes. As I was coming on the Swisher exchange, a jeep was going fifty miles per hour, and I told her that the traffic was terrible (going both north and south) and to hang on a minute until I could get around the jeep. It was almost military in appearance. The fellow driving was young and had a crew-cut and sunglasses. He turned to look at me as I passed him.

In a few minutes, I was looking at the Iowa River/Coralville Dam area when I felt a slight pressure on my forehead. I thought that was weird as I never have headaches. It wasn't really a headache, but rather a pressure lasting a few seconds. Suddenly, my voice felt strangely hoarse and my throat dry, so I told my friend I was going to hang up as I would soon be near Iowa City. The 1-80 and the Iowa City interchanges, with the traffic, meant that I really had to concentrate. I took a sip of my 7-Up, clipped my phone on the side of my bag, and looked up.

Emmet suddenly found himself sixty miles farther down the road than he thought he was. Had he traveled unexpectedly through some kind of multidimensional portal? (*Art by Ricardo Pustanio*)

I was astonished to see that it was suddenly dark, and instead of the heavy traffic, only three vehicles and some steep hills that I did not recognize were visible.

Keep in mind that it was only about 7:10 P.M. and still quite bright. I had my sunglasses on, and just a moment before the traffic had been bumper to bumper.

I drove about three miles or so, and I tried to see something that would explain things. Then I came upon a sign that said "Ottumwa/Mt. Pleasant 1 mile." WHAT? I had somehow got turned around. In one mile, I was in Mt. Pleasant. It was dark and 8:20.

I did an immediate turnaround, called my wife, told her where I was, and that I was badly frightened and disoriented. At first she was very angry and did not believe me. When she realized that something was wrong, she called me every ten minutes to get a progress check until I was home.

After the call to her, I called my friend to explain where I was. She said that only five minutes or so had elapsed since I had hung up. How could I have traveled over sixty miles in only five minutes? I don't know—but traveling at the sixty-mph speed limit, between Mt. Pleasant and Iowa City, it took fifty-three minutes to get home.

This means that I passed the North Liberty exit, the 1-80 interchange, three Iowa City exits, the Hills exit, Riverside/Casino exit, Ainsworth exit, Columbus Junction exit, Washington exit, and one mile of single-lane travel south of Ainsworth—all with no recollection.

Talking to my friend shortly thereafter, a thought occurred to me. I asked her, since it was only about five minutes since I had talked to her that day, what had happened to *her* hour? It had been about 7:15 or so when I had last talked to her, but to her it was only about five minutes after I had hung up and called her back and was in Mt. Pleasant. What happened to her hour?

She doesn't know and doesn't want to think about it. But is it possible that an area can time jump and you are unaware of it because you are stationary? I recognized what had happened as I was traveling a distance that was measurable, but not in time. As I am a fanatic when it comes to distance, time, and landmarks, I realized that something was wrong.

Anyway, my wife will not let me drive the family car out of Iowa City after dark as she is worried I will get lost. *I wasn't lost!* It is a straight shot from Cedar Rapids to Iowa City and from there to Mt. Pleasant, no turns, no stop signs, no stoplights, you can't get lost!

I always thought it would be "cool" to encounter an experience like this, but when you are not expecting it, it is not cool. It is more than frightening, because you have no control over it.

A DOOR TO ANOTHER DIMENSION IN AN ARIZONA RV PARK

Dr. Dave Oester and Dr. Sharon Oester are the coauthors of twenty-nine books and the cofounders of one of the oldest and largest Internet-based ghost research organizations, the International Ghost Hunters Society. They traveled full-time in their RV coach for twelve years before settling down at their Coyote Moon Ranch in the mountains of Northern Arizona. During those twelve years, they visited America's most haunted sites and recorded more than 5,200 ghost voices; they have more than 1,000 recordings of ghost voices posted on their website www.ghostweb.com.

Our friends the Oesters informed us of a dimensional shift that occurred when they were staying in an RV park in Kingman, Arizona. Sharon was the principal percipient of the dimensional phenomenon, so she was elected to tell us of the experience.

It was a beautiful Friday afternoon, and we had spent a quiet day just hanging out around the RV park. Nothing out of the ordinary had happened. It was silent, warm, and sunny in the Southwest. It felt like a good day to just kick back and enjoy our surroundings, which is exactly what we decided to do.

The evenings were cool, and as the sun started to set, we settled down for the evening and continued to enjoy the silence around us. Though this may sound somewhat hokey, we don't find many places that offer such peacefulness while blocking out the sounds of the busy world.

I had trouble sleeping. After tossing and turning until 1:45 A.M., I found myself wide awake so I got up to get a drink of water and returned to bed deciding I would look out at the star-filled sky. I find it relaxing to watch the stars when everyone else is sound asleep.

I raised the blind on the window beside my bed and looked out into the darkness. To my surprise, I found the sky was dark blue, and I couldn't see any stars at all. It looked almost eerie in that the sky wasn't inky black. Then I realized that it was only two days after the full moon so naturally the sky would be lighter and the stars harder to see. The cool air felt good blowing gently through the screen so I left it open and looked around the RV park.

As I watched out the window, I realized that our elderly neighbors across the road had a light on. These folks go to bed at sunset and get up at first light. Rarely do they have lights on, so I wondered if something was wrong.

As I watched, I discovered a light moving around the living room at the front of the trailer facing the road. I watched as the light moved around the room, bouncing and flickering as it slowly moved along the walls.

It had to have been a flashlight they were using, and again I wondered what was wrong. Had someone broken in? Had they heard a noise and decided to check the room? Was there a problem with the electrical system in the trailer? They do have full electrical hook-up, so why would they use a flashlight in the middle of the night?

As all these questions ran through my mind, I saw someone standing in a doorway inside their trailer. The figure was in light-colored clothing, like a long, grey robe, not unusual attire for that hour of the morning. I couldn't make out any facial features at all, and decided I really needed to find a good pair of binoculars so I could see better! (This is called the Gladys Complex, as in the TV sit-com *Bewitched.*)

The light continued to move around, shining around the windows and walls as the figure stood watching. This went on for more than five minutes before all went black in the trailer once again.

I watched for a few minutes longer to see if anyone left the trailer. No one came out and the light didn't come back on.

I could clearly see all of the odd events taking place through the large side window on the trailer, and I was wide awake even at that hour. The whole thing seemed very odd, which held my complete attention. Everything seemed to be okay and the folks had gone back to bed.

> The light continued to move around, shining around the windows and walls as the figure stood watching.

On that Saturday morning, we got up and as the day began. I told Dave about the events that took place earlier that morning. I explained what I saw, and he thought it odd they would be up and using a flashlight at that hour as well. I told Dave about seeing the grey-clad figure through the window and how I could see better if I had binoculars, at which point he laughed at me.

As I drank my morning coffee, I opened the window blind and watched as people started coming outside to begin the day. The old man across the road came out of his trailer, as he does every morning, and walked his bag of trash to the dumpster. The guy next door to him rode off on his bicycle and the lady in the next trailer came out to walk her dog. It was a normal, beautiful day and, once again, everything was peaceful.

As I watched people going about their morning business, my mouth dropped open and I nearly spilled my coffee. I said, "Oh, my gosh!"

Dave asked me what was wrong. It took me a few minutes to find my tongue as I stared out the window. As I looked at the trailer across the road, the same one I had observed at 1:45 A.M., I realized the window I had seen, the light within, and the figure didn't exist. There is no large window on the side of the trailer; it is a solid metal-sided wall.

We have discussed dimensional shifting many times in the past. Sometimes we see things that seem perfectly normal—and only later realize what we saw couldn't have happened on this plane of existence. We live in a very mysterious world where many things can't be explained away by our limited knowledge. These things continue to happen and sometimes we just happen to be at the right place at the right time to observe them.

VISITING THE ASTRAL WORLD

When Paula was thirteen, she fell desperately ill with a rare blood disease, and after a long period of convalescence she was placed in a hospital. Her parents were very devout Roman Catholics, and as she slipped in and out of consciousness, Paula heard her mother talking about their taking her to Lourdes or some healing shrine in the United States. That's when Paula knew her condition must be very serious.

Late one evening, after her parents had both left her room to go to the hospital cafeteria to get something to eat, Paula overheard a doctor and a nurse freely discussing her prognosis just outside the door of her room. The doctor had made the same assumption as her parents, that she was sleeping, but Paula could clearly hear him telling the nurse that it was doubtful that Paula would survive the night. He was confiding in the nurse that he was summoning the courage to tell her parents and how the part of medicine that he hated was the task of informing hopeful parents that all hope for their child had passed. The nurse sympathized with the doctor and said that she would call a priest to administer last rites.

Paula told us that it was at that point that she began to pray with every ounce of what little strength of will and purpose that she had left. She asked God to heal her, and in her thirteen-year-old state of innocence and belief, she fully expected to receive a miracle.

Paula said that she clearly remembered feeling as if her hospital bed was tilting crazily. And then it was as if the entire room was spinning.

"I seemed to leave my bed and float up toward the ceiling," she said, "but I could see that I was really still on the bed. My consciousness, though, my spirit, was up on the ceiling looking down on the physical me."

At her birthday celebrations when Paula was very little, her father would often take a balloon, blow it up and tie the end, then rub it against his sweater or shirt to build up static electricity. Once he had performed this little ritual, he would stick the balloon up on the ceiling or on the wall way up high where none of the children could reach it. That was how Paula felt then, like a balloon stuck on the ceiling of the hospital room.

Paula was confused, then frightened: Had she died?

If the doctor was right, then she had died without even getting to say good-bye to her mom and dad. That made her feel very sad.

If she had died and this was God's idea of the miracle for which she had been praying, then the Almighty's concept of the miraculous certainly did not coincide with her own.

Paula felt herself moving through the ceiling.

"It actually kind of tickled as I felt myself sort of oozing upward through the construction materials of the ceiling," Paula remembered. "And then, whoosh! I was somewhere 'way out in space.'"

At first there seemed to be nothing but darkness all around her. It was much better floating above her body in the hospital room, and she wanted to go back.

Then Paula heard someone calling her name. "I recognized the voice as that of my Grandma, who had died about four years before. I couldn't see her, so I called out for her to come and get me."

A slim shaft of light pierced the darkness, and it seemed as though far, far away, Paula could see an image of her grandmother. She seemed to be beckoning to her, and Paula could hear her urging her to move toward the little speck of light.

Paula remembered that at this point in the experience she was convinced that she had died. "I was saddened because of leaving my parents and my friends, but I had always really liked Grandma. She had always held me on her lap when we came to visit, and she would make special chocolate chip cookies with marshmallows for me. So I thought that if I would be with Grandma, then death wouldn't be so bad."

As soon as the slightest thought of acceptance of her transition came to her, Paula found that she began to fly toward the light with much greater speed. She could see a small cottage with a beautiful flower garden. Grandma had always loved flowers. And she could smell chocolate chip and marshmallow cookies.

Paula's flight was suddenly blocked by three tall figures in lavender robes. She clearly recalled that one had a beard, so he was definitely male.

"I think the others were female," she said, "but they could have been androgynous beings. None of them really looked like my thirteen-year-old concepts of angels. They looked to me more like people from the time of Jesus and the disciples."

The bearded entity told Paula that she could not join her grandmother on the Other Side.

"I was upset by this announcement," Paula said. "I thought he meant that I was going to be taken to some other place, that I would be separated from Grandma, that I wasn't good enough to be with her."

> The bearded angelic figure informed Paula that she would not be returning to the same body. They would heal it before she left their sacred dimension.

The being explained that what he meant was that it was not yet Paula's time to stay in heaven. He said that she must return to her body.

Paula told him that was impossible. She had heard the doctor telling a nurse that she was dying. Besides, she had been so terribly ill that she really didn't want to go to that diseased little body of hers. The bearded angelic figure informed Paula that she would not be returning to the same body. They would heal it before she left their sacred dimension.

"As strange as it seems," Paula told us, "it was at that point that all three of the angels opened their mouths and began to sing this most incredibly beautiful song. My entire spiritual essence began to vibrate and to glow. I remember somehow feeling at one with the angel-song and, well, everything—the angels, God, the universe. The next thing 1 knew, I was opening my eyes in an oxygen tent. Mom and Dad were standing there with tears in their eyes, and the doctor seemed really surprised."

Paula heard the nurse telling her parents that it was a miracle.

The doctor shook his head and said in a tone of amazement, "I feared we might lose her, but thank God, she's come back!"

Paula knows for certain that "something happened" to bring about a miraculous cure of a blood disease that her doctors had decreed was incurable.

"And that is about as technical and scientific as the doctors were able to be: Something happened and the disease disappeared," Paula summarized the official diagnosis with a slight satirical tone.

For the next four or five years, Paula was regularly examined by doctors to be certain that her disease was truly "in remission."

"By the time that I was nineteen, they finally pronounced me officially cured," said Paula, now a healthy thirty-year-old mother of two. "It may have taken the doctors six years to accept the miracle, but I accepted it the instant God gave the angels permission to heal me and I became one with that incredibly beautiful angel-song."

Had Paula's soul essence really gone to the popular conception of Heaven, a place where one's dear deceased love ones await the newly arrived soul? Or had she entered a dimension of Time and Space that mystics and spiritualists have for centuries termed the Astral Realm, a kind of in-between universe where Spirit Teachers exist to instruct their earthling charges?

Concern over Changing Weather Patterns in the Astral World

Susan H. of Pennsylvania witnessed a low over-flight of a strange glowing object in the sky when she was five years old. She stood on her front lawn, spellbound, as the bright light came speeding over the rooftops in her neighborhood.

As an adult, Susan has a degree in chemistry, and she is the technical manager of an industrial laboratory. She is married, with no children—a level-headed woman with her feet solidly on the ground. And yet she reports a vision, a dream of being taken to a large group of people who are gathered in a strange city in some other world or in some other dimension in the astral domain. The citizens of that reality seem concerned and speak with great agitation about recent reports of odd patterns of dramatic weather changes on planet Earth. Susan knows about the reports, but she is not anxious, because to her they are normal and expected.

"I responded to the milling group in a very matter-of-fact manner, saying, 'Yes, things are changing—because *they* are here.'"

At this point in the dream she gestures upward to a clouded sky where two, possibly three, golden submarine-type spacecraft have appeared. "I had been totally aware of their impending arrival."

The citizens of the other reality observed our world and were disturbed by the climatic changes that are occurring. (Art by Ricardo Pustanio)

Susan says that the vision shifts, and she is transported with a large number of people on board one of the craft. "Each of us has a small collection of things with us in various types of knapsacks, suitcases, and so forth. We are in this huge room that seems to have some curves to it. We receive a message to go to the view port. All of us are unafraid, accepting and expectant.

"We leave our stuff along the corridor and proceed to the view port. We are hovering high enough, so that a sense of the curvature of the Earth can be seen, but we are not so high that we cannot see that we are over the water with the shoreline in full view. We are told that they will begin a rotation of the spaceship and that we will see that there is nothing to be concerned about, such as falling down because of gravity. The ship begins to rotate. As we watch the shoreline move during the rotation, we are amazed and excited, and feeling somewhat unnatural. We are astonished when we stay in one spot with respect to the motion of the ship.

"It was an incredible feeling, and one which I distinctly recall to this day," Susan said. "It was almost like the kind of amusement park ride that strives to disorient through optical illusion. After the rotation, we were told to make ourselves comfortable, and we returned to the corridor outside the view port and sat on the floor. I had the sense that we were going on a long voyage, but one which I knew was not going to take long."

AN ASTRAL PROJECTION OR AN ACTUAL PHYSICAL ENCOUNTER?

Mary is a freelance writer from Salem, Ohio. At around the age of ten she experienced an astral projection or an actual physical encounter. It is all hazy to her now, but she remembers at night seeing a large spaceship hovering about twenty feet off the ground in her backyard.

A door opened in the bottom of the craft, and a light beamed down. A woman in a white gown appeared to Mary. Mary, reared as a Roman Catholic, somehow assumed that the woman was Joan of Arc. She was not afraid of the glowing woman, and the entity gave her a message that she still, even as an adult, cannot understand very well.

But Mary remembers that the woman said that she knew that she was lonely and that she would give her a playmate who would always be with her. The woman said that she would have to go back.

Mary cried because she didn't want the glowing woman to go. The woman stood in the beam of white light again and cloned herself, thus making an exact duplicate of her physical form. This duplicate was the woman, but she now appeared as she would have as a little girl.

The beautiful woman in the white gown appeared to the ten-year-old Mary as an astral projection, though it looked as if she was emerging from a spaceship. (*Art by Ricardo Pustanio*)

When she was eleven, a man appeared in her room and lifted Mary's soul essence to join him in a spaceship. She remembers that it was all white, except for a purple object on a low white table. Mary does not remember what the entity told her, but he had black hair cut in an ancient Egyptian style.

As she grew older, Mary understood that the experience aboard the spaceship seemed to have been done by astral projection. Today, in adulthood, Mary says that "they" have often guided her and her husband to various places. Once they saw seven craft, including a mothership. Two other witnesses confirmed their sightings, and the experience was reported to a local UFO-investigating group.

In 1998, Mary and her children saw a large ship hovering over their house. It was shaped like a diamond with one end cut off, and it had hundreds of gadgets in its underside. It was slow-moving and appeared two hundred or more feet long. It disappeared as if it vaporized.

Mary describes the two entities with whom she has special contact since childhood as "extremely good-looking humans." They have an aura around them and they glow, but they appear to be solid. Although she has been in contact with them for years, their age always appears to be roughly twenty-six to thirty years old. The hair of both male and female is cut in a page-boy style. The man has black hair, and the woman's is a golden blond. The woman wears a long white gown with a rounded neck. The man wears a white pantsuit garment. Both of them are very kind.

"They are not permitted to tell me everything, but they give hints so I can get the answers to my questions. They help me with my life. I don't receive contact with them very often, but they are watching me. They give me advice, which I try always to follow."

Mary reported that once her guides directed her husband and her to a nursing home in the area where they suggested that her elderly father might be comfortable. What a perfect place, she thought, for aliens to be in charge. It would be ideal. It would not be detected, and they would be able to gain a great deal of Earth information from the elderly people.

⌐⇒⎯⟋⟍⎯⇐¬

PARAPHYSICAL BEINGS AND ALTERED STATES OF CONSCIOUSNESS

Dreams, astral projection, other worlds. It is clear to us that many people are receiving instruction and teachings from intelligences representing themselves as alien beings, angels, or ancient masters. If it is possible that the human essence can soar free of the accepted limitations of time and space imposed by the physical body and truly engage in "astral flight," "soul travel," or the more academic "out-of-body experience," then it may well be that the paraphysical aspect of humankind may more easily interact with paraphysical intelligences. Indeed, many accounts that tell of a subject having been taken aboard a UFO may be descriptions of a mental/spiritual/nonmaterial experience, rather than an actual physical/material one. And it is quite likely that the individual undergoing such an encounter is first placed into an altered state of consciousness.

An altered state of consciousness is a brain state wherein one loses the sense of identity with one's body or with one's normal sense perceptions. A person may enter an altered state of consciousness through such things as sensory deprivation or overload, neurochemical imbalance, fever, or trauma. One may also achieve an altered state by chanting, meditating, entering a trance state, or ingesting psychedelic drugs.

The testimonies of those high-profile mystics and meditators who claim that their ability to enter altered states of consciousness has brought them enlightenment or transcendence are generally regarded with great skepticism among the majority of scientists in Western society. Descriptions of mystical revelations become almost florid as self-proclaimed seers and mystics attempt to translate their psychedelic drug or trance state experiences into the language of a technically oriented society.

However, in the opinion of many open-minded psychologists and students of the individual mystical experience, science must abandon the notion that waking, rational consciousness is the only form of any value and that all other kinds are pathological.

William James, the great pioneer of the study of consciousness, wrote in *The Varieties of Religious Experience* that what we call our "normal waking consciousness" is but one special type of consciousness, while all about it, separated by the slightest of barriers, "there lie potential forms of consciousness entirely different." While many individuals may go through life without suspecting the existence of these states of consciousness, "… apply the requisite stimulus, and at a touch they are there in all their completeness…. No account of the universe in its totality can be final which leaves these forms of consciousness disregarded."

Real Encounters, Different Dimensions, and Otherworldly Beings

We suggest that continued research into altered states of consciousness may well reveal that humankind's most important discoveries, its highest peaks of ecstasy, and its greatest moments of inspiration occur in reverie, in dreams, and in states of consciousness presently ignored by the professional world and the general public.

⸺⁜⸺

VARIOUS TYPES OF CONSCIOUSNESS DESCRIBED

Researchers who study aspects of human consciousness have suggested that within the course of a single day an individual may flicker in and out of several states of consciousness. In 1968, Dr. Stanley Krippner, at that time director of the Dream Laboratory at Maimonides Medical Center in New York City, sent Brad his paper on what he believed to be the twenty states of consciousness. This list has proven extremely useful to us through our many years of research, and we present a condensed version of Dr. Krippner's list for the benefit of all serious-minded students of the paranormal.

The Six States of "non-reflective consciousness," characterized by the absence of self-consciousness, include the following:

1. *Bodily feelings*, which are induced by normal bodily functioning and are characterized by non-reflective awareness in the organs and tissues of the digestive, glandular, respiratory, and other bodily systems. This awareness does not become self-conscious unless such stimuli as pain or hunger intensify a bodily feeling.

2. *Stored memories*, which do not become self-conscious until the individual reactivates them.

3. *Coma*, which is induced by illness, epileptic seizures, or physical injuries to the brain, and is characterized by prolonged non-reflective consciousness of the entire organism.

4. *Stupor*, which is induced by psychosis, narcotics, or overindulgence in alcohol, and is characterized by greatly reduced ability to perceive incoming sensations.

5. *Non-rapid-eye-movement sleep*, which is caused by a normal part of the sleep cycle at night or during daytime naps, and is characterized by a minimal amount of mental activity, which may sometimes be recalled upon awakening.

6. *Rapid-eye-movement sleep*, which is a normal part of the nighttime sleep cycle, and is characterized by the mental activity known as dreams.

The reflective, or self-conscious, states of consciousness are the following:

1. *Pragmatic Consciousness*, the everyday, waking conscious state, characterized by alertness, logic, and rationality, cause-and-effect thinking, and goal-directedness. In this level of consciousness, one has the feeling that he or she is in control and has the ability to move at will from perceptual activity to conceptual thinking to idea formation to motor activity.

2. *Lethargic Consciousness*, characterized by sluggish mental activity which has been induced by fatigue, sleep deprivation, feelings of depression, or certain drugs.

3. *Hyperalert Consciousness* is brought about by a period of heightened vigilance, such as sentry duty, watching over a sick child, or by certain drugs, such as amphetamines.

There are many different states of consciousness that we can experience, ranging from the unconscious to the hyperalert and rapturous consciousness. (Art by Ricardo Pustanio)

Levels or types of consciousness with varying degrees of what could be considered an altered state might include the following:

1. *Rapturous Consciousness*, characterized by intense feelings and overpowering emotions and induced by sexual stimulation, the fervor of religious conversion, and the ingestion of certain drugs.

2. *Hysterical Consciousness*, induced by rage, jealousy, fear, neurotic anxiety, violent mob activity, and certain drugs. As opposed to rapturous consciousness, which is generally evaluated as pleasant and positive in nature, hysterical consciousness is considered negative and destructive.

3. *Fragmented Consciousness*, defined as a lack of integration among important segments of the total personality, very often results in psychosis, severe neurosis, amnesia, multiple personality, or dissociation. Such a state of consciousness is induced by severe psychological stress over a period of time. It may also be brought about temporarily by accidents and psychedelic drugs.

Real Encounters, Different Dimensions, and Otherworldly Beings

4. *Relaxed Consciousness*, characterized by a state of minimal mental activity, passivity, and an absence of motor activity. This state of consciousness may be brought about by lack of external stimulation, such as sunbathing, floating in water, and certain drugs.

5. *Daydreaming*, induced by boredom, social isolation, or sensory deprivation.

6. *Trance Consciousness*, induced by rapt attentiveness to a single stimulus, such as the voice of a hypnotist, one's own heartbeat, a chant, certain drugs, trance-inducing rituals, and primitive dances. The trance state is characterized by hypersuggestibility and concentrated attention on one stimulus to the exclusion of all others.

7. *Expanded Consciousness*, composed of four levels:

   A. The sensory level, characterized by subjective reports of space, time, body image, or sense impressions having been altered.

   B. The recollective-analytic level, which summons up memories of one's past and provides insights concerning self, work, or personal relationships.

   C. The symbolic level, which is often characterized by vivid visual imagery of mythical, religious, and historical symbols.

   D. The integrative level, in which the individual undergoes an intense religious illumination, experiences a dissolution of self, and is confronted by God or some divine being.

—∽∿∿∽—

ASTRAL TRAVEL AND OUT-OF-BODY EXPERIENCE

There is an enormous body of literature dealing with out-of-body experience (OBE), and numerous accounts of the phenomenon are to be found in mystical and religious traditions. Possibly it is a kind of OBE brought about by the subtle or not so subtle influence of the Other that may provoke experiences with the astral worlds.

Spontaneous OBEs often seem to fall within eight general categories:

1. Projections while the subject sleeps

2. Projections while the subject is undergoing surgery, childbirth, tooth extraction, etc.

3. Projection at the time of accident, during which the subject receives a terrible physical jolt and seems to have his spirit literally thrown from his body

4. Projection during intense physical pain

5. Projection during illness

6. Projection during pseudodeath, also known as the near-death-experience (NDE) wherein the subject "dies" for several moments and is subsequently revived (Dr. Elisabeth Kubler-Ross, Raymond Moody, and Dr. P.M.H. Atwater are authors who deal with this phenomenon in great depth)

7. Projection at the moment of death, when the deceased subject appears to a living percipient with whom he has an emotional link

8. Conscious out-of-body projections in which the subject deliberately seeks to project his spirit from his body

Now, it would appear, another category must be added: projection during which the subject feels that he or she has been taken aboard a spaceship or to another world and has interacted with an alien intelligence.

Consider this account of the kind of UFO-OBE that results in a recognition between strangers sent to us by a correspondent named Jacob:

When I answered the door, I saw my friend Charles standing there along with a man I did not know, whom Charles introduced as James, a friend from work. James had a look of shock on his face. For most of the evening he kept staring at me, and I finally insisted that I know why.

Reluctantly at first, James finally said he had had a weird dream about someone he'd never met before, and he had recognized me as the man in the dream. He said that in the setting of his dream, he had been in a clearing with a lot of other people. They seemed to be waiting for someone or something. He did not know anyone there except

RICARDO PUSTANIO 2012

Spontaneous astral projections can be initiated at times when the body is going through trauma or is near death or during sleep, but there are also cases of deliberate OBEs. *(Art by Ricardo Pustanio)*

Real Encounters, Different Dimensions, and Otherworldly Beings

me. He said that I smiled at him and made him feel calm and peaceful. He trusted me. Then everyone began to look up.

The sky was clear and star-studded except for a large circular patch directly overhead. Then he noticed that there was a large oval object blotting out the sky. As he realized this, an opening appeared in the center of the object, and a blue-white light spilled out.

He felt strange and he looked around to see how the others were reacting. Then he noticed that everyone was floating up toward the opening, one by one.

He blacked out and came to in a dome-shaped room. The other people appeared to be awakening at the same time. Everyone had been placed in one of the chairs that lined the walls in three tiers. Across from them were electronic panels with flashing lights, dials, switches, and cabinets. In the center of the cabinets were two seats in front of what appeared to be control panels. Behind this area was a brilliant light. In the exact center of the room was a column, or pole, running through the floor and ceiling. A low railing, about three feet high, encircled the column.

> He felt strange and he looked around to see how the others were reacting. Then he noticed that everyone was floating up toward the opening, one by one.

James looked at the other men and women, and they appeared to be as confused as he was. He felt as though someone were missing. Then everyone turned and looked toward the center of the room. There stood a man in a close-fitting, one-piece, silvery spacesuit that covered his hands and feet. He wore a globe over his head that obscured his features.

"Welcome aboard, friends," the man in the spacesuit said, as he reached up and removed the globe.

And James said that it was I in the silvery spacesuit!

I have now experienced this sort of thing again and again over a period of a year and a half. The shocked stranger, the stare, the same dream, down to the most minute details.

After the fifth or sixth time, I began thinking, "Oh, no, not again!" I can't say how many times this has happened. I have lost track.

In discussing this dream-recognition phenomenon further, the following additional comments and details were produced: One person having a dream about a future meeting with a stranger is an occurrence not at all unfamiliar in the literature of psychic phenomena. But we are speaking of a situation in which approximately a dozen men and women experienced the same dream, identical to the smallest detail, all climaxing with the meeting of the same man. This bends the laws of chance out of all proportion and possibility.

Jacob continued with his account, writing that he began asking those individuals who claimed that they knew him from a UFO dream to draw a floor plan of the dome-shaped room. Allowing for differences in artistic ability, Jacob said, they all drew the same, identical floor plan.

Jacob then had them mark the position that they had occupied on the three tiers of seats, hoping that some of them would mark the same position. But none did. Each one had a different location in which he or she said they had been sitting.

He then asked them to describe the suit that he had been wearing. Again, the descriptions were identical.

Just about every detail that Jacob could possibly think of, he asked—and they all agreed.

Jacob added another interesting facet: "I asked each one of them *when* they had had the dream, and none could remember. This puzzled some of them. Surely they could recall vaguely if it had been a week, two weeks, a month. But they had no idea whether it had been the night before or a month before. Apparently, the dreams were not normal dreams."

TAKEN BY TWO MEN IN BLACK

Hugh, another correspondent, admitted that he had carefully considered what he was relaying when he at last decided to share the following account with us.

It was in the fall of 1959. I was sitting in my lounge chair, reading, dozing. Yet I was tense, nervous, restless. Something seemed to be in the back of my mind that I seemed to have forgotten but shouldn't have.

Suddenly I looked toward the door. I knew someone was on the other side. I laid my book down, got up, went to the door, opened it a crack, and looked out.

There were two men there dressed in black. They could have been identical twins, they looked so much alike. They were dark complexioned with Asian-slanted eyes, but they were definitely not Asian. Remember, this was in 1959, long before people started talking about "Men in Black."

They never said a word, but I heard inside my mind: "Are you ready?"

I don't know why, but for some reason or other, I indicated that I was ready to go. Since it was very hot that night, I had stripped down to my birthday suit, so I reached for a pair of walking shorts. Again, I heard inside my head: "That will not be necessary. No one will see you." Strangely enough, that seemed to satisfy me.

We stepped out into the hall, then instantly we were on top of a hill in back of the apartments. I was rather surprised that the scene had changed so quickly. I noticed the headlights of a car coming down the street, and I ducked behind the two men. I didn't want to be seen running around naked.

I heard some laughter in my mind: "We told you no one would see you. Try it!"

I boldly stepped around in front of them, propped my hands on my hips, daring anyone to see me. The car, with a man and a woman in it, passed a few feet from us. They didn't even look in my direction. It was as if we weren't there. That surprised me.

I turned to say something to my companions, and they were looking up. I followed their gaze and realized that something was suspended above us. As I did so, an opening appeared in its center, and blue-white light came tumbling out of it.

I felt a queasy sensation in the pit of my stomach, like when you are in an elevator or an airplane that is dropping too fast. I could see the apartment houses and the ground receding below us. We were floating up toward whatever that thing was. I blacked out as we were approaching the opening.

When I came to, I was lying on my side facing a wall.

I rolled over on my back and sat up. I was in an oddly-shaped room. The best way I can describe it is like a wedge of pie with the point bitten off.

The whole room was bare except for some kind of projection on which I was sitting. Everything seemed to be made out of a blue-gray material. While the walls were very hard, the surface on which I was sitting was soft, even though everything seemed to be made of the same material. The room was bathed in a soft glow; there were no shadows anywhere, and there was no light source that I could see.

I heard a female voice say, "He's awake now."

I looked around to see if I could spot a speaker, a TV camera, or something, but again I saw nothing but blank walls and a ceiling.

About this time on the short wall—the one bitten off the end of the pie wedge—a door appeared and opened. I could see into a hallway. Although the hall was dark, there was blue-white illumination that appeared as though it were coming from some great distance.

Two shadows flitted across the doorway. I couldn't tell anything about their shapes. The movement was too rapid and too distorted.

But I got a mental impression, if you will, of two people approaching—a man in the front and a woman in the back—carrying a tray full of some kind of surgical instruments and hypodermic syringes.

The next thing I knew, I was back in my apartment, in my chair, reading my book. I gave a shudder and thought how sleepy I was. I went to bed, laughing about what a vivid imagination I had.

When I awakened the next morning, I regarded the whole episode as a strange dream. But when I reached for the book that I had left on my desk, I found that it had disappeared. For two days I searched the apartment without finding the book that I had been reading when the bizarre experience interrupted me.

> If this book did indeed vanish from our apartment and then reappear, the question is *how?*

When my roommate, a special agent of the FBI, returned from a trip, I challenged him to prove his effectiveness by finding the missing book. We turned the apartment upside down, searching for the vanished volume.

We started at one end of the apartment, and we moved, dusted, waxed, and cleared everything all the way to the other end. We found things we had forgotten about, things that we'd thought we had lost someplace, but no sign of the book.

Then, about one week later, we suddenly found the missing book on the edge of the desk, right where I had left it.

If this book did indeed vanish from our apartment and then reappear, the question is *how?* Which goes back to that dream sequence again. If it really happened, how did I get back in the apartment, since when I pulled the door closed behind us, it locked automatically—and I had no key in my birthday suit!

If we assume for a moment that the dream sequence really occurred, it brings up some interesting points. For one, the possibility of teleportation. When I was let out into the hall, we were instantly on top of the hill. There was no time lapse. It was an instantaneous thing.

If we did teleport, why didn't we teleport directly to the UFO? The only explanation I can reason out is that somehow or other the UFO was shielded or had some kind of radiation that prevented teleportation and we had to be levitated inside.

When I dream, I usually know, even in my dream, that I am dreaming. But in this case, I didn't have that knowledge, or even that feeling, of a dream. It was dreamlike because I had so little control over my actions, but there was no sense of time lapse between the moment I was reading my book and the moment I looked up at the door. If I had nodded off to sleep in those seconds, I would assume that there would have been a feeling of change; yet there didn't seem to be any. The only change seemed to be that I suddenly lost control of myself and became more of a robot than anything else.

I think a lot of us have been controlled telepathically, somehow or other, by the UFO intelligences. That's just a feeling I have. I have no proof.

That's the trouble with the whole UFO phenomenon. What concrete evidence is there? All the weird things that have occurred around UFOs seem to be leading us more into the area of parapsychology and religion.

And perhaps, we propose, that is exactly where the Other has been intending to take us all along.

THE FLEXIBLE DIMENSIONS OF THE DREAM WORLD

Rachael M., of Glendale, California, states that at the age of six she had a dream of being on another planet. She still remembers how beautiful it was. The colors were vivid and clear, and there were more varieties of colors than there were on Earth. The main color of the planet, she recalls, was a glorious yellow.

"That may be difficult to imagine, but just as our main colors here—the blue of the sky, the green of plant life, the brown earth—blend to make this wonderful planet, so on that world did the colors blend in the most wonderful way," she said.

When Rachael was ten years old, her father passed away. The loss of her father was devastating to her. She began to feel more and more alienated from people around her.

"I felt completely different because of that dream and others like it that I had every month or so," she told us. "I could not think the way most people thought or talk the way they talked. I couldn't understand the little girls squealing when the little boys chased them, nor could 1 understand the chase. Later on, 1 couldn't understand changing boyfriends in a week or anything that was done only as a status symbol. I don't understand the value of gossip, and I've never understood group or racial prejudice. I've always felt so alone, with such a deep longing inside, as if I didn't belong with these people here on Earth, but I haven't known where I belonged. I still feel that way. I have people I love, sure, friends I care about, but I feel deep down that it may be many lifetimes before I can see those whom I truly know, those beings who *are* love. I don't know—maybe it's a memory of the beginning."

RICARDO PUSTANIO 2012

The beings who visited Rachael looked human but had a fluorescent glow. (Art by Ricardo Pustanio)

Rachael firmly states that she considers Earth to be very beautiful, but ever since that powerful dream when she was six, and the series of dreams that she continued to receive, she has never thought of herself as an Earthling or felt truly at home on this planet. During the last several years, although she has come to love the Earth even more, she has become even more convinced, because of dreams, that she is of extraterrestrial origin. In fact, she thinks that all humans are.

She wonders if the Cro-Magnon may have been a leftover from some other world, starting over here on Earth. And could the Star People be the enlightened brothers from the same part of the universe? Could a deep sense of love have brought all people together again?

She has been told in a psychic reading that she spent three hundred years on Venus in preparation before coming to Earth and that she comes from a place in the stars called Soropa. Rachael has also been told that somewhere in space there is a very large spaceship in which there is a body that she occupied in a previous lifetime lying in a state of suspended animation.

When Rachael was eighteen years old, she met Glenn, whom she later married in 1967. Shortly after they met, Glenn told her that when he was twelve years old he had been entrusted with some information from the stars. At last she had found someone with whom she could communicate, someone to whom she could relate.

Rachael ponders frequently a dream that she had in August 1968 when she, Glenn, and their six-month-old son, Eric, lived in a small apartment in San Diego. Glenn was on a midshipman cruise; he was in the Navy at that time. Their apartment was a second-floor corner with a fire escape outside the window.

> One night it seemed so real to dream that I was awakened by three beings in the room with me. There were two men and one woman. They looked like us except that their skin had a fluorescent glow. The woman had long red hair and violet eyes. They did not talk, but they communicated with me telepathically. They said they wanted me to go with them.

We left through the window where a starship hovered beyond the balcony. I went with them into the interior of the ship. We must have floated rather than walked. I don't remember my feet moving at all.

They directed me to go into what I knew to be a mind probe chamber. There was a glasslike cylindrical tube, probably about three feet in diameter, that came down from the ceiling. Inside it was an instrument about eight inches in diameter. It looked something like a dentist's X-ray machine. There were no wires or anything visible.

One of the beings stepped into the circle, and the tube came down to surround his body.

Then the instrument touched the top of his head to probe his mind.

I asked them why they wanted me to do this, and they said that there was some information that they needed, information that I had buried in my memory, and they could only get it from me. I had the feeling that it was some kind of formula.

I was more than a little uneasy. If I refused to cooperate, they were going to force me. But from somewhere within me, I found a kind of power of my own. I told them they could not force me to enter the mind probe. I put up my own shield of protection. I used a kind of mental force to keep their minds from touching mine. I told them that they had to let me go, and I was able to move past them out of the ship.

The next thing I remember is awakening in the dark in the corner of our tiny kitchen, crouched on my knees and scared half to death.

In yet another dream, Rachael experienced what she thinks now may have been a past life aboard an immense starship.

"I had a little cubicle, probably fifteen feet or so in diameter. There were instruments all around the inside. My job was to scan a section of the universe, looking for anything unusual. It was probably something like a radar unit. It seems to me that this ship was stationary, maybe like a space station.

"What happened in the dream is that someone came into my room and asked me if I knew how to turn on a power switch. I said that I did and left the room with him. There was a switch between an outer and inner wall which I activated, then I went back to my job."

Real Encounters, Different Dimensions, and Otherworldly Beings

Rachael was quite astonished when, in December 1982, Glenn began to channel a voice that identified itself as a being from another world. Rachael asked if she could use the name Alpha in referring to the entity, and the being said that that was fine since she needed a point of reference. Alpha explained to Rachael that he represented multidimensional entities from near the central Sun. When Rachael asked if they had bodies like humans, Alpha replied, no, they had bodies of light.

Alpha and other beings, which later channeled through Glenn, spoke of the Circle of Brotherhood, of being from a race that died from a genetic disease. They said repeatedly that humankind must unite their minds and join the Brotherhood.

Rachael said that one night she dreamed that entities from the planet Xerces in the star system Xandor visited her. The beings declared that their home was three hundred million light years away. They told her that they would be coming to Earth very soon.

When we last heard from Rachael in 2007, she was still continuing to have her strange outer-space dreams—dreams that seemed to comprise a bizarre series of visits in her sleep for more than forty-five years.

DREAMS—THE MOST COMMON PARANORMAL MYSTERY

Whether in ancient or in contemporary times, dreams are a mystery of the mind that everyone has experienced and, on occasion, quite likely pondered the meaning of. Whether these sleep time adventures are considered voyages of the soul, messages from the gods, the doorway of the unconscious, or accidental by-products of insufficient oxygen in the brain, down through the ages thoughtful men and women have sought to learn more about this intriguing activity of the sleeping consciousness.

In 1899, Sigmund Freud, a Viennese psychiatrist and the founder of psychoanalysis, brought dreams into the realm of the scientific community with the publication of his monumental work, *The Interpretation of Dreams*, in which he maintained that the dream is "the guardian of sleep" and "the royal road" to understanding man's unconscious. Freud's theory was basically that the dream was a disguised wish-fulfillment of infantile sexual needs, which were repressed by built-in censors of the waking mind. Through the use of a complex process of "dream work," which Freud developed, the dream could be unraveled backward, penetrating the unconscious memory of the dreamer and thereby setting the person free.

Jung found startling similarities in the unconscious contents and the symbolic processes of both modern and primitive humans. (*Art by Bill Oliver*)

Swiss psychiatrist Carl G. Jung, a student and later dissenter of Freudian techniques, added new dimensions to the understanding of the Self through dreams. In Jung's opinion, the unconscious was far more than a depository for the past—it was also full of future psychic situations and ideas. Jung saw the dream as a compensatory mechanism whose function was to restore one's psychological balance. His concept of a collective unconscious linked man with his ancestors as part of the evolutionary tendency of the human mind.

Jung found startling similarities in the unconscious contents and the symbolic processes of both modern and primitive humans, and he recognized what he called "archetypes," mental forces and symbology whose presence cannot be explained by anything in the individual's own life, but seemed to be "aboriginal, innate, and inherited shapes of the human mind." Jung believed that it is crucial to pay attention to the archetypes met in dream life. Of special importance is the "shadow," a figure of the same sex as the dreamer, which contains all the repressed characteristics one has not developed in his conscious life. The "anima" is the personification of all the female tendencies, both positive and negative, in the male psyche. Its counterpart in the female psyche is the "animus."

The most mysterious, but most significant, of the Jungian archetypes is the Self, which M.-L. von Franz describes in Jung's *Man and His Symbols* (1964) as the regulating center that brings about a constant expansion and maturing of the personality, "… and the fulfillment of that process … the 'Cosmic Man' who lives within the heart of every individual, and yet at the same time fills the entire cosmos."

In April 2012, author William Kern sent us an in-depth exploration of a dream that certainly demonstrates the psychic integration of the personality of an extremely creative individual. Kern served twenty years in the U.S. Navy as a photojournalist and documentary motion picture cameraman, participating in many NASA unmanned and manned space missions. Kern served ten years in the intelligence community prior to and during the Vietnam conflict. He has written and published eight novels, including, *The Morningstar Conspiracy*, *The Windmills of Mars*, and *The Man Who Fell from a Clear Blue Sky*. He has also compiled information for other books, including, *Secret Societies and the Founding of America*, *UFOs: Another Point of View*, and *Introduction to Conspiracy*. He is currently the layout artist and ad designer for *Conspiracy Journal* (available online at http://therealmidori.com).

⟞⟝⟞⟝⟞

THE AWFUL DREAM

By William Kern

Behold, I show you a mystery; we shall not all sleep, but we shall all be changed.

I was born into this world dead, a breach-born child. The doctors (I was told) worked for some time to revive me, which was quite a feat back in 1936. If it is true, as the prophets say, that we live two lives—first when we are born and again when we die—then I have already lived twice. I have some pre-birth memories.

About ten years ago, just before my mother died, I described a house to her and asked her where we lived and how old I was. It is the house detailed in my book, *The Windmills of Mars*. It was on Adams Avenue in Evansville, Indiana. My mother stared at me for some time and said, "You couldn't possibly remember that house. We only lived there for two weeks and you were only 10 months old."

I then related the story of "my dream" of seeing myself as an adult walking across a desert toward myself as an infant, of falling and dying and of seeing or feeling an anomalous cloud rising out of the dead adult me and entering the infant me.

And that is when she told me that from the time I was revived until the time we lived at that house so briefly, I cried day and night ("wailed," she said), but after we left that house and moved into the new house, all my crying and wailing stopped. She said she believed "that was when you received your soul."

I am moved by waves of feelings, lonely in the harsh shadows that run like fear beside me, darkness in which I am lost but cannot hide. I tremble to share the vision of what I see and hear in the darkness, share with someone, just one someone who might understand the deep, mysterious, unuttered screams that rise in my throat like bile and are choked into my guts before I can say them.

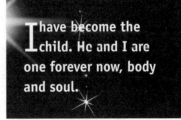

I have become the child. He and I are one forever now, body and soul.

I've seen life and death beyond the limits of human fear, outside the prison of my soul, free from the arrows of pain. I have breathed life before, the blood of it has run through me hot and furious, the memories of it are caught in the web of my brain, strong and enduring. Its seed has infected me, running through the very essence of all that I see and do in this life. It devours me until I am transformed.

Can you remember when you died and how old you were? Can you remember when you were reborn?

I can.

In the distance, I see a child lying upon the ground, a sleeping infant who is dreaming of an adult male walking across the wastelands dressed in a shimmering garment and near to death. As I approach the infant I know that I am losing consciousness; I am dying, the clock is ticking, time is running out, and the poker is in the fire. My cosmic second has ended and I fall to my knees and just before I collapse upon the red, cold sand, I can see that the infant is me.

I lie on my back, sleeping in a dimly lighted room, with my head turned to the left. A cool sheet is beneath me. Faint light enters from an uncurtained window. Far away, walking toward me across a barren, red desert, I dream of a male figure dressed in a shimmering uniform. He appears and vanishes like a mirage in the rising thermals, always and ever drawing nearer and nearer. After what seems hours the man is beside me, looming above. He raises his hand to his brow, rolls his eyes skyward and sinks wearily to his knees, falls dead, face down, into the cold sand, the light of understanding drained from his weary countenance.

As he falls, I see that I am the man.

At the same moment, an anomalous cloud bursts from the still, adult figure, whirling and rising above me, then rushes downward, exploding within me silently, painlessly.

This house has a green roof. It is painted white, chipped and peeling. There is a brick carport and a sagging garage beneath a broad catalpa tree behind; tall maples line the street beside and in front. The ceilings are high, the windows tall, the wallpaper is stained and faded. There are two stairways, one in the living room foyer and one at the rear entrance. They lead to rooms on the second floor. I know the rooms are there although I have never been on the second floor, have never seen the stairs.

I am in the bedroom of a ten-month old infant boy. He sleeps fitfully on his back, his head turned to the left. He is dreaming of a man walking toward him across the broad, awful desert. He was breach born and dead, this tiny boy, revived after long, anxious minutes.

I have become the child. He and I are one forever now, body and soul.

I am the dreamer and the dreamed, dead and reborn.

I will remember the dream all my life but of the events that have occurred before this night I have no memory.

—◁◁◁◁◁ ᔈ ▷▷▷▷▷—

RE-OWNING THE FRAGMENTS OF OUR PERSONALITY IN DREAMS

Friedrich (Fritz) Perls, the founder of Gestalt therapy, believed that dreams are "the royal road to integration." In his view, the various parts of a dream should be thoroughly examined and even role-played to gain self-awareness and to integrate fragmented aspects of the personality into wholeness. According to Dr. Perls, the different parts of a dream are fragments of our personalities. Since our aim is to become a unified person without conflicts, what we have to do is to put the different fragments of the dream together. We have to re-own these projected, fragmented parts of our personality and re-own the hidden potential that appears in the dream.

The Gestalt approach to learning about ourselves through dreams lies in a concerted attempt to integrate our dreams, rather than seeking to analyze them. This can be accomplished by consciously reliving the dreams, by taking responsibility for being the people and the objects in the dream, and by becoming aware of the messages contained in the dream.

Dr. Perls found that in order to learn from our dreams, it is not essential to work out the entire dream structure. To work even with small bits of the dream is to learn more about the dreamer. In order to "relive" a dream you must first refresh your memory of it by writing it down or by telling it to another person. Write it or tell it as a story that is happening now, in the present tense.

Dr. Perls uses the present tense in all of his Gestalt dream work. In his view, dreams are the most spontaneous expression of the existence of the human being. One might perceive dreams being very much like a stage production, but the action and the direction are not under the same control as in waking life. Each part of the dream is likely to be disguised or to bear a hidden message about the dreamer. When the message comes through, the individual will feel that shock of recognition that Gestalt calls the "Ah-ha!" moment. Dr. Perls concludes that every dream has a message to reveal to the dreamer.

Tuesday Miles is an experienced psychic medium who is known to have had exceptional experiences with spirit entities. Tuesday's psychic abilities are multidimensional, which means that she can see spirit manifestations on all levels of the veil. Tuesday lives in a very active haunted house; she knows what it feels like having some unseen force enter into your life. One thing Tuesday teaches each of her clients is how to empower themselves. Tuesday believes that if you stand as a victim, the ghost will treat you as a victim, just as any human bully would do. Tuesday has made a promise that she has yet to break—if someone needs help with a paranormal situation, she will not turn her back on the client. She will do everything that she can to get that person some help. Tuesday Miles' personal website is www.Tuesdaymiles.com.

Dr. Perls concludes that every dream has a message to reveal to the dreamer.

In her very intriguing "My Letter to a Priest," Tuesday shares with us a series of four dreams that constitute an extremely haunting scenario of the unconscious interacting with universal symbols.

My Letter to a Priest

By Tuesday Miles

Dream Night One

We have spoken before on the phone. The reason for my email to you is about a dream I had that lasted for four nights in a row. After the first night, I awoke in a panic, gasping to breathe. I let out a scream and then started touching myself to see if I was real and awake.

I looked over at the clock. I had been asleep for six and a half hours. I know at least six hours was in a dream state. This dream was the longest one I had. For four very long nights, for three to six hours straight, I dreamed. On the next night, I would walk into the new dream at exactly the spot where I had left off the night before.

Warning: If you spook easy, you might not want to continue reading my story.

On the first night, it seemed like the minute my head hit the pillow, I was floating downward, standing at the end of this town, and it reminded me of an old Western abandoned town. I saw no one standing on the street. I saw no people roaming around the stores. I was curious where all the people were, so I started walking very slowly down this street, glancing over my shoulder, trying to be sly about it.

The ground had been torn up, with old paving on it. The shops were old, barely put together. The signs on the stores had Bible verses written all over them, some in English, some in Spanish. I was reminded of old Mexico City. It was still daylight out, and the sky had some orange and blue clouds that seemed to be getting lower and lower.

At first I did not hear any sounds coming from the town. I shivered, looking behind me as I walked slowly down the middle of this town, carefully investigating the insides of the shops. As I was passing the first few of them, I felt my eyes shifting back and forth. I was starting to feel the fear coming off my body like steam from an iron.

My eyes popped open. I sat right up in bed. What the hell was that all about?

Dream Night Two, as It Continues

I was a little bit afraid to go to sleep. I have had dreams before which lasted a couple of days. Each time I would sleep, I would go right into the dream I had left the night before.

I was back in the town, standing next to a restaurant. Inside, there were three sets of tables. Each had two chairs that looked like somebody had been sitting there, then pushed the chairs out and left very quickly. There were tacos and burritos left on plates, barely a bite taken from them.

I walked into another room where they did the dishes. The water was still running, I turned it off. As I did so, the radio that had just static coming from it was now making moaning and growling sounds. In the corner of the room, I saw a baseball bat. I picked it up and swung at the radio, knocking it to the floor.

Any minute now, I thought, somebody is going to jump out and say, "BOO! The joke is on you." Oh, how I wished and prayed this was just a joke. I knew something was terribly wrong.

It was at this point I tried to wake myself up. I called out my name, "Tuesday, Wake up, Wake Up!" I turned around to check if someone or something was following me. I saw no one behind me. I glanced over at the next building. The lettering on the glass windows of the stores had changed. There were words, but they seemed to be backward, dripping with blood. "Oh my f ... ing God!" I slapped my hand over my mouth as soon as I said that. What the hell was going on here? I made no apologies for my foul mouth. It was comforting to me. I was smelling fear, and I knew it was my own. No one was around to help me. In my head I was taking notes. Why had the townspeople left everything behind?

The sun seemed to be right in my eyes, and I felt dehydrated, as I licked my lips, trying to catch my own sweat for hydration. As I neared the next set of stores, I saw that the front window had a painted upside-down cross on it. It looked as if it was freshly painted, because the paint was still running from it. The cross was painted white, but there was red paint running from it ... or was it something else?

My eyes popped open. I was awake and very thirsty. I was pushing my husband awake, asking him to please get me something to drink.

Dream Night Three: The Take-Over

I thought about the dream that I had two nights in a row. It bothered me all day long. When I went to bed, I tried to stay awake, but my eyes could hardly wait to close.

This time it was different. I felt as if I was a puppet. I had control over my eyes, but no control over my body. I looked down, and I could see my legs and my feet, but I was wondering why I could not feel them walk. I was floating just barely off the ground. A voice told me to "Be Quiet," so I did not say another word until I was spoken to. People were running and hiding. Nobody was speaking to me, and the writing on the store windows seemed to become more violent. The sky was gray now; there were storms above the clouds, but not at street level.

Now the shop windows had drawings on them of a beast with thick red horns on its forehead and on the back of its head. Its eyes were yellow. I felt like I had to vomit. I could feel fear coming from within me. I wanted to run the other way; I could feel this heaviness from my chest.

"You must trust me, and trust in you. Show no fear. If you trust in me, I will offer protection." Those words to this day still haunt me, even though it was coming from

The voice of the seer told her that it needed her body so that it could have eyes to see the Beast. (*Art by Ricardo Pustanio*)

a source from the heavens above. But what was waiting for us was indescribable. I could now hear the screams from people, echoing through this small town. Some on their knees praying. Others were crying, asking to be saved. I closed my eyes as tight as I could.

Then a voice said to me, "Open your eyes!" I said that I would not until the voice told me why it had control over my body. The answer came that it was the voice of a seer who needed my eyes to see the Beast.

The ground started to shake, and I could hear this really loud thump. People were screaming that someone save them. The growling sounds from the Beast were louder, deeper, closer now. I knew that we could not leave these people. I looked over to the left of me and saw this huge church—all made of bricks, no windows in it, just a front door.

I shouted at everyone to run to the church, but nobody seemed to hear me. Then the seer said, "They cannot hear you. Give your voice to me!"

I woke up, gasping for air, crying about what I just witnessed. Implanted in my head was the pure ugliness of the beast. I knew what that was, who that was. I started to become angry, my adrenalin was just throbbing, growing intense. I could feel my gut as if I had on combat gear. My body felt protected. During the whole time I was hearing this sound coming from behind us. It was like a flapping sound of a dove, or an eagle.

In the dream I had noticed almost every place in the town had some sort of religious music or preaching coming from it. I lay awake, reviewing what I dreamed. I was curled up in my bed with the covers over my head, thinking I am safe now, but the recall of the intense night three of dreaming caused me to recall more of it.

As I remembered looking up at a glass window and recalling the writing on it, it now appeared as if the Bible verses were backward and written in Latin. I remembered that a painted cross on one of the windows was upside-down and the paint was still running from it. I could feel my stomach starting to feel sick. I was nervous, and I was scared.

The writing was becoming clearer: *Venator daemonum Daemonis Daemon Diaboli Lucifer: Luciferi.*

Now wide awake, I jumped out of bed to look up the spelling of what was on the window. No! This cannot be true, No way ! The Devil—THE DEVIL. I am never going back to sleep—ever!

Dream Night Four: The Last Night

I am now awake and recalling the dream that I just had. As I walked farther down the street, people were running and hiding. No one was speaking to me, and the writing seemed more violent. The weather was now grey. There were storms above the clouds, but not yet at street level.

The writings on the businesses' glass front windows now were drawings of a beastly looking creature, skinless, red, thick horns on the forehead and on the back of the head, with yellow eyes. I could feel fear coming from me. I will not run the other way.

It is now 3:30 A.M. I cannot keep my eyes open. I fall back asleep and into the dream.

I no longer saw myself in the dream. I was now looking through somebody else's eyes. I felt protected. Something else had taken control, a higher divine energy. My eyes were able to see where we were going. I could see people in front of us. Anybody who saw the new "me," dropped to the ground and covered his or her eyes. I felt as if I was floating. No longer were my feet hitting the ground.

> Next, I was in the church, and I could hear a deep growling sound of something speaking in Latin, but backwards.

I tried to wake up. I could hear myself call out loud for my husband (he said later that he did not hear me). I was fighting to wake up. The more I fought, the more I would go back into the dream and it would continue.

I came to this very old church. My eyes were burning; I tried to wake up again, yelling my own name aloud. I just could not gain control of myself and wake up. Next, I was in the church, and I could hear a deep growling sound of something speaking in Latin, but backwards. The thing was speaking to the body my eyes were looking from. My eyes were blurry from burning, and I felt this sickness come over me, as this horrible voice was coming closer to the body I was in.

Just then I woke, sitting straight up. I had to run to the bathroom where I was sick to my stomach.

That afternoon, I tried to stay awake. My mind, body, and spirit were exhausted. I lay down to take a nap, making my husband swear to wake me up after thirty minutes had passed. I did not dream. For whatever reason I had this dream, I still do not understand. I try to push it out of my memory, store it in the back of my mind. I pray this was the last of it.

UNDERSTANDING YOUR DREAMS

Dr. Stanley Krippner, formerly of the Maimonides Dream Laboratory in New York City, says if one were to lie quietly in bed for a few moments each morning, the final dream of the night would often be remembered. In Krippner's opinion, no dream symbol carries the same meaning for every person. Despite certain mass-produced "dream interpretation guides," the research in the Dream Laboratory indicates that only a very skilled therapist, working closely with an individual over a long period of time, can hope to interpret dream symbolism with any degree of correctness. Even then the therapist's interpretations would hold true for only that one subject.

Jung spoke of "archetypal images" in man's "collective unconscious." In this part of the mind, Jung believed, were images common to all people everywhere. People living in different times and different places have dreamed of "wise old men," "earth mothers," "mandalas" (circles within a square), and other "archetypes."

Jung's theories are rejected by many psychologists and psychiatrists as being too mystical, but Krippner believes Jung's hypotheses really are not in conflict with what the dream researchers call "scientific common sense." There must be something structural in the brain comparable to the structural form of other body parts. If so, this structure would develop along certain general lines even though an individual was isolated from other human beings.

According to a general consensus among dream researchers, the Number One rule in understanding one's dreams is to understand oneself. It is only by knowing oneself as completely as possible that any individual will be able to identify and fully comprehend the dream symbols that are uniquely his or her own.

MIND TRAVELING THROUGH TIME AND SPACE

One of the most unusual cases in our files of mind traveling through time and space involves a mother projecting out of her body, a dying son, and the spirit of his deceased friend. This account also offers a dramatic demonstration that the essential self within us does survive physical death.

⊶⊷

IN A DREAM, A DEAD YOUTH HELPED HER RESCUE HER SON

In 1972, times had grown very hard for the Levesque family of Aurora, Colorado. When Paul, the breadwinner of the large family, was terribly injured at work, his wife, Nancy, was left with the sole responsibility of providing for six children—all under the age of seventeen.

"Paul's employer was underinsured, and we had no insurance of our own," Nancy Levesque said. "What money we did receive didn't last long after all the medical bills had been deducted. Paul was left bedridden, and we didn't know at that time if he would ever be able to walk, to say nothing of being gainfully employed, ever again."

"I was a thirty-seven-year-old high school graduate with practically no work experience outside of the home," Nancy explained. "What kind of job could I get that would be able to bring us enough money to keep our heads above water financially?"

Michael, their seventeen-year-old son, picked up as many small, part-time jobs as possible. "Michael wanted desperately to be able to help his dad and me support the family. He had always been a really conscientious boy, and when he saw that his part-time jobs just weren't helping all that much, he insisted on dropping out of high school in his senior year and looking for full-time employment."

Nancy and Paul would not listen to such a proposition. Somehow, they told Michael, the family would get by on the money that she was making as a part-time, short-order cook and the dollars that he was bringing home with his many small, part-time jobs.

But then came the terrible day when Nancy found the money and the note that Michael left behind.

"He said that he could not stand being unable to help us more," Nancy said. "Since he was the oldest, he wrote that he was going to strike out on his own and try to get a good job in a larger city. He would send every cent home that he could. In the meantime, he was leaving behind his special little nest egg of $35.10."

> Before she could say a word, her visitor spoke in urgent tones: "The boy is sick ... come quick!"

They were sick with worry. Michael was not a very tall boy, and he didn't weigh more than 135 pounds. He looked even younger than he was. He was naive and trusting—and he would probably be taken advantage of and exploited by too many unscrupulous employers. Or worse, he could easily be victimized by thugs on the road.

Nancy, Paul, and the five children left at home prayed each night during family devotions for the Lord to keep a safe watch over their "big brother" Michael. The days passed into months, and no word arrived from their son. The worst part, Nancy said, was not knowing whether Michael was alive or dead.

"A thousand dreadful possibilities tormented me," she said. "I prayed to hear from him until it seemed as though my every breath became a prayer."

Incredibly, a year passed without word from their son.

And then, one night, eighteen months after Michael had left home, Nancy Levesque had her most unusual dream.

"It was just too real to have been an ordinary dream. What it really was, we may not yet be able to understand."

According to Nancy's account, she was awakened in the dream by an insistent knocking at their back door. She got out of bed, fastened her bathrobe about her, and made her way through to the kitchen. She opened the door to find a young Chicano boy standing there, shivering with the cold.

Before she could say a word, her visitor spoke in urgent tones: "The boy is sick ... come quick!"

Without thinking to question him further, Nancy motioned the boy, who was about the age of Michael, to come inside.

While he waited for her to join him, she rushed to gather all of the spare sheets and bath towels in the house. All thought of sleep fled as she piled this linen collection into two huge bundles. She took one and handed the other to the boy.

They threw the bundles over their backs and walked out into the night. Nancy specifically remembers closing the door quietly behind her, so as not to awaken her husband and children, and then carefully closing the gate so the dog would not follow her.

Then, with the boy leading the way, they started to walk "quickly and with a gliding motion."

They hurried through the streets until they reached open country, then "we fairly skimmed over the roads, uphill, downhill, so fast we seemed to fly."

They climbed mountains and crossed them "as if with wings"—then just as quickly, they descended.

"We crossed rivers as if we stood on tiny canoes that scooted us across the water without getting our feet wet."

Nancy and her young escort seemed to travel for hours over mountains, open country, forests. Never once did they halt for drink or food, but kept moving relentlessly forward.

Nancy often found herself looking down on country that she had never seen before, but had read about in books and magazines.

"The trees were large," she recalled. "From the wide-spreading branches festoons of gray moss hung down like shimmering veils."

Then the road that they had been following wound up and down, over hummocks and through swamps. Finally, they came to a long, low building.

"The boy is here," the young Chicano guide said. And then they were inside, and the lad was leading her up a short, steep stairway, covered with dust and cobwebs.

They entered a windowless room, illumined only by the light from the cracks between the clapboard walls and the broken places in the roof. The place was heavy with a moldy, damp smell.

"Oh, Mom!" Nancy heard a familiar voice cry out faintly. "You've come!"

Her heart beating faster, Nancy rushed forward to discover her son Michael lying on a bare floor in a far corner of the attic. She fell to her knees, clutching her missing son to her breast, noting with alarm that his body was burning hot and that his face was dry and parched with fever.

"Oh, Mom," Michael moaned. "I'm so sick! I'm so sick with fever."

Nancy Levesque lost no time. She turned to the Chicano lad who had brought her there to ask him to bring buckets of cold water.

She got busy gathering refuse from the floor which she wrapped into a pallet. Then she spread a cool, clean sheet over it.

Although Michael was a full-grown boy, she lifted him like a baby to settle him onto the hastily constructed bed.

By this time, Michael's friend had returned with the water. She dipped the towels and sheets one by one into the buckets of cool water, wrung them out lightly, then packed them around Michael's feverish body.

Hours later, she finally relaxed, knowing the fever had broken. She could tell that the worst of her son's illness was over.

"Go to sleep, son," she said. "You'll get better now."

Without saying another word, Michael drifted immediately into a deep sleep.

Nancy sat quietly beside him, holding his hand, until she, too, slept.

She awoke in her own bed, tired and exhausted, every bone in her body aching.

Nancy was so weary that when she attempted to get out of bed, she found that she could not move. Again and again she made an effort to get out of bed, but she was too exhausted to lift her head from the pillow.

She called to Paul to tell him how completely enervated she was, and she told him about her strange dream.

"And don't tell me it was just a nightmare," she warned her husband. "Somehow, I know that I was really there with Michael. Paul, he's sick. I know it. Maybe he's dying. And he is somewhere a long, long way from here."

Paul told her to stay in bed and rest. The girls would help with breakfast and the other daily chores.

Nancy rolled over and slept the entire day, barely getting up in time to get to her job.

Two days later, the Levesques received a telegram from a county hospital in another state: "Come quickly. Your son frozen—possible amputation."

Nancy borrowed money from her sympathetic employer and boarded a bus for the journey to the little mountain town in Oregon where Michael was hospitalized. He suffered the amputation of a foot, but he recovered his full health.

One day, several weeks later, after Michael had returned to their home, Nancy decided to tell him about the strange dream that she had experienced.

Michael listened to the part about the Chicano boy who had knocked at the door, but when she began to describe the bizarre journey, he interrupted her.

"Let me give you some very important background information here, Mom," Michael said. "The boy's name is Alfredo Maqueda, but I called him Jose. You know, 'No way, Jose.' I know that somehow he saved my life. I guess he's saved my life twice now."

Michael explained that he had been eating a sandwich in a fast-food restaurant when he glanced up to see a Chicano boy, about his own age, watching him through the window with such a hungry look on his face that Michael could not bear it. He motioned for the lad to come inside, and he ordered a sandwich for his companion.

> "The boy's name is Alfredo Maqueda, but I called him Jose. You know, 'No way, Jose.' I know that somehow he saved my life. I guess he's saved my life twice now."

Michael had left the restaurant and bade farewell to the Chicano, who was also wandering the country, looking for some kind of work.

Later that night, as he was walking past an alley in a rough part of town, two thugs jumped out of the darkness and blocked Michael's path.

They demanded whatever money he had, his coat, and even the shoes that he was wearing.

Suddenly, the young Chicano pushed himself between Michael and the hoods. "No way," he insisted, brandishing a length of pipe under their noses. "No way you gonna take this boy's money. No way! Now you get away, or I'll wrap this pipe around your heads!"

"Believe me," Michael told his mother, chuckling at the memory of Alfredo's fierce defense of him, "those punks hit the road."

Alfredo had smiled and told Michael: "No way I let them scum hurt you."

Michael christened his newfound friend "No Way, Jose," and the two of them teamed up together.

They picked up odd jobs here and there, always backing each other up. When the weather got colder, they decided to work their way south to a warmer climate.

The two teenage boys got as far south as Florida and were living there when one of the devastating hurricanes that periodically rip into the coastal regions hit that southern state.

Michael and Alfredo had been camping on the beach when a hurricane caught them unexpectedly. A huge wave had reared up and crashed down on them, sweeping them off their feet. Another angry wave hit them, and they were now at the mercy of the storm.

"Somehow, Jose got hold of me and managed to pull me onto the beach," Michael said, tears welling in his eyes. "I don't know how he did it, but he got me to a place where I was able to get a good hold on a branch or something."

"Just as I turned to see how Jose was making it, another wave swept him out to sea. I never saw him again. He had saved me … then lost his own life."

Michael began to work his way back toward Colorado and his parents' home, but when someone offered him a job at a forestry camp in Oregon, the money seemed too good to pass up. Maybe now, for the first time, he would be able to save enough to send home to be of help to his family's financial situation.

Then he had come down with the illness, the terrible fever. He tried to keep working, but one day he had collapsed and had spent the night in the forest, exposed to freezing temperatures. The next morning when his foreman found him, he had rushed him to the county hospital.

Michael spent most of the time in an unconscious or semiconscious state. Once he did come to, he realized he was in a hospital and that he was ill, that he might lose his life.

In his fevered mind, Michael believed himself to be shut up in some musty, dirty, old attic covered with cobwebs and crawling spiders.

Most of the time his body felt as if it were covered with hot coals. "But I did not want to die. And, like a frightened little boy, I wanted my mother!"

"Oh, Mom," Michael began to cry, "whenever I could think at all, I wanted you. And I prayed—or tried to pray that you would come … that somehow God would send you to me so that you would take care of me."

Michael knew that he had left his physical body on numerous occasions. "I could see my body below me, and I knew that I was dying."

Then one night he had awakened to find No Way Jose standing at his bedside. "Amigo, it does not go so well for you. What can I do to help you?"

Michael did not question the reality of his dead friend standing there speaking to him and asked Jose to bring his mother to him. "Please, Jose. Please. As fast as you can. I really don't think I can last much longer."

Michael fell into a semiconscious state and found himself back in that detestable attic place. He was lying on the bare floor, surrounded by refuse and debris. The place was damp and smelly, and he knew that he was sicker than ever before.

And then before his painfully burning eyes, he saw No Way Jose come into the attic with his mother.

Michael was able to recount to Nancy all that she had done that night to save him and how Jose had worked to help her. Finally, he had heard his mother tell him to sleep, and he had drifted into the sweet oblivion of a healing slumber.

He had awakened in the hospital where a nurse stood taking his pulse. At last he was rational enough to give her his parents' address in Colorado.

Nancy and her son compared the dates of their two extraordinary experiences, and they found them to be the very same. The night that she had had her bizarre "dream" had been the night that Michael had passed the critical stage of his illness. He had awakened that morning with a normal temperature, thus encouraging the medical personnel to proceed with the required surgery.

"Michael has always insisted that some way or somehow, I had actually been there with him that night he was so near death," Nancy concluded her account. "And I wholeheartedly agree. Someway or somehow, his friend Jose—Alfredo Maqueda—had come from Beyond to bring me to my son's side."

THE ACCEPTED VIEW OF REALITY
LEAVES OUT A SIZEABLE PORTION

For well over three hundred years, Western science has been fixated upon the concept that everything in the universe is subject to physical laws and exists only in terms of mass and energy—matter being transformed by energy into a variety of conditions and shapes that come into existence only to pass away eventually in time and space.

From time to time, however, there have been some highly regarded scientists who have protested that such a view of the universe leaves out a very sizeable portion of reality. British philosopher and mathematician Alfred North Whitehead observed that a strictly materialistic approach to life completely ignored the subjective life of humans—or that area of existence which we commonly term the spiritual. It in no way accounted for emotions—the feelings of love between a man and a woman; the magnificent joy upon hearing a Beethoven symphony; the sense of beauty in sighting a rainbow; the inspiration of religious thought. According to the major tenets of Western science, these things are mere transient illusions—things that people imagine for themselves or dream for themselves—while the only true reality consists in the movement of atoms blindly obeying chemical and physical laws.

On one occasion during one of our late-night discussions, Professor Charles Hapgood, of Keene State College in New Hampshire, remarked upon this lopsided worldview: "This soulless 'world machine' was created for us three centuries ago by the genius of Descartes, Newton, and their predecessors. It has proved very useful for the development of physical science."

Some scientists such as British philosopher and mathematician Alfred North Whitehead recognize that the universe includes more than just the material world that adheres to definitive laws of nature. There is a spiritual side that coexists with the "real" world. (*Art by Ricardo Pustanio*)

"Whitehead's attempt to construct a philosophy that would include the experience of peoples' inner lives within the framework of 'reality' has apparently made little dent in our contemporary science, which remains rigidly devoted to this seventeenth-century 'world machine.' Everything must still be explained in terms of the physical action of material bodies being acted upon by external forces."

SUBJECTING SPIRITUAL EXPERIENCES TO SCIENTIFIC SCRUTINY

In the early 1970s, Brad corresponded with the highly respected British marine biologist Sir Alister Hardy, D.Sc., F.R.S., Emeritus Professor at Oxford, who readily conceded that science can no more elucidate the "inner essence" of spirituality than it can the nature of art or the poetry of human love. But he steadfastly maintained that "an organized scientific knowledge—indeed, one closely related to psychology dealing with the records of man's religious experience … need not destroy the elements of religion which are most precious to man—any more than our biological knowledge of sex need diminish the passion and beauty of human love."

Sir Alister, an exacting scientist, regarded himself as a "true Darwinian," but he granted that the DNA code that determined the physical nature of an individual might not give us a complete account of the evolution process. The mental, the nonmaterial side of life, he admitted, "turns out to be of cardinal importance within the process of Darwinian evolution."

Contending that spiritual experiences could be subject to scientific scrutiny, Sir Alister generously provided Brad with data that he had collected for his Religious Experience Research Centre, which he had established at Manchester College in England. Numerous accounts detailed ecstatic transfiguration experiences, the hearing of inspirational voices, feelings of Oneness with the universe, lucid dream experiences, and near-death projections to other dimensions of awareness.

Here are a few representative selections from Sir Alister's files:

"A marvelous beam of spiritual power shot through me, linking me in rapture with the world, the Universe, Life with a capital 'L.' All delight and power, all things living, and time fused in a brief second."

"It seemed to me that, in some way, I was extending into my surroundings and was becoming one with them. At the same time, I felt a sense of lightness, exhilaration, and power as if I was beginning to understand the true meaning of the whole Universe."

"In the darkness, I cried, 'Oh, God, Oh, God. Please help,' then burst into tears…. From that night onward, a strange calm came over me as I felt the tug of an unseen hand guiding me and leading me to do things I would not otherwise have done."

Sir Alister admitted that some people were offended by his attempt to apply the scientific method to something as delicate and sacred as religious experiences. On other occasions he had been scolded for not being satisfied with the evidence of spiritual experience to be found in the Bible and in the works and lives of the mystics and the saints.

As might be expected, Sir Alister did not view God anthropomorphically, as some great father image sitting on a golden throne in Heaven, but he expressed his firm belief in "extrasensory contact with a Power which is *greater than*, and in part lies *beyond the individual self.*"

"A biology based upon an acceptance of the mechanistic hypothesis is a marvelous extension of chemistry and physics," he said, "but to call it

Biological evolution might not provide us with a full look into our evolutionary process. There is also spiritual evolution. (*Art by Ricardo Pustanio*)

an entire science of life is a pretense. I cannot help feeling that much of man's unrest today is due to the widespread intellectual acceptance of this mechanistic superstition when the common sense of his intuition cries out that it is false."

Sir John Eccles is another highly esteemed scientist who declared that evolution alone cannot explain our awareness of ourselves. Winner of the Nobel Prize in Physiology or Medicine in 1963, Sir John was the complete scientist, philosopher, and metaphysician. As the scientist who demonstrated the transmission of electrical impulses in the brain, he was well-acquainted with the workings of humankind's mental machinery, and he became increasingly convinced that there must have been the intervention of some transcendental agency in the infusion into humankind of Soul.

Simply stated, he maintained that the brain and the mind are separate entities which interact, but it is only the brain that is the product of genetic evolution.

In an interview with Sandy Rovner of the *Washington Post* (April 1981), Sir John explained his hypothesis in this way: "I am an evolutionist, of course, but I don't believe that evolution is the final story.... If you look at the most modern texts on evolution, you find nothing about mind and consciousness. They assume that it just comes automatically with the development of the brain. But that's not an answer. If my uniqueness of self is tied to the genetic uniqueness of self that built my brain, the odds against myself existing are ten to the ten-thousandth against.

"It is just too improbable to wait around to get the right constructed brain for you. The brain is a computer, you see. Each of us has a computer, and we are the programmers of this computer. ... But the soul is this unique creation that is ours for life. It is us. We are experiencing, remembering, creating, suffering, imagining. All of this is processed here with the soul central to it."

Dr. Robert Crookall, a British biologist and botanist, was one of the great pioneers in the clinical study of near-death and out-of-body experiences. In 1969, he did Brad the great honor of recognizing some of his early work in the field by initiating a correspondence with him and by sending him a number of his books and papers on the subject. In 1969, Brad had only recently begun distributing the Steiger Questionnaire of Mystical, Paranormal, and UFO Experiences, and he was enormously pleased that Dr. Crookall had looked with favor on his efforts.

Dr. Crookall theorized that what metaphysicians had labeled the astral or the etheric body—the soul—is normally "enmeshed in" or "in gear" with the familiar physical body so that most people are never aware of its existence.

"But many people have become aware of [the Soul Body], for with them [during out-of-body and near-death experiences] the Soul Body separates or projects from the physical body and is used, temporarily, as an instrument of consciousness."

According to Dr. Crookall, this "Soul Body" consists of matter, "... but it is extremely subtle and may be described as 'superphysical.'"

Dr. Crookhall perceived the physical body as animated by a semi-physical "vehicle of vitality," which serves as a bridge between the physical body and the Soul Body. This, he believed, was the "breath of life" mentioned in Genesis.

In some people, he speculated, "... especially (though not necessarily) saintly people," the Soul Body may be less confined to the physical flesh than it is in persons of a more sensual nature, thus making it easier for the aesthetic to achieve out-of-body experiences.

Real Encounters, Different Dimensions, and Otherworldly Beings

"With some very few people," Dr. Crookhall theorized, "and these may be either saintly or sensual, the vehicle of vitality is loosely associated with the physical body, and it may readily project part of its substance."

⊶⊷

SHE MANAGED LITERALLY TO SQUEEZE TWO DAYS INTO ONE

In 1981, Mrs. Patricia Fellar worked as a cook in a restaurant in Tempe, Arizona, while her husband, Louis, was completing his work on his doctorate at the university.

Her daily schedule was a busy one, requiring her to rise every morning at 4:45 A.M. if she wanted any breakfast for herself before she began cooking for everyone else, including Louis and the kids, seven-year-old Lisa and ten-year-old Tammy. Louis also worked part-time at a filling station, so he needed a solid breakfast before he went in at 6:30 A.M., and Patricia had always believed in the kids having a nutritious breakfast to fill them with positive energy for school.

During the heavy tourist season over the winter months when the "snow birds" from the frigid states came to Arizona, Patricia's workload seemed to increase to such a degree that it appeared as though the days would stretch into weeks. During this period, she would be so exhausted when she came home that all she felt like doing was falling into a deep, weary sleep.

And after a month or two of the increased work load, the combination of cooking at the restaurant and caring for two small children soon conspired against housework. Patricia, normally a very conscientious housekeeper, would wince when she saw the laundry piling up, the dust gathering, the floors of their rented apartment growing in grime. She knew that Louis was trying to help out in the spic-and-span department, but he spent all afternoon in classes, his evenings studying, and his mornings working at the gas station.

"Dear God," she began praying aloud, "if only I could afford a day off to catch up with the housework and get the extra rest that I can feel my body is beginning to demand."

On a Thursday night in February, Patricia came home with a fever. She knew it was the darned bug that was going around. Nearly everyone at work had been out with it. But she couldn't afford to take any sick time.

She took her temperature and saw that it was 103.4 degrees. Not at all good for a woman to be running such a high fever. She took a couple of aspirins and went to bed without mentioning anything to Louis.

Patricia could not recall when she had ever felt so bone tired. "Even before I set my alarm clock, I felt as though my conscious self was slipping out of my body. I figured that I must really be sick and starting to hallucinate, because I felt as if the 'real me' was standing apart from my physical body, just kind of checking things out."

Because she felt so tired and so "weird," Patricia was extremely concerned about her being able to get up in time in the morning. Before turning out the light, she checked and rechecked her alarm clock to be certain that it would go off at the right time.

On Friday morning she awoke and looked at her clock.

She sat bolt upright when she read *seven-thirty*.

She was two hours late.

The alarm had not gone off!

As her mind spun with possible explanations, the only one that made sense was that Louis had felt her fever during the night, assessed how ill she was, and had decided to shut off her alarm and let her sleep. And—bless his heart—he had also got Lisa and Tammy up and quietly got them off to school.

As she slowly got dressed, feeling really quite good and wondering what her next course of action should be, Patricia all at once decided that this must be the day off for which she had been praying so earnestly to God. This must be the day that she was supposed to catch up on her housework—and if that meant losing her job, then so be it. Another of the restaurants in the Arizona college town had already approached her about coming to work in their kitchen, so if her boss didn't like her taking a day off once in a blue moon, then it was meant to be. And knowing her husband's thoroughness, she just knew that he had already called in sick for her.

> "Even before I set my alarm clock, I felt as though my conscious self was slipping out of my body."

First she went to work on the bathroom, scrubbing all the fixtures until they were bright and shiny.

Next she launched a full-scale attack on the kitchen with its dishes, cupboards, and floor—all to be cleaned.

Finally, she attacked the small dining room, where a large basket of ironing awaited her.

All in all, Patricia Fellar dusted, scrubbed, waxed, washed, folded, and ironed until she could say with full satisfaction that her house was clean. Slick as a whistle!

And then the alarm went off.

With an abrupt sense of confusion, Patricia reached for the clock. *It was four-forty five!*

Real Encounters, Different Dimensions, and Otherworldly Beings

She sat up and saw Louis pull the covers over his head to catch a few minutes more of snoozing time.

She looked in on her children and saw that they were still sleeping.

Patricia shook Tammy awake and asked her what day it was.

Tammy's eyelids fluttered into wakefulness, and she stretched and yawned before she answered with a giggle. "Mommy, it's Friday. You always know what day it is! You're teasing me!"

Patricia Fellar did not know what day this *day* was. How could it be Friday, when yesterday, Friday was her stay at-home cleaning day? Today had to be Saturday!

Louis was up, heading for the bathroom for his morning shower. "You feeling better, honey?" he asked. "I could tell that you had a pretty high fever during the night."

Patricia nodded. She felt better. Then she had to ask: "What day is it today, Lou?"

"It's TGIF, babe. Thank God It's Friday. Why, did you lose a day?"

Patricia looked around the house in stunned amazement. Everywhere she saw the obvious results of her labors—clean floors, ironed and folded clothes, polished fixtures.

She hadn't *lost* a day. Rather, she had *gained* one!

When she thought back, it suddenly occurred to her that in a very real sense, time had not seemed to exist. She had worked an entire "day" without having seen Louis, the girls—or without having fed them ... or herself, for that matter. She had worked like a madwoman without food or drink or rest. And her fever had completely disappeared.

Somehow, Patricia Fellar stated in her fascinating account to us, she had managed to live two days in one.

"I have always been intrigued by the true nature of time," she wrote. "Is it truly a dimension unto itself? Or maybe I had entered another aspect of physical time when that terrible fever projected me out of my body and into another dimension of reality? I have lots of questions that I would like someone to answer, but the proof lay in the physical evidence of the tangible results of my nonexistent day's work!"

VOYAGES DURING NEAR-DEATH EXPERIENCES

Jack provided our files with a detailed account of his near-death experience when he was severely injured after an explosion in the chemistry laboratory in which he is employed. Jack had always prided himself on being a solid materialist, a practitioner of pure science. Until his near-death experience, he said bluntly, he would not likely have discussed spiritual matters. After hearing us on a late-night radio talk program, he sent for our questionnaire on paranormal and mystical experiences, but he admitted that his universe "was now a great deal larger than it had been before his near-fatal accident."

According to Jack, he remembered nothing after one of his coworkers in the laboratory managed to shout a brief exclamation of warning before the explosion shattered the building. "I was astonished when I saw what appeared to be the traditional representation of an angel flying off with what looked as though it might be Peter, my lab partner."

"And then I was even more astonished when I saw that I—or some part of me—was also being borne aloft by someone or something in what appeared to be a gown of shimmering white. 'Absurd!' I thought. 'I don't even believe in such things!'"

"It didn't seem to matter. And it certainly didn't seem to matter what my thoughts were to the silent entity who was lifting me upward. I remember seeing a bright light, feeling a kind of almost sensual, ecstatic sensation—and then I was seated near a lovely forest stream on what appeared to be a marble bench. A tall, imposing figure was seating beside me."

Jack asked if he might inquire exactly what was going on.

Real Encounters, Different Dimensions, and Otherworldly Beings 333

The being shrugged, then smiled warmly. "Don't you think it is rather evident, Jack? Look around you. As you might to be quick to say, 'This doesn't look like Kansas.'"

Jack recalled snapping back: "Well, if you're supposed to be an angel, where are your wings?"

"If you want wings, you'll get wings. I didn't think such traditional trappings would appeal to a disciple of science such as yourself," the angel replied.

"Forget the wings. The white robe is enough," Jack told him.

"If you prefer a business suit, I can arrange it with but a moment's thought," the angel explained.

Jack wrote in his report of the experience that he was surprised to find that his angel was not at all pompous or holy.

"In some sense, I am the nonphysical aspect of yourself," the angel told him. "But it is now my task to expand your consciousness and to help you attain a better balance before you return to your body."

"You mean," Jack wanted to know at once, "that I am not dead?"

"Well, you are going to have to cut down on contact sports for a while," the angel replied, "but you will live. We've more or less taken advantage of the accident to get you apart so that we can set you back on the path with greater equilibrium."

Jack pointed out that the angel continued to make references to his being "out of balance."

Just what was it, he wanted to know, that he was doing that was so wrong?

The angel assumed the manner of a teacher. "You've emphasized your intellect to the exclusion of your emotions and your spiritual growth. If you are to fulfill your true mission on Earth, you must recognize the importance of the nonphysical aspects of existence."

"For centuries now," the angel continued, "it seems that not many humans are given to know the truth of things. Yet we look forward and foresee a world of humans living in a greater vibration of the Light than exists on Earth today.

"In that glorious day to come," the angel said, "humans will see and understand how near we of the heavenly kingdom are to them. Meanwhile, we do our part, ever watchful, ever hopeful—and if our heavenly joy is often mixed with sadness, it is because we cannot yet walk hand-in-hand with you on Earth. But we know that we are coming closer and closer together—and all is working according to the great Divine Plan."

"In that glorious day to come," the angel said, "humans will see and understand how near we of the heavenly kingdom are to them." (*Art by Bill Oliver*)

The angel smiled at him, and Jack was certain that he had seen his face somewhere before.

"Perhaps in dreams," the being acknowledged. "And certainly when you were a small boy. You are my ward, you see; so let us take advantage of this time for me to present certain teachings for you to take back with you.

"While we are pleased that you work with earth sciences, we want to instruct you to explore deeper into those fundamentals that are of a spiritual origin. Your science is only beginning to acknowledge the unseen realms. If you would place more emphasis on the nonmaterial aspects of existence, then our two worlds would be able to draw closer together.

"One thing that humans must keep in mind: the Universe was not created for them alone, any more than the sea was created for the use of one particular fish or the air was created for the pleasure of one particular bird.

"Humans invade both sea and air and consider them their own kingdoms to conquer and to use. To a certain extent, they are correct. Humans, by permission, rule Earth and the dominion over which their Maker has placed them.

"But there are beings greater than humankind; and as humans rule the lesser entities and use them for the development of their faculties and personality, so do the greater beings rule humankind and use them.

"If humans kept the hierarchy of beings more clearly in mind, then they would better appreciate the gift of free will that has been given to them. And be assured that this gift is one that no one of the heavenly hierarchy may ever take from humankind. And they would not if they could, for by so doing their own substance would be deteriorated in quality and they would become less capable of their own advancement. Humans are, and must ever remain, beings of free will."

Jack had many questions, but each time that he made a sound or movement that signaled an interruption, the angel silenced him with a glance.

"I soon came to understand," Jack said, "that my angelic teacher was very much aware of our limitations of time and that he wished to make the best use of our moments together."

The angel next explained that the one great power that animated all those who served the Living Creator God in the heavenly dimension was that of Divine Love.

"In this dimension," Jack's celestial tutor said, "power means an issuing forth of love—and the greater the power, the greater the love which is sent forth. When you return to Earth, my ward, see to it that your work becomes one with our own. We have only one object set before us—the betterment of all life and all things. We follow this, our mission, with humility and simple trust in Divine Love. And we take great delight in assisting all human entities who become our fellow workers in the one great assignment in the universe of the Living God.

"Do not become discouraged. From our perspective, we see far more than you humans of the effects of evil—war, murder, rape, poverty, so-called genetic cleansings, exploitation of the weak. And yet we do not despair, because we are able to see more clearly the meaning and the purpose of all these things. And thus seeing, we know that humankind will one day ascend to the higher spheres of service and from this point of higher elevation continue its evolution as spiritual beings."

Jack concluded his account by stating that he had been badly burned and injured in the laboratory fire. He had been unconscious for two days, and for several hours, the attending physicians did not expect him to live. His laboratory partner, Peter, had been killed outright by the blast.

"I am now a very different person," he said. "My wife and my children take delight in this, for I now take much more time to 'smell the roses.' I am less of a workaholic.

"I like to think, as my angel advised me, that I have become a much more balanced individual, acknowledging both the physical and nonphysical aspects of reality—and I see no conflict in serving both facets of the universe."

Whether Jack was communicating with an angel, his own higher-self, or some teaching aspect of the Other, we cannot say for certain. What we can state from our research, and our reading of thousands of such accounts from the correspondents who filled out our questionnaire, is that the near-death experience very often becomes a mechanism of moral instruction for many individuals. Since 1967, we have distributed questionnaires to readers of our books and to those who have attended our lectures and workshops. Of the more than thirty thousand people who have returned completed forms, 72 percent state that they have had a near-death experience; 95 percent report out-of-body experiences; and 86% percent testify to an illumination experience.

⚬

WHAT LIES BEYOND PHYSICAL DEATH?

Even the most devout high priests of the materialistic religions of test tubes, chemical compounds, and mathematical formulas still cannot answer the ultimate question—*What lies beyond physical death?*

The doctrine of immortality is an integral part of all the major world religions, but, as Professor Charles Hapgood once explained to Brad, if a physical scientist is true to his basic principles, he cannot accept it.

"To the physical scientist," Professor Hapgood continued, "if he or she is consistent, life can exist only within a physical frame, a mortal body—and death is the end of the life of the individual. Some scientists compromise by accepting both points of view, because their instincts or desires tempt them to hope that life goes on, but they cannot be consistent. The consistent materialist has to regard death as the end."

It may be all well and good for some researchers to stop here, but such action does nothing to answer several perplexing questions raised by the phenomenon of near-death experiences (NDE), such as, What is it *within* us that is projected to other dimensions of reality during near-death experiences?

The answers that come to us from those men and women who have experienced an NDE are subjective, of course, but they do provide us with valuable clues.

Nearly all of those who have undergone an NDE express an awareness of some type of body image. Many state that they see themselves as "golden bowls" or globular or egg-shaped spheres of some sort, which may eventually assume the more familiar shape of their own physical form. A good many

What worlds lie beyond this one after we die? What do we take with us after our physical forms perish? (*Art by Bill Oliver*)

reporting cases of near-death refer to the existence of a "silver cord" of great elasticity which appears to connect the spiritual body to the physical body.

Throughout the centuries there has been a rather remarkable consensus regarding the NDE, which seems to have been reached informally by those scholars and metaphysicians who have kept records of such experiences, and by those men and women who underwent an NDE at the moment of serious accident, during an illness, in times of extreme exhaustion, or other physical crisis points. The largest body of collected, subjective evidence seems to support the description of a spiritual body that is more or less egg-shaped with an orangish glow.

Those of Christian orientation who have undergone the NDE sometimes quote Ecclesiastes 12:6–7 as scriptural testimony to the reality of the spiritual body and its ability to separate itself from the flesh:

"Or ever the silver cord be loosed, or the golden bowl be broken, or the pitcher be broken at the fountain, or the wheel be broken at the cistern. Then shall the dust return to the earth as it was: and the spirit shall return unto God who gave it."

————

ERNEST VOWS TO KEEP HIS "RECORD BOOK" CLEAN AFTER AN NDE

Ernest thought that he would die when the other automobile struck his at the intersection in Nogales, Arizona. "What seemed to be the real me, was somewhere above the crash looking down on all the confusion," he wrote in the lengthy letter that accompanied his report to us. "I watched the other driver get out of his car and shake his head, as if he were dazed by the blow. Other than a cut on his forehead, he seemed all right. I saw the police and a crowd arrive, and I could see my bleeding body slumped forward against the steering wheel. I thought that this was it, I was really dead."

Ernest wanted to see his wife, Marisol, one last time. Then he discovered that all he had to do was to form the thought, and he was there beside her. For a few moments, he watched her fixing their dinner. She was completely unaware of either the accident or his spirit body there beside her.

"I thought of my only child, my son, Edward, from my first marriage," Ernest said. "In an instant I was bobbing above him in my spirit body, observing him as he sat at his desk in his office in Mesa. I felt no real sorrow at leaving Marisol and Edward, but I was thankful that I was somehow given the opportunity to see them one last time."

It was at that point that Ernest felt something tugging at his right hand. "I should really say my 'right side,'" he clarified, "as I didn't really seem to be any longer in human form. I actually looked more like a kind of egg yolk floating above the physical 'me' in the car below."

The "something" that was tugging at him appeared to Ernest to be either an angel or one of the saints.

"He didn't have wings, and he was dressed in a long, flowing robe. He had a full beard and long, shoulder-length hair." Ernest remembered that the two of them seemed to be sitting in some kind of room, "kind of like a waiting room in a doctor's office."

The spiritual guide was very direct in his words to Ernest. "Now you understand why you must not carry hatred in your heart," he said in a low, rumbling bass voice. "You never know when your life is going to be taken from you; and if you harbor hatred, such negative energy weighs heavily upon your soul."

Ernest knew at once that the saintly figure was referring to an animosity which he felt toward one of his coworkers in the office. He was certain that the man had deliberately lied about him to their boss and had cost him an important promotion. Ernest had cursed the man to his face, even threatened him in the parking lot. He had told Marisol that he would get even with the man if it took him the rest of his life.

Now, it appeared that his life was over, and the hatred he bore the man was weighing his soul down. Maybe even to Hell!

"As a churchgoing man, you have heard often of the unconditional love of Jesus for his enemies," the being said. "Like so many other men, you have marveled at this aspect of Divine Love, the ability to forgive one's enemies.

"Jesus' first commandment to his human flock was that they love one another. This is the greatest commandment—and the hardest for humans to keep. People always agree in moments of quiet and peace that to love one another is good. But when it comes time to translate that sentiment into action, how they sadly fail.

"And yet, my son," the bearded teacher continued, "without love, nothing in all the universe could endure. Without love, everything would fall into decay and dissolution. Humans must realize that it is the love of God that energizes all that is. You will be able to see the fruits of God's Divine Love everywhere—once you learn to look for it.

"When one man hates another, he is likely to cease being able to love anyone as completely as he should. The larger the hatred grows, the more difficult it becomes to love anything at all.

"The human propensity toward hatred is one of the most difficult things to overcome for your advancement toward the heavenly realms," the entity said. "Not until a human has learned to love all others without hating anyone is he or she able to progress toward the Light. In this higher sphere, my son, love is light, and light is love. Those who do not love must move in dark places where they are apt to lose their way completely.

"My son, just as you think of God with reverence, awe, and love, so you must think of your fellow humans with reverence, respect, and love. Do this, knowing that we of the heavenly realms are watching you and steadily charting your progress toward the spiritual kingdom. Understand that we mark down with precision the workings of your inner mind. As you are on Earth, so will you be when you are awakened here for your final and ultimate projection from the physical body."

With that statement, Ernest was led to understand that he was not yet dead. He told the heavenly being that indeed he had reacted in an uncharitable way toward his fellow worker. He promised that he would make amends and that he would do his very best never again to harbor such hatred in his heart.

The bearded one smiled and nodded knowingly at him—and then Ernest felt a tugging and a pulling sensation.

"I was being literally sucked back into my physical body," he said. "I perceived a brilliant, swirling blur of color—and I landed in my body with a spasmodic jerking of my muscles."

Ernest heard someone chuckle and say, "Hey, doc, what was in that needle? It really snapped him back to life."

Ernest heard another man laugh, and then he opened his eyes to see what appeared to be a dozen or more people pressing forward to view the accident scene.

He caught a glimpse of the back of a police officer herding the curiosity seekers back from his damaged car, then a sickening rush of pain caused Ernest to lapse back into unconsciousness.

"This time I met no bearded teacher in outer space, and received no further admonishments," Ernest said. "When I awakened several hours later in a hospital, Marisol was holding my hand."

Ernest did add a meaningful postscript to his account: "A couple of weeks later, when I was back at work, I did some checking around and I learned that I had wrongfully accused my coworker of having bad-mouthed me to the boss. I offered my sincere apologies—and thank heaven, he accepted them. We have since become good friends. I thank God every day that I was given another chance, and I am going to work very hard to keep my record book clean and my heart clear of hatred."

WHY PEOPLE ARE BEGINNING TO PAY ATTENTION TO THE NDE

Perhaps the reason why so many men and women are beginning to take notice of such phenomena as the near-death experience, angels, and other mystical occurrences may be due to the fact that, in the Western world, our non-rational needs have been denied for decades. Materialism, competition, power politics, and commercial exploitation can be endured for only so long before the human soul cries out for meaningful spiritual expression.

More Westerners are recognizing that near-death experiences and other otherworldly and spiritual experiences may be valid parts of our existence. (*Art by Ricardo Pustanio*)

The increase in such experiences may result from the time of great transition that many sensitive men and women feel is fast approaching. Some perceive that our entire human species may be standing on the precipice of a great leap forward in our physical and spiritual evolution.

Although the Western world has never encouraged the individual mystical experience, for those of us who collect such accounts of encounters as you have read in this book, it seems clear that we are all potential mystics, just as there are potential artists, poets, and musicians.

The philosopher-psychologist William James once observed that the fountainhead of all religions lies in the mystical experience of the individual. All theologies, all ecclesiastical establishments are but secondary growths superimposed.

BRAD STEIGER'S NEAR-DEATH EXPERIENCE

Brad became a firm believer in the survival of the human spirit at the age of eleven when he underwent a dramatic near-death experience and was left with the firm conviction that the human soul is imperishable—and we need not fear death.

Brad has a blurred memory of losing his balance, falling off the farm tractor that he had been driving, and landing in the path of the implement with whirling blades.

He remembers pain as the machine's left tire mashed his upper body and broke his collarbone. And then he no longer felt any pain as the blades clutched at his head and ripped at his scalp and skull. He had left his body, and he was now floating many feet above the grisly scene in the field below.

He recalls a fleeting moment of feeling relief when he perceived that his seven-year-old sister, June, who had been riding with him, managed to bring the tractor under control without endangering herself, but he was becoming more detached about such earthly matters by the moment.

"I had some sense of identification with the mangled Iowa farm boy that I saw lying bleeding beneath me on the hay stubble below, but I was growing increasingly aware that that unfortunate lad was not who I really was," Brad recalls. "The *real me* now seemed to be an orangish-colored ball that appeared intent only on moving steadily toward a brilliant light. At first, because of my religious orientation as an Evangelical Lutheran, I believed the illumination to be Jesus or an angel coming to comfort me, but I could distinguish no distinct forms or shapes within the bright emanation of light. All I seemed to feel was an urgency to become one with that magnificent light.

"Strangely, though, from time to time my attention seemed to be divided between moving toward the wondrous light and descending back toward the hay field.

"I opened my eyes, blinked back the blood, and became aware of my father, shocked, tears streaming down his face, carrying my body from the field."

And then Brad discovered a most remarkable thing: He could be in two places at once. He could exist physically in his father's arms as he carried Brad's terribly injured body from the field; and at the same time, he could be above them, watching the whole scene as if he were a detached observer.

When he became concerned about his mother's reaction to his dreadful accident, he made an even more incredible discovery: The Real Brad could be anywhere that he wished to be. His spirit, his soul, was free of the physical limitations of the human definitions of Time and Space. He had but to think of his mother, and there he was beside her as she labored in the kitchen, as yet unaware of his accident.

He put the newly found freedom to other tests. He thought of the friends with whom he planned to see the Roy Rogers/Gene Autry double-feature that night in the local small town theater. Instantly he was beside each of them as they worked with their fathers on their own farms.

And then he was back with Mom, trying to put his arms around her, wanting her to be able to feel him. Disappointed, he was forced to conclude that she could neither see nor feel him. His normally very attentive mother had absolutely no awareness of his spirit form.

It was August 23, 1947, his parents' anniversary. The family had been trying to finish work early so that they could eat at a local restaurant before the double-feature began. He had certainly given Mom and Dad a wonderful anniversary present.

And his sister! He had probably scarred her for life. A seven-year-old girl having to watch her brother being run over and killed.

Killed. That was when it occurred to Brad that he was dying.

He had an awful moment of panic. He did not want to die.

He did not want to leave his mother, father, and sister.

"And then the beautiful light was very near to me," Brad said, "and I perceived a calming intelligence as a being composed of pure light projected a peculiar, three-dimensional geometric design that somehow instantly permeated my very essence with the knowledge that everything would be all right.

"The very sight of that geometric design somehow transmitted to me that there was a pattern to the universe and a meaning, a Divine Plan, to life.

"My panic and my fear left me, and I experienced a blissful euphoria, an incredible sense of Oneness with All That Is. I was ready to die and to become one with the light.

"But even though I was at peace with what appeared to be the fast-approaching reality of death, I had misinterpreted the reason why the intelligence within the light had shown me the geometric representation of the Divine Plan. It seems that an integral part of my mission on Earth was to testify to others about what I had been shown."

> "The very sight of that geometric design somehow transmitted to me that there was a pattern to the universe and a meaning, a Divine Plan, to life."

In the August 12, 1973, issue of the *National Enquirer*, the farm family's former physician, Dr. Cloyce A. Newman, was interviewed about Brad's near-death experience that had occurred twenty-six years before. Dr. Newman, who was living in retirement in Homestead, Florida, told of his shock when Brad's father carried him into his office and how he had rushed them by car to St. Mary's Hospital in Des Moines, about 140 miles away: "He was very seriously injured and on the verge of death. We managed to get him to a specialist and it saved his life."

Brad was in and out of the body during those 140 miles, and he did not come back with any serious intention of staying in that domicile of flesh until the surgery was about to begin. At that point, it seemed as though some energy was insisting that he return to participate in the medical procedure.

Brad came back with such force that he sat up, shouted, and knocked an intern off-balance. He continued to struggle until the soft voice of a Roman Catholic nun pacified him long enough for the anesthesia to take effect.

Although Brad's life force remained in the eleven-year-old body to cooperate with the surgery, his Real Self left to spend the next twelve hours in a delightful park in another dimension, complete with bandstand, ice cream vendors, and smiling, pleasant people.

"About 1982," Brad recalled, "I was attempting to describe the series of geometric designs to a number of other men and women who had undergone near-death experiences. When I found myself unable to provide a meaningful description of the pattern, I stated that the designs—so clearly envisioned by me to this day—appeared to be ineffable, beyond human description. Two or three of the group stated that they understood what I was attempting to explain, for they, too, had been shown some kind of tranquilizing, yet revelatory, geometric object—and they also found it impossible to describe it in mere words.

"It was not until 1987 when Sherry began to conduct seminars utilizing, in part, computer-derived images of fractal geometry that I saw designs that very closely approximated what I had been shown during my near-death experience. The central purpose of her seminar was to demonstrate the sacredness and the multidimensional oneness of all creation.

"From the perspective of my now 77 years, I can see that my near-death experience at the age of eleven was a most fortunate one. Certainly one of the questions that every thinking man and woman eventually asks is, 'Is there life after physical death?' I was blessed to have that eternal puzzler answered for me in the affirmative before I entered my teens.

"I was shown through my powerful near-death experience that there is an essential part of us, perhaps most commonly referred to as the soul, that does survive physical death. This knowledge has greatly influenced my attitude toward life, as well as toward death.

"And I am far from alone in having been granted this emancipating awareness, this life-altering assurance."

THE MANY NDES OF SHERRY STEIGER

Sherry has survived a number of near-death experiences and/or very close calls when it appeared that the Angel of Death might be coming to take her to the Great Mystery.

In her infancy, she nearly died of pneumonia.

At the age of six, when she suffered a severe bout of rheumatic fever, she was bedridden for nearly a year. Doctors said it was a miracle that she survived. She was only allowed minimal physical activities for many years until she was given a more complete bill of health.

At the age of nine, medical personnel accidentally gave her a near fatal overdose of ether when she was in the hospital to have her tonsils removed.

When she was about twenty-four, Sherry survived a shark attack off the coast of South Padre Island, Texas. She was pulled under the surface of the water three times by her monstrous adversary.

"I saw the horror in the faces of swimmers coming to rescue me before the huge 'something' grabbed me for the second time. I thought I would surely die.

"I found out later when the sea park ranger pulled a shark's tooth from my foot that the monster must have been toying with me before it made me its main dinner course. When it pulled me under for the third time, I was shown a review of all the major scenes of my life. It is just incredible to think how you can see all of your life in what is perhaps only two or three seconds of linear time.

"Surely I would have drowned if I had even suspected my sea attacker was a shark! At the time, all I thought was a very big fish!"

Real Encounters, Different Dimensions, and Otherworldly Beings   345

Sherry remembers going under for the third time and then falling into unconsciousness. She came to briefly in the rangers' station. Not knowing what happened, she looked down and saw that she was covered with blood. Whoever her rescuer had been was no longer in sight. After the ranger pulled out the shark's tooth embedded in her left foot, he immediately issued a shark warning and cleared the beaches of all swimming.

Years later, specialists in dolphin research with whom Sherry was working heard her story and theorized that a team of dolphins may have arrived on the scene to surround the shark and saved Sherry from being an entrée for a predator of the deep. Dolphins are the only marine animals known to fearlessly take on sharks.

She was twenty-eight when she suffered a heart "episode" and was told by three eminent cardiologists that she must have surgery at once—or die within twenty-four hours.

At the age of thirty, a kidney infection sent her temperature soaring to 106 degrees. She was in and out of a coma and packed in ice for ten days.

There is no question in Sherry's mind that the close calls with death had a profound effect on her. She had no conscious recall of what occurred during her NDEs, but in review she wonders if the experiences may have taken shape in her subconscious with the manifestation of repeated dreams.

As a child, the closest thing she ever had to nightmares were dreams of geometric shapes that would rush at her at tremendous rates of speed. The sense of movement would grow faster and faster, and then it would seem to her as if the shapes were somehow pushing against her, exerting great pressure on her body. It was as though each shape had a weight to it, and at a certain point she would wake up screaming. Her mother, who would always enter the bedroom to see what was wrong, would comfortingly say that Sherry was just having a bad dream. She would always inquire what the dream was about, and Sherry's answer was always the same, "Lights and shapes were coming at me." There was no monster to describe, no Boogie Man, no one chasing her, or any of the other typical bad dreams that children experience.

It was not until Sherry saw the motion picture *2001: A Space Odyssey* that she perceived anything like the geometric patterns and lights that she had seen moving rapidly toward her in her childhood nightmares. There, in the amazing "light show" sequence when the astronaut Bowman enters dimensional hyperdrive as the ship approaches Jupiter, she saw an amazingly accurate cinematic representation/re-creation of the personalized "light show" that she had seen since she was a small child.

"The viewing of this movie triggered memories of my childhood dreams/nightmares, and they suddenly made sense to me. It was as though I had also encountered a 'hyperdrive' in which I was traveling through space at a high rate of speed. This may also have been what happened in my near-death experiences. That one incredible sequence in Stanley Kubrick's masterpiece of cinema was like a healing of my spirit. Those memories that had haunted and confused me for so long now seemed a great deal less frightening, and I never experienced those 'nightmares' again."

During the mid-to-late 60s, at the Lutheran School of Theology at Chicago, Sherry was fortunate to take courses from Dr. Elisabeth Kubler-Ross who, in 1969, would become internationally famous for her pioneering work with the dying and with her book *On Death and Dying*. Sherry was immediately taken by her professor's research into the death process, for even during her undergraduate work in nursing,

Dr. Elisabeth Kubler-Ross (left) with Sherry Hansen Steiger.

she had the firsthand opportunity to observe that dying patients often experienced an encounter with the supernatural. On occasion, when patients would "come back to life" after a near-death experience, Sherry had witnessed that their lives were often transformed by what they had seen on the Other Side. Dr. Kubler-Ross was later on Sherry's board of directors for her Butterfly Center for Transformation.

Sherry took an interest in studying many other spiritual disciplines and in evaluating numerous alternative, wholistic healing modalities. In the latter years of the 1970s, through her Butterfly Center for Transformation, Sherry was invited to participate in an early study of what makes healing work. Once a month she traveled to Bethesda, Maryland, where she became involved with a group of prestigious doctors, many from the National Institutes of Health. She became deeply involved in the research, examination, and testing of such remarkable faith healers as Olga Worrall, holy men from India, and Native American tribal medicine people. In 1978, Sherry was one of the initial participants of the Wholistic Healing Board through the National Institutes of Health, Bethesda, Maryland.

TAKEN TO A SACRED PLACE BY A LIGHT BEING

Although Sherry had begun meditating in the early 1970s, she became a more disciplined and serious meditator as the years progressed. It was during an astonishing five-hour meditative experience in 1985 that she was given an additional spiritual impetus, beyond that of her Butterfly Center for Transformation, to pull together a unique experiential program of the Transcendence of Life.

Sherry remembered that her Real Self was met by an angelic Light Being who escorted her through a beautiful mystical adventure. Although she issued an immediate disclaimer that no words can ever come close to describing what she saw, she states that, audacious as it may sound to many, she truly felt that through the holiness of her experience it was as if she saw or touched the sacred space of God.

Sherry said that the Light Being who guided her through the experience was loving and caring. "The Being did not seem to have a gender, but I felt as though I knew him/her."

She was in a place that perhaps could best be described as a diamond or crystal city (or planet) where she beheld unearthly beauty and colors and lights unequaled by those on Earth.

"Perhaps I beheld the New Jerusalem as described in the Bible. All I can say for certain is that its beauty was beyond anything I've ever dreamed possible. It was like a crystal or diamond planet, reflecting and refracting the purest, most brilliant colors. The light all around was effervescent, as if it were alive. As if the light itself was alive and that light was the very essence of love. This love was deeper and more complete than anything experienced here on Earth. I myself seemed to become diamond-like or as a living crystal as I became fused with the light. I became the Light. All is light. All is love."

This dramatic visionary experience expanded her life mission. Sherry became more compelled than ever before to find a way to convert her ineffable experience into a teaching program that would enable others to apprehend the perfection and the Oneness of Life, and understand that God's promise to humankind is, indeed, real. Life does continue after death.

"The most important thing in life that we can do is to be loving and to meet an experience with love," she said.

Shortly after she received the powerful vision, she was led to her research on fractal geometry, a "new" mathematics. By 1988 she had assembled a powerful, multimedia presentation entitled "Sacred Geometry: The Nature of Life," utilizing slides and computer-derived images of fractals along with slides and videos of nature—Earth and Space—meticulously timed to special music and light sequences.

Brad has stated how it was not until he had viewed Sherry's presentation that he saw designs which closely approximated the geometric images that he had been shown during his own childhood near-death experience.

In addition to testifying that the viewing of such images prompted tears to form in their eyes and healing energy in their physical bodies, countless seminar participants said that the geometric shapes had also triggered memories of their own earlier near-death experiences, which they had not been able to put into words until they had experienced Sherry's presentation. Many of these individuals also stated that they, too, had experienced dreams or nightmares as children in which they had seen "shapes of light" coming at them. Many participants indicated the experience had touched a chord within them that inexplicably caused them to burst into tears. During each presentation, an audible combination of gasps, awe, and crying were heard. Many also reported a strange heat and perspiration along their entire spinal column.

"Somehow, my out-of-body viewing of the New Jerusalem—or whatever it truly was—filled me with a heightened and expanded sense of oneness with All-That-Is and allowed me to visit the dimension of spirit from which my soul may have come to Earth," Sherry said. "Perhaps that is the true spiritual home for all of us—a place we call 'Heaven' where we truly shall be one with God—one with love."

ON STAGE IN THE MAGIC THEATER

When Brad was a child, he saw what is commonly referred to as an elf—or in the Scandinavian traditions of his family, a nisse, looking in the kitchen window of their Iowa farm home. "I believe that I must have surprised him as much as he did me," Brad said, "but he quickly regained his composure and gave a rather a conspiratorial smile, as if we were sharing a secret that was profound in its simplicity. Then he vanished."

Brad has never forgotten that smile or the nisse's compelling eyes. "I have walked many a strange path and turned many a bizarre corner in the hope that I might once again meet my multidimensional friend," Brad said. "On several occasions, when I somehow sensed his presence, I quickly glanced over my shoulder, hoping to catch a glimpse of him. Although I have not yet seen him again, I know that he occasionally makes his presence known by acts of elfish mischief."

In the seventy-three years since his encounter with the mysterious entity, both Brad and Sherry have met and corresponded with hundreds of men and women who have experienced an interaction with beings that appeared to them as spirits, elves, holy figures, or extraterrestrial visitors. These people are sincere in their recounting of their experiences and are unshaken by the disbelief or doubts of others.

While in many instances there is little or no physical evidence to demonstrate any kind of proof of the encounter to skeptical materialists, the individuals who received such unexpected visitations from nonmaterial beings are left with an unyielding conviction that their lives have been forever changed. For some reason, which they may never fully understand, they underwent an individual mystical experience with some facet of the supernatural.

They were somehow invited to participate in a very personal, very subjective, extremely illuminating experience that is as intimate, as life-altering, as revelatory, as unifying as the human psyche can perceive.

ONE STRANGE NIGHT IN IOWA IN 1940

In 1988, Brad and Sherry, together with their friends, Dr. Patricia-Rochelle and Reverend Jon Terrance Diegel, attended an art show in Sedona, Arizona, of the paintings of their mutual friend, Luis Romero. As Brad examined one painting of what appeared to be an alien entity, he experienced a very strange kind of déjà vu.

"This is the closest I have seen to the entity that I witnessed as a child," Brad told Luis, who had heard the story of Brad's childhood encounter at a recent lecture.

Luis smiled and said, "I rather thought that you would have such a shock of recognition when you saw this work."

He went on to tell Brad that he had been commissioned to do the painting to the specifications of a woman who had had an encounter with the alien as a child and who had continued to interact with that particular being.

"Luis had no sooner told me that he had painted that work for a UFO contactee when the lady under discussion walked into the art show," Brad said. "Her name was Sharon Reed, and to my astonishment, she had spent her childhood in West Bend, Iowa, just a few miles from our family farm where I had seen the smallish entity looking in our kitchen window. While Sharon and I had never met each other while growing up, we obviously had a very fascinating friend in common.

"As we compared notes, we discovered that we had both seen the entity at approximately the same time, and while we cannot say it was exactly the same night, it had to have been within a few days of each other's experience."

It would seem that on one strange night in Iowa in 1940 "something" was trolling for inquisitive children. We can only guess how many other boys and girls saw something very unusual looking in their windows that night, something that would change their lives forever.

As an adult, Sharon practiced meditation for many years, and in the summer of 1975, while she was sitting very much at peace inside of herself, a vision suddenly appeared and blocked out all awareness of anything else in the room around her.

The room in which she was sitting was the living room of her California home, a beautiful room with many large windows for viewing the lovely scenery outside. This room was on the top floor of her tri-level house, and the view to the sky, the lake, and the hills was totally unobstructed by the other houses.

At first when the vision appeared before her, Sharon felt shock and surprise at what she was feeling and seeing. The vision appeared as a large light penetrating the room. Within the body of light was a large screen for viewing, much the same type of screen on which one would watch home movies. Appearing on the screen was a long, strangely shaped object that seemed to be floating in space.

She had never seen such an object before, and her mind was asking a thousand questions. She felt no panic or fear within her, only calmness and curiosity. She sensed that this object was from another world, another place in time, and the next thing she remembers is that she was standing *inside* the cigar-shaped object.

One night in Iowa in 1940 a being of some kind set out on the task of finding inquisitive human children. (**Art by Ricardo Pustanio**)

She was directed to a central, glass-like dome standing alone in the center of this room. Inside the dome was a large book that seemed to be supporting itself in midair. She could not touch the book, because the glass dome was completely encasing it.

She was aware of beings who directed her attention to the book. They were polite, and they seemed eager to have her view it. As she stood before the dome, the book opened, but the letters of the book were unrecognizable to her.

Nonetheless, as she scrutinized the strange script, she could feel the knowledge of what they represented flowing into her mind. She could not interpret their meaning consciously, but she knew that somewhere inside of her the knowledge was being deposited.

As she studied each page, the book seemed to come alive, and the pages began turning over slowly. She continued to read each page as it was presented to her.

She stood transfixed in front of the glass dome, viewing the strange book and reading its messages. She became more aware of the beings who were in the room with her, and as she gazed at them, a strong feeling of calmness developed within her. She felt a strong bond with the entities.

When she finished reading the book, she said thank you to the beings who were so kind and intelligent. Although they appeared physically very different from her, that difference didn't seem to matter—for they had shared something very important together.

Sharon knew inwardly that what she had been given to read was implanted within her. Somewhere within her there was a space that had been reserved just for this experience and for the storage of what she had been given to understand.

Since that time Sharon has had many contact experiences with the beings. "There have been many stories published that tell of cruelties being done to Earth beings who are abducted and taken aboard a spaceship. Some people have told of painful tests that have been performed on them. This is an example of how fear can influence the mind and cause persons to perceive what has happened to them in an incorrect analysis."

The visitors from Gilanea (the place by which they have identified themselves to Sharon) have not brought physical harm to any Earth being.

Sharon was told that when the entities with whom she had contact approached earthlings, they did so with compassion, patience, and wisdom; Earth beings were sent thought waves that penetrated their brain with a soothing, anesthetic-type effect. Fear was erased so that the Earth beings would not be harmed by their own fears, which could cause stress on their physical bodies. Earth beings were then able to meet the space visitors on an informative and mutually beneficial basis.

Earth beings who have previously been contacted by the space visitors of Gilanea would have no fear of meeting the entities again. They have met positive space beings. Those who have encountered the benevolent entities know deep within their inner selves of the beauty, love, and compassion extended to them; and they know the space visitors to be highly special beings, whose love for all creation is a love that is unknown here on planet Earth.

Sharon Reed was told that the space visitors dwell on seven different dimensions. Their advanced technology would enable them to completely control Earth beings if they so desired. However, their absolute respect for the laws of the universe governs all their acts, and they do not seek superiority and power through control. Their Planet Earth Probe Mission has been an extremely long and difficult task, and their many messages to Earth have seemed at times to be almost desperate. As a parent to a child, they hope that Earth beings are listening to them, but only time will tell if the human race has responded.

The beings told Sharon that they are presently working with many of Earth's children through mind coding. These children, if planet Earth survives, will grow to become individuals of great accomplishment. They will be individuals with a strong inner belief in *what* they are doing and with a full knowledge of *why* they are performing their particular missions. There will be great changes among the many cultures that inhabit planet Earth.

While many contactees, such as Sharon Reed, have found their encounter with an alien, an elf, or a cosmic visitor to be positive and instructive, we must always be very conscious of the reality that not all multidimensional beings are positive and helpful to their human hosts.

In the account below, our friend Brandie tells of an early experience with a fae, a humanoid mystical creature of extraordinary powers whose kind predates the rise of humans on the planet. In common usage, the fae is synonymous with fairies or the wee people, but they definitely are not in the same family as Tinker Bell. Brandie's experiences with the fae turned out to be both frightening and potentially dangerous to her spiritual health.

⋙⋘

MIDNIGHT CLASSES TAUGHT BY A DEMANDING FAE INSTRUCTOR

By Brandie

This episode with an otherworldly being happened basically against my will, and in retrospect I believe that I was under some heavy enchantment at the time.

I was just a child, about eight, living in Dorchester, Massachusetts. The first visitation occurred after my grandma had tucked me in bed, leaving the door open and the window cracked. The room had these semi-huge bay windows, and on that night it was particularly windy. I remember lying there, looking out of the window at the bright moon and the trees just tossing violently.

I started to doze off, but something woke me. It was like a sound on the wind that started off really faint. I had to strain to catch it before I realized that it was music.

It wasn't like any music that I heard before or found familiar. It had an odd quality to it. I remember it sounding like a lot of wind instruments, and the strange music was intertwined with singing. It sounded unbelievably beautiful, yet sad.

I lay, just listening, and the music began to get louder and louder until it drowned out the wind. My ears were aching with the sound, and I began to feel defensive. The strange music had gone from a sweetness to a smothering sound that tried to drown me in it. After that I just blacked out.

Later on, I remembered a lot of haziness and green. A twilight green that swamped my vision. And there was something that called me, yearned for me, so I followed. I was compelled to follow.

Real Encounters, Different Dimensions, and Otherworldly Beings   355

When I woke up I found myself on the leather couch underneath the stairway in a little room off the hallway. It was pitch black, and the area was freezing. I woke up disoriented, drained, not knowing how I ended up there.

I sensed a presence, though I couldn't see clearly in the dark. I was frightened, yet curious. The figure seemed to hide in the shadows. It seemed tall, and I eventually learned that it was male. The only name I ever had for him was "Gene" or "Ghene." That first time, he laughed at me, and the sound of it was unpleasant.

Being together with Ghene in the darkness scared me, so I ran and left the room under the stairway and ran back to my room.

> What freaked me out was that this nightly meeting between us existed in a bubble. Time was never affected, nor did it ever pass midnight.

The night encounters began to happen repeatedly under the guise of my "sleepwalking." It would always begin by my being summoned by the same faint melody. I must have been under a spell, for when I was called and sleepwalked, I spoke to no one and remembered nothing. It all seemed like a foggy dream. I became so desperate not to follow the pattern that I tried to tie myself to the bed.

That didn't work at all.

What freaked me out was that this nightly meeting between us existed in a bubble. Time was never affected, nor did it ever pass midnight. Always I was called at midnight, and I always returned without time seeming to have passed at all. So many hours passed it seemed, but never did the clock leave midnight. Somehow I knew instinctively that Ghene was fae-like.

He wasn't a ghost or a bodiless spirit. He was very real and wicked when angered. I'd always wake up feeling weak, and I think he used some of my energy.

Somehow he saw this forced relationship as a trade-off. He would talk to me and try to teach me things. Truthfully, I cannot remember anything we discussed, but I remember him grabbing my wrist one time. I had begun to backtalk. He didn't like it, and his touch was so cold.

As I reflect back on this experience from my childhood, I see that Ghene's behavior was bizarre, yet interesting. Obviously, he worked by a different set of rules from humankind. He was capricious, fickle, moody, amusing, and ever vigilant. He told me never to tell or to talk to anybody about our meetings, because he would know. The seriousness of that threat wasn't lost on me at all. This episode may have messed up my relationship for life with all otherworldly people, but especially the fae. I don't trust them, because their motives are unknowable and crazy. Sometimes Ghene scared me purposely; other times he kept silent, just staring.

Mostly, I felt like a pet to him, and that may not have been too far from the truth. Ghene constantly summoned me to the point where I was exhausted and just wanted to sleep. My grandma would wonder why I wasn't as playful in the morning as I used to be. I tried telling her about Ghene, but she didn't listen, nor did my cousin.

One morning I sucked up some bravery and went downstairs to the little room under the stairs. Somehow that area of the house had a forbidding aura to it and the heavy atmosphere frightened me. I would always zoom by to avoid the little room unless I had to get something from there. It looked harmless enough—a couch, a small desk with a typewriter. I entered the room until I felt a ripple of fear and a sense of foreboding like I was being watched. So I left.

The next night when he summoned me to the room, I challenged him. He was incensed, and he glared at me with strange otherworldly eyes.

I hardly remember the challenge, but it was surreal.

I remember running away, up the stairs to my room, hearing him yell after me. I passed out on the edge of the bed.

I woke up the next morning, hearing a slight commotion, and looking down the stairs. I saw the small hallway area was trashed. Ghene must've done so in anger. He never bothered me again

As a side note, I had begun to build a very strong connection with Ghene. It was almost like an invisible string that led me to him and formed a bond somehow. When we moved not long after I had freed myself from Ghene, I was really depressed, not from just leaving friends, but oddly enough from leaving him. I felt like I betrayed him.

BRAD COMMANDS AN INVISIBLE INTRUDER TO LEAVE

One night in 1972, as I sat in my office, desperately working over my faithful 1923 Underwood typewriter, I heard the heavy sound of footsteps at the top of the stairs.

A quick glance told me that no one was there.

A few moments later, my favorite painting of Edgar Allan Poe was lifted from the wall and dropped to the floor.

I became irritated. I had to work to meet a deadline on a magazine article. I had no time to play. Papers began to rustle off to my side. A single sheet became airborne.

I had had enough. I looked up from my typewriter, rolled my eyes upward in disgust, and shouted: "Just cut it the hell out!"

Everything stopped. There was literally the sound of silence. The very air seemed less crowded and oppressive. I went back to my writing without taking any further notice of anything other than the work at hand.

Every kind of intelligence, regardless of how high or how low, wishes to be recognized. Nothing shuts up any thinking entity faster than to *ignore* it.

But I *hadn't* ignored it. Rather, I had *commanded* this poltergeist-like force. I had refused to go along with its framework of reality, and my own change of attitude—from passive annoyance to a touch of fear to impatient rage—had apparently done the trick.

In weeks to come I wondered about the other less fortunate victims of poltergeist phenomena, hostile entities, and demonic attacks. Perhaps they were taken off guard and had simply gone along with the "game," refusing to see themselves as the equals of their otherworldly adversaries. The cessation of odd activity in my office had been so abrupt that it was almost like some kind of lesson was terminated. Could it be that some intelligence was trying to teach me something all along—and satisfied that I had learned it, departed for other pupils?

Is it possible that even some of the ostensibly nastiest of entities may be tutors of a sort? May they manifest to teach us that it is possible to command other forces by a sheer effort of will? Of course they may appear to threaten, but when confronted by a firm refusal—or in my case—defiance, do they simply move on? It would sometimes seem that they are deliberately bullying us into revolt, using childish, annoying methods to get us to stand up and take charge of our lives. Is this, in fact, the point of so many of these encounters?

⬤⬤⬤

WE ALL HAVE THE ABILITY TO ACCESS UNIVERSAL LAWS

The universe is governed by physical laws that never fail, by forces that work without the interaction of human consciousness. Many of these energies, these powers, go beyond the present understanding of our sciences and technologies, so we call them "supernatural."

What the angels, the spirit guides, the extraterrestrial entities, and all the other impersonations of the Other may be telling us is that even though we cannot yet explain these mysterious forces, we do have the ability to tap into the energies governed by these universal laws. We have the ability to utilize the infinite current of this force and channel it into positive actions of prayer, mystical expression, healing, and positive interaction with other people.

It has been postulated by some that the entire universe may be a single hologram. It may well be that information about all of the cosmos is encapsulated in each part of it. And that includes each of us human beings. We may all be unfolded images of aspects which exist in a higher reality.

In his book, *Wholeness and the Implicate Order* (2002), physicist David Bohm of the University of London urges contemporary men and women to become aware that the modern view of the world has become fragmented, especially in the sciences, but also in the execution of our daily lives. In science's efforts to divide our universe into stars and atoms, it has separated us from nature. In humankind's penchant for dividing itself into races, nations, ethnic groups, political parties, and economic classes, we have fragmented ourselves from any underlying wholeness with each other.

The benevolent beings teach us that the essential Self within each of us has eternal awareness, eternal consciousness, eternal wisdom, and eternal existence. These multidimensional intelligences state that we have within us the ability to interact with a Supreme Consciousness more powerful than our own, whose boundaries are without limits, whose awareness comprises all of the universe. The human mind and body are not distinct from their environment and their universe.

> It has been postulated by some that the entire universe may be a single hologram.

Throughout the ages, our most revered masters, prophets, and mystics have received glimpses of an interconnected universe and the powers that are available to us through the unknown force that permeates All-That-Is. As our teachers from many cultures sought to better understand this force, to better define it, they have given it names such as *prana, mana, ki, chi, wodan, the Holy Spirit,* the *ruach ha-kodesh.* The Algonquins' *Manitou,* the Lakota's *Wakan Tanka,* the Sufis' *Baraka,* Plato's *Nous,* and Aristotle's *Formative Cause* are all names, terms, and concepts used by prophets, seers, and shamans in their attempts to identify and define the supernatural energy.

In some way that we have not yet fully defined, the human psyche serves as a conduit for this force that, in turn, enables us to perform miracles of healing, enlightenment, and illumination. With access to this unknown energy, we can overcome all obstacles that may seek to interfere with the accomplishment of our attaining higher awareness. Each one of us can become a conduit through which this unknown force flows. We can become co-creators with the Great Mystery.

THERE IS A PURPOSE, BALANCE, ORDER, AND UNITY IN ALL THINGS
By Sherry Steiger

As Sherry said in her mission statement for The Butterfly Center for Transformation:

Sherry Steiger meditates in Sedona, Arizona. She believes that, as we learn more, religious and scientific understandings of the universe will merge. (*Photo by Timothy Green Beckley*)

In our dynamic universe nothing is static. There is a purpose, balance, order, and unity inherent in all things. Gaps between religion and science are closing.

The exploration of our subatomic reality has forced us to drastically modify our basic concepts of reality. Matter is revealed not as passive and inert, but as bundles of energy, moving in a continual dance of transformation. What appears to be solid is not; scientists are saying patterns of energy reflect patterns of mind.

All things man-made were first a thought in someone's mind. Laboratories all over the world are discovering how we can learn to control our thoughts and even regulate our heart beat and bodily functions. There is continual, mounting evidence that life (consciousness) exists after death—less and less that it does not. Clear evidence of a human energy field (aura) suggests that field to be brighter and larger when a person is in prayer or meditation. Evidence of that same energy field around plants reveals that they can respond to human thoughts and emotions.

People pronounced clinically dead, who have come back to life, have been transformed by the dead-and-beyond experience. Many such near-death experiencers seem to be recalling that the judgment by a being of light is concerned primarily with how much that person *loved* during life on earth. Love is the highest definition, which includes compassion, service, and self-lessness. Love is seen as the strongest force in the universe—and not to love brings suffering.

The material for our creative transformation is inside us and exists in us, equally accessible to everyone. As the oak tree is inherent in the oak seed, as the butterfly in inherent in the caterpillar, the Kingdom of God is *within* us. What keeps us from being more creative, sensitive, resourceful, and loving is a frame of mind that exists in seeing only the commonplace in the familiar. We become frozen in the ice of our own conservatism and the world congeals around us.

We must learn to see with all our senses, intuitive and rational. The creative loving way must be learned: even though it is inherent within us, it is not the normal way of the world and it actually has been buried deeper within us. To really see with all of our senses, to be really integrated, we must shift our attitudes. Some attitudes add to our blindness, others enhance our ability to see clearly. As we explore our attitudes and beliefs, actions and interactions, we can begin to remove the blinders on our journey. We can become more fully integrated, alive persons. We can become free, creative, positive shapers of our destiny, not victims of our past. We believe in celebrating this process, this rebirth and awakening, this freedom to be new creatures transformed.

CLOSING THOUGHTS

by Brad Steiger and Sherry Hansen Steiger

In the pages of this book, the reader has met men and women who have reported interactions with beings who presented themselves as angels, spirit guides, devas, hooded masters, totem spirits, or as extraterrestrial visitors. These individuals are sincere in reporting the accounts of their experiences and are unshaken by the disbelief or doubts of others. And it is at the time of that initial contact with the Unknown, the Other, that the experiencer first understands that reality may have many more facets than previously imagined.

As we have mentioned often in this book, there are good and bad entities in every dimension, earthly or otherwise. Evil does exist; negative beings do exist; and we must always learn to practice discernment and refuse to enter into their game so we are not deceived.

Perhaps preparation for a dramatic time of upheaval, a transition of our world, and a transformation of our species is what all of the many "real encounters" that humankind has experienced down through the ages have been all about. Perhaps once we correctly fathom the meaning of the Other, and its total relevance to our lives, we will perceive how an evolved Intelligence, whose manifestations we have been for centuries mistakenly labeling as our gods and our demons, has been challenging us, teaching us, and preparing us to recognize our true role in the cosmic scheme of things.

FURTHER READING

Ghosts, Near-Death Experiences, and Life After Death

Asala, Joanne, editor. *Scandinavian Ghost Stories*. Iowa City, IA: Penfield Press, 1995.

Auerbach, Lloyd, and Annette Martin. *The Ghost Detective's Guide to Haunted San Francisco*. Fresno, CA: Linden, 2011.

Baird, A.T, editor. *One Hundred Cases for Survival after Death*. New York: Bernard Ackerman, 1944.

Bayless, Raymond. *The Other Side of Death*. New Hyde Park, NY: University Books, 1971.

Carrington, Hereward. *The Case for Psychic Survival*. New York: The Citadel Press, 1957.

———, and Nandor Fodor. *Haunted People*. New York: New American Library, 1968.

Clark, Jerome. *Unexplained! Strange Sightings, Incredible Occurrences, and Puzzling Physical Phenomena*, third edition, Detroit/London: Visible Ink Press, 2012.

Copper, Arnold, and Coralee Leon. *Psychic Summer*. New York: The Dial Press, 1976.

Crawford, W.J. *The Psychic Structures of the Goligher Circle*. New York: E.P. Dutton & Company, 1921.

Crookall, Robert. *Intimations of Immortality*. London: James Clarke Company, Ltd., 1968.

———. *More Astral Projections*. London: Aquarian Press, 1964.

Ebon, Martin, editor. *True Experiences in Communicating with the Dead*. New York: New American Library, 1968.

Estep, Sarah Wilson. *Voices of Eternity*. New York: Ballantine Books, 1988.

Flammarion, Camille. *Death and Its Mystery after Death: Manifestations and Apparitions of the Dead; The Soul after Death*. Translation by Latrobe Carroll. New York and London: The Century Co., 1923.

———. *Haunted Houses*. London: T. Fisher Unwin, 1924.

Fiore, Dr. Edith. *The Unquiet Dead*. New York: Doubleday, 1987.

Fodor, Nador. *These Mysterious People*. London: Rider & Co, 1935.

———. *Mind Over Space and Time*. New York: The Citadel Press, 1962.

———. *The Haunted Mind: A Psychoanalyst Looks at the Supernatural*. New York: New American Library, 1968.

———. *Between Two Worlds*. New York: Paperback Library, 1967

Garrett, Eileen. *Many Voices: The Autobiography of a Medium*. New York: G. P. Putnam's Sons, 1968.

Goode, Caron B. *Kids Who See Ghosts: How to Guide Them through Fear*. San Francisco, CA/Newburyport, MA: Weiser Books, 2010.

Hauk, Dennis William. *Haunted Places*. Reprint edition. New York: Penguin USA, 1996.

———. *International Directory of Haunted Places*. New York: Penguin, 2000.

Holzer, Hans. *Yankee Ghosts*. New York: Ace Books, 1966.

Kerman, Frances. *Ghostly Encounters: True Stories of America's Haunted Inns and Hotels*. New York: Warner Books, 2002.

Kolb, Janice Gray. *Compassion for All Creatures*. Nevada City, CA: Blue Dolphin Publishing, 1997.

Krippner, Stanley, with Etzel Cardena and Steven J. Lynn. *Varieties of Anomalous Experience: Examining the Scientific Evidence*. Washington, DC: American Psychological Association, 2000.

Jacobson, Laurie, and Mark Wanamaker. *Hollywood Haunted*. Los Angeles: Angel City Press, 1999.

LeShan, Lawrence. *The Medium, the Mystic, and the Physicist*. New York: Viking Press, 1974.

May, Antoinette. *Haunted Houses and Wandering Ghosts of California*. San Francisco: San Francisco Examiner Division, 1977.

McComas, Henry C. *Ghosts I Have Talked With*. Baltimore, MD: The Williams & Wilkins Company, 1937.

Monroe, Robert A. *Far Journeys*. Garden City, NY: Doubleday, 1987.

Murphy, Gardner. *The Challenge of Psychical Research*. New York: Harper & Row, 1970.

Norman, Michael, and Beth Scott. *Historic Haunted America*. New York: Tor Books, 1996.

———. *Haunted Heritage*. New York: A Forge Book, Tom Doherty Associates, 2002.

Pitkin, David J. *New England Ghosts*. Chestertown, NY: Aurora Publications, 2010.

Price, Harry. *Poltergeist Over England*. London: Country Life, Ltd., 1945.

———. *The Most Haunted House in England*. London: Longmans, Green & Co, 1940.

Ramsland, Katherine. *Ghost: A Firsthand Account into the World of Paranormal Activity*. New York: St. Martin's Press, 2001.

Rider, Fremont. *Are the Dead Alive?* New York: B.W. Dodge & Company, 1909.

Sitwell, Sacheverell. *Poltergeists*. New York: University Books, 1959.

Smith, Alson J. *Immortality: The Scientific Evidence*. New York: Prentice Hall, 1954.

Smith, Susy. *Haunted Houses for the Millions*. Los Angeles: Sherbourne Press, Inc., 1967.

———. *Prominent American Ghosts*. New York: Dell, 1969.

Spence, Lewis. *An Encyclopedia of Occultism*. New Hyde Park, NY: University Books, 1960.

Stallings, Nancy L. *Show Me One Soul: A True Haunting*. Baltimore, MD: Noble House, 1996.

Steiger, Brad, and Sherry Hansen Steiger. *Hollywood and the Supernatural*. New York: St. Martin's Press, 1990.

———. *Montezuma's Serpent and Other True Supernatural Tales of the Southwest*. New York, 1992.

Steinour, Harold. *Exploring the Unseen World*. New York: The Citadel Press, 1959.

Stevens, William Oliver. *Unbidden Guests*. New York: Dodd, Mead & Company, 1957.

Stonehouse, Frederick. *Haunted Lakes: Great Lakes Ghost Stories, Superstitions, and Sea Serpents*. Duluth, MN: Lake Superior Port Cities, Inc., 1997.

Sullivan, Lawrence E, editor. *Death, Afterlife, and the Soul*. New York: Macmillan Publishing Company, 1989.

Tucker, George Holbert. *Virginia Supernatural Tales*. Norfolk, VA: Donning Company, 1977.

Turnage, Sheila. *Haunted Inns of the Southwest*. Winston-Salem, MA: John F. Blair, 2001.

Tyrrell, G.N.M. *Apparitions*. New York: Collier Books, 1963.

Uphoff, Walter, and Mary Jo. *New Psychic Frontiers*. Gerrards Cross, Bucks, UK: Colin Smythe, Ltd., 1975.

Watson, Lyall. *The Romeo Error*. New York: Dell Books, 1976.

White, Steward Edward. *The Road I Know*. New York: E.P. Dutton, 1942.

Willis-Brandon, Carla. *One Last Hug before I Go: The Mystery and Meaning of Deathbed Visions*. Deerfield Beach, FL: Health Communications, Inc., 2000.

UFOs, Flying Saucers, and Alien Intelligences

Adamski, George. *Behind the Flying Saucer Mystery (Flying Saucers Farewell)*. New York: Paperback Library, 1967.

Barker, Gray. *They Knew Too Much about Flying Saucers*. Adventures Unlimited Press, 1956.

Beckley, Timothy Green. *Subterranean Worlds*. New Brunswick, NJ: Inner Light, 1992.

———. *Jimi Hendrix: Starchild*. New Brunswick, NJ: Inner Light, 1992.

———. *The American Indian UFO-Starseed Connection*. New Brunswick, NJ: Inner Light, 1992.

———. *The UFO Silencers*. New Brunswick, NJ: Inner Light, 1990.

Binder, Otto. *What We Really Know about Flying Saucers*. New York: Fawcett, 1967.

———. *Flying Saucers Are Watching Us*. New York: Tower, 1968.

Bowen, Charles (ed.). *The Humanoids*. Chicago: Henry Regnery, 1969.

Bryant, Alice, and Linda Seeback. *Healing Shattered Reality: Understanding Contactee Trauma*. Tigard, OR: Wild Flower Press, 1991.

Clark, Jerome. *The UFO Book: Encyclopedia of the Extraterrestrial*. Detroit, MI: Visible Ink Press, 1997.

———, and Loren Coleman. *The Unidentified*. New York: Warner Paperback Library, 1975.

Chester, Keith. *Strange Company: Military Encounters with UFOs in World War II*. San Antonio, TX: Anomalist Books, 2007.

Commander X. *Nikola Tesla-Free Energy and the White Dove*. New Brunswick, NJ: Inner Light, 1992.

———. *Ultimate Deception*. New Brunswick, NJ: Inner Light, 1992.

———. *Underground Alien Bases*. New Brunswick, NJ: Inner Light, 1991.

Constable, Trevor James. *The Cosmic Pulse of Life*. Santa Ana, CA: Merlin Press, 1976.

Cooper, Milton William. *Behold a Pale Horse*. Sedona, AZ: Light Technology, 1991.

Crystal, Ellen. *Silent Invasion*. New York: Paragon House, 1991.

Dennett, Preston. *UFOs Over New York: A True History of Extraterrestrial Encounters in the Empire State*. Atglen, PA: Schiffer Publishing, 2008.

Downing, Barry H. *The Bible and Flying Saucers*. New York: Avon, 1970.

Drake, W. Raymond. *Gods and Spacemen in the Ancient West*. New York: New American Library, 1974.

Edwards, Frank. *Flying Saucers-Serious Business*. New York: Lyle Stuart, 1966.

Fawcett, Lawrence, and Barry J. Greenwood. *Clear Intent: The Government Cover-up of the UFO Experience*. Englewood Cliffs, NJ: Prentice Hall, 1984.

Fry, Daniel. *The White Sands Incident*. Madison, WI: Horus House, 1992

Fuller, John. *Incident at Exeter*. New York: G.P. Putnam, 1966.

Good, Timothy. *Above Top Secret: The Worldwide UFO Cover-up*. New York: William Morrow, 1988.

Hayakawa, Norio F. *UFOs: The Grand Deception and the Coming New World Order*. New Brunswick, NJ: Civilian Intelligence Network/Inner Light, 1993.

Huyghe, Patrick, and Harry Trumbore. *The Field Guide to Extraterrestrials*. New York: Avon Books, 1996.

Hynek, J. Allen, and Jacques Vallee. *The Edge of Reality*. Chicago: Henry Regnery, 1975.

———, and Philip J. Imbrogno, with Bob Pratt. *Night Siege*. New York: Ballantine, 1987.

Jacobs, David M. *Secret Life: Firsthand, Documented Accounts of UFO Abductions*. New York: Touchstone, 1999.

Jung, C. G. *Flying Saucers: A Modern Myth of Things Seen in the Sky.* New York: New American Library, 1967.

Kean, Leslie. *UFOs: Generals, Pilots and Government Officials Go on the Record.* New York: Crown, 2010.

Keel, John A. *Strange Creatures from Time and Space.* New York: Fawcett, 1970.

———. *The Mothman Prophecies.* New York: Saturday Review Press, 1975.

Keyhoe, Donald E. *Flying Saucers from Outer Space.* New York: Henry Holt, 1953.

LaViolette, Paul A. *Secrets of Antigravity Propulsion: Tesla, UFOs, and Classified Aerospace Technology.* Rochester, VT: Bear and Company, 2008.

Mack, John E. *Abducted.* New York: Charles Scribner's Sons, 1994.

Menger, Howard. *From Outer Space to You.* New York: Pyramid, 1967.

Palmer, Raymond A. *The Real UFO Invasion.* San Diego: Greenleaf, 1967.

Randle, Kevin D. *Invasion Washington: UFOs Over the Capitol.* New York: HarperTorch, 2001.

———. *Case MJ-12: The True Story Behind the Government's UFO Conspiracies.* New York: HarperTorch, 2002.

———. *Conspiracy of Silence.* New York: Avon Books, 1997.

———. *A History of UFO Crashes.* New York: Avon Books, 1995.

Randle, Kevin D., and Donald R. Schmitt. *UFO Crash at Roswell.* New York: Avon Books, 1991.

———. *The Truth About the UFO Crash at Roswell.* New York: M. Evans, 1994.

Redfern, Nick. *On the Trail of the Saucer Spies: UFOs and Government Surveillance.* San Antonio, TX: 2006.

———. *The NASA Conspiracies: The Truth Behind the Moon Landings, Censored Photos, and the Face on Mars.* Pompton Plains, NJ: New Page Books, 2011.

Ruppelt, Edward J. *The Report on Unidentified Flying Objects.* New York: Doubleday, 1956.

Saunders, David R., and R. Roger Harkins. *UFOs? Yes! Where the Condon Committee Went Wrong.* New York: New American Library, 1968.

Schellhorn, G. Cope. *Extraterrestrials in Biblical Prophecy and the New Age Great Experiment.* Madison, WI: Horus House, 1990.

Sitchin, Zecharia. *The 12th Planet.* New York: Avon, 1978.

Steiger, Brad, *Strangers from the Skies.* New York: Award, 1966.

———, *Atlantis Rising.* New York: Dell, 1973

———. *Mysteries of Time and Space.* Englewood Cliffs, NJ: Prentice Hall,1974.

———, ed. *Project Bluebook.* New York: ConFucian Press/Ballantine, 1976.

———. *The Gods of Aquarius: UFOs and the Transformation of Man.* New York: Harcourt Brace Jovanovich, 1976.

———, and Joan Whritenour. *New UFO Breakthrough.* New York/London: Award/Tandem, 1968.

———, and Joan Whritenour. *Flying Saucer Invasion: Target Earth.* New York/London: Award/Tandem, 1969.

———, and Sherry Hansen Steiger. *Starborn.* New York: Berkley, 1992.

———, and Sherry Hansen Steiger. *The Rainbow Conspiracy.* New York: Kensington/Pinnacle, 1994.

———, and Sherry Hansen Steiger. *UFO Odyssey.* New York: Ballantine, 1999.

Stevens, Wendelle. *UFO Contact from the Pleiades.* Tucson: UFO Photo Archives, 1982.

———. Sherry Hansen Steiger, and Alfred Bielek. *The Philadelphia Experiment and Other UFO Conspiracies.* New Brunswick, NJ: Inner Light, 1990.

Stonehill, Paul. *Soviet UFO Files: Paranormal Encounters Behind the Iron Curtain.* Barnsbury, Guilford UK: Quadrillion Publishing, 1998.

Story, Ron. *The Encyclopedia of Extraterrestrial Encounters*. New York: New American Library, 2001.

Strieber, Whitley. *Communion*. New York: Beech Tree/William Morrow, 1987.

Trench, Brinsley Le Poer. *The Flying Saucer Story*. New York: Ace, 1966.

Warren, Larry, and Peter Robbins. *Left at East Gate: A First-Hand Account of the Rendlesham Forest UFO Incident, Its Cover-up, and Investigation*. Introduction by Budd Hopkins. New York: Cosimo Books, 2010.

Wee People, Fairies, and the Sidhe

Booss, Claire, editor. *Scandinavian Folk & Fairy Tales*. New York: Gramercy Books, 1984.

DuBois, Pierre. *The Great Encyclopedia of Fairies*. Illustrated by Roland Sabatier and Claudine Sabatier. New York: Simon & Schuster, 2000

Froud, Brian. *Good Faeries, Bad Faeries*. New York: Simon & Schuster, 1998

Gordon, Stuart. *The Encyclopedia of Myths and Legends*. London: Headline Books, 1994.

Keightley, Thomas. *The World Guide to Gnomes, Fairies, Elves, and Other Little People*. New York: Random House, 2000.

Mack, Carol K., and Dinah Mack. *A Field Guide to Demons, Fairies, Fallen Angels, and Other Subversive Spirits*. New York: Henry Holt and Company, 1999

Larousse Dictionary of World Folklore. New York: Larousse, 1995.

Rose, Carol. *Spirits, Fairies, Leprechauns, and Goblins: An Encyclopedia*. New York: W.W. Norton & Company, 1998.

Simek, Rudolf, *Dictionary of Northern Mythology*. Translated by Angela Hall. Rochester, NY: D.S. Brewer, 1993.

Spence, Lewis. *The Fairy Tradition in Britain*. London: Rider and Company, 1948.

Monsters and Cryptids

Armstrong, P.A. *The Piasa or the Devil among the Indians*. Morris, IL: 1887.

Carrington, Richard. *Mermaids and Mastodons*. London: Arrow Books, 1960.

Corrales, Scott. *Chupacabras and Other Mysteries*. Murfreesboro, TN: Greenleaf Publications, 1997.

Bord, Janet, and Colin Bord. *Unexplained Mysteries of the 20th Century*. Chicago: Contemporary Books, 1989.

Byrne, Peter. *The Search for Big Foot: Monster, Myth or Man?* Washington, DC: Acropolis Books, 1976.

Clark, Jerome, and Loren Coleman. *The Unidentified*. New York: Warner Paperback Library, 1975.

———, and Loren Coleman. *Creatures of the Outer Edge*. New York: Warner Books, 1978.

Coleman, Loren. *Curious Encounters*. Boston and London: Faber & Faber, 1985.

———. *Mysterious America*. Boston: Faber & Faber, 1985.

———. *Mothman and Other Curious Encounters*. NY: Paraview Press, 2002

Dash, Mike. *Borderlands*. New York: Dell Books, 2000.

Dinsdale, Tim. *Loch Ness Monster*. Fourth edition. Boston: Routledge & Kegan Paul, 1982.

Eisler, Robert. *Man into Wolf*. London: Spring Books, n.d.

Ellis, Richard. *Monsters of the Sea*. New York: Alfred A. Knopf, 1994.

Green, John. *On the Track of the Bigfoot*. New York: Ballantine Books, 1973

Heuvelmans, Bernard. *On the Track of Unknown Animals*. New York: Hill & Wang, 1958.

Hurwood, Bernardt J. *Vampires, Werewolves, and Ghouls*. New York: Ace Books, 1968.

Jones, Alison, editor. *Larousse Dictionary of World Lore*. New York: Larousse, 1995.

Keel, John A. *Strange Creatures from Time and Space*. Greenwich, CT: Fawcett Publications, 1970

———. *The Mothman Prophecies*. NY: Tor Books, 2002.

Mackal, Roy P. *The Monsters of Loch Ness*. Chicago: The Swallow Press, 1976.

———. *Searching for Hidden Animals: An Inquiry into Zoological Mysteries* Garden City, NY: Doubleday, 1980.

———. *A Living Dinosaur? In Search of Mokele-Mbembe*. New York: E. J.Brill, 1987.

Masters, R. E. L, and Eduard Lea. *Perverse Crimes in History*. New York: The Julian Press, 1963.

Melton, Gordon J. *The Vampire Book: The Encyclopedia of the Undead*. Farmington Hills, MI: Visible Ink Press, 1998.

Sanderson, Ivan T. *Abominable Snowmen: Legend Come to Life*. Philadelphia: Chilton Company, 1961.

Steiger, Brad. *The Werewolf Book: The Encyclopedia of Shape-shifting Beings*. Detroit, MI: Visible Ink Press, 1999.

———, and Sherry Hansen Steiger. *The Gale Encyclopedia of the Unusual and the Unexplained*. Farmington Hills, MI: Thomson-Gale, 2003.

———. *Real Vampires, Night Stalkers, and Creatures from the Darkside*. Detroit, MI: Visible Ink Press, 2010.

———. *Real Zombies, The Living Dead, and Creatures of the Apocalypse*. Detroit, MI: Visible Ink Press, 2010.

Dreams

Freud, Sigmund. *The Interpretation of Dreams*. New York: Basic Books, 1955.

Jung, C. G. ed. *Man and His Symbols*. London: Aldus Books, 1964; New York: Dell Publishing, 1968.

Krippner, Stanley. *Dreamtime and Dreamwork: Decoding the Language of the Night*. Los Angeles: Jeremy P. Tarcher, 1990.

Pearce, Joseph Chilton. *The Biology of Transformation: A Blueprint of the Human Spirit*. Rochester, VT: Inner Traditions International, 2002.

Sechrist, Elsie. *Dreams: Your Magic Mirror*. New York: Dell Publishing, 1969.

Targ, Russell, and Harold E. Puthoff. *Mind-Reach: Scientists Look at Psychic Ability*. New York: Delacorte Press/Eleanor Friede, 1977.

Tart, Charles, ed. *Altered States of Consciousness*. New York: John Wiley & Sons, 1969.

———. *Body Mind Spirit: Exploring the Parapsychology of Spirituality*. Hampton Roads, 1997.

Angels and Spirit Guides

Alper, Matthew. *The "God" Part of the Brain*. New Hartford, NY: Rogue Press, 2001.

Anderson, Joan Wester. *In the Arms of Angels: True Stories of Heavenly Guardians*. Chicago: Loyola Press, 2004.

———. *Where Angels Walk*. New York: Ballantine Books, 1993.

Atwater, P. M. H. *Beyond the Light*. New York: Avon, 1997.

Bach, Marcus. *The Inner Ecstasy*. New York and Cleveland: World Publishing, 1969.

Bennett, Hal Zina. *Spirit Animals and the Wheel of Life*. Charlottesville, VA: Hampton Roads Publishing Company, 2000.

Burnham, Sophy. *A Book of Angels*. New York: Fawcett Columbine, 1995.

Ensley, Eddie. *Visions: The Soul's Path to the Sacred*. New Orleans: Loyola Press, 2001.

Evans, Hilary. *Gods, Spirits, Cosmic Guardians: A Comparative Study of the Encounter Experience*. Wellingborough, Northamptonshire, UK: The Aquarian Press, 1987.

Goldman, Karen. *Angel Encounters: Real Stories of Angelic Intervention*. New York: Simon & Schuster, 1995.

Harner, Michael. *The Way of the Shaman*. New York: Bantam Books, 1982.

Hastings, Arthur. *With the Tongues of Men and Angels: A Study of Channeling*. New York: Holt, Rinehart, & Winston, 1991.

Hirschfelder, Arlene, and Paulette Molin. *The Encyclopedia of Native American Religions*. New York: MJF Books, 1992.

Kinnaman, Gary. *Angels Dark and Light*. Ann Arbor, MI: Servant Publications, 1994.

Lissner, Ivar. *Man, God and Magic*. New York: G. P. Putnam's Sons, 1961.

Moolenburg, Dr. H.C. *Meetings with Angels*. New York: Barnes & Noble, 1995.

Morse, Melvin. *Parting Visions: Uses and Meaning of Pre-Death*. New York: Villard Books, 1994.

Oesterreich, T.K. *Possession: Demonical & Other among Primitive Races, in Antiquity, the Middle Ages, and Modern Times*. New Hyde Park, NY: University Books, 1966.

Ring, Kenneth. *Life at Death*. New York: Coward, McCann & Geoghegan, 1980.

Steiger, Brad. *Guardian Angels and Spirit Guides*. New York: Plume Books, 1995.

———. *Totems: The Transformative Power of Your Personal Animal Totem*. San Francisco: HarperSanFrancisco, 1997.

———. *Angels Around the World*. New York: Random House, 1996.

———, and Sherry Hansen Steiger. *Angels Over Their Shoulders: Children's Encounters with Angels*. New York: Fawcett-Columbine, 1995.

Van Dusen, Wilson. *The Presence of Other Worlds: The Findings of Emanuel Swedenborg*. New York: Harper & Row, 1974.

INDEX

Note. (ill.) indicates photos and illustrations.

Numbers

2001: A Space Odyssey, 346

A

Abandondero, 119

abduction stories, 19–22, 21 (ill.), 43–67

accessing universal laws, 358–59

accidents or alien attacks, 99–100

Acorn, 126

Adamski, George, 17–18, 23–25, 24 (ill.)

Agharta empire, 107

Ahrimanes, 74 (ill.), 74–75

aircraft designs, morphing, 9–11, 10 (ill.)

Aldebaran aliens, 114

Algonquins, 359

Alien Impact (Craft), 190

Alien Research Group, 162

aliens

being mistaken for, 17 (ill.), 17–18

blue, 58–59

impregnating earth women, 62 (ill.), 62–66

meeting, 34–39

sexual experience with, 51–53, 52 (ill.)

shape-shifting, 50–51

Alkaid, 94–95

Allen, Dan, 2–4, 178–181, 238–242

Alpha, 308

American Association for Electronic Voice Phenomena, 270–72

American Philosophical Society, 1

ancient sea gods or ancient alien USOs, 91–92

Angel, 255

angelic helpers and messengers, 201–18

angels, comparison between space beings and, 27

angels, relationship between fairies and, 128–29

animal totems and nature spirits, communicating with, 235–250, 237 (ill.), 239 (ill.), 246 (ill.), 248 (ill.)

Antura, 34–39, 35 (ill.)

Apol, 193

Arakarimoa, 96–97

Aratoba, 96

ARE (Association of Research and Enlightenment), 69

Argentine Navy, USOs evade, 87–88

Argo, Melissa, 187–88

Aristotle, 197, 359

Arizona RV park, door to another dimension in an, 285–87

Arnold, Kenneth, 1, 86

Aryans, 111, 113–14, 117–18

Ashtar, 27

Association of Research and Enlightenment (ARE), 69

Astral Light, the, 111

astral world, visiting the, 289–304

Atlans, 96, 111, 118–19

attacks or accidents, alien, 99–100

attention to NDEs, paying, 341–42

Attila the Hun, 92

Atwater, P.M.H., 81, 250, 299

aUI, the Language of Space (Weilgart), 149, 151

Avery, Don, 29–33

Avery, Peggy, 29, 31, 33

awful dream, the, 310–12

Azhazha, Vladimir, 90

B

babies, alien-earth hybrid, 62 (ill.), 62–66

baby's life saved by angel, 213–14

Bain, Squadron Leader, 90

balance in all things, 359–361

ball lightning, orbs as, 78

Barbara K., 95

Barker, Gray, 169–170, 196

Barrett-Pellington, Jennifer, 197

Bates, Sir Alan, 196

Batman, 194

Battle of Somme, 110

bed, the thing on Johnny's, 174–78, 175 (ill.)

bed and breakfast, haunted, 189

beginners, spirit recording for, 269–270

beings of terror, unknown, 155–181

believers, angels making people into, 210–11

Bell, Art, 179

Bender, Albert K., 169–170

Bennett, Marcella, 194, 196

Bergier, Jacques, 113

Bermuda Triangle, Flight 19 and the, 97–99, 99 (ill.)

Bernard, Raymond, 108–9

Bernhardt, Clarisa, 217–18, 218 (ill.)

Bernstein, Marge, 189–192

Berosus, 91

Beyond the Light (Clark), 69

Bigfoot, 185, 185 (ill.), 187–88, 188 (ill.), 281

bird, spirit guide taking form of a, 242–43

bird songs, spirit voices among, 266–67

B.K., Mrs., 77–78

Black Sun, the, 111–12

Black-Eyed Kids, 169

Blavatsky, Mme. Helena, 111

blind, angels leading the, 206–9, 207 (ill.)

Bloom, Orlando, 127

blue aliens, 58–59

BOAC (British Overseas Airways Corporation), 6

Boericke, Charmaine Yarune, 123

Bohn, David, 359

Borley Rectory, 260

Borovikov, B., 101

Bourie, Ric, 133

Breakthrough: An Amazing Experiment in Electronic Communication with the Dead (Raudive), 266, 268

British Association for the Advancement of Science, 100

British Overseas Airways Corporation (BOAC), 6

Brockway, Cathy, 161–64, 167–68

Brotherhood, 308

Bryant, Ernest, 24

Buckle, Eileen, 24

Buddha, 92

Bulwer-Lytton, Edward, 111

Burke, Ronald, 86

Burroughs, William, 198

butterfly, spiritual totem in form of a giant, 243–46

Butterfly Center for Transformation, 232, 347–48, 359

butterfly people in Joplin, Missouri, 216–17, 217 (ill.)

Byrd, Richard E., 109

C

cabin, ghastly attack in the, 178–181, 179 (ill.)

cabinets, tapping, 258–59

Caddy, Eileen, 246–47

Caddy, Peter, 246–47

Campbell, Joseph, 11

cancer, angel healing, 212–13

Cardano, Gerolamo, 197

Carrington, Hereward, 261

Cassidy, Kerry, 85

Casteel, Sean, 19–22

Cayce, Edgar, 222

Ceto, Sanni, 16

Chakra Suite, 223

Chambers, Big Lou, 107

characteristics common to abductees, 54

Charles XII, King, 117

cheer, ghost bringing one, 254–55

Chi, the, 111

Chief Eagle, Dallas, 236

Children of the 5th World (Atwater), 81

China, abduction in, 58–59

Christ, 92

The Christian Philosopher (Mather), 108

The Chronicles of Narnia: The Lion, the Witch and the Wardrobe (Lewis), 129

Chronos, 91

Circle, 308

Clark, Fay, 69–71, 236

Clark, Mary, 69

Coast to Coast A.M., 156, 179

Coleman, Loren, 195–96

The Coming Race (Bulwer-Lytton), 111

Communion (Strieber), 21–22, 57

Confucius, 26

Congress of Scientific Ufologists, 172

Conroy, Mr., 135

consciousness, states of, 295–98, 297 (ill.)

Constable, Trevor J., 72–75

contact with space brothers and sisters, 23–42, 24 (ill.)

contactee, profile of a UFO, 25–27

contactees, silent, 29–33, 30 (ill.), 31 (ill.), 32 (ill.)

contactees and spirit mediums, similarities between space, 27–28

Corso, Col. Philip J., 9, 11

cosmic gospel, 25–28

Council of Cosmic Tutors, 88, 93

Council of Seven Lights, 27

Craft, Michael, 190

critters and orbs, sky, 69–82

Crookall, Robert, 329–330

Crookes, Sir William, 194, 261

Crowhurst, Donald, 95–96

cruise ship, light following a, 84–85

Crystal, 225–26

D

Daley, John, 107

DAP (German Workers' Party), 110–12

Darkness Walks: The Shadow People Among Us (Offutt), 275

Davenport, Peter, 83

The Day After Roswell (Corso), 9

The Day the Earth Stood Still, 25

De Laurier, John M., 106

dead, electronic communication with the, 264–66, 270–72

Dead Sea Scrolls, 229

death, angel comforting living after, 204–5, 242–43, 319–325

death experiences, near- (NDEs), 299, 333–349, 335 (ill.), 338 (ill.), 341 (ill.), 360–61

demonology, 191–92, 192 (ill.)

Demyanko, Major-General V., 100–101

Dennett, Preston, 86–87

Descartes, Rene, 325

Devas, 79, 246–250, 248 (ill.)

Dickson Springs, Tennessee, Bigfoot at, 187–88

Diegel, Patricia-Rochelle, 352

Diegel, Rev. Jon Terrance, 352

dimensions, people and places from other, 273–287

dimensions of the dream world, flexible, 305–18, 306 (ill.), 309 (ill.), 315 (ill.)

Dinking, Scott, 106

The Divine Animal (Westcott), 92

doctor's contacts with angels, 214–16

Dossey, Larry, 223

Dow, 11

Dowd, Elwood P., 130

Dream Laboratory, 296, 317

dream world, flexible dimensions of the, 305–18, 306 (ill.), 309 (ill.), 315 (ill.)

Dream-Machine, 198–99, 199 (ill.)

Drexler, Anton, 110–11

drowning, angel save from, 211 (ill.), 211–12

Duff, Gordon, 85–86

Dunbar, William, 1–2

E

Ea, 91, 91 (ill.)

Earth Mother, 121–137, 235, 237

Easter Rebellion, 135

Eccles, Sir John, 328–29

Eckart, Dietrich, 111

Edinger, Edward E., 80

Edison, Thomas, 264–66

Ego and Archetype (Edinger), 80

Einstein, Albert, 9

Elder Gods, legends of the, 107–8

Elder Race. See Aryans

electronic voice research, 268

elemental sighting at Stones River Battlefield, 189–191, 190 (ill.)

Eleoneai, 99

Elijah, 229–234, 230 (ill.)

Elohim. See Aryans

Encyclopaedia of Psychic Science (Fodor), 188

Epp, Joseph Andreas, 115

ESP Research Associates Foundation, 268

Estep, Sarah Wilson, 270–72

evolution, alien-earth hybrids accelerating human, 65–66

extraterrestrials walking among us, 12 (ill.), 12–22, 15 (ill.)

F

Fae, the, 355–57

fairies. See wee people

Fairies (Froud), 121

faith keeping shadow people at bay, 277–79

Federation of Planets, 39, 41

Fellar, Lisa, 330–31

Fellar, Louis, 330–32

Fellar, Patricia, 330–32

Fellar, Tammy, 330–32

Fellin, David, 106

Fenrir, 112

Findhorn community, uniqueness of the, 246–49

Findhorn Foundation, 247

Firkon, 24

flexible dimensions of the dream world, 305–18, 306 (ill.), 309 (ill.), 315 (ill.)

Flight 19 and the Bermuda Triangle, 97–99, 99 (ill.)

Flight into Freedom (Caddy), 247

Florida Keys, USO off the, 88

Fluff, 126

Flying Saucers and the Three Men (Bender), 170

Flying Saucers Are Hostile (Steiger and O'Connell), 171

Flying Saucers Have Landed (Adamski and Leslie), 23

Fodor, Nandor, 188, 261

footprints, ghostly, 255–58, 258 (ill.)

Ford, Gerald, 217

forest creatures, 139–153, 140 (ill.), 143 (ill.), 145 (ill.), 146 (ill.), 149 (ill.)

Forman, Simon, 197

Frankel, Todd C., 216

Freeman, Col. George P., 172

Freud, Sigmund, 308

Froening, David, 9

Froud, Brian, 121

Ft. Sill, Oklahoma abduction, 43–53

Fuller, R. Buckminster, 225

G

Gaddis, Vincent, 98

Gaia, 34

Garduno, Claudia Trujillo, 255

German Workers' Party (DAP), 110–12

Gestalt therapy, 312–13

Ghene, 356–57

Ghost Box, 162–66, 187, 255–58, 257 (ill.)

ghosts, 251–272

Gifts of the Angels, 223

gods from the sea, old, 83–101

Golden Sun, the, 112

Gordon, Stan, 244

Gˆring, Hermann, 112, 115

gospel, cosmic, 25–28

Grandmother Twylah. See Nitsch, Twylah

Great Mystery, 153, 199, 235–36, 345, 359

Greeley, Horace, 108

Greys, 16

Gudrun, 114

guides and teachers, encountering spirit, 219–234

Gulf Master, 100

Gysin, Brion, 198

H

Habermohl, Otto, 115

Hall, Manly P., 222

Halley, Edmund, 108

Halo Paranormal, 162

Halpern, Steven, 221–23, 222 (ill.)

Halstead, Allan, 141–42

Halstead, Lynette, 141–43

Halstead, Millard, 194

Halstead, Scott, 141–43

Halstead, Tonya, 142

Handwerk, Brian, 78

Hanning, R.D., 99–100

Hansen, Sherry. See Steiger, Sherry

Hapgood, Charles, 325, 337

Harder, James, 54–55

Hardy, Sir Alister, 326–27

Harrer, Karl, 111

Harrison, Chandra, 162, 187

Harvey, Roy, 106

Hattie D., 95

Haunted and Paranormal Investigations, 183, 211

haunted office, 258–59

To Hear the Angels Sing (Maclean), 247

Heart of the Deep, 44, 44 (ill.), 47 (ill.), 52 (ill.)

Heike, 114

Hidden Folk, 132–33, 136

Hill, Barney, 55–57

Hill, Betty, 55–57

Himmler, Heinrich, 112, 115

Hitler, Adolf, 109–16, 111 (ill.), 150

Holbein, Hans, 156

The Hollow Earth (Bernard), 108

hollow earth hypothesis, 108–9, 109 (ill.)

Holt, Alan, 9

Holy Mystery, 236

home, the orb that followed her, 77–78

Hopkins, Budd, 20–22

Howard, Captain, 6–7

Hubler, Graham K., 78

humankind, transformation of, 66 (ill.), 66–67

hybrid babies, alien-earth, 62 (ill.), 62–66

Hyre, Mary, 195

I

Iasos, 221, 223–26, 228

immortality, question of, 264

impregnating earth women, aliens, 62 (ill.), 62–66

inheritance from a poltergeist, 260–61

inner earth, master race from, 103–19

instructor, midnight classes by a Fae, 355–57

intelligences, monsters as, 199–200, 200 (ill.)

intelligences, wee people as community of, 136–37

The Interpretation of Dreams (Freud), 308

"interrupted journey" abduction, prototype for the, 55–57, 56 (ill.)

Introduction to Conspiracy (Kern), 310

Intruders (Hopkins), 22

invisible intruder, 357–58

Ireland, wee folk in, 135–36

Iron Sky, 114

J

Jackson, Mahalia, 266

Jackson, Peter, 126

James, 230

James, William, 226, 261, 295, 342

Jastrow, Lorrie, 139–141

Jefferson, Thomas, 1–2

Jehovah, 40

jellyfish, abduction by a huge, glowing, 43–53, 44 (ill.), 47 (ill.)

Jensen, Norman, 106

Jesus, 26, 221, 230, 291, 340, 342

Joan of Arc, 293

John the Baptist, 230

Johnson, Carl, 95

Johnson, W.J., 99

Jones, James Earl, 55

Jonsson, Olof, 152–53

Joplin, Missouri, butterfly people in, 216–17, 217 (ill.)

A Journey to the Center of the Earth (Verne), 108, 110 (ill.)

Jung, Carl G., 309, 318

Jurgenson, Friedrich, 266

K

K, Captain, 88–89

Kakar, 96

Kalson, Stan, 231

Kammler, Hans, 114

Kantor, MacKinlay, 262

Keel, John A., 171–73, 191–97

Kehoe, Richard, 86

Kellog, Rhoda D., 80

Kennedy, Robert F., 268

Kern, William, 310–12

Khan, Genghis, 92

Kingman, Arizona UFO sighting, 29–33, 30 (ill.), 31 (ill.), 32 (ill.)

Kirkland, Betty, 125–26

Klaatu, 25

Kluski, 188

Knights Templar, 115

Kohler on Strike (Uphoff), 268

Krippner, Stanley, 296, 317–18

Krishna, 26

Kubler-Ross, Elizabeth, 299, 347, 347 (ill.)

Kubrick, Stanley, 347

L

Lakotas, 359

Lamoreaux, Michael, 268–69

lands sacred to wee folk, 131 (ill.), 131–36

Langsford, W.A., 106

Laughton, A.L., 100

laws, accessing universal, 358–59

Lawton, Oklahoma abduction, 43–53

learning experiences, real encounters as, 22

learning from forest encounters, 147–152

LeMay, John, 15

Leslie, Desmond, 23

letter to a priest, 313–17

Levesque, Michael, 319–325

Levesque, Nancy, 319–322, 324–25

Levesque, Paul, 319–320, 322

Lewis, C.S., 129

Liberty, 95

Life Beyond 100—Secret of the Fountain (Shealy), 215

Light Beings, 213, 219–220, 347–49

lightning, orbs as ball, 78

Little Gasparilla Island, 83–84

Little Gray Man, 117

living UFOs, 69–75, 70 (ill.), 73 (ill.)

Lodge, Sir Oliver, 261

Long Island Sound, USOs off of, 89

Los Alamitos Naval Air Station, 87

Lost Boys with the Black Eyes, 279 (ill.), 279–280

lost in another dimension, getting, 283–85, 284 (ill.)

Lucchesi, Dominick, 169–170

Lucifer, 128

Lumpur, Kuala, 261

M

Mack, John, 21

MacLaine, Shirley, 217

Maclean, Dorothy, 246–47

magic theater, on stage in the, 351–361, 353 (ill.), 360 (ill.)

Magill, Herman, 105

Mallette, Charlie, 196

Mallette, Steve, 194, 196

Man and His Symbols (von Fram), 310

The Man Who Fell from the Sky (Kern), 310

Mann, Thomas, 151

Manu, 91

Maqueda, Alfredo, 323–25

The Mass Murderer (Steiger), 147

Massachusetts Institute of Technology, 43

master race from inner earth, 103–19

Mather, Cotton, 108

Mathieu, Louis, 116–17

Maury, Alfred, 197

May, Barbara, 17–18, 23

May, Hoyt, 17–18

Meadows, Mary-Caroline, 231–33

Medical Renaissance—The Secret Code, 216

Medicine Power: The American Indian's Revival of His Spiritual Heritage and its Relevance for Modern Man (Steiger and Nitsch), 236–37

Mediterranean Sea, UFO in the, 83, 84 (ill.)

Meeks, Mr. and Mrs. Earl, 106

meeting an alien, 34–39

Men in Black, Three, 59, 156, 169–174, 196, 301–4

Mendoza, Benjamin, 193

Menger, Howard, 170

Mere Christianity (Lewis), 129

mermen, face to face with the, 100–101

Mesewa, 108

A Midsummer Night's Dream, 128, 130

Miles, Tuesday, 313–17

mind, power of the, 39 (ill.), 39–41

mind traveling through time and space, 319–332

Minerve, 96

Ministry of Universal Wisdom, 27

missing time experience, 59–62

Missouri, multidimensional vortex in, 280–81

Mitchell, Edgar, 153

Monsanto, 11

monsters, encounters with, 183–200

Moody, Raymond, 299

Moore, Tom T., 34–39

Moose River Mine disaster, 104–6

Morell, Theodor, 112

The Morning of the Magicians (Pauwels and Bergier), 113

The Morningstar Conspiracy (Kern), 310

morphing aircraft designs, 9–11, 10 (ill.)

morphing UFO, reports of, 6–9

Mossman, Tam, 227

motel, unusual, 281–83

Mother Sea, 226

Mothman, 194–97, 195 (ill.), 245

Mothman and Other Curious Encounters (Coleman), 195

The Mothman Prophecies [movie], 196–97

The Mothman Prophecies (Keel), 193, 195

motives of USOs, 93–97, 96 (ill.)

MS Norwegian Pearl, 85

Mt. Ranier, UFO sighting on, 2–4, 86

MUFON (Mutual UFO Network), 54, 84

Muhammad, 92

multidimensional beings, angels as, 205–6

multidimensional vortex in Missouri, 280–81

music to uplift the spirit, 221–26

mutation, creating a human, 112–13

Mutual UFO Network (MUFON), 54, 84

Myers, Fredric W.H., 261

mystery, dreams as a paranormal, 308–10

mystical experiences, angels as more than, 209–10

mystics, all people as potential, 226, 226 (ill.)

mythological symbol, UFO as a living, 11–12

N

Napoleon Bonaparte, 116–17

"The Narrative of Arthur Gordon Pym," 108

NASA, 9

National Institute of Oceanography, 100

National UFO Reporting Center, 83–84

Native American beliefs

and communicating with animal totems and nature spirits, 234–37

and contact with space brothers and sisters, 34

and encountering spirit guides and teachers, 219

and encounters with a menagerie of monsters, 186, 199

and the master race from the inner earth, 108

and meeting strange creatures in dark forests, 143, 152

and wee people, 130–31

nature spirits and animal totems, communicating with, 235–250, 237 (ill.), 239 (ill.), 246 (ill.), 248 (ill.)

nature spirits in Sedona, Arizona, 123–24

Nazis, master race of the, 109–16

Nazis, relationship with Weilgart, 150–51

near-death experiences (NDEs), 299, 333–349, 335 (ill.), 338 (ill.), 341 (ill.), 360–61

Nefertari, Queen, 48

Nellis Air Force Base Bombing and Gunnery Range Complex, 7–8, 8 (ill.)

New Age music, 221–26

New Mexico Art League and Gallery, 254

New Orleans, haunted bed and breakfast in, 189

New UFO Breakthrough (Steiger and O'Connell), 171

New Zealand, USOs in, 88–89

Newman, Cloyce A., 344

Newman, Robert C., 95

Newton, Sir Isaac, 325

Nicholas, Captain Jacques, 88

Nichols, Sandy, 161–69, 255–58, 256 (ill.)

Nitsch, Bob, 238

Nitsch, Twylah, 130, 235–38, 236 (ill.)

North, Donald I., 196

Nothdurft, Rev. Milton, 69

nun, angel taking form of a, 201–2

O

occult and shadow people, the, 276–77

O'Connell, Joan, 171

Odic force, the, 111

Oester, Dave, 285–87

Oester, Sharon, 285–87

office, haunted, 258–59

Offutt, Jason, 275

Old Ones, 107, 116 (ill.), 116–17

Oldham, Bret, 162, 164–66

Oldham, Gina, 162, 164–66

On Death and Dying (Kubler-Ross), 347

Opening Doors Within (Caddy), 247

Operation Trojan Horse (Keel), 191–93

orbs and sky critters, 69–82

order in all things, 359–361

Orgone, the, 111

Orsic (Orsitch), Maria, 113–14

Orthon, 23–24, 24 (ill.)

Osiris, 48, 48 (ill.)

Ouija Boards, using, 265, 276

out-of-body experiences, 298–301, 299 (ill.)

Oyoyewa, 108

Oz Factor, 185

P

Palmer, Ray, 117, 119

paraphysical beings, 295–96

Parker, Arizona UFO sighting, 29–33, 30 (ill.), 31 (ill.), 32 (ill.)

Parsons, Estelle, 55

Paul VI, Pope, 193

Pauwels, Louis, 113

Pavai, Will, 134

Pellington, Mark, 197

Pendragon (Steiger), 260

Pendragon, John, 260

Perls, Fritz, 312–13

Perry, John W., 11

personality, fragments of in dreams, 312–13

perverse talents of the poltergeist, 262–64

Pete, Ira, 94

Peter, 230

Peterson, Abby, 45–46, 49, 53

Peterson, Becca, 45

Peterson, Z., 43–53

Phelps, Michelle, 188

physical death, what lies beyond, 337–38

physical encounter or astral projection, 293–94, 294 (ill.)

Pilkington, Robin, 196

plants, finding nature spirits of, 246–49

plastic reality, poltergeists and our, 259–260

Plato, 80, 359

Pleiadians, 35, 37–39

Poe, Edgar Allan, 108, 357

Pointer, Eugene, 184–85

Poltergeist over England (Price), 260

poltergeists, 251–272, 260 (ill.)

Posada, Greg, 184–85

power of the mind, 39 (ill.), 39–41

praying mantis, spiritual totem in form of a, 246, 246 (ill.)

Predicting the Past: An Exploration of Myth, Science, and Prehistory (Wescott), 92

Price, Harry, 260–61

priest, letter to a, 313–17

The Prime Directive, 39, 41

profile of a UFO contactee, 25–27

Project Camelot, 85

prototype for the "interrupted journey" abduction, 55–57, 56 (ill.)

A Psychic Explores the Unseen World (Sterner), 266

Psychic Feats of Olof Jonsson (Steiger), 152

psychokinetic manifestations, 261–64

psychonauts, 65

Puharich, Andrija, 39–41, 65–66

purpose in all things, 359–361

R

race from inner earth, master, 103–19

racial memories of an underground advanced civilization, 117–19

Rains, Claude, 69

Ramu, 24

Randles, Jenny, 185

Raphael, message from angel, 217–18, 218 (ill.)

Raudive, Konstantin, 266–69

Rauschning, Hermann, 113

Raynes, Brent, 162, 186–194

Raynes, Joan, 162

Real Self, the, 344, 348

reality, limited view of, 325–26, 326 (ill.)

reality, poltergeists and our plastic, 259–260

Rebikoff, Dmitri, 88

"record book," keeping clean after NDE, 339–341

recording spirit voices, 251–272, 257 (ill.)

Red Jacket, 237

Red Man, 116–17

Redfern, Nick, 197–99

Reed, Sharon, 352–55

Reich, Wilhelm, 72

Reichswehr, 110

Reinventing Medicine and Healing Words (Dossey), 223

religious view of angels, 205–6

rescue of living by dead, 319–325

Ress, Patricia, 59–62, 135–36, 202–3

A Return to Love (Williamson), 223

Reveals the Mysteries, 34–35

Revelation, Book of, 22

Revelation: The Birth of a New Age (Spangler), 247

Revelation: The Divine Fire (Steiger), 227–28, 231

Ring series (Tolkien), 126

Riou, …douard, 110

road, forest creature on side of the, 143 (ill.), 143–44

Roberts, August C., 169–170

Roberts, Patricia, 211

Roberts, Paul Dale, 58–59, 183–84, 211–12, 258–59

Robertson, David, 105

Roddenberry, Gene, 39–41, 41 (ill.)

Romero, Luis, 352

Roswell, UFO crash in, 9–11, 23, 86

Roswell UFO Museum, extraterrestrial visitor to the, 13–17, 15 (ill.)

Roswell USA (LeMay), 15

Rovner, Sandy, 329

Ruby E., 94

rules of the wee folk, disrespecting, 132–36

Russian Navy, USO encounters with the, 90

RV park, door to another dimension in an Arizona, 285–87

S

Salter, Marcus, 134–35

Sanderson, Ivan T., 196

SaradUris, 148

Scadding, Alfred, 104–6

Scarberry, Roger, 194

Schneider, Rudi, 113

Schneider, Willy, 113

Schriever, Rudolf, 115

Schulmann, W.O., 114

Schupe, Dagmar, 16

Schupe, Rick, 16

Schwarz, Berthold, 188

scientific scrutiny, subjecting spiritual experiences to, 326–330, 328 (ill.)

scientist, spirit guide's encouragement to become a, 221

The Scoriton Mystery (Buckle), 24

Scott, Sir Walter, 129

SE 140, 95

sea, old gods from the, 83–101

Secret Societies and the Founding of America (Kern), 310

Sedona, Arizona, nature spirits in, 123–24

Self, the, 309–10, 359

Seneca tribe, 130, 235–37

Serpent People, 108

Sevenfold Peace Foundation, 212

sexual experience with an alien, 51–53, 52 (ill.), 62–65

Shadow People, 273–79, 274 (ill.), 276 (ill.), 278 (ill.)

Shag Harbor, USOs in, 90

Shakespeare, William, 128, 130

Shakespeare Psychognostic (Weilgart), 151

shape-shifting aliens, 50–51

shape-shifting UFOs, 4–9, 5 (ill.)

Shapiro, Robert, 34

Shaver, Richard, 117–19

Shaver Mystery, 117

Shawano County, Wisconsin, werewolves of, 184 (ill.), 184–85

Shealy, C. Norman, 214–16

Sheldon, Paul, 89

Sherman, Harold, 268

Siegmeister, Walter, 108

Sigrun, 114

silent contactees, 29–33, 30 (ill.), 31 (ill.), 32 (ill.)

Silkies, 91

Silveroe, 95

Simon, Benjamin, 57

Sirians, 34–38, 43–53

Sitwell, Sacherverell, 263

Six Root Races, 111

sky critters and orbs, 69–82

Slenderman, 155–161, 159 (ill.), 169

Smith, Wilbert B., 98–99

Solgonda, 27

Sommerville, Ian, 198

soul, encountering other half of one's, 226–234

Soul Body, 329

space, mind traveling through time and, 319–332

space brothers and sisters, contact with, 23–42, 24 (ill.), 220

Space Kids, 65

Spangler, David, 136, 247–49

Spirit Box. See Ghost Box

spirit guides and teachers, encountering, 219–234

spirit medium, Hitler as a, 113–14

spirit mediums and space contactees, similarities between, 27–28

spirit voices, recording, 251–272, 257 (ill.)

spiritual experiences to scientific scrutiny, subjecting, 326–330, 328 (ill.)

Spiritual Frontiers Fellowship, 69

Sprinkle, R. Leo, 54

squeezing two days into one, 330–32

St. Fillans, the rock of the wee folk at, 134–35

Stanford, Captain Alfred, 89

Star People, 30 (ill.), 30–31, 33

Star Trek, 36, 39, 41

Star Wars, 61

Stardancer, 239 (ill.), 239–242

Starseeds, 65

Starship Enterprise, 39

statistics, abductee, 54–55

statistics, interactions with wee people, 125–26

Stefansdottir, Erla, 133, 136

Steiger, Brad

and communicating with animal totems and nature spirits, 236–37, 240, 247–49

and contact with space brothers and sisters, 29, 34

and encountering spirit guides and teachers, 226–234

and ghosts, poltergeists, and recording spirit voices, 260–61, 266, 268

and the master race from the inner earth, 119

and meeting strange creatures in dark forests, 147–48, 151–53

and mind traveling through time and space, 326–27, 329

and near-death experiences, 337, 342–45, 348

and on stage in the magic theater, 351–52, 357–58

photo of, 236 (ill.)

and sky critters and orbs, 69, 71–73, 75–77

and unknown beings of terror and the dark-side, 169–171, 173

and visitors from extraterrestrial worlds, 4

Steiger, June, 342

Steiger, Marilyn, 227

Steiger, Sherry

and communicating with animal totems and nature spirits, 240, 247–49

and encountering spirit guides and teachers, 231–34

and near-death experiences, 344–49

and on stage in the magic theater, 351–52, 359–361

photos of, 236 (ill.), 347 (ill.)

and unknown beings of terror and the dark-side, 173

and visitors from extraterrestrial worlds, 4

The Steiger Questionnaire of Mystical, Paranormal, and UFO Experiences, 125, 329

Steinmetz, Charles Pro-teus, 265

Sterner, Kay, 266

Stick Man, 161–69, 163 (ill.)

Still Water, 34

Stone Age, monsters in the, 185–86

Stonehill, Paul, 101

Stones River Battlefield, elemental sighting at, 189–191, 190 (ill.)

Strangers from the Skies (Steiger), 147

Strickler, Lon, 103

Strieber, Whitley, 21–22, 57–58, 62

subterranean culture, evi-dence of, 104–7, 105 (ill.)

Sufis, 359

Sumerians, 114

Sun Wheel, the, 112

Surge, Victor, 155

Sutphen, Dick, 34

Swartz, Tim R., 4–6, 12

Swastika, the, 112

Swope, Pastor Robin, 155–161, 174–78, 213–14

Symmes, Captain John Cleve, 108

T

Tafel, Paul, 111

Taft, Tennessee, wee man in, 191

taken away to other worlds, 43–67

Talbot, Michael, 28, 200

talents of the poltergeist, perverse, 262–64

Tannebaum, Ted, 196

tapping cabinets, 258–59

teachers, encountering spirit guides and, 219–234

Tennessee, Stick Man sightings in, 161–69

Tennessee Spirits, 187–89

terror, unknown beings of, 155–181

Tesla, Nikola, 265

Theo, 34–35

They Knew Too Much about Flying Saucers (Barker), 170, 196

Third Reich, 113

Thomas, Angela, 251–54

Thomas, Joe, 86

Thomas, Ricky, 194

Three Men Seeking Mon-sters (Redfern), 197

Throne, Henry, 106

Thule Society, 110–12, 114

Thunder Beings, 237 (ill.), 237–38

time, experience of miss-ing, 59–62

time and space, mind traveling through, 319–332

Titans, 118–19

Tolkien, J.R.R., 97, 126–27

Tonal Alchemy, 223

tornado victims, angels comforting, 216–17, 217 (ill.)

Torres, Noe, 144–47, 145 (ill.)

Toyofuku, Melanie, 66

Transactions of the Ameri-can Philosophical Society, 1–2

transformation of humankind, 66 (ill.), 66–67

Traute, 114

travel, astral, 298–301

triangle-shaped UFO, 2–4

Trimaran, 95–96

truck, angel in a white, 202–4, 203 (ill.)

Trujillo, Antonio, 254

Trujillo, Matilde Fernandez, 254
Twietmeyer, Ted, 280
Two Guns, 237
Tyler, Liv, 127
Tyrrell, G.N., 192

U

UFOs
abduction stories, 19–22, 43–67
diary, 29–33, 30 (ill.), 31 (ill.), 32 (ill.)
encounters with orbs, 75–82, 76 (ill.), 80 (ill.)
first sightings of, 1–2
as intelligences, 200
living, 69–75, 70 (ill.), 73 (ill.)
as living mythological symbols, 11–12
Nazi program, 114–15
or old gods from the sea, 83–101
orbs as, 79–81
profile of a contactee, 25–27
shape-shifting, 4–9, 5 (ill.)
triangle-shaped, 2–4
UFOs: Another Point of View (Kern), 310
UFOs Over California: A True History of Extraterrestrial Encounters in the Golden State (Dennett), 87
understanding your dreams, 317–18
underwater extraterrestrial base investigation, 85–87
Unified Field Theory, 9

unity in all things, 359–361
universal laws, accessing, 358–59
unknown beings of terror, 155–181
Uphoff, Mary Jo, 268
Uphoff, Walter, 268–270
Ury, Gary, 196
Ury, Thomas, 194, 196
USOs, 86–101, 88 (ill.)
U.S.S. Thresher, 93, 94 (ill.)

V

vacation home, creatures invading, 141–43
Van Tassel, George, 27
Vandenburg Air Force Base, 85
The Varieties of Religious Experience (James), 295
vegetables, huge, 246–49
Verne, Jules, 108
Victoria, Queen, 66
Virgin Mary, 28, 255
Vision 4, 89
visiting the astral world, 289–304
visitors from extraterrestrial worlds, 1–22
Vista, 224–25
Vivas vat, 91
voices, recording spirit, 251–272, 257 (ill.)
Voices of Eternity (Estep), 271
von Fram, M.I.., 310
vortex in Missouri, multidimensional, 280–81
Vril, the, 111–14, 115
Vrilerinnen, 113–15

W

Wagner, Beverly, 143
Wagner, Jim, 143
Wamsley, Mr. and Mrs. Raymond, 194
warning to future humankind, Shaver's, 118–19
Watson, Beverley Hale, 212–13
Watts, Alan, 225
weather patterns in the astral world, changing, 292 (ill.), 292–93
Webb, David, 54
wee people, 121–137, 122 (ill.), 124 (ill.), 127 (ill.), 191
Weilgart, Wolf, 147–152
Weilgartner, Hofrat, 150
werewolf, encounter with a, 197–99
werewolves of Shawano County, Wisconsin, 184 (ill.), 184–85
WERT (Weilgart-Ethos-Rhyme-Test), 151
Wescott, Roger W., 92–93, 107
Weston, Rev. Mark, 69
Wetlash, 183
Wexford, trouble at the fairy mound of, 133–34
Whitehead, Alfred North, 325–26
Whiteman Air Force Base, 280–81
Whitmore, John, 66
Wholeness and the Implicate Order (Bohn), 359
Williamson, Marianne, 223
Wilson, E.J., 13–17
Windle, Chris, 134

The Windmills of Mars (Kern), 310
Wisconsin, wee people in, 122–23
Wise, Robert, 25
Wizard of Oz, 79
Wolf, Priscilla Garduno, 254–55, 255 (ill.)

Wolf Age, 112
Wolf Clan, 235, 237–38
The Women of the West History Trail, 254
Woods, James O., 73–74
worlds, taken away to other, 43–67
Worrall, Olga, 347

Wright Patterson Air Force Base, 11

Y

Yahweh, 108
Yamski, 25
Yeats, W.B., 129